TO BE USEFUL
TO THE WORLD

Women in Revolutionary America, 1740–1790

AMERICAN WOMEN
1600–1900

Series Editor: Julie Roy Jeffrey, Goucher College

Other Titles in This Series

TO BE USEFUL TO THE WORLD

Women in Revolutionary America, 1740–1790

Joan R. Gundersen

Twayne Publishers
An Imprint of Simon & Schuster Macmillan • New York

Prentice Hall International
London   Mexico City   New Delhi   Singapore
Sydney   Toronto

To Be Useful to the World: Women in Revolutionary America, 1740–1790
Joan R. Gundersen

Copyright © 1996 by Joan R. Gundersen

Twayne Publishers
An Imprint of Simon & Schuster Macmillan
1633 Broadway
New York, New York 10019

Library of Congress Cataloging-in-Publication Data

Gunderson, Joan R.
    To be useful to the world : women in revolutionary America,
1740–1790 / Joan R. Gundersen.
        p.   cm.   — (American women, 1600–1900)
    Includes bibliographical references and index.
    ISBN 0-8057-9916-8 (hardcover)
    1. United States—History—Revolution, 1775–1783—Women.
2. Women—United States—History—18th century.   3. United States—
Social life and customs—To 1775.   I. Title.   II. Series.
E276.G86   1996
973.3'082—DC20   96-36313
                                                                              CIP

The paper used in this publication meets the minimum requirements of American National Standard for Information Sciences—Permanence of Paper for Printed Library Materials. ANSI Z39.48-1984. ⊚ ™

10 9 8 7 6 5 4 3

Printed in the United States of America

CONTENTS

LIST OF ILLUSTRATIONS   vii
FOREWORD   ix
PREFACE   xi
ACKNOWLEDGMENTS   xv

CHAPTER ONE
The Worlds of Their Mothers   1

CHAPTER TWO
Women on the Move   16

CHAPTER THREE
The Silken Cord   38

CHAPTER FOUR
Mistress and Servant   58

CHAPTER FIVE
Dutiful Daughters and Independent Minds   77

CHAPTER SIX
Sisters of the Spirit   94

CHAPTER SEVEN
"An Injurious and Ill Judging World"   113

CHAPTER EIGHT
The Garden Within   132

CHAPTER NINE
Daughters of Liberty   149

CHAPTER TEN
Mothers of the Republic   169

NOTES   185
BIBLIOGRAPHICAL ESSAY   249
INDEX   263

ILLUSTRATIONS

Deborah Read Franklin   9

Sarah Franklin Bache   17

Forceps used by physicians in assisting at childbirth,
   late eighteenth century   56

Colonial loom   65

Needlework bed hangings   67

Christiana Campbell's tavern   72

Joseph Brant, Margaret Brant's son   85

Title page of an early edition (1773) of Phillis Wheatley's poems   91

Mercy Otis Warren   92

Title page of *The Female Review* (1797)   145

FOREWORD

For much of the twentieth century, American historians have explored the political, economic, social, and cultural events of the first 300 years of the nation's existence with a focus on men as historical actors. In the last 25 years, however, many scholars have concentrated on uncovering the experiences of early American women as individuals and as members of families and communities. This shift of perspective has had a dynamic impact on the study of the past. Women's history has raised new questions about the American experience, challenged the ways in which historians have conceptualized issues and problems, and even called into question the usefulness of familiar chronological divisions.

Each of the volumes in Twayne's "American Women 1600–1900," like those already published in its series "American Women in the Twentieth Century," draws upon a rich body of scholarship in women's history as the basis for an interpretive study of the lives of women of different classes and races during a specified time period. Each presents a readable narrative suitable both for undergraduates and general readers. In the extensive documentation, graduate students and those with particular research interests will also find a valuable introduction to the significant primary and secondary sources in the field and to its scholarly debates.

In *To Be Useful to the World*, Joan R. Gundersen explores the period between 1740 and 1790 when Americans fought for and won their political independence. As the formative event in the nation's history, the American Revolution has, of course, generated hundreds of studies, many of the more recent ones dealing with the experience of women. Gundersen's work reflects the maturation of this new field of interest. The debate over whether the Revolution had a positive or negative impact on women's lives, she suggests, is too simple. While she clarifies the ways in which gender roles changed between 1740 and 1790, she argues that the Revolution was only one of the forces affecting women's situation. Alterations in American society were under way well before the beginning of hostilities, and the revolutionary period itself was too brief to allow any thorough social transformation. More important, her analysis of white, Native American, and African-American women demonstrates that events not only had a differential impact on women of different races and classes but also that their impact was not merely positive or negative. If migration to the frontier offered opportunities to white women, it was at the expense of Native American women. New standards of respectability constricted all white women's activities, conferring on some the mantle of moral authority and on others (poor white women and women of color) the label of deviancy. When white upper- and middle-class women became consumers instead of producers, they traded the gender-integrated world of work and family for a more confined gender-segregated world of domesticity, privacy, and dependency. Although collectively "women found no great improvement in their status" by 1790, Gundersen writes, "the Revolution brought both promise and new restraints" into their lives.

Gundersen's subtle and arresting analysis contributes to our understanding of women during the revolutionary period. She sheds light on important historical questions and, in the process, brings many of her subjects vividly to life.

Julie Roy Jeffrey
Goucher College

PREFACE

This work is unabashedly a synthesis. It could not have been written without the many excellent studies by early Americanists who have spent the last 25 years reshaping our understanding of eighteenth-century America. I could not have attempted to write an explicitly social history of women during the era without the pioneer efforts of Linda Kerber and Mary Beth Norton, who 15 years ago outlined women's social and political experience. Similarly, I owe a debt to the young scholars whose gender-sensitive studies of American Indian history provided me with a fresh understanding of women's lives among Indian peoples. Although I have freely borrowed their research, the conclusions and connections are mine, for good or ill.[1]

In 1740 the British "New World" empire was a growing collection of colonies sprawling from Newfoundland to the Caribbean. After two centuries of exploration, and a century and a half of settlement, the British American colonies were both mature societies and societies still being formed. Those who lived in the colonies—immigrant or native born, African, European, or American Indian, male or female—all encountered a world both old and new at the same time. The colonies differed in climate, geography, length of experience within the empire, and density of American Indian population. Each colony had a unique mix of ethnic groups and religions. To explore the lives of women and their roles in the late eighteenth century in those British colonies that became the United States is thus to explore many stories.

Despite the differences, however, by 1740 a set of colonial cultures had developed with recognizable shared characteristics, including some patterns of women's lives and roles. Change, paradoxically, served as one of the constants in British colonial life. The economic, social, and political changes of the era of the American Revolution reworked women's roles so that the daughters of the Revolution lived in a new world very different from that which their mothers knew, and yet very familiar. This book explores the depth and meaning of those changes for women.

For many years women's historians have debated whether the American Revolution improved women's status or not. Hidden beneath the discussion was a definition of "women" limited to white middle- and upper-class women. Although black women appear in these studies, they are absent from the conclusions. American Indian women rarely appear. It is my contention that when we step back to look at the multiple peoples who lived and interacted within the bounds of the new United States, the outcome of the Revolution is more complex. It appears as a series of trade-offs. Women both gained and lost, but not equally, and one woman's gain might be intimately tied to another's loss. Paradoxically, some of the greatest changes appear in areas that seem continuous, because the meaning assigned to familiar actions changed.

These historical debates often hinge on whether or not the colonial period was a "golden age" for women, but the traditional dates for the Revolution (1763–1789) provide barely enough time for a single generation to reach adulthood, much less measure social change. Hence this work traces the lives of three generations of women beginning with those who were adults in 1740. Born in the colonial period, many lived to see independence declared, and are thus part of the Revolutionary era. Their daughters came of age during the protests leading to the War for Independence, and raised families in the tumult of the Revolution. The book closes with hints of the future for the heirs of the Revolution, the granddaughters of the original women. Chronologically, then, this book begins with a chapter about the first generation, then moves to a series of topical chapters tracing the changing lives of the first two generations over the whole period, and closes with two chapters on the War for Independence, its aftermath, and implications for the third generation.

All three generations lived in a world at war. From 1740 to 1790, peace appeared more as short periods of regrouping than as an end in itself. Throughout the last half of the eighteenth century France and England were locked in a power struggle that did not conclude until the final defeat of Napoleon in 1814. From 1739 to 1748 Britain was at war first with Spain and then also with France in what began as the "War for Jenkin's Ear" and became the War of the Austrian Succession. In 1754 clashes on the Pennsylvania frontier began another war, which again broadened into a European conflict. From the colonial point of view, the Seven Years' War (as Europeans referred to it) lasted nine years, until 1763. In 1774 frontier fighting began again, followed the next year by the armed rebellion that became first the War for American Independence and then a world conflict as France, Spain, and Holland became involved. Only six years after signing the formal peace treaty ending the War for American Independence, Britain and France clashed again, and the United States struggled to avoid being dragged into the war. If the warp of the fabric of war was the struggle between the great powers of Europe, its woof was threads of conflict spun in the colonies. Competition for Indian lands and tension between local rule and an orderly empire provided raw fiber for the American Revolution. Thus war and its aftermath provided the canvas on which women stitched their lives in late eighteenth-century North America.

My goal has been to shift the perspective on the American Revolution so that it includes all women living within the bounds of what would become the United States in 1783. Rather than see ethnic groups in isolation, however, I have sought connections. Marriage, migration, revivals, and the events of war were experiences both shared and uniquely felt by women whether their ancestors had come from Europe, Africa, or the Americas. As colonial societies defined norms and deviancy for women, they constructed versions of "otherness" informed by their understandings of women from cultures, races, and classes different from their own. All women felt the effects of the new definitions of womanhood that emerged during the Revolution, but with different effects. It mattered greatly whether one was an American Indian, an enslaved African, an impoverished widow, or the daughter of a prosperous merchant or planter.

In the hopes of making the connections and differences tangible, I chose to highlight three households. For two of these I owe debts to the scholars whose research provided the basic outlines of their lives. The third comes from my own ongoing research in a Virginia community. Such a focus both clarifies and limits. Their lives serve as points of entry for topics that affected many women. The women in the three households cannot stand for all women, but they can introduce us to many of the issues.

The households were chosen deliberately. I wanted women whose lives could be connected to Revolutionary events, who lived in geographically different regions, and who could introduce the experiences of Indian, African, and European women. Margaret Brant is one of the very few eighteenth-century Indian women whose children's lives are also well documented. By working with the Brant family, I could also illustrate cultural interaction on the frontier and include a Loyalist family. Deborah Franklin offered the possibility of tracing the roles of an urban artisan-class woman. Her daughter, Sarah Bache, was an active member of the social and political elites during the Revolution. Long overshadowed by the most famous member of their household, Deborah and Sarah Franklin offered a fresh approach to the Revolutionary leadership, and specific windows into courtship and marriage. Elizabeth Porter's household brought the story south, and allowed exploration of immigration, the Great Awakening, a mid-range planter family, and the experience of enslaved Africans. It is my hope that their experiences will help personalize the Revolution for the reader.

Strictly speaking, these households are not typical. This is not a random sampling of families. Deborah and Sarah Franklin, after all, shared their lives with one of the most famous men in America. The very fact that we can trace Margaret Brant's life makes her unusual among her Indian contemporaries. The prominence and wealth of her son and daughter set the family further apart from the norm. Elizabeth Porter and her daughters have more claim to being typical members of a small planter class, but that class itself included only a portion of Virginians. Peg and Amy are as typical of Virginia's African community as any two women can be. But even atypical women can have "typical" aspects of their lives. It is my hope that I have paid due respect to both the typical and the unique in the lives of each of the women whose stories I have borrowed.

ACKNOWLEDGMENTS

This book has been more than five years in the making. Originally conceived of as a leave project for my sabbatical in 1989, the project took much longer when I instead began duties as Founding Faculty at a new state university. I would like to gratefully acknowledge the support given to me in this project, first by the History Department and student assistants at St. Olaf College, and then by President Bill Stacy of California State University, San Marcos, who provided summer support and a course release time to help make this book finally happen.

I would also like to acknowledge the patience of the editorial staff at Twayne, who believed in my project enough to wait for my manuscript, and to thank Julie Roy Jeffrey, who offered very helpful comments on the first draft. A whole network of scholars, especially Madeleine Marshall, helped with illustration research. The debt I owe my husband, Robert Gundersen, is beyond measure. He finally made it all happen by sending me to a lake resort, out of reach of university and family duties, where I could write without interruption for two summers. He has been my "in-house" computer consultant and a constant supporter.

CHAPTER ONE

The Worlds of Their Mothers

In 1740 someone wishing to visit the British "New World" empire would have had to construct an itinerary covering the Caribbean, Bermuda, and a string of colonies stretched along the North American coast from Newfoundland to Georgia. British influence and claims extended inland to the lands owned and occupied by a variety of American Indian groups. By 1763 the empire had expanded even further at the expense of France and Spain. That very success, however, led to the empire's unraveling. British attempts to reorganize this sprawling empire led 13 of the colonies to resist and eventually declare their independence.

The American Revolution was more than a war for independence. Revolutions involve major changes in all areas of life. Many of these changes began separately from the events leading to independence, but simultaneous events seldom run on parallel, untouching tracks. Changes in one area result in adjustments or reactions in others.

How did these changes affect women living through them, and what role did women play in these events? Did the Revolution better women's lives, make them worse, or simply make them different? To answer these questions requires an understanding of what women's lives were like before the Revolution began. Thus this book begins with a visit to three pre-Revolutionary households and the women who lived in them.

Elizabeth Dutoy Porter, Deborah Read Franklin, and Margaret Brant never met, and they certainly never corresponded, for only Deborah could sign her name. They lived in separate colonies—Virginia, Pennsylvania, and New York—and moved in separate social circles. Yet their lives and the households they lived in illustrate both the common elements and different contexts of women's lives in the British-American colonies in 1740. Married, and about the same age, each was the mistress of a household and contributed to the family income. All bore daughters who would be mistresses of households during the Revolution. These daughters (and their siblings) would help shape a new society quite different from that of their mothers. Their households' experience can help us understand the parameters of women's lives on the eve of the American Revolution.

Elizabeth Dutoy Porter lived her whole life in the Virginia piedmont, the rolling wooded area between the first set of falls on Virginia's tidal rivers and the Appalachian Mountains. In the eighteenth century, Virginians poured into the piedmont, cutting plantations from the woodland to grow tobacco, corn, and other grains, and to raise livestock. Probably born on her parents' farm overlooking the James River in the small settlement of Manakin, Elizabeth had by 1740 never seen a town of more than 200 people. Manakin had about 125 residents spread over 10,000 acres. In 1740 it was 20 miles to Richmond, the nearest town. It was just a small collection of houses and stores at the falls of the James River. Neighbors gathered on Sunday at King William Parish Church for religious services and to visit, conduct business, and exchange gossip. The local county seat consisted of a courthouse and a tavern. Elizabeth's world was bounded by rural paths and roads connecting farms and leading to the nearby ferry across the James. When she traveled, it was to visit relatives in the surrounding counties. Since Elizabeth had inherited the family farm, she was more likely in 1740 to welcome returning family members to her home than to travel to see them in their new homes on adjoining frontier lands.[1] Although at first glance Elizabeth Dutoy Porter's life was intensely local, it was also culturally diverse. American Indians had abandoned Manakin only a few years before Elizabeth's parents settled there. Some Indians were servants in the Manakin community when Elizabeth was young.[2] Her parents had arrived in Virginia as part of an organized resettlement of French Protestants who had been refugees in Europe for nearly two decades. Thus, the Virginia-born Elizabeth grew up in a French-speaking community. By age 30 she headed an English-speaking household. The cultural and linguistic mix was further enriched by the importation of African-born slaves. Elizabeth's parents and family were among the early slaveholders. Thus Elizabeth Dutoy Porter lived at the intersection of at least four cultures—English colonial, French Protestant, African, and American Indian.

The Porter household of 1740 sheltered three generations of kin and workers. Married about 11 years, Elizabeth and Thomas Porter awaited the birth of a child in the fall. They had three living children—John, age 6; Elizabeth, 4; and two-year-old Dutoy, just recently weaned. They shared their home with Elizabeth's mother, Barbara de Bonnett Dutoy, and Elizabeth's brother, Isaac Dutoy. Completing the household in 1740 were three African slaves, including Peg and Joseph who had been with the Dutoy family since 1723.[3] The lives of the adult women of the Porter household reveal the threads of dependence and independence woven into the fabric of women's roles.

In 1740 Barbara de Bonnett Dutoy had been a widow for 16 years. Born in France, she fled to England with her parents to escape religious persecution. Barbara moved to Virginia in about 1700, when the crown granted French refugees land in the colony. She married Pierre Dutoy at about the time they both emigrated, and they lived together for about 20 years before Pierre died. Barbara's life was filled with great contrasts. Suspended between the French traditions of her family and the English ways of her land of refuge, Barbara grew up in an urban environment and then moved to a struggling rural settlement on the American frontier. Although viewed by the outside world as impoverished refugees, within the Manakin community Barbara and Pierre were among the elite. Barbara raised not only her own three children (Elizabeth, Marianne, and Isaac), but also an orphaned nephew, Anthony Benin, and another orphan, Jean Pierre Bilbaud.[4]

The pattern of her widowhood was typical of many eighteenth-century women. Barbara, with a little help from her nephew and ward, farmed the land until her daughter Marianne married neighbor John Lucadou in 1732. Then the nearly 50-year-old Barbara turned over management of the farm to Thomas and Elizabeth Porter. This was a natural decision, for Pierre Dutoy had specified that Elizabeth should receive the farm upon her mother's death. Barbara retired to be a dependent in the household she had managed for many years. Like many older widows, she never remarried, and she lived out her remaining years surrounded by family and neighbors.[5]

Elizabeth Dutoy married Thomas Porter when she was about 19. For ambitious but landless Thomas, the marriage brought economic opportunity. Elizabeth was due to inherit the 61-acre family farm and slaves when her widowed mother died. Marriage to Elizabeth also gave Thomas access to the tight-knit social community of King William Parish. By 1740 Thomas was well settled in the community. The county court regularly appointed him to appraise the estates of his Huguenot neighbors, and in 1750 Thomas became one of the first non-Huguenot members of the King William Parish Vestry. Thomas and Elizabeth's nearly 40-year marriage was marked by their attempts to acquire adequate land to give each of their children a suitable inheritance.[6]

Thomas and Elizabeth had a son, William, before they had been married a year. Two years later daughter Elizabeth was born. Both children died, however, before 1740. At 17-month intervals Elizabeth then had John, another Elizabeth, and Dutoy. Now in her 30s, Elizabeth Dutoy Porter began spacing her children farther apart. William (the child she was carrying in 1740) was born 33 months after Dutoy. Sarah, Ann, Marie, and Isaac followed at similar intervals. After 24 years of marriage, 10 pregnancies, and eight living children, the 43-year-old Elizabeth finally finished bearing children. Her experience (the patterns of spacing, the number of children, and traditional family naming patterns) was common among native-born Chesapeake women in the eighteenth century. They chose family names linking children to grandparents, parents, and siblings. The Porters maintained a link with Elizabeth's family by making her surname a first name. Because the Porters' brothers and sisters followed similar customs, the children shared names with cousins, aunts, and uncles. Family ties weighed more heavily than individualism. Elizabeth's family was much larger than that of her mother Barbara. Better life expectancy, resistance to endemic disease, and a rising standard of living all helped to explain the larger families typical of second and third generation settlers.[7]

Elizabeth oversaw a busy household. The women not only cared for the usual garden that supplied vegetables for their table, but they kept a large flock of geese, and sheep. They used the feathers to make beds, and spun wool and flax for thread. Barbara and Elizabeth wove fabric on the family loom for others in the area. There were cows to milk and meals to prepare in the separate kitchen fireplace. Thomas was often in the fields supervising the tobacco cultivation, so Elizabeth or Barbara often transacted family business with neighbors, buying and selling garden goods and farm surpluses, and accepting payment for small debts.[8]

Elizabeth was not isolated. With a homestead close to King William Parish Church and the Manakin ferry, and next door to Elizabeth's sister Marianne Lucadou's farm, Elizabeth had frequent visitors. Elizabeth periodically saddled one of the family horses and made neighborly calls on other women, to exchange local produce and news, visit the sick, attend at childbirth, or celebrate a wedding. The Porters were active members of the King William Parish, where services in 1740 were conducted in French and English by the parson of a nearby Anglican parish. Elizabeth's father had served on the King William vestry until his death in 1726. Brother Isaac was elected to the vestry in 1746 and her husband Thomas in 1750. Although neither Elizabeth nor Barbara could write, they may have been able to read, and the family owned a small library.[9]

The Porters' small, plain frame farmhouse was appropriate to their status among the bottom quarter of piedmont slaveholders. Built by Peter Dutoy, the house was most likely two rooms with a breezeway in between. There may have been a separate barn and a kitchen. The few beds and chairs and the simple table could be pushed to the side during the day so that the women could spin or weave, and the family could do other tasks. Little Elizabeth, John, and Dutoy probably slept with their parents, or perhaps with their grandmother. Where Peg and the other slaves slept is uncertain. They may have gone to the kitchen and barn or slept in the house.[10]

Peg and Joseph were almost certainly African born. Ironically, that meant that they had traveled much more widely both in the world and within Virginia than their mistress, Elizabeth Porter. They had been purchased by Pierre Dutoy in about 1723, when the piedmont was becoming the major destination in Virginia for African-born slaves. Slaves on both large and small plantations learned English and other plantation skills quickly.[11] On small plantations, slaves spent much of their time working with whites. By 1740 nearly one-third of Virginia slaves lived in the piedmont. Peg's presence in the tobacco fields helped ensure that Barbara Dutoy, Elizabeth Porter, and her daughters would not be called to help with the crop. Barbara Dutoy hired out Peg in 1726, 1730, and 1732 to provide income for the household. The majority of slaves hired out in Virginia were women; often they were sent from their home plantations by widows seeking a cash income. Thus disruption of one woman's life (Peg's) helped to sustain another's (Barbara's) during a time of family transition.[12]

Peg was lucky to have the company of Joseph, for many small planters owned too few slaves to have them marry on the plantation. Many slaves became part of "commuter" marriages, meeting with their spouses only on Sundays or when they could slip away in the evening for a few hours. Other slaves in the piedmont married American Indians who worked on the plantations or lived in the area. Virginia colonial law and custom left African slaves outside the legal systems of marriage. As property, they could not legally give the consent necessary to marry. Before the American Revolution, ministers married only a handful of enslaved blacks in Virginia, and those had become active church members. Peg and Joseph were also removed from their traditional systems of courtship and marriage. African customs varied widely, and those enslaved came from many cultural groups in Africa. There were simply too few slaves in the piedmont area in the 1720s to form a community that could reproduce any particular African tradition. Peg and Joseph were truly in a new world. Despite the restrictions on slaves inherent in any system of unfree labor, and the fears of owners that slaves would run away or rebel, slaves like Peg and Joseph traveled between plantations with some frequency. In the early years of piedmont settlement, for example, many slaves lived on quarters with absentee owners. Slaves traveled to the home plantation with messages or to report mistreatment by overseers.[13]

In 1740 Peg, like her mistress, was pregnant. It is likely that Pierre Dutoy had purchased Peg and Joseph in 1723 expecting them (and perhaps requiring them) to live together and reproduce. Thomas Porter registered the birth of a slave child, Amy, in September. Two years later, in May of 1742, Dick was born.[14] The black women of King William Parish had fewer children than white women, saw more of their children die in infancy, and were at greater risk of miscarriage due to the farm labor they continued to do right up until the birth of the child. Most black children were born in the spring (like Dick), when tobacco culture put heavy work demands on slaves, thus adding to the risks of childbirth.[15]

It is not clear Peg and Joe had any say in their own names. Because some Africans resisted being given a new name, owners sometimes settled for an English name that resembled the African name in sound or meaning. Peg and Joseph bore such compromise names. With the birth of children, however, Peg and Joseph once again faced a struggle for control. Their success could be measured in the separate naming traditions evident among slave families on Porter farms by 1767.[16]

The women of the Porter household thus brought diverse experiences to the everyday routines of rural life. Although she lived and worked in the household, sharing chores with the other women, Peg's perceptions of family and community were different from those of Barbara Dutoy or the Porters. All were technically dependent, but Barbara Dutoy and Elizabeth Dutoy Porter had also exercised the authority of a mistress of the household. Barbara Dutoy may have found her role as dependent widow either constraining or a relief after the burdens of widowhood. For Peg, the contrast between her life and the lives of Elizabeth Porter and Barbara Dutoy was stark. Peg worked in a household with and for other women, but she was subordinate to them. She had to fit the care of her own family and household into the cracks between her tasks for the Porters.

In 1740, war was only a distant backdrop to life in King William Parish. The Virginia Governor had led a force from Virginia into the war, but none of the Porters seem to have enlisted. The frontier remained quiet, and distant campaigns had little effect on the Virginia tobacco economy. In Massachusetts (especially in Boston, where there was heavy recruiting for expeditions to Canada), the war brought economic stagnation, heavy debt, and a new class of poor—the widows and orphans of men killed. In Philadelphia, however, the war touched off an economic boom that helped fuel a 75 percent growth of that port city.[17] Deborah and Benjamin Franklin prospered along with their city.

Like the Porter household, the Franklins of Philadelphia had workers and extended family living with them in 1740. Mrs. Read, Deborah's widowed mother, had moved in with the couple shortly after they married in September 1730. Benjamin had a son, William, born in 1730 or 1731, to an unnamed mother. William lived with Deborah and Benjamin. In 1740 Deborah took in her orphaned niece and namesake, Deborah Croker. Deborah and Benjamin's only son had died at age four in 1736, and their only other child, Sarah, would not be born for several years. Thus William and young Deborah filled important gaps in the family circle. In addition, the Franklin household included apprentices and a servant.[18]

Philadelphia, however, was very different from rural Virginia. By 1740 Philadelphia had surpassed Boston as the largest city in the British American colonies. The city was a commercial port, and Deborah could hear many languages spoken on the streets. Immigrants used Philadelphia as a gateway to Pennsylvania and the southern backcountry. The city supported several newspapers, and kept up on happenings in England. Like an unsure adolescent on the brink of maturity, Philadelphia in 1740 was poised to develop its own intellectual and artistic traditions. While Elizabeth Dutoy Porter had to saddle a horse or walk winding rural paths to visit a neighbor, and faced a full day's ride to the nearest store, Deborah Read Franklin could easily run next door for a few words with a neighbor, or walk down the street to a local market.[19]

Deborah's father, James Read, had been a prosperous carpenter who had business reverses shortly before his death. Deborah and her family attended Christ Church, and her friends included daughters of the most influential families in Philadelphia. Plump, cheerful, attractive, and good-natured, Deborah met Benjamin Franklin when he first arrived in Philadelphia as a journeyman printer. The young couple had seemed close to marriage when Franklin left for England in hopes of securing a printing press and patronage. What followed was nearly disastrous for her.[20] In England, Benjamin forgot about Deborah and explored the pleasures of London. Assuming herself abandoned, Deborah consented to marry a potter named Rogers, who proved to be a bigamist and soon left the colony. Rogers disappeared before the Reads could take any legal action. Absolute divorce with the right to remarry was not possible in Pennsylvania, except for marriages between parties too closely related. The 1705 divorce law allowed divorce *a mensa et thoro* for bigamy, adultery, sodomy, and buggery, but such a divorce was more like a legal separation, granting Deborah control over her own finances, but not the right to remarry.[21] Deborah and her family chose not to seek such a decree, with Rogers long gone from Philadelphia. Neither single nor married, Deborah was caught in a legal bind, saddled with debts from the marriage her financially strapped father could not pay. Her predicament was not unique. In Connecticut, where divorce was legal, petitioners for divorce cited desertion as a reason in 64 percent of cases. In some instances the couple had simply separated, but a majority of these cases involved women whose situations were not unlike Deborah's.[22]

When Franklin returned from England, he renewed his suit to Deborah only after failing to negotiate a more prestigious match. Given Deborah's previous marriage, a church ceremony was out of the question, so the couple simply set up housekeeping as a married couple, knowing that their union was recognized under common law. Within a year, Franklin had brought his infant son William into their household. While some historians have speculated that William might have been the son of Benjamin and Deborah, born at a time when Deborah might technically have been considered married to another man, others have argued that William had a different mother. In either case, his presence added another factor of risk to their new union.[23]

Matthew Pratt painted this portrait of Deborah Read Franklin at the request of her husband. *Courtesy of the American Philosophical Society Library.*

The Franklin's common-law marriage did not bar them from respectable company. Disparaging comments might appear in private letters, but open disapproval was muted. It is hard to say whether Deborah avoided public social events to prevent social snubs or because she had little interest in them. She continued to visit her prominent friends and take communion at church. Franklin's marriage was not a minus in his political career. In every seaport city were women unsure if their husbands were dead or alive. Some chose to remarry, as Deborah had. What mattered to the Franklins and their neighbors was that the couple successfully negotiated the roles assigned to husband and wife in colonial society. Similarly, the presence of William in the Franklin household did not cause major scandal. Despite laws against fornication, bastardy, and adultery, many colonial couples married after the birth of children, especially on the frontier and in the South. By the 1740s prosecutions for bastardy throughout the colonies were used more to secure child support than to punish women. Since Benjamin Franklin took responsibility for his son, the courts had little reason to be concerned. Benjamin Franklin's open acknowledgment of William and 44-year marriage to Deborah kept gossip from having much sting.[24]

Deborah Read was an asset to a young man setting up in the printing business. She helped maintain her family's good social connections with her regular attendance at Christ Church, and brought Benjamin into contact with leading Anglicans, including evangelicals such as George Whitefield. At home, she ran the stationery store that the Franklins opened in conjunction with Benjamin's printing business, and when Benjamin was appointed postmaster for the colonies, Deborah oversaw much of the postal business. In 1743, six months pregnant with Sarah, Deborah ran both the printing shop and the post office while Benjamin visited family in Boston. Her mother also added to the family income, selling herbal medicines from the stationery store. In the early years of their marriage, Deborah made the cloth she fashioned into clothing for the family. By 1740, however, the Franklins were beginning to enjoy some of the imported luxuries available in Philadelphia. When a successful Franklin turned to scientific and political pursuits, Deborah kept an eye on the business, even when he was away for years at a time.[25]

It is difficult to determine who else was in the Franklin household in 1740. Relatives, apprentices, and servants moved in and out of the household, helping with work and family chores. Nine-year-old Deborah Croker, Deborah Franklin's niece, had just joined the household. Benjamin's nephew James moved in shortly after the Franklins' son Francis ("Franky") died of smallpox in 1736. In August 1743 Deborah safely delivered a daughter, whom they named Sarah. Apprentices lived with them much of the time. Deborah, like many Philadelphia women, hired other women for specific tasks such as laundry or extra sewing, but surviving records do not indicate what help Deborah had by 1740, nor whether it was day or live-in. In 1740 the Franklins were not well enough established to invest in slaves, but in years to come they would do so.[26]

The 1740s were good times for the Franklins despite the backdrop of war. Philadelphia prospered from outfitting ships and military expeditions, but the war did not seem very close. By 1748 Benjamin Franklin's finances were secure enough for him to retire from active printing at age 42 to pursue more steadily his interest in science and politics. Franklin's partner took over the printing business, and Franklin had additional income from other sources. By 1750 the Franklins were members of the elite. Their annual income was then more than £2,000 a year, twice the salary of the governor of Pennsylvania. Deborah did not retire when Franklin did: she remained active in the shop and in the post office business. The household continued to require care.[27] This, however, lay in the future, and the Franklin household of 1740 was not that different from those of other prospering urban families.

Despite her rural background, Elizabeth Dutoy Porter would have found much that was familiar had she ever visited the Franklins. Both Elizabeth and Deborah found their days filled with the routines of family and housekeeping and with activity designed to increase the family income. Each attended the Anglican parish where she had been baptized as a child, and looked forward to living the rest of her life in the community where she was born. Both could draw on their mothers' support in running extended households. Both, despite their responsible roles, were technically subordinate to their husbands. Deborah, however, bought at market things that Elizabeth might have made, and the city provided Deborah with quicker access to friends and news.

The life of Margaret, a member of the Mohawk tribe, might at first seem to have little in common with that of Elizabeth Porter or Deborah Franklin, but the Mohawks and many other eastern Indian nations lived in a society in constant dialogue with European settlements in the New World. By the eighteenth century, many Indians lived in areas that resembled cultural patchwork quilts, with clusters of settlers of different European and colonial backgrounds scattered between Indian settlements. Crops, goods, and ideas passed back and forth between Indians and European colonists. The Mohawk, one of the five original nations of the Iroquois Confederacy, occupied an area in upstate New York. The Iroquois were a buffer between French Canada and the settlements of Europeans in New York. Nearby were Schenectady and Albany, both settled first by the Dutch and now attracting both English and German settlers. With homes in western New York, members of the Iroquois nations moved back and forth from New York to villages along the Ohio River and Lake Erie, and war parties raided as far south as South Carolina and north into Canada. After a half-century of war with French Canada, the Iroquois had allied with the British, but by mid-century were trying to map out a more independent diplomacy.[28]

Throughout the 1740s the area occupied by Indians east of the Mississippi saw numerous changes. Indian settlement along the Ohio River had created new towns with mixed populations including Shawnee, Delaware, and occasional Iroquois. By the mid-1740s, the Iroquois were at war with the Catawba of the Carolinas, and the Mohawks had split from the neutral policy of the other Iroquois to become allies of the British in their wars with France. The Great Lakes and Ohio Valley regions were in chaos. New French policies toward the Indian tribes further destabilized the situation.[29]

Margaret thus lived her life at the intersection of European colonial and Mohawk culture. Her son Joseph Brant later claimed she was the daughter of a Huron adopted into a Mohawk family as a replacement for someone killed during war. This is quite possible. Iroquois customs of personal revenge and mourning demanded the taking of prisoners. Women in the bereaved family then decided if the captive would be adopted or killed. Usually women and children were adopted and became full family members. In the last half of the seventeenth century the Mohawks adopted the remnants of several Huron villages into their tribe. Margaret's mother may have been among these villagers. The family that adopted Margaret's mother was not among the Mohawk elite who chose the traditional leaders. Whether Margaret's father was a chief taken to England on a visit is irrelevant to her status. Under Mohawk customs, social status was determined by the mother's status and family.[30]

Margaret lived at Canajoharie Castle, one of the major Mohawk villages. It had about the same population as the Manakin community where Elizabeth Porter was born. Probably born between 1710 and 1720, Margaret was only a few years younger than Elizabeth Porter and Deborah Franklin. Canajoharie was in major transition at the time of her birth, as its residents abandoned longhouse living for small cabins. Average household size ranged from five to 10 people. Waves of German immigrants arriving after 1712 added to a European population that already outnumbered Mohawks. By 1740 there were 10 settlers of European and African descent for every American Indian in Albany County. Fort Hunter, built about the time Margaret was born, had an Anglican chapel and missionary. Margaret's family periodically traveled the 30 miles to Fort Hunter to trade. William Johnson, who arrived in 1738, was among the traders drawn to the fort. He would have a tremendous impact on the Iroquois and on Margaret's family in years to come.[31]

Trade goods were an integral part of Mohawk life, and hunting was as important for the furs and skins it provided as it was for the meat. Mohawks used the cash or credit they received for furs and skins to purchase trade goods. Margaret cooked in metal pots of European manufacture, and wrapped herself in trade blankets. Mohawk women decorated clothes and wampum belts with Venetian glass beads rather than shells and dyed animal quills. Margaret made clothes from cloth bought from traders, and worked the cornfields with an iron hoe bought from the same source.[32]

The decision to have their children baptized was one of the ways Margaret and her husband Peter blended the customs of two worlds. Many of the Hurons adopted by the Mohawk had been converted by Jesuits. By the early eighteenth century Mohawks often took their children to local Protestant ministers for baptism. The Society for the Propagation of the Gospel staffed the Fort Hunter chapel with a missionary, and Margaret grew up in a community practicing both traditional spirituality and Christianity. Anglican missionary Henry Barclay baptized Margaret's daughter Mary (Molly) in 1735 at Fort Hunter, and he baptized children of Margaret and her second husband Peter in 1741 and 1742. Another Protestant minister baptized her son Joseph when the Anglican chaplaincy was vacant. Although she sought baptism for her children, Margaret chose traditional Mohawk marriage ceremonies for three of her four marriages, and took part in other traditional ceremonies.[33]

Iroquois families followed matrilineal rules, tracing kin and clan membership through female lines. Households formed around female kin. Under Iroquois traditions, women controlled their village fields. While men might clear stumps from fields, women, children, and men too old for the hunt worked together on planting, hoeing, and harvesting. Twice a year, the Iroquois would move to hunting villages, where Margaret and other women would dress and preserve the meat killed by the men. The rest of the year women tended their fields of corn, beans, and squash; they also gathered berries, nuts, fruits, roots, and other native plants. In spring they would move for a few weeks to a sugaring camp to collect sap for maple sugar. Many of these tasks would have been familiar to Elizabeth Porter or Peg. Just as life in the Porter household revolved around seasons of planting, so did Margaret's.[34] In European settlements, however, white women did not usually own the fields or plant the grain crops, although they might help hoe or harvest. Given the annual hunting moves to the Ohio River, Margaret regularly traveled much farther than Elizabeth Porter or Deborah Read Franklin ever ventured.[35]

By 1740 Mohawks had shifted almost entirely from the longhouse clusters of kin to an extended nuclear family.[36] Margaret's household included her husband Peter and her daughter Mary, who was about four. Margaret, like Elizabeth Porter and Peg, was pregnant in 1740.

Her infant Jacob was baptized at Fort Hunter in 1741. It is likely that at least some of Margaret's other relatives lived with them. Margaret bore at least five children. Mary was the only surviving child of her first marriage. Peter and Margaret's only surviving child was Joseph, born in 1744. About that time, Peter and children Jacob and Christina died in one of the many devastating epidemics that decimated the Mohawk population. Margaret's third marriage to Lykas appears to have had no issue; he died in 1750 while on a raid against the Catawba in South Carolina. Margaret's last recorded child, another Jacob, was born in late 1752 or early 1753. She married Jacob's father, Brant Canagaraduncka, in September 1753 in an Anglican ceremony at Canajoharie Castle. This marriage scandalized both the Indian and the English communities. Brant Canagaraduncka shocked Mohawk kin by marrying too soon after the death of his previous wife. Anglicans were more concerned about the fact that Margaret and Brant had conceived Jacob before Brant's wife died. Margaret had to confess adultery and ask forgiveness before being readmitted to communion.[37]

King George's War added to the disruptions in Margaret's life. Most of the Indian nations tried to remain neutral in battles between the European powers, but competing traders struggled to win the attention, allegiance, and trade of Indians throughout the Ohio River and Great Lakes regions.[38] White settlers living near Margaret fled to Albany during the war. Margaret lost at least two children and a husband to the epidemics spread by the war. In addition, the Iroquois were at war with the Catawba of South Carolina throughout the 1740s. Margaret's husband Lykas was a late casualty of that war.

Nothing better symbolizes the intersection of two worlds in Margaret's life than her name. Surnames in European society identified paternal kin. First names tied European colonists to maternal and paternal kin. For Mohawks, membership in a clan determined kinship. Mohawk names represented events or attributes. The British records provide no clue to Margaret's Mohawk name, only the name she received at baptism. Her children also had both Mohawk and Christian names. Mary, for example, was also Degonwadonti or "Several-against-one."[39] Christian Mohawks sometimes combined Indian and Christian names to provide the first and last name required by European tradition. Americans of European descent identified Mohawk women by the names of the men with whom they associated. Thus, after Margaret married Brant Canagaraduncka in 1753, British and colonial records list her and all her children with the surname Brant.

Elizabeth Dutoy Porter, the African slave Peg, Deborah Read Franklin, and Margaret Brant represented the major varieties of women's experience in 1740. Although Peg and Elizabeth Porter worked side-by-side in the same household and were present for the births of each other's daughters, the two women in many ways lived in different worlds. When Peg helped Elizabeth stuff a feather mattress, she knew that she would never sleep on such a bed, and that both the mattress and her daughter might be presented as gifts when Elizabeth's daughters married. Although Margaret, Deborah, and Elizabeth all worshiped at Anglican churches, Sundays reminded Elizabeth of her French refugee heritage and Margaret of an alien culture gaining power in her homeland.

As adult women, their experiences were both unique unto themselves and typical of those of many women who lived and worked in the British American colonies of 1740, and who made decisions that would affect their families and women's roles for the next 30 years. Had Deborah Franklin decided to accompany her husband on one of his trips to visit relatives in New England, she would have found an urban culture that she understood. Granted, Boston did not offer theater, dances, and concerts the way her native Philadelphia did, but Deborah Franklin did not partake of such amusements once married. The majority of churches might have been Congregational, but Deborah would have found a daily attention to piety—the saying of grace and family prayers—that were familiar to her. Elizabeth Porter's daily routines of household and farm duties would have been familiar to rural women throughout the colonies. Prosperous families would have had servants or slaves, like Peg, doing many of the heavier chores. Margaret's moves, the high family mortality rate, and the direct effects of endemic war would have been familiar to American Indian women anywhere east of the Mississippi. Their daughters Elizabeth (and Ann, Sarah, and Marie), Amy, Sarah (Sally), and Mary (Molly) would come of age under their mother's guidance in Revolutionary America. The variety of ways in which they were affected by the changes of the Revolutionary era help us see what was lost and what was gained by women. By 1790, their granddaughters would be shaping a new world in which women's lives and work would carry quite different meanings than they had in 1740, even when the work looked familiar. Time and again women would exchange a privilege for a constraint, a limitation for a freedom.

CHAPTER TWO

Women on the Move

In 1763, when Sarah Franklin was 20, she accompanied her father Benjamin to visit his family in New England. This trip was a longer version of the family visits an eighteenth-century woman made to maintain kinship and to meet others approved by her kin. Sally was, after all, of an age to marry. Her visit illustrates one of the many reasons women might travel in Revolutionary-era America. Although Sally and Benjamin traveled together, gender helped ensure that they experienced the trip differently. Most women's experience of mobility was shaped by factors beyond their control, and the Revolution magnified the effects of these factors.

Late eighteenth-century America was a society in constant motion. Women took part in all forms of travel—seasonal moves as part of a work cycle; family, church, and business visits; immigration; or migration to the frontier or to cities. War and political/economic changes regularly pushed women into the ranks of migrants, refugees, and a floating population of poor seeking work or support.

Whatever the reason for leaving home, as women joined the flow of migrants, their gender shaped that experience profoundly. Child care and household duties meant that women traveled less frequently and for either longer or shorter periods than men. Many trips were tied to uniquely female events such as childbearing and weaning. Outnumbered by men in most kinds of travel, women were more likely to be

This portrait of Sarah Franklin Bache was painted during her trip to England after the American Revolution. *The Metropolitan Museum of Art, Wolfe Fund, 1901. Catharine Lorillard Wolfe Collection.*

involuntary migrants, were at greater risk sexually than men, and were more likely to be part of a family group.

Travel and migration were part of broader social and economic forces that affected women's lives. The same economic forces that fueled migration led families to reduce the control daughters and women had over inheritances. Migrants from Europe left behind many of the traditional practices that gave women authority and control over property. In community after community, the old residents and new arrivals struggled to reconcile different gender expectations. Nowhere was this more evident than on the frontier and in the pressures on Indian society.[1]

The Franklin, Porter, and Brant households illustrate the types of physical mobility that an eighteenth-century woman might experience. Deborah Franklin seems never to have left Philadelphia, but that does not mean she remained isolated in her home. Deborah visited neighbors, shopped at the markets, and spoke with travelers regularly while running a store and postal shop. Although Elizabeth Porter, two of her daughters, and Amy, the slave, similarly limited travel to local visits, the Porters' definition of *neighborhood* covered a larger area. Elizabeth made at least five county court visits during her life. Another Porter daughter moved after marriage to an adjoining county, thus providing family women an incentive to extend their visiting.[2]

The remaining six women took part in major moves. Three women traveled widely within America. Sarah Porter Hatcher emigrated to Kentucky. Margaret and Mary Brant moved among a variety of Indian communities and trading posts in New York and the Ohio Valley, eventually becoming Loyalist refugees during the War for Independence. Three women crossed the Atlantic. Sarah Franklin Bache's travels went well beyond her trip to New England. A refugee during the Revolution, Sarah visited London after the war. Elizabeth Porter's mother, Barbara de Bonnett Dutoy, was a Huguenot refugee who finally settled in Virginia. The African Peg was a survivor of the slave trade. Mobility for these women was both voluntary and involuntary, short-term and permanent. They adjusted to new lands and interacted with those who arrived later. Four of the five most mobile women were among those most often overlooked by historians generalizing about women in this era (an immigrant, two American Indians, and an African).[3]

Barbara de Bonnett Dutoy's travels began as an infant, when her parents hid Barbara and her sister in saddlebags to cross the French border. One of the children was wounded when a soldier thrust a sword into the bags. The de Bonnetts were among the 200,000 Huguenots who chose to leave France rather convert to Catholicism after the Revocation of the Edict of Nantes in 1685. In 1700–01 the de Bonnetts joined an organized, publicly financed expedition of Huguenots who had received a grant of land in Virginia from the English crown.[4]

Having experienced two dramatic moves in her youth, Barbara spent the rest of her life in King William Parish, Virginia. She married and raised her family in an immigrant community slowly adapting to the culture and conditions surrounding them. Unlike her husband, she had little contact with English neighbors. She was a source of cultural continuity in an alien land, and her dramatic escape from France became family folklore. British law set Barbara's experience further apart from that of her husband Pierre. The men of King William Parish sought naturalization from the Virginia legislature. Women did not, for their status depended on their husbands'. In France, Barbara would have retained separate rights to property she inherited or brought to a marriage, and a share in property acquired during marriage. Under Virginia common law, Barbara had only a one-third life interest in such property, unless her husband chose to will her more (which he did) or had created an equity trust at marriage (which he did not).[5]

Religious refugees such as Barbara Dutoy were an important minority among eighteenth-century immigrants. After 1740 religious refugees were mostly German pietists, who formed small frontier enclaves of German culture from New York to the Carolinas. Among these groups the Moravians were especially well-organized. In the 1740s the Moravians sent small groups of men to North Carolina and Pennsylvania to prepare for the arrival of families and single women. By 1762 Moravians were unique among immigrant and frontier communities in having nearly balanced sex ratios. By the end of the Revolution, women outnumbered men. A continuous source of curiosity to outsiders, the Moravian's unique gender arrangements held special attraction for women.[6]

Despite the threats of war, both the Continent and Britain sent large numbers of immigrants to the mainland New World colonies. At least 55,000 Protestant Irish, 40,000 Scots, 30,000 English, 12,000 German and Swiss, and 84,500 Africans arrived in North America during the quarter-century before independence. Smaller numbers arrived from France, Italy, Greece, and the Caribbean. Joined by migrants from more settled areas, the immigrants spilled into areas already settled by American Indians. By 1770, while 2,300,000 people lived east of the Allegheny Mountains, only 100,000 of them were Indians. Of the rest, 500,000 people were of African descent and 1,700,000 of European.[7]

Women were approximately one quarter of the immigrants from Europe and Africa. Women, married and single, came from Europe mostly as members of family groups. Two out of every five immigrants arriving as part of a family group were women. They were only one out of seven of other immigrants. In contrast, enslaved Africans like Peg had been torn from their families, spouses, and communities. Even if African slave traders originally acquired small groups of kin or neighbors, the workings of the trade ensured that these groups were dispersed. Women traveling as individuals were more vulnerable to abuse, more likely to spend time as unfree labor, and more likely to be a small minority among a large group of men.[8]

Arriving singly, as part of either well-organized expeditions or more spontaneously arranged groups of friends and relatives, family groups settled together or near family and friends. Women traveling in groups could help each other with meal preparation, household duties, or childbirth. For example, when a group of 280 Scots headed for North Carolina in 1774 the 30 mothers with nursing infants could help each other. For German women, companionship translated into lower shipboard mortality than for men (2.53 percent and 3.56 percent respectively).[9]

Immigration helped feed rapid colonial expansion after 1750. In the quarter-century before the start of the War for Independence, Euro-American settlement doubled the land area occupied by Europeans and Africans in the preceding century and a half. Both European immigration and the slave trade poured new people into the mainland colonies during the third quarter of the eighteenth century. By 1770 over 10 percent of the white population were immigrants. British leaders, fearing Old World depopulation and uncontrolled colonial growth, passed measures designed to discourage immigration—to no avail. Growth continued during the Revolution as waves of settlers arriving on the frontier formed three additional states by 1800.[10]

All immigrants went through a period of adjustment to new climates, crops, social customs, and language. Eighteenth-century colonists suffered a period of "seasoning," especially in the Chesapeake, as they were struck by malaria, yellow fever, and other diseases. Mortality for immigrants was high. From 1738 to 1756, 61 out of every 1,000 German immigrants to Pennsylvania died in the first year, a death rate 66 percent higher than that for established residents. The round of debilitating diseases was especially hard on women. Although malaria could reduce fertility, it also increased the risk of death for those who became pregnant.[11]

Immigrants clustered by nationality in different areas. Scots families settled in Pennsylvania, Nova Scotia, and the southern backcountry. Germans were scattered in the interior from New York south through the Carolinas. From 1748 to 1759 more than 5,000 immigrants from Germany and Switzerland arrived in South Carolina's backcountry, for example.[12] English immigrants preferred Maryland, with New York, North Carolina, and Nova Scotia next in popularity. Georgia was a struggling frontier that attracted settlers from all areas, especially Protestant Irish.

The Franklins' Philadelphia was one of the busiest receiving centers for immigrants, especially those who came as servants. Philadelphians bought a disproportionate number of female servants, employing them in household work such as gardening, dairying, washing, and cooking. Quakers, trying to avoid owning slaves, shifted to servants after 1750. Even so, the supply of female servants exceeded the demand enough that ship captains were frequently directed to import fewer women. Potential purchasers of female domestic servants often required letters of recommendation for the servant. By 1773 captains were asked not to bring anymore at all.[13]

The majority of women servants in a cargo were sold a month later than the majority of men. Special conditions could increase the demand for women servants. For example, women skilled in spinning, weaving, and sewing sold as rapidly as men in a new settlement in Georgia where few settlers had those skills. In Maryland, small farmers eager for labor exempt from the tithe bought women servants to work in the tobacco fields. The British government twice disallowed Maryland laws removing the tithe exemption for white female servants. Slaveholders thought the exemption unfair since female indentured servants were doing the same work as taxed female slaves.[14]

A servant's arrival in the colonies extended the traditional migration patterns of young adults from tenant and yeoman families seeking work away from home. They were familiar with farmwork and had household skills. Women often traveled in small groups to market towns and then to regional centers or London. Some were then recruited by ship captains acting as colonial labor brokers. Those recruited signed indentures (contracts) setting a specific period of service in exchange for passage. Because women were more tightly grouped in age in their late teens, on average they negotiated shorter contracts than males.[15] Redemption became a growing alternative to formal indentures in the eighteenth century. Upon reaching the colonies without a contract, the redemptioner had a set length of time to repay, or "redeem," passage. They negotiated their own contract exchanging service for repayment, or contacted relatives already in the colony who paid. If they failed, the captain sold them as servants to compensate for the passage.[16]

Although single servants were forbidden by law to marry until they completed their service, married couples and families, especially German, Scots, and Irish, used service as an immigration strategy.[17] One member of a couple might come to the colonies in service, hoping to bring the other later. Many families gambled that the sale as redemptioners of one or two family members (often girls) would pay for the passage of all. Married servants preferred urban areas. Deborah's Philadelphia housed over 140 married female servants in 1772. Married servants placed economic necessity and social norms at odds. Despite a 1765 Pennsylvania law forbidding the separation of married servants, couples were separated.[18] Many runaway servants were desperate pregnant women searching for their husbands.

Some women came to Maryland and Virginia involuntarily as convict servants. England was willing to commute the death sentences of those convicted of a variety of less violent offenses if the convict was willing to be "transported" as a servant to the colonies. Although controversial because colonists feared criminals would repeat their crimes, convicts served longer terms of service than most other adults. Thus they offered a longer return (if they lived) on the initial purchase price. The inclusion of such property crimes as theft on the list of capital offenses ensured a supply of women eligible for transportation.[19]

While American folklore focuses on stories of the indentured servant who gained wealth and fame in the colonies, the reality was quite different. For a woman, becoming an indentured servant was very risky. Servants usually arrived weak from the voyage and poorly clothed. Ship captains were eager to unload their human cargo quickly, before disease and hungry servants ate up their profits. Because women's contracts sold more slowly than men's, ship captains often sold them in lots at auction or pressured women to take less desirable terms of indenture. Indentured servants were most likely to work for small planters whose own standard of living was low. With no capital to set up in business, single women who finished their indentures had few options in the eighteenth century. Most either married or competed for day labor with slaves and servants. Wages were low, and former women servants on their own eked out a precarious living.[20]

Far removed from the protection of family and friends, women were at greater risk than men of sexual and physical abuse. Harsh masters raped, whipped, or starved servants; some women bartered sexual access for better treatment. Sexual abuse was so common that many colonies passed laws extending the service of a servant who bore a child. Because seventeenth-century masters had abused women servants and then benefited by claiming the extended service, the statutes usually specified that the extra time would be done with a different master. Some desperate serving women concealed a pregnancy and abandoned or killed their newborns in efforts to escape longer terms.[21]

Slavery and indentured service went hand in hand. The same Maryland counties that were the best markets for slave labor were also the best customers for imported servants. Although some servants held highly skilled jobs as tutors or craft workers, most provided labor for household and farm duties. Slaves performed the same tasks. The difference was cost and length of investment. Servants might cost only £7–10, while a young adult slave might sell for five times as much. The higher price bought lifetime service and, if the slave were female, the possibility of increase. Marginal farmers bought servants or recently imported African children (a girl cost £15–20) to reduce labor costs. By 1755 slaves were far more common than servants in Virginia, but servants still accounted for about 20 percent of the unfree labor force.[22]

Peg was among the more than 58,918 Africans brought to Virginia from 1725 to 1775. Over one-third of all people who arrived in the British mainland colonies from 1760 to 1775 came as slaves. Even so, only 7 percent of slaves imported to British colonies went to those on the mainland. Pierre Dutoy probably purchased Peg at Bermuda Hundred, a major point of entry for African imports not too far from Manakin. As one of only 390 Africans (mostly male) living in the Virginia piedmont during the 1720s, Peg began her life in the colonies as a minority within a minority—female and African.[23]

When Peg came to Virginia she had already survived two great risks. The slave trade in Africa had an even higher death rate than the middle passage to the colonies. Peg was among the relatively few women whom African slave traders did not reserve for sale in Africa. After mid-century, traders began offering more women to British and American ship captains looking for slave cargoes. Weak and traumatized by the African trade, Peg probably crossed the Atlantic between January and May on a crowded ship allowing her half the between-decks space allotted to European immigrants. Although as a woman Peg may have had access to the upper deck unchained, that made her vulnerable to sexual abuse by the crew. The risks of the middle passage declined in the late eighteenth century, however, as ships became faster and more specialized. Overall death rates on late eighteenth-century slave ships (16 percent mortality from the Bight of Benin, and less from other areas) were comparable to those on ships transporting soldiers or convict labor from Europe.[24]

By 1740 the area around the Porter plantation had become prime tobacco land. Amy grew up in a fast-growing community with constant new arrivals from Africa, 7,302 to the piedmont in the 1750s alone. The piedmont and the frontier absorbed almost all the Virginian slave population growth from 1755 to 1782. In 1755 almost 40 percent of the areas' adult slaves had been born in Africa. The trade shifted to Maryland ports after Virginia imposed a duty to limit importation. Although reduced by half after 1765 through boycotts and war, the trade revived in the 1780s. Twenty-seven percent of those enslaved in neighboring Chesterfield County in 1782 were African born, despite the war's disruption of the trade, births of Virginia-born slaves like Amy, and flight to invading British army lines in 1780. After 1790, natural increase satisfied the demand for slaves.[25]

Young Amy, unlike her mother, did not feel like a minority. By adulthood, Africans outnumbered whites at the Porter household, and about half the slaves were female. Colonists saw tobacco cultivation as appropriate work for women and children. Not surprisingly, then, women and children made up a higher proportion of the late eighteenth-century slave trade with Africa. By 1750 one-sixth of those imported were children, and by the 1760s girls outnumbered boys among new arrivals to the central piedmont.[26] Although all the British colonies used slaves before the Revolution, Maryland, Virginia, the Carolinas, and Georgia received most of the imports. By 1776 South Carolina, French Louisiana, Virginia, and Georgia all had a black population equal to or greater than the white population.[27]

By the 1750s, the Franklins were among the urban slaveholders of the north. Urban areas contained only 2–8 percent of any middle or New England colony's population, but out of every 10 urban residents, two to four were black. By 1745 New York City was 21 percent black. Two neighboring counties also had substantial black populations. Since urban work included many jobs deemed suitable for women, whites were more willing to purchase or keep female slaves. The result was a more even sex ratio in these middle and northern urban areas than in the South.[28]

Urban enslaved women lived scattered throughout the city in their masters' households, rather than in a black residential enclave. Many, like the poet Phillis Wheatley, arrived as children and became thoroughly acculturated. Wheatley, probably born in Senegal, was about seven or eight when John and Susanna Wheatley purchased her as a domestic in 1760. Although educated by the Wheatley family, Phillis never crossed a subtle racial line. She ate her meals sitting at a separate table near the family. Alone, she sat between slavery and freedom, African and European cultures, but not really *in* either.[29]

As Deborah Franklin walked through her city in the 1740s, she saw many more directly imported Africans than she had as a child. About one-tenth of the population were slaves. Most of the women who arrived in Pennsylvania as part of the slave trade were of similar age and set to similar tasks as those coming from Europe as servants. Most Pennsylvania slaves lived in Philadelphia or surrounding dairy areas. Originally they had arrived in small lots picked up by ship captains trading among the British colonies in many kinds of goods. By mid-century specialized ships brought slaves directly from Africa to Philadelphia. Philadelphians and other northerners temporarily turned to slaves to replace indentured servants who enlisted during the Great War for Empire. Following the Great War for Empire, Philadelphians turned away from bound labor. By 1775 the slave population had dropped to almost half of its 1767 total. Poor free whites now sought many of the jobs previously filled by servants and slaves. The trend away from slavery continued. The Philadelphia Sarah Franklin Bache knew in 1790 had few slaves, no new imports, and a small, but growing, free black community.[30]

No matter what their status, the immigrant generation bore fewer children than those who grew up in the colonies. Disease, harsh conditions, delayed marriages, and death of spouses helped depress the fertility of all immigrants to the New World. For African women, childbearing and family formation were even more problematic than for European immigrants. Small piedmont plantations offered little opportunity to find a spouse. Couples could be separated by the practice of hiring out or by a planter's decision to send one member of a couple to work land owned by the family in another location. It took time to meet men from neighboring plantations. Because African women continued to do field work throughout much of a pregnancy, the risk of miscarriage was high. Immigrant blacks maintained African traditions of extended periods of breast-feeding, which also lowered their chances of conceiving.[31]

The higher fertility of native-born couples in maturing communities caused a different problem. Throughout the eighteenth century, older settlements found themselves with more young adults coming of age than there were parcels of good available land. Families tried to settle all of their children in the community by splitting the family land and farming it more intensively, by claiming marginal land, by providing some sons with alternative trades, or by buying land from neighbors who decided to leave. Ultimately, some children moved to frontier areas or floated from community to community looking for work.

As land became more scarce, daughters were less likely to receive any gifts or bequests of land from their parents. Increasingly they inherited cash, slaves, or moveable property such as beds or livestock. Ownership of moveable property passed to their husbands upon marriage, unlike land, in which they retained a partial life interest. Widows also received diminished bequests. While widows before 1740 often received more than their dower share, after that date they were increasingly limited to dower (a one-third life interest in the land), or to a bequest obligating a child to provide a certain level of support and space to the widow. In a world of finite resources and growing numbers of claimants, women's claims took last priority.[32]

The land squeeze sent many families to the frontier. Frontier areas attracted both families and single males, but few single women. Movement to the frontier thus unbalanced sex ratios in both old and new areas, creating a female majority along the coast and reducing women's marriage prospects. Men who went to the frontier ahead of their families helped to further unbalance ratios. Frontier Orangeburg in South Carolina had 118 men for each 100 women. In French settlements along the Mississippi (which became part of the British Empire as a result of the Seven Years' War) there were as many as 222 males for every 97 females.[33] Black families also felt the strain and separation, for many whites brought young male slaves to help with the heavy labor of settlement.[34]

The Porter household illustrates changing family strategies as land pressure increased. In 1726 when Pierre Dutoy died, King William Parish was not far from the frontier. His will distributed his 861 acres among three children, a nephew, and Barbara, his widow. Barbara received a life interest in all 861 acres, including the home plantation. Daughter Elizabeth inherited the home plantation of 61 acres upon Barbara's death. Other heirs received unimproved nearby frontier lands—daughter Maryanne, 300 acres; son Isaac, 400 acres; and nephew Anthony Benin, 100 acres. Because Barbara received a life interest in all the land, she decided when her children and nephew would begin to manage it. Pierre Dutoy was able to give his daughters and son equivalent bequests because nearby frontier land was available at minimal cost.[35]

Thomas and Elizabeth Porter had to work harder to acquire land for their large family. When Thomas died, sons Isaac, William, and John, and married daughter Elizabeth Porter Branch, received land in Manakin. Daughters Sarah Porter Hatcher and Ann Porter shared a tract in frontier Albemarle County. By the 1790s they had moved west to claim that land. Elizabeth Porter used her will to try to even things out for daughter Mary, who had received no land. She left a son three slaves if he would pay his sister £30. However, this passed immediately to Mary's husband with no dower protection for Mary. Elizabeth Dutoy Porter remained in her childhood home until she died, but her inheritance was both proportionately and absolutely less than what her mother Barbara Dutoy had received as a widow. Thomas left her only a life interest in the farm willed her by her own father. As coexecutrix of the estate, Elizabeth had to share the decision-making with two of her sons.[36] Thomas Porter tried to provide nearly equal estates for his children, but limited the control of his widow Elizabeth and had to short his youngest daughter.

The next generation used even more restrictive strategies. Because Elizabeth Porter Branch died before her husband Daniel Branch wrote his will in 1782, he did not need to consider provisions for her. There were, however, four sons and three daughters living. The Branches lived on the land they had inherited from Thomas Porter and some adjoining land they purchased from Porter at the time of their wedding. This time the 301-acre estate passed intact to son Daniel. The other children inherited slaves and moveable property only. The sons were to receive an additional slave each if they paid each daughter £30.[37] Thus the bequest Daniel Branch's daughters received passed immediately to the control of their husbands.

If land scarcity lowered women's economic status in more settled areas, it also sent young men and families in search of areas with greater opportunity. Elizabeth's sister Maryanne and her second husband left Manakin for frontier land. Grandson Thomas Branch moved to less-settled Amelia County by 1792 in search of land. Young families moved back and forth across county lines renting land or working for wages. In the Chesapeake, approximately one-quarter of the young men left their home counties between 1750 and 1760.[38]

Population centers moved westward in nearly every colony from 1750 to 1775. Pennsylvanians not only pushed onto the Chesapeake frontier, but more than 2,000 families left for the southern backcountry each year. New England migrants scattered in all directions. In the 15 years preceding independence, 283 new towns were founded in New England, mostly in New Hampshire, Vermont, and the district of Maine.[39]

The British government controlled frontier growth. The Proclamation of 1763, intended to prevent Indian discontent by containing white settlers, quickly eroded as colonists ignored it and renegotiated the boundaries set by the Proclamation. In April 1773, the Privy Council ordered colonial governors to stop all granting of land. The American Revolution swept away any British restraints, and migration to frontier areas accelerated. Indians once on the boundary between Euro- and Indian America (like Margaret and Mary Brant) found themselves surrounded by white settlers. Western Indians, used to contacts of trade and diplomacy, now found themselves face-to-face with settlers intent on transforming the land. The contest for Indian lands merged in complex ways with the War for Independence. The frontier war continued for a decade after Britain and the United States had agreed to peace.[40]

Marie Porter's marriage to Daniel Guerrand in 1770 made neighbor Daniel Trabue a distant kinsman. Trabue scouted Kentucky in 1774 at the close of a short war with the Shawnee. The next year, white settlers organized a government in Kentucky, thus merging the struggle for independence with that between Indians and whites for control of the area. By 1800 one-eighth of the population of Virginia and Maryland moved into Kentucky and Tennessee. Sarah Porter Hatcher and her husband Thomas became the first of Elizabeth Porter's direct descendants to join the flow to the west.[41]

The Revolutionary frontier was an area of cultural contact and transition where women often served as the bridges between cultures. Indians and whites together had already created a cultural "middle ground" with its own rules of interaction, cultural accommodation, and negotiation for trade and diplomacy. Women—captives, wives of traders, and eastern Indians moving west—helped construct the rules for cultural interaction on the "middle ground." Both gender and racial lines remained fluid as American Indian and European cultures borrowed, adapted, and rejected parts of the other's culture.[42]

The "middle ground" in western New York was under constant pressure from settlers. By 1757 more than 4,550 people of European background had settled in Mohawk country. Sir William Johnson, the British Indian agent (and soon to be Molly's spouse), actively recruited German and Dutch immigrants. He also negotiated major land cessions from the Mohawk. As European settlement increased, Mohawk numbers declined from disease. By 1771 Albany County had 406 Mohawk in two villages, and 42,706 whites and blacks. The Mohawk adapted to sedentary farming, but this increased the risk of disease and depleted their numbers even more. Margaret and Molly Brant were now a minority in their own land.[43]

The dwindling Mohawk population struggled to maintained traditions. Cultural accommodation increased. By 1771 most Mohawks, like

Margaret and Molly, were nominal Christians. Missionaries encouraged men to assume women's farm duties on individual, fenced plots of land, and to raise domesticated animals rather than hunt. This displaced women as owners and workers of fields, and eroded the power of clan matrons who oversaw women's agricultural work and distributed harvest surpluses at councils and festivals. Despite resistance from women, by 1760 some Mohawks hired white men to plow their fields in order to farm more intensively. Others, such as Molly and Joseph Brant, purchased slaves to help farm. As men began using horses to haul firewood, women gave up a tiresome task, but also lost part of their symbolic control of the home fires.[44]

Margaret spent her whole life adapting to these changes. European disease and wars with European causes widowed her and killed at least two children. To feed her children, Margaret sold (Euro-American) liquor and gathered ginseng to sell to whites. When she married Brant Canagaraduncka in 1753, the Anglican missionary at Fort Hunter performed the ceremony. The couple built a frame house rather than a traditional dwelling. Margaret's children accommodated even more. Joseph attended European mission schools, first at Canojhorie and later in Lebanon, Connecticut. Symbolic of the cultural pressure faced, Margaret's oldest children entered the world as Joseph and Mary Brant, linked to their stepfather's rather than their mother's kinship group.

Margaret and her children were leaders in the Mohawk cultural accommodation, blending old and new. Margaret lived in a small home (10' × 16') with glass windows and a barn. She served traditional foods, but on ceramic dishes. Joseph could read and write English and argue Christian theology if necessary, but he remained active in Mohawk councils and took seriously his duties to matrilineal kin. When in 1774 the widowed Molly returned to live next door to her mother, she arrived wearing silk hose and gowns and accompanied by two maids and two male servants. Mary filled her large (20' × 40') Dutch-style home with Chinese porcelain and fine furniture. Despite her obvious delight in the trappings of Euro-American society, Molly remained a Mohawk matron and moved back and forth between the two cultures.[45]

Few Indians made the spectacular leap between two cultures that Molly Brant made. Stubbornly retaining matrifocal kin groups and the traditional seasonal move, Indians joined the floating labor poor on the edges of Euro-American society. Others traded with the whites who surrounded their tiny reservations. Women found a ready market for their skills in basketry, sewing, and farming.[46] Indians constantly adapted European items to their own use. For example, Catawba buildings used British-style square logs set vertically with a central smoke hole rather than a chimney. Indian dress mixed European blankets and traditional skins or layered European clothing in unique ways.[47]

Under the pressure of mid-eighteenth-century settlement, some Indian groups merged or centralized, while others fragmented. Villages lay abandoned. Epidemics sped up the merger process by wiping out two-thirds to half of several southern groups. Women collectively owned the fields at these villages and women maintained the household structures of the village. Each consolidation thus shook the foundations of women's lives. The new settlers changed all that was familiar by renaming places, damming streams, and building fences.

Trade and settlement pressures resulted in major shifts of the Indian population in the late eighteenth century. In about 1720, Great Lakes Indians built Ohio Valley towns that attracted Indians from many groups. Eastern Algonkians, many English-speaking (and some Christians), moved to the Ohio Valley mixed towns after Pontiac's Rebellion. Some tribes moved to be closer to trading centers in Natchez, Mobile, and New Orleans. Women's skills in agriculture, basket weaving, and animal-hide preparation made this trade possible. The search for the ever-scarcer game moved winter hunting camps several hundred miles from summer villages. Mixed villages and trading centers expanded cultural exchange.[48]

Women who married white Indian traders were important cultural mediators. Indian traders followed an old European tradition of using marriage to further diplomacy and trade. Traders' wives bridged two worlds, interpreting customs and conversations for their trader husbands, and gaining access themselves to many trade goods. By the 1770s more than 300 traders and settlers resided in or near Chickasaw and Choctaw towns, and another 300 in Creek villages. Most of the traders lived with Indian women, many in long-term, stable relationships. In some cases the traders purchased Indian women captured in the frequent raids between southeastern Indian groups. After the Revolution, loyalist traders moved with their families to Creek country, where they became large slaveholders on their wives' lands.[49]

Marriage to a trader was not without risk. Catawba Indians required family consent when a woman wished to marry a trader because traders sometimes abandoned women. Molly Brant had to weigh the risks and benefits carefully when Sir William Johnson approached her. Johnson had a history of short liaisons with Indian women, and a long-term one with his housekeeper. Molly's family would gain prosperity and status among the Mohawk from their connection with Johnson. Joseph's ties to Johnson, and the education Johnson arranged for him, helped Joseph rise to leadership among the Mohawk. Johnson, in return, gained greater credibility with the Iroquois through Molly's connections to the tribe and her role as a clan matron.[50]

Some traders took advantage of their economic power or misinterpreted Indian customs of ritual exchange (which could include sex). By the late eighteenth century, women's offers of sex following trade had been commodified. Women exchanged sex for rum, which they then sold to other Indians at high prices. Once women controlled the rum trade, they exchanged furs rather than sex for rum. By the 1760s Indian leaders began denouncing the trade, and complained that traders were sexually abusing respectable married women. The traders apparently could not distinguish between women or kinds of offers.[51]

The children of mixed marriages benefited from a form of dual citizenship, claimed both by matrilineal tribes and patrilineal Euro-Americans. The children grew up bilingual and familiar with both cultures. They married into both cultures, or mediated between them. One such mixed-blood Creek woman, Mary Musgrove, helped shield Georgia from Indian wars throughout the 1730s and 1740s. Men born to such mixed marriages became influential leaders by the time of the Revolution in the new blended villages of the Ohio River Valley and among the Creek.[52]

Women captives also bridged the cultural gaps between Euro-American customs and Indian customs. The nearly constant warfare after 1740 increased the number of captives and the need for Indian families to replace the casualties of war and diseases through adoption. Indian women adopted after capture helped provide cultural ties across tribal lines. White captives often translated, taught skills such as knitting, sewing, or weaving, and married in their adopted communities.

Both Europeans and Indians took captives during wars, but they treated them differently. Whites either took no captives or sold the captives as slaves. Cherokee captives taken during the Revolution were sold as slaves in Charleston, South Carolina.[53] Whites considered rape an extension of war, and often raped Indian women. Captive-taking was embedded in Indian rituals of war. Captives might be sold, tortured and killed in rituals of revenge and mourning, or adopted into families. Many American Indians followed customs of ritual purification as part of war, and warriors abstained from sex until after they had returned to their village. Thus the rape of white women was uncommon.[54]

Captivity began with violence and traumatic shock. Most women saw family members killed in the fight leading to capture. Raiding parties needed to move quickly. Those captives who could not keep pace did not survive. Women, usually captured with other family members, were often too burdened with infants or pregnancy to help themselves or others. Thus pregnant Margaret Erskine had to watch her Shawnee captors tomahawk her crying child in 1779. The elderly, infants, and pregnant women were most at risk. Judith Ford, a former neighbor of Elizabeth Porter Branch, did not survive the 1780 march as a captive to Detroit from Martin's Station in Kentucky. The raiders often separated captives into smaller groups, or traded them to other Indians. Others saw members of their group tortured and killed upon arrival in the Indian Village.[55]

One of the most difficult things for many white colonists to accept was that not all whites who were captured and adopted by Indians wanted to return to "civilization" when peace arrived. Their original families scattered or dead, and colonial customs a distant memory, the captives had built new lives among the Indians. Although originally hoping for a rescue, Mary Jemison (captured in 1755) voluntarily remained with the Seneca, marrying first a Delaware and then a Seneca. The daughter of hard-working Irish immigrants, she thought life was easier among the Iroquois.[56]

Indian women played important roles in determining which captives lived or died, and oversaw rites of adoption. When the British began negotiating with Indian leaders for the return of captives during the Seven Years' War, they found themselves negotiating with clan matrons. Even a leader as knowledgeable about Iroquois customs as William Johnson was taken aback by the prominent role women expected to play in these negotiations.[57]

The last half of the eighteenth century saw a west constantly at war. Throughout the 1740s Iroquois and Catawbas were at war. The Upper Creeks attacked the Cherokee in 1748. A two-decade conflict between Cherokee and Shawnee stretched into the 1770s. Although most tribes were officially neutral during King George's War, the Great War for Empire was harder to avoid. Despite official Mohawk neutrality, some joined the British cause. The Shawnee and Seneca allied with the French, while the Cherokee shifted positions several times. The wars brought captives and casualties to Indian villages, sent refugees scurrying from war zones, and led to further consolidation of depleted villages.[58]

By 1760 a precarious peace had been restored through individual treaties with Indian groups, only to be shattered in 1763 when the Ottowa leader, Pontiac, launched a united effort against the British by Ohio Valley Indians. Frontier peace officially returned in 1765, but individual acts of violence continued. In the first six months of 1766, whites and blacks killed 20 Indians. The British were unable to punish the murderers, and Indians began revenge killings.[59] The war left unhealed divisions among the Cherokee and a split among the Iroquois that would haunt these groups when war resumed in the 1770s.

Overall, these wars devastated those involved, especially women and children. Hunger stalked the frontier throughout the 1750s. Armies often targeted Indian crops. Women suffered directly since they owned the crops and fields. Marie le Roy, a Delaware, remembered eating bark, grass, and acorns after her village was destroyed in the fall of 1756. The Indian requests of European nations for food and clothes in order to fight gained a new urgency in 1758 and 1759. Supplies served as reparations for those who had died and offered relief from impending famine.[60]

The 1740s were difficult times for Margaret, but she married Brant and moved into Johnson's charmed circle just before the Great War for Empire. Johnson stayed with Margaret's family while negotiating with the Mohawk in 1752 and 1753. By the end of the war Mary had borne Johnson a son. In 1760 she became mistress of Johnson Hall, where she remained until his death in 1774. Mary and the Brants were invaluable to Johnson during the war, helping to enlist the Mohawk on the British side and to procure a large land grant in 1759. Mary also became an influential clan matron. Thus Margaret and Molly moved from poverty and marginality to wealth and power during the course of the two wars.[61]

Warfare on the frontier created refugees of many kinds. Neutral Indians often sought safety in vain, as Euro-Americans failed to distinguish between villages at peace and at war, or to recognize shifting alliances among Indians. Twice Pennsylvanians murdered bands of neutral Indians. In 1755 frontier units slaughtered the entire Moravian-convert Indian village of Gnadenhutten. Moravians at Bethlehem sheltered other Indians who then fled to them for protection. Following the cold-blooded murder in 1763 of Conestoga Indians in Lancaster, Pennsylvania, Quakers helped some Lenape flee to New Jersey.[62] During the war, Mohawk villages swelled with Canadian Mohawk refugees and those from other tribes.

Colonial settlers, especially women and children, also streamed east as refugees. The frontier war reached within 30 miles of Philadelphia. Settlers also moved to the South Carolina backcountry, where the Cherokee kept an uneasy peace (thanks in part to the efforts of Cherokee leader, Nancy Ward) until late in the war. Disease followed refugees and troops. Frontier troops returning from Cherokee country were the likely source of a major smallpox epidemic in Charleston, South Carolina, that killed over 700.[63]

The colonial wars impoverished many women. At the end of King George's War, widowed women who flocked to Boston and other port cities overburdened poor relief and philanthropy. According to a 1742 census, 1,200 women, or one-third of the adult females in Boston, were widows. Over the next decade, drought, smallpox, and fire would add to Boston's woes. The fire of 1760 left more than 100 widows homeless, of whom 82 percent had been among the city's poor before the fire. Towns began to "warn out" strangers, a majority of whom were women without family to support them. Thus women became part of a floating population of poor that increasingly troubled leaders on the eve of the Revolution. The War for Independence soon added to the problem.[64]

When the War for Independence renewed conflict along the Canadian border, both Americans and British sought support from the Iroquois, shattering Iroquois unity. The Seneca and Oneida largely supported the Americans, but Mary Brant worked continuously to make the Mohawk, Seneca, and Cayuga British allies. Margaret, Mary, and their family fled to the Cayuga in 1777, when Americans learned that Mary had passed the British information at the battle of Oriskany. Patriots gleefully plundered Mary Brant's home, loading wagons with her silver and her silk dresses. As Mohawk villages faced reprisal raids over the next several years, women and children joined Margaret and Mary as refugees.[65]

From 1777 to 1780, Mary Brant entertained visiting Indian delegations at Fort Niagara and traveled to recruit British support. When Niagara became too crowded with refugees in 1780, she moved to a house on Carleton Island. As much a civil war for the Iroquois as for the European settlers of America, mixed groups of Indians and whites marched on campaigns against other Indian and white settlements. The Brants paid a high personal price during the war: Mary lost her mother, her son Peter, her stepson William Johnson, and her daughter-in-law.

At the end of the war, Mary Brant resettled in Kingston, Ontario, with other Mohawk loyalists, on lands granted by the British. Mary Brant was now an exile from her own land.[66]

If the war on the northeastern frontier was a civil war, in Kentucky and the Ohio Valley it was a bitter, no-holds-barred struggle for survival with causes beyond the War for Independence. White encroachment on their land convinced many Shawnee and Creeks to ally with the British during the war. When the Treaty of Versailles officially ended the War for Independence in 1783, the Indians continued to resist. The struggle continued until 1792, when, defeated at Fallen Timbers, Indians signed treaties relinquishing most of the contested lands.

In this contest for land, there were no noncombatants. The Indian conflict reopened in 1774, with a colonial expedition against the Shawnee led by British Governor, Lord Dunmore.[67] The inability and unwillingness of many settlers to distinguish Indian allies and neutrals from those at war with the new government drove more Indians into open war with settlers on the frontier. The Seneca initially allied with the Americans. By 1777 enough Seneca had been murdered by their allies, however, to turn them against the new nation. In November 1777 Virginia militia captured and murdered the Shawnee leaders who had been holding some villages out of the conflict. In 1784 they killed many in a Shawnee village that had just negotiated peace. Militia killed neutral chiefs (and their relatives) working to keep their villages from joining the British. In a chilling repeat of an earlier massacre, militia executed over 90 Moravian Indians, mostly women and children, in March 1782 at Gnadenhutten.[68]

The taking of captives during the War for American Independence, as usual, focused on women and children. One raid in Kentucky by a combined British and Shawnee force in 1780 resulted in 170 Kentucky women and children being taken as captives to Canada. Creek raids on Georgia, South Carolina, and Florida brought enslaved Africans to Creek lands where they became slaves of their Indian captors. White women were also Creek captives.[69] After 1780, the pressures of relentless war meant that the Shawnee increasingly chose to kill white women and children rather than take captives. At Cherry Valley in New York, the Iroquois broke ranks and began killing indiscriminately, in part to retaliate against whites who had violated their paroles to take part in raids against Iroquois villages.[70]

Eastern campaigns also displaced women. As the daughter of a signer of the Declaration of Independence and wife of the postmaster for the new nation, Sarah Franklin Bache had to flee Philadelphia in December 1776 and again on September 17, 1777, just four days after giving birth to a daughter. Sarah settled in Manheim, Lancaster County, until the British left Philadelphia in 1778.[71] Many loyalist women soon became refugees, like Mary and Margaret Brant. Women either endured long separations from their loyalist husbands or joined them behind British lines as refugees. Mobs drove some women from their homes. Some loyalists went to Britain, where they lived precariously, petitioning for compensation. Other women resettled in Nova Scotia, Florida or the Bahamas.[72]

Beginning in 1776, African-American women and men escaped to British lines. In 1779 General Henry Clinton issued a general order offering freedom to slaves willing to help the British. About two-fifths of those who escaped were women. Many of the women brought young children with them or had children while under British protection. Children born in the British camps were free. At the close of the war the British had to decide what to do with the several thousand former slaves now under their protection. They returned fugitive slaves who had escaped after the signing of the preliminary peace treaty, and those claimed by loyalists. Of the 2,800 black refugees who resettled in Nova Scotia, 936 were adult women.[73]

Despite the seeming chaos of the years from 1740 to 1790, certain larger patterns emerged. Women were a minority of free and unfree migrants to new areas. Immigrants of all races had a different pattern of childbearing than women who were raised in the colonies. Colonial growth in more settled areas reduced women's chances there for inheritance and marriage. In the backcountry, men continued to outnumber women, and both Indian and African women felt the effects of being a double minority. The expansion of colonial settlement brought both cultural adaptation and friction. Women served both willingly and unwillingly as bridges between different cultures. War on the frontier inevitably brought patterns of capture, fleeing refugees, starvation, and dislocation. Women made up the majority of refugees, captives, and victims of famine.

The Revolution accelerated the patterns of prewar migration. Fighting on all fronts brought waves of refugees and captives. The scale and geographic sweep of the War for Independence meant that the dislocation touched the lives of many more women than that of earlier colonial wars. The turmoil of the Revolution allowed some women to escape from slavery and turned others into refugees and exiles in their own land. Frontier fighting took on a more vicious cast as retaliations escalated, Euro-American migration to the frontier accelerated, and hunger stalked Indian villages. The frontier war also defied peace, continuing for 10 bitter years after the United States and European powers signed a peace treaty. Women, winners and losers alike, had been uprooted by the Revolution in profound and irreversible ways.

The trade-offs of the Revolutionary era are starkly evident for women. If moving west helped relieve land pressures reducing eastern women's options, it came at a direct cost to American Indian women, who were displaced by the settlement, and to the African-American women whose families were divided to provide the labor in new areas. If the replacement of indentured servants with paid, day labor offered women more control over their lives and working conditions, the women who worked in this way were part of a growing, marginalized class of the poor. If visiting helped sustain ties of kin and friendship, it did so along increasingly stratified lines of race and class. Women's Revolutionary-era mobility produced clear winners and losers, sharply divided by lines of race and class.

CHAPTER THREE

The Silken Cord

Marriage "gave a Complexion" to a woman's life in eighteenth-century British America, whatever her race or social status.[1] It redefined a woman's legal status, economic opportunities, family networks, and family and community roles, and it directly affected her reproductive history and health. The experiences of the mothers and daughters of the Brant, Porter, and Franklin households illustrate both the continuities and the shifting social and ideological contexts in which women made basic decisions about family. Historians do not agree on the causes of these changes, but the Revolution certainly influenced them. By 1790, the social context of marriage and family for women was quite different than it had been in 1740.

Generally, women of the eighteenth century spent most of their lives as married women. Deborah Read Franklin and Elizabeth Dutoy Porter each entered relationships that survived more than 40 years. Peg and her mate Joseph had at least 20 years together on the Porter farm before Peg died. Epidemics and war disrupted Margaret Brant's married life. Even so, when she died at about age 60, more than 27 of those years were as a married woman.

For all groups in American society, wedding celebrations were important social occasions, an intersection of social customs, coming of age, and religious beliefs. The importance of the occasion was set off by new clothes, feasting, and (when not contrary to religious beliefs) dancing. Women played important roles in planning and orchestrating these social rituals, which were often held at home. A couple's first appearance at religious services after marriage was often a major event.[2]

Family income and connections helped define women's marriage choices. Both Elizabeth Dutoy and Deborah Read based marriage on practicality and companionship. Given that Margaret's economic status improved with each marriage, she might have agreed. Peg faced marriage without family help and with constraints that made marriage optional, fragile, and important. By 1752 Deborah Franklin, Elizabeth Porter, Margaret Brant, and Peg all had daughters or wards of marriageable age. Their family lives would be profoundly affected by the wars for empire and independence that dominated the age. However, they made their marriage choices without knowledge of the Revolutionary years to come.

The daughters of Elizabeth Porter deviated only slightly from the patterns of courtship and marriage of their parents. Elizabeth, Sarah, Anne, and Marie all married between ages 16 and 19, choosing men (Daniel Branch, Thomas Hatcher, Charles Sampson, and Daniel Guerrant, respectively) who lived nearby and were older by several years. Their two brothers also followed tradition. The girls married in order of age, and none was pregnant at marriage. Death, however, ended at least four of the marriages prematurely. Ann Porter Sampson and Magdalene Chastain Porter (Elizabeth Dutoy Porter's daughter-in-law) spent at least a dozen years each as widows.[3] Although marrying slightly younger than the norm, the Porter daughters were typical in the age and residence of their new husbands, and even in the time of year they married.[4]

In 1754, at the age of 23, Deborah Franklin's niece, ward, and namesake Deborah Croker married printer William Dunlap. The Franklins promptly arranged for William to take over one of the Franklin printing enterprises. The Dunlaps named their first child Frances, in honor of the Franklins' deceased son. Like her aunt, Deborah looked after her husband's business when he was away, and helped in the shop. When William Dunlap sought ordination as an Anglican priest in 1766, Deborah's life took an unexpected turn. William took a Virginia Parish in 1768. She died in Virginia in 1775. For Deborah Croker Dunlap, marriage to a rising member of the middle class had required separation from her family, despite the best efforts of the Franklins.[5]

Like her cousin, Sarah Franklin was in her early 20s when Richard Bache sought her hand in 1767. Deborah Franklin was "obliged to be father and mother" in the resulting negotiations, since Benjamin was in England. Sally's half-brother William alerted his father that he feared the English-born merchant Bache was a fortune hunter. Deborah and Sally ignored Benjamin's concerns, and the couple married in October. Despite Sarah's status as a potential heiress, there was no formal marriage settlement, probably because the absent Benjamin was still trying to prevent the marriage. Benjamin Franklin used his will to provide Sarah with a separate estate. In the Franklin family, parental authority bent to Sarah's choice. After Richard Bache met with his father-in-law in England, Franklin gave him £200 and a power of attorney to share oversight of the Franklins' affairs with Deborah.[6]

By marrying at 23, Sally and Deborah deviated from the experience of most women from their class and region. Women living south of Pennsylvania married earlier than those to the north. Economic factors affected marriage ages everywhere. Women and men whose families cared about economic security for a couple, but could not easily supply it, married later. Those with handsome marriage settlements could marry earlier. Black and white women with few or no economic assets to protect generally seemed to have married or begun bearing children in their teens. Race, class, and regional differences declined in the late eighteenth century, however, and median marriage ages for women from all groups converged in the 18–22 age bracket.[7]

Margaret's daughter Mary (Molly) was 17 when the British trader and Indian agent Sir William Johnson began staying with the Brants. Johnson had relationships with several women, including Molly. His German servant housekeeper, Catharine Weissenberg, bore him three children, and he married Catharine in 1759 just before she died, ensuring the legitimacy of those children. A pregnant Molly moved to Johnson's impressive home shortly after Catharine's death. In Mohawk eyes, she and Johnson were married. Under English law they were not. Johnson referred to her as his housekeeper and to their children as "natural" in his will. Molly was the official hostess and mistress of Johnson Hall until William Johnson died in 1774. Then she and her eight children returned to Canajohorie to live in luxury with fine furnishings and clothes and four servants.[8]

Kin were important for marriage negotiations among most Indian groups. Clan matrons often acted as go-betweens. Among some Indians, courtship involved gifts to the woman's family. Because courtship could include sexual experimentation, Molly's pregnancy before joining Johnson at Johnson Hall was not an issue among the Mohawks, although it certainly would not have pleased the Christian missionaries whose services Molly attended.[9]

Peg's daughter Amy also came of age by 1760, but there is no evidence that she married. Thomas Porter owned 19 slaves by 1767, making him a substantial slaveholder, but Porter's holdings gave Amy little choice of a spouse within the plantation community. Of the seven adult men on the plantation, five appear to have been married to others on the plantation. At least one of the remaining five may have been Amy's brother. Thus, unless she could find a way to meet a man from another plantation, she had no options. Even after moving to Daniel Branch's plantation as part of Elizabeth's inheritance, she did not marry.

Amy's difficulty in finding a mate was not unusual for those enslaved on Chesapeake farms, for most slaves lived in small clusters (or quarters) with imbalanced sex or age ratios, or with a population of kin that custom eliminated as potential mates. Although black men generally outnumbered black women in the colonies, a particular small farm could reverse that ratio. The uneven sex ratios also led to marriages between Indians and Africans in some areas of the colonies. Indian populations seem to have had more women than men, and so the two groups complemented each other.[10] Although Manakin had once been an Indian Village, by 1750 Indians were gone. Thus Amy did not have this option.[11] Amy was an exception in that she did not eventually find a mate. The sex-ratio difference did eventually help women find husbands on nearby plantations. Given the few opportunities for travel, it just took longer than it did for white women.[12]

Courtship customs in the last half of the century shifted so that young adults of European background took more initiative in finding mates. Control of the formalities of marriage became stricter. A redefinition of marriage accompanied the changes in courtship. Whereas Deborah Franklin and Elizabeth Dutoy Porter thought of marriage as an economic partnership with a major goal of providing property for offspring, their granddaughters more likely viewed marriage as a form of companionship based on affection.

Because marriage had social, familial, and economic implications, it was never left solely to the discretion of the courting couple, whatever their race. Old and new patterns of courtship existed side-by-side in the last half of the century, but under all circumstances families had some role. Families sought to protect their children by finding the best possible economic and social match available. For women of the upper class, such as Sarah Franklin, the neighborhood provided too restricted a net-

work for courtship. Elite families used periodic extended visits and letters to sustain their more geographically dispersed network of family
and friends. Sarah and her father's visit to New England relatives when
she was 20 was a perfect opportunity to meet a new pool of family-
approved young men. Had Sally found a family-approved mate on the
trip, she might have married immediately.[13] Conversely, families worried about outsiders such as Richard Bache. Courtship for women of
the upper class brought the possibility of relocation beyond the easy
reach of kin, and thus heightened family concerns about a wise choice.[14]

Even groups with unique customs of courtship or marriage were
affected by shifting understandings of marriage. Both Moravian and
Quaker women needed church approval for a marriage. The Quaker
women's meeting screened couples seeking to marry. Although young
people might fill the meeting room with friends, hoping to influence
the decision, the women's meeting ensured that the parents consented
and that each member of the couple was in good standing. The meeting
disowned those who married outside the denomination; these were
often women without enough standing to find a match in the limited
Quaker marriage pool. In the 1750s, Quakers turned inward, enforcing
marriage rules more strictly and increasing disownments. Moravians
originally exercised even stricter control over marriage. The community sometimes matched couples and then cast lots to see if God
approved. Many men and women remained single. By the 1770s, however, the Moravian communities began allowing families to live
together and granting young people slightly more initiative in mate
selection, thus becoming more like their fellow pietists, the Quakers.[15]

By midcentury, many white families had shifted the initiative in finding a mate from the family to the individual. Control was limited to
accepting or rejecting the choice already made. Young people occasionally courted without parental knowledge. Families continued to take
the granting of permission seriously, but used delay tactics rather than
outright negatives. Benjamin Franklin, for example, suggested a trip to
England for his daughter Sally when trying to delay her marriage to
Richard Bache.[16]

Marriage was thus neither an independent act divorced from family,
nor a parental decision forced on children. Many young couples came
to Gloria Dei Lutheran Church near Philadelphia to be married without their parents. Although the minister would marry a woman over 18
and a man over 21 who were free of indentures, he would refuse if the
family had property. A quarter of the couples who came to the church

did not meet these standards. The young couples showed a high degree of independence from family, but the minister clearly believed that parents did have a say under certain circumstances.[17]

Consent was an issue for Peg and Amy as well, both in terms of giving their own consent and in seeking permission to marry. It was Pierre Dutoy's wishes that mattered to Peg, who was cut off from her family. Pierre Dutoy may have ordered Peg and Joseph to live together. If so, there was no one to whom Peg could have appealed. Despite being orphaned early, Amy grew up with the support of community and kin. Amy would have had to seek approval from both her community and the Porters/Guerrants to marry, and she also ran the risk of being forced to marry against her will.[18] Thus, ironically, although slave marriages had no legal status, the process of receiving consent to marry might be more complex than those of couples of European descent.

Thus the daughters of the Porter, Franklin, and Brant households picked their way through a changing social landscape offering them both increased choice and risks. Women had more independence in choosing a mate, but the standards of behavior during courtship had also shifted. In the Anglican colonies, dancing provided a means of courtship. As the night wore on, the couples would move from the stately minuets to the livelier country dances, reels, and jigs. Other times were more private. Even careful Quaker parents would retire to bed, leaving their son or daughter to entertain another young man or woman. The New England custom of bundling (having a courting couple climb into bed next to each other fully clothed) provided a more controlled setting for courtship than a haymow or the barn, but a curtained bed still provided privacy. Even daughters of the elite enjoyed considerable freedom, so that one young man and woman from the Virginia elite spent "Hours together" in each other's arms, including one unchaperoned night on the young man's bed. A North Carolina suitor was even more blunt. He complained to a male friend that he had only stayed with one woman since the friend left, but that he was going visiting on Saturday and "will hump them for you."[19]

One sign of changing customs was a dramatic rise after mid-century in premarital pregnancies in some areas. Eighteenth-century white society officially frowned on sexual intercourse outside of marriage, but the enforcement of statutes was limited. Most prosecutions singled out lower-class women whose children might become public charges. Servant women remained vulnerable.[20] Many couples used pregnancy as leverage in securing parental approval for a marriage. In fact, premarital pregnancy correlates closely with the marriage of a younger daughter (out of turn), and a greater difference in the ages of bride and groom. Many couples tried to divert attention from an early birth by delaying baptism or having the baby baptized away from the church where they were married. Since a man could abandon the woman after getting her pregnant, the woman bore a greater risk. Some desperate women then sought abortions.[21]

European society had long treated formally betrothed couples as almost married and tolerated intercourse by those who were formally engaged. By the time of the American Revolution, when war disrupted some of the usual family controls, over one-third of the brides in some New England towns were already pregnant on their wedding day. In Sarah Franklin's Philadelphia, one-quarter of middle-class brides, over half of lower middle-class women, and a third of poor women were pregnant on their wedding day. The upper class had much lower pre-marital pregnancy rates. After the Revolution the greatly varying pre-marital pregnancy rates converged toward the 16 percent–24 percent range for all groups except the middle class, of which about one-third were pregnant before marriage. Widows, living away from parental supervision and already sexually initiated, were among those most likely to be pregnant at marriage.[22]

Many adults were concerned by the rise in premarital pregnancy. In the 1750s a few New England towns tried without success to ban bundling, and the clergy led an attack in the 1770s that put them at odds with rural mothers and daughters who approved of the custom. The controversy revealed shared assumptions that both men and women had sexual feelings and desires, and that young couples would try to satisfy these feelings. Older systems of external control by family, neighborhood, church, and state had loosened. Now the couple, especially the woman, needed to internalize control. This new ethic of virtue took time to establish. A new code of chastity emerged after the American Revolution providing a crucible in which public and private virtue could be melded into a new ideology of women's roles.[23]

Rather than strictly enforcing anti-fornication and bastardy laws, leaders in the late eighteenth century regulated marriage, creating a clear distinction between legal and customary forms of marriage. All the colonies (and later the states) regulated marriage, strengthening mechanisms (such as licenses, or the public posting of marriage banns) designed to prevent secret marriages. Nonetheless, these legal regulations provided only a thin layer of decorum over a set of fluid customs sanctioned by late eighteenth-century communities. Before the Marriage Act of 1753, both England and the American colonies recognized as married any couple openly living together.[24] Thus, although Deborah and Benjamin Franklin's decision to live together troubled the local Anglican parson, their daughter Sarah was not considered illegitimate. After 1753, however, "common-law" marriages had less legal standing.

Marriage customs among Indians ranged from bride purchase and arranged marriages to practices giving women the deciding power in a relationship. In all cases, community or kin participated. The Mohawk traced kinship through female lines, giving women central decision-making roles in courtship and marriage. After marriage, the man lived with his wife's kin. Courtship could involve sexual experimentation. The records reveal little about either Margaret's courtship experiences or her daughter Molly's, except that both were pregnant at the time of a marriage.[25]

The growing emphasis in white society on specific rituals, religious or civil, that left behind a legal written record of the beginning of a marriage, was only a trend. White couples on the frontier, far from courts and churches, often "legalized" relationships long after a relationship had begun. Unchurched lower-class couples who could not afford a license simply ignored legal niceties.[26] The emphasis on legal forms, however, fit neatly with a growing legal and print culture and a commercial economy that needed individual relationships to be clearly documented. It also provided a counterbalance to changing courtship customs. If families controlled courtship less, then society defined the outcome more rigidly.

When we look at the whole population, and not just at free, white, middle- and upper-class families in settled areas, the variety of marriage forms is obvious. Slaves formed long-term relationships without the benefit of church services, banns, or licenses. (Although there were exceptions, most slaves could not legally marry.)[27] On the other hand, communities created rituals to recognize slave marriages, and whites recognized and recorded these relationships in numerous everyday records. In Virginia and South Carolina, where half the populations was enslaved, slave customs *were* the most common form of marriage.[28] Not until marriage reforms after 1750 did a gap emerge between the marriage customs of those of European and African descent. Then white access to "legal" marriage reinforced racial hierarchies.

Relationships between American Indians, or between Indians and those of European descent, posed a similar challenge. Although Molly

Brant's relationship with William Johnson had no legal standing in New York, Mohawks considered it a valid marriage. Equally telling, visitors and British officials negotiating with the Iroquois also recognized her as his wife. As European-descended settlers insisted on the unique legitimacy of their marriage customs, both the marriages of Indian couples and Indian-white unions lost status. By 1800 "polite" society considered such unions immoral.[29]

Although the percentage of never-married women dropped during the eighteenth century, the number of single women increased after 1750 due to population growth and larger numbers of widows. Women had both fewer options for marriage and less inclination to marry. In the Moravian community at Bethlehem, where single women and widows had important roles, over two-thirds of the women chose not to marry or remarry from 1764 to 1803. If women wanted to marry, they could have gone to the Moravians at Salem where there were men looking for wives.[30] The widow was the most common single woman. Scattered evidence suggests that only about a quarter of widows remarried before the Revolution, and this dropped to one-fifth after the war. Suitors sought younger women or prosperous widows. More even sex ratios reduced a widow's chances of remarriage. By 1750 the average widow was 50 when her husband died (like Elizabeth Porter) and could expect to live at least a decade longer. Women remarried only half as often as men. Many women were in no rush to remarry, refusing offers of marriage even when they were financially advantageous.[31]

By the 1770s, younger women could see advantages to being single.[32] In numerous writings, women and men adopted the political rhetoric of the day to describe women's marital state. Marriage was the end of liberty. Numerous writers used the phrase "Daughter of Liberty" to refer to single women, or contrasted women's power as "absolute Monarch" in courtship with their subjugation afterward.[33] Women's actions followed their words: The generation that came of age after 1760 had a visible group of never-married women. The process of winning independence helped make married women's dependent status more noticeable and, for some, less desirable.[34]

Married women's legal status was an important factor in making women dependent. The law viewed single, adult women (*feme soles*) as independent individuals competent to sue, make contracts, and dispose of property in the same way as men. Married women's independence was suspended through coverture. Husbands controlled the property of a *feme covert* with certain restrictions, and gained immediate control of moveable property, except for a small amount of "paraphernalia" (personal clothes, jewels, and tools protected from seizure for debts and excluded from his estate at his death). In most areas, dower rights gave women a life-interest share of the couple's real estate. Legal transfers of property required waiver of dower, and women occasionally sued successfully for compensation when the transfer had not included her waiver. It was possible to set up a trust that would give a woman control over property, thus overriding coverture.[35]

During the Revolution a few women asked for changes in property rights. When Abigail Adams wrote to her husband John in 1776 asking him to "remember the ladies," she was asking for a change to coverture. Lucy Ludwell Paradise of Virginia lobbied for a law that would have given every married woman a marriage settlement protecting the property she brought to a marriage.[36] Instead, the new states gave husbands more control of and access to the wife's property. Virginia had classified slaves as real property through most of the century. Thus, Virginia families used entail to protect from spendthrift husbands the major form of property (human) given to daughters at marriage. Between 1776 and 1792, the Virginia legislature passed a series of laws changing slaves to personal property and forbidding entail. Although court decisions made it easier to create a separate estate for a married woman by allowing a direct grant rather than a trust arrangement, after the war creditors of husbands successfully broke marriage settlements to attach the woman's assets. Several states eliminated or limited dower and paraphernalia, again giving creditors access to the property.[37]

One reason families intervened in courtship was that they often gave children their "portion" at marriage. Prudent parents often made agreements before a courtship progressed too far, so it would be easier for the couple to break up if the families failed to agree on the settlement. Benjamin Franklin, for example, stopped courting one woman because her parents were not willing to discharge the debts Franklin had incurred in setting up his print shop.[38] Most marriage settlements were informal, or were direct gifts to the couple of land, slaves, and property. Families seldom recorded such settlements in court, but parents sometimes confirmed these gifts in their wills, or granted married children only token amounts since they had already received their "share" of the estate at marriage.[39]

When an orphaned heiress or a widow married, however, a formal settlement was more common. Most formal settlements before the Revolution (82 percent in South Carolina) protected property a woman brought to marriage, and most granted the woman some control over the property through trust arrangements. By the end of the century some couples created separate estates by simple agreement between themselves. Women, however, lost some autonomy as more marriage settlements gave husbands joint control of the property. In 1795 the courts of Pennsylvania ruled that unless a marriage agreement explicitly reserved property for the "sole" use of the woman, the property belonged to the husband and wife jointly, even if contrary to the intent of the granting party.[40] Separate trusts were uncommon in New England, and creditors undermined separate equity trusts through suits designed to access assets in such trusts. Thus, ironically, married women lost protection of their separate estates through a growing emphasis on companionate marriage and commercial economy.

The growing emphasis on the formal boundaries of marriage affected its dissolution as well as its creation. Because both American Indian and African-American marriages occurred outside the parameters of English/American law, the rules for their dissolution remained fluid. American Indian customs for many groups allowed divorce at the discretion of either member of the couple. Rather than see this flexibility as positive, whites interpreted the ease of divorce in Indian society as proof of Indian immorality and lack of "civilization."[41]

For most African-American couples the real struggle was to maintain a relationship despite tremendous disincentives. Separation was both too easy and too difficult. Sale, family estate division, and work assignments could separate couples who wished to remain together. For African-American women in forced relationships, however, there was no way to dissolve an unwanted union.

If a couple were incompatible, they had few options in white communities. English law recognized three ways for a couple to separate: absolute divorce with right to remarry, a legal separation without right to remarry, and separate maintenance and property settlements agreed to by the couple in equity court.[42] English law gave spiritual courts run by Anglican bishops jurisdiction over absolute divorce. The colonies had neither a bishop nor a spiritual court. Thus most colonies had no way to grant absolute divorce. The New England colonies (where marriage was a civil contract rather than a sacrament) were the only exceptions.

Many couples used desertion as a means of ending a marriage, and, like the Franklins, they remarried without seeking a divorce. Other couples drew up articles of separation without court approval. Some clergy even recorded these documents in church records.[43] By 1800, however, such actions had become chiefly the resort of poorer couples, for "polite" society increasingly equated legality with respectability and virtue.

Couples in colonies without divorce laws could seek court-ordered separations, or divorce through private acts passed by the legislature. Private laws were rare. For example, the Virginia legislature passed no such acts before the Revolution. In Massachusetts the General Assembly passed six private divorce acts between 1755 and 1757, when the governor and council refused to award absolute divorces and granted only separations. These varied enough from English custom to catch the attention of officials in England, who considered disallowance. In 1773 the legislature in Pennsylvania passed a general law providing a method to seek absolute divorce with rights to remarry, but the crown disallowed the law.[44]

In New England absolute divorce was possible throughout the colonial period, but colonial laws produced different results. Rhode Island and Connecticut had divorce statutes. Massachusetts allowed the governor and council to act as a divorce court. Rhode Island and Connecticut, then, granted divorce on grounds of desertion, but Massachusetts did not. Since this was women's most common complaint, Massachusetts handled proportionately fewer divorce cases than Connecticut or Rhode Island.[45] Other grounds for absolute divorce included adultery and fraudulent contract.

By mid-century actions in a number of colonies suggest a changing view of divorce. The number of petitions for divorce increased in colonies where divorce was possible, and, at least in Massachusetts, women brought more of the suits. The language of the Massachusetts petitions also changed to include emphasis on affection as a component of a marriage relationship. By 1775 women began to have success with petitions charging their husbands with adultery. Colonies outside New England saw pressure for divorce proceedings. British officials had to disallow legislative acts of divorce not only in Pennsylvania but in New Jersey and New Hampshire. Virginia also discussed a divorce bill in 1772.[46] The British reacted to the rising interest in divorce by instructing royal governors in 1773 not to approve any private divorce bills.[47]

The Revolution freed states to expand divorce options. Pennsylvania's 1785 act expanded grounds for divorce to include bigamy, impotence, desertion, sexual incapacity, adultery, and cruelty. Two years later New York authorized the chancery court to grant divorce in cases of adultery, and separations for cruelty and desertion. Since grounds were still limited, some New York couples sought Connecticut divorces.[48] The Chesapeake and southern colonies did not pass general divorce laws after the Revolution, and by 1790 only Maryland had passed even a single private divorce act (to a man whose wife bore a mulatto child). Instead these states continued to allow courts to provide legal separations with some form of property rights for women.[49]

Changing laws were both the cause and the effect of increasing suits for divorce. Because women were successful, other women filed suit. Before the war the most common divorce applicant was a woman deserted by her husband. After the war, as the courts reopened, the number of divorce suits increased and the reasons shifted. Women began charging their husbands with adultery. Wives left abusive husbands, who then sought divorce. When a South Carolina man advertised his wife's desertion in the paper, she countered with her own advertisement, bluntly stating, "I never eloped, I went away before his Face when he beat me." Some clergy were concerned about the rising divorce rate and lobbied for tougher laws in Connecticut. The only response was a 1797 law requiring courts to try to get both parties to come to court.[50]

Women did not enter the divorce process lightly and spent years in terrible situations before seeking a way out. Mary Cooper of New York characterized her 40 years of marriage as "harde labour and sorrow, crosses of every kind," but she never considered separation. Her daughter Esther, however, did separate from her husband in 1769.[51] The Coopers' options were limited by New York's laws, but even in more liberal Connecticut Abigail Bailey endured years of abuse and adultery (including incest) by her husband Asa before seeking a divorce in 1793.[52] Certainly the economics of divorce was a disincentive. In a legal separation women could receive property settlements, dower awards, and rights to basic maintenance under the common law "law of necessities." Some courts insisted husbands honor debts incurred by their separated wives.[53] Divorce awards to women left them with little or no property and no financial support. Connecticut, for example, did not grant alimony to women until after the Revolution, and then in no more than 10 percent of cases. Most women forfeited even dower rights through divorce.

Historians trying to make sense out of the changing patterns of divorce have suggested a connection among increasing numbers of divorce petitions, ideas of companionate marriage, and women's rising expectations and self-esteem.[54] Revolutionary rhetoric on republican virtue may have aided women charging husbands with bigamy or adultery. Other historians have argued that no change in women's attitudes was necessary, since the success of one woman in getting a divorce could encourage others to petition.[55] As marriage reform led to a focus on precise legal definitions of marriage, divorce offered the counterbalance, a precise definition of the end to a legal relationship. Respectable families could no longer afford to live in a gray area of informal separation or desertion. Whatever the reasons, by 1790, women of European descent in a growing number of locations saw at least a faint chance that they could legally terminate abusive and nonfunctional marriages. Still, divorce remained an option chosen by only a few.

Thus race, class, and region shaped women's concerns as they contemplated marriage. A white woman had to plan for a lifetime of marriage, given the limited options for divorce. In contrast, enslaved women worried about involuntary separation from their spouses. All women knew that death ended many marriages prematurely, and that they might go through courtship several times, as did Margaret Brant. Each woman had to calculate the odds and weigh them against the economic and emotional draws of marriage.

Childbirth and child raising usually followed closely on the heels of marriage. Elizabeth Dutoy Porter bore 10 children between 1730 and 1753. The youngest was still a minor living at home when Elizabeth died in 1772. In this respect, little changed between her generation and the next. However, family roles and the definitions of marriage, family, and motherhood all changed substantially in the last half of the eighteenth century. Thus, although the daughters experienced the same landmarks of family formation their mothers had, both the context and meaning of the events had changed.

Middle- and upper-class families constructed a new worldview based on sentiment and the home as private space. The family was not a private firm, but a source of companionship and nurture. The ideal relationship between husband and wife ought to be "a silken Cord of Mutual Love and Tender sympathy and Affection."[56] The idea of marriage as friendship was widespread by the middle of the century. Without using the words "companion" or "friend," Benjamin Franklin expressed this ideal in a song he wrote on a challenge.

> I beauty admire but virtue I prize,
> that fades not in seventy years.

> Am I loaded with care, she takes of a large share,
> That the burden ne'er makes me to reel;
> Does good fortune arrive, the joy of my wife
> Quite doubles the pleasure I feel . . . .

Companionate expectations cut across race and class. The epitaph a free black wrote for his wife, "by her fidelity his friend," echoed the sentiments in Franklin's song.[57] Despite the expectation of friendship, the husband was still expected to have final authority.

A woman's relationship to her husband, however, was not her sole family role. In the third quarter of the eighteenth century a married woman was expected to be a "Virtuous tender and affectionate wife and parent, a humain [sic] mistress and a kind Neighbor." Earlier the formulation would have emphasized duty over virtue.[58]

This image of an ideal wife shifted the standards that Deborah Franklin and Elizabeth Porter learned as young women. The wife as helpmeet and housewife, an economic contributor to the family economy, was subsumed by an image emphasizing psychological and personal traits.[59] Even the language of divorce petitions shifted from describing a good wife as a woman who "managed her Domestic affairs with Industry & frugality" to expectations of companionship and cooperation.[60]

Women's roles increasingly were tied to virtue in the later part of the eighteenth century. As one woman explained in verse in 1778

> Shall Men the slave of vice, the tools of art?
> Stand public guardians of the female Heart.
> With wisdom lead us, or to duty warm?
> Improve our morals, or our manners form?
> Direct us when to advance, or when to retire
> The proper find, the delicate inspire?
> Ah specious shew, if justly they condemn
> Your error lyes my Sex, in copying them.
> Take but their high example for your guide
> You sink to ruin, and from virtue Slide
> Fall from the dignity by heaven assign'd
> The native standard, of the female mind.[61]

Making women paragons of virtue required some vigorous mental gymnastics. Women had long been associated theologically with Eve, the fall from grace, and temptation. By the 1780s, the ideal young woman was described in terms of her physical appearance (young, full-bosomed, small-waisted, and raven-haired), thus emphasizing latent sexuality. For most adult women of the late eighteenth century, sexual intercourse was not latent, it was a reality (even in courtship). The ideas linking women to morality had not yet displaced assumptions that women were sexual beings who found pleasure in intercourse. Paradoxically, Revolutionary emphasis on the "pursuit of happiness" helped promote sexuality as a form of pleasure, even as the emphasis on domestic virtue put restraints on sexuality.[62]

After 1775, as new ideas about the family merged with republican political theory, married women assumed a new role as republican wives and mothers. Images of woman as the temptress Eve faded, and married women became models of private virtue and self-sacrifice who would influence husbands and shape sons into good citizens. As the new nation changed the metaphor for political society from that of parent and child to that of a marriage, courtship and marriage gained political meaning. The new metaphor left men in charge but made private virtue a public good.[63]

A messy set of law suits in Virginia in 1772 and 1773 illustrate the partial transformation of ideas about marriage in Revolutionary America. On May 21, 1771, Dr. James Blair, from a prominent Virginia family, married Kitty Eustace, a New York woman with equally stellar connections. Almost immediately Kitty Eustace Blair left her husband and sued for separate maintenance. When James Blair died at the end of 1772, Kitty Blair claimed the widow's dower in his estate. For at least two years, as the law suits wound to conclusion, Virginia's elite discussed the definition marriage.[64]

Two areas of concern in the case are especially revealing: the role of family and friends, and the ambiguous attitudes toward sex. Kitty Eustace's mother had clearly pushed her daughter to marry, and tried to force a reconciliation. Kitty seemed as concerned about her friendship with James Blair's sister Anne—whom she referred to as "Sister of my Heart"—as she was about James. As Kitty explained to Anne, she had married James because

> "I knew it was perfectly agreeable to the best of parents, & that I loved & valued your Family one and all of then, at the same time [had] no particular objection to your Brother."[65]

Kitty exercised her marriage choice to please her mother, and saw marriage more as acquiring a whole family than an individual husband. She continued to solicit Anne's friendship in the midst of the scandal. Throughout the remainder of 1771 and all of 1772, the couple used various friends and kin as go-betweens and advisors. Neither beginning nor ending a marriage was done in isolation; both were complicated decisions involving family and friends.

The issue of sexuality was more problematic. The marriage had never been consummated. During one reconciliation attempt, Kitty bolted from the bed, resulting in countercharges of impotence and lack of virginity. Kitty argued that intercourse without full reconciliation was "legal Prostitution." Lawyers for the couple drafted arguments on the validity of an unconsummated marriage. In the end even the law was ambiguous. The original court ruled against Kitty's dower claims. On appeal, however, the court ruled that Kitty was the legitimate widow of James, despite lack of marital relations.[66] The original court decision made sexuality an integral part of marriage. Edmund Pendleton, one of the lawyers opposing Kitty Blair, had argued that marriage had three purposes: procreation, prevention of fornication, and enjoyment of mutual society. The decision on appeal made marriage a contract completed upon the exchanging of promises between two willing individuals. It both desexualized marriage and emphasized individual will and companionship.

Given that most women had childbearing histories spread over at least 20 years, marriage was hardly platonic. Elizabeth Porter and Margaret Brant both had their first children in the early 1730s and their last children after 1750. Elizabeth's children came regularly every two and a half years. Health and family circumstances created variation in childbearing. Deborah and Benjamin Franklin had only two children together, and these were born more than a decade apart. Peg also appears to have had only two children during her 20 years on the Dutoy and Porter plantations.

Women who came of age after mid-century, and who were raising families during the Revolution, behaved much like their mothers unless outside events interfered. Death of a spouse broke the childbearing patterns of four of Elizabeth Porter's children. Deborah Croker Dunlap also had only five children before dying in 1774. Molly Brant and Sarah Franklin Bache each had eight children.[67]

During the Revolutionary War, economic hardship, separation from spouses, and an unwillingness to bring children into a politically uncertain

world combined to lower birthrates overall for the Revolutionary generation. Many married three to four years later than women early in the century, and they typically bore five to six children. Since most couples
desired at least five children, even women who used some means to prevent conception spent more than 10 years of their adult lives in a cycle of
pregnancy, birth, and lactation. A woman might easily expect that it would
be 40 years from the birth of her first child until the last one came of age.[68]

Women had some ability to control their reproductive lives. During
the Revolutionary War, for example, the average age of a Philadelphian
woman at the birth of her last child dropped from 40 to 37. A number
of women had no children during the war.[69] Breast-feeding for at least a
year (reinforced by traditions of abstinence during nursing) helped set
the typical pattern of births at every two years. Some women stretched
birth intervals by breast-feeding longer. Douching, coitus interruptus,
and abortion were all means available to some women to reduce fertility
in late eighteenth-century America. Abortion, or "taking the trade,"
was not illegal before "quickening" (roughly three months), and
although medically risky, women did exercise this option.[70]

Despite the physical demands of household tasks, women continued
with regular chores and traveled until late in their pregnancies. Medical
complications could make pregnancy draining. For example, Molly
Carroll, from one of Maryland's leading families, became addicted to
laudanum taken to ease the pain from complications after her fifth child
was born in 1776. For most women, however, pregnancy was part of
the normal cycle of married life.[71]

Rituals surrounded childbirth. Women prepared special childbed
linen. Sometimes mistresses provided it for favored slaves. During
labor, guests ate "groaning beer" and "groaning cakes." Most women
gave birth surrounded by "a house full of people" (mostly supportive
women), including those of their family. Women traveled in advanced
stages of pregnancy in order to be with a mother or sister when the
time came to give birth. While pregnancy may have been viewed as
normal, the actual childbirth was treated as an illness. A woman in labor
was "unwell." After childbirth, middle- and upper-class women rested
for several weeks to a month ("lying in") while other women cared for
the house. Indian women, enslaved blacks, indentured servants, and
poor working women had the support of others during birth, but could
not or did not follow lying in customs.[72]

Although women were concerned about the risks of death during
childbirth, they survived most pregnancies and had life expectancies

Physicians used forceps similar to these when intervening in late-eighteenth-century childbirth. *Courtesy of the Colonial Williamsburg Foundation.*

only slightly lower than men of the same class. Puerperal fever was so rare in late eighteenth-century New England that some doctors had never seen an epidemic. Mortality rates for births assisted by both midwives and physicians in the late eighteenth century appear to have been 3.3 percent or less. Studies from earlier in the century suggest that perhaps 10 percent of adult female mortality was associated with childbirth.[73]

Skilled midwives knew how to turn babies in breech deliveries and could remove obstructions in the birth canal. If birthing became dangerous, the family or midwife might call on a surgeon to dismember and remove the fetus. After 1750 more physicians and surgeons added obstetrics to their practices. Unlike midwives, they could use forceps to aid a difficult birth. Unfortunately, in the hands of an unpracticed physician, forceps increased the risk of tears and infection. Two important changes of birth customs accompanied the arrival of male physicians on the birth scene. First, the social and collective nature of childbirth was modified, as doctors took charge and neighboring women limited their visits to before or after the birth. Second, by the nineteenth century many women were less willing to accept prolonged and painful labor as natural, and may have asked the doctor to speed delivery by intervention. These changes isolated women, allowed male medical management of birth, and increased the risk of maternal death.[74]

Infant and child survival did not match that of the mother in childbirth. Most women of both generations in the Porter, Franklin, and Brant households experienced the sorrow of burying a child.[75] In general African Americans and American Indian communities had higher rates of child mortality than did settlers of European descent. African-American children might be given away as infants or put to work very young, and they generally received poorer food, clothing, and housing—all factors creating greater risk. In addition, their mothers were often in advanced stages of pregnancy during the strenuous spring planting season, thus contributing to lower birth-weight babies and greater risk. Children were exceptionally vulnerable to the epidemics and periodic scarcity that played havoc on American Indian groups.

As the century came to a close, the granddaughters of Deborah Franklin, Elizabeth Porter, and Margaret Brant were young adults seeking to build families. With greater freedom to choose a mate, they were also expected to exercise more self-control in their behavior. If they remained single, they had more company. The emotional leverage provided by close companionship in marriage was necessary to offset the heightened disabilities of coverture with fewer compensatory protections through trusts and dower. Childbirth was growing both more risky and less painful in certain difficult cases. Greater expectations of women's virtue and a stricter legal demarcation of marriage helped set standards for respectability that gave some women increased moral authority and set others (especially the poor, American Indian, and enslaved blacks) firmly beyond the realm of respectability. In a Revolutionary era, family changes resulted in major trade-offs of benefits and drawbacks, producing a new world neither clearly better nor worse, but decidedly different from the world women knew in 1740.

CHAPTER FOUR

Mistress and Servant

Before 1790, the United States was overwhelmingly rural, and the daily tasks of almost all women were tied to agriculture, as Mary Brant, Elizabeth Porter Branch, and her servant Amy well knew. As part of an urban mercantile or trade household, Deborah and Sarah Franklin were in a decided minority. Whether rural or urban, however, women contributed to a family economy tied to a growing commercial system, and produced goods and services that made them truly "useful unto the world." Almost all women worked in eighteenth-century America, and although women worked at the same tasks in the nineteenth century, the interpretation of women's roles after 1790 limited recognition of women's economic contributions. By the end of the century the changing ideology of family and women's roles and a growing commercial economy allowed upper- and middle-class women to shift their efforts from production to consumption.

When Elizabeth Porter and Deborah Franklin married, their roles as household managers resonated with economic overtones. As wives, they were responsible for processing raw goods and creating products with economic value. They were helpmeets in a family enterprise dedicated to creating a living for the household and to acquiring the goods necessary to successfully launch each of their children into adulthood. Most debt was interest free, merely a way to keep track of obligations between families in a cash-short society. As slaves, Peg and Amy were simultaneously contributors to the Porter household economy, family assets, and managers of their own household economies. Margaret Brant was no one's helpmeet, but an independent producer. She was a grower of food and a processor of products trapped or hunted by her husband, but although her work was different, her participation in the economy did not set her apart from Elizabeth or Deborah.

By the time the grandchildren of these women came of age, women were consumers of trade goods, and nurturers of families in a domestic sphere separate from the economy. Only tasks that produced cash seemed to have economic value, and new forms of interest-bearing, negotiable debt had changed economic relationships.[1] Women's production continued, but its economic contribution was invisible.

Many women participated in family businesses and accounts and in local markets, and people generally assumed women capable of running family concerns. In fact, even British advice books available in the colonies made that assumption. One abused wife considered it a sign of reconciliation when her husband gave her physical control of all his money, keys, notes, deeds, and papers. Although many women participated in the economy, others had less direct involvement. Some women, insecure about their decisions, sought men's advice or removed themselves from the market economy, including shopping. Married women who filed loyalist claims after the war often had little knowledge of family finances, net worth, or business affairs. They knew what they owned, but not its value.[2]

Because women's work kept them closer to the house, wives and daughters often received payments owed to their families. When financial dealings took place in an office at home or at the kitchen table, women heard much of what went on. Women testified in court on business matters, although later in the century women avoided court by relying on male lawyers or agents. As widows they learned to handle complicated estate administrations. The ability to be recognized as a *feme sole* trader allowed some married women the right to act in their own right, and to sue and be sued independently of their husbands.[3]

Eighteenth-century women might not have known their net worth, but they knew the everyday details of running the family farm.[4] If we remove racial and cultural blinders to look at the whole population living within the boundaries of the future United States in 1783, women were at least as involved in farming as men. Most American Indian and black women farmed. European women participated through gardening and tending to the poultry and livestock. Since these activities, when pursued by men, are considered farming, there is no reason to assume they are not farming when pursued by women.

Well over nine-tenths of the colonial population lived in households directly engaged in agriculture, and women provided essential labor in tending crops and animals. Black women like Peg and Amy worked regularly in fields and gardens. In the Chesapeake and the South, 95 percent of enslaved women worked in the fields.[5] It is clear that Virginia's lawmakers considered Peg and Amy part of the labor market, because Virginia's tithe laws taxed African women over age 16 and all males of the same age. Widows whose husbands had left them slaves found it easier to live on income from slaves rented to others rather than work a farm themselves. Many of those hired out were women. Scattered court records suggest that even advanced pregnancy did not relieve women of their field duties, a fact that may have contributed to low birth-weights and higher infant mortality.[6] Slave women planted and transplanted rice and tobacco, hoed and tended the crops, and worked in the harvest. African women who had worked in rice cultivation before reaching the Carolinas contributed much to the development of the crop in the Americas. As older settled areas turned to wheat farming, planters shifted women to tobacco fields and cornfields in areas farther west. Since men did the plowing, women's labor was less essential to wheat production, and the prices for women slaves dropped in wheat areas. Slaves in many areas also had small garden patches of their own and livestock to care for when finished with their assigned work.[7]

Successful farmers planted a series of crops that were harvested through late summer and fall. Experiments by Eliza Lucas in the 1740s resulted in South Carolina rice plantations adding a winter crop of indigo. During the winter slack time elsewhere, enslaved women were shifted to agricultural processing and domestic production. Women used the winter months to slaughter animals, salt meat, and make sausage, as well as work on the carding, spinning, and weaving of cloth from flax and wool gathered earlier in the year.[8]

Women of European descent also worked in the fields. On small farms, women added planting, hoeing, and harvest chores to their other household duties. Families purchased the labor of others to relieve female family members of fieldwork. Peg's presence may well have spared newly-married Elizabeth Porter the task of weeding and pinching suckers in the family tobacco fields.[9] Small farmers in Maryland purchased tithe-exempt female indentured servants for the same tasks. During the Revolution wives of enlisted men sometimes had to return to the field to plow and hoe in order to support the family. In Pennsylvania, where grain crops predominated, the demand for indentured women was less. Servant women, however, still did agricultural work as dairymaids, tending fruit and vegetable gardens or caring for poultry.[10]

Women's gardening was an important part of eighteenth-century agriculture. Gardens supplied the family table with vegetables and fruits and relieved the monotonous winter diet. Over the course of 1772 and 1773, one Long Island farm woman picked blackberries, apples, quince, and peaches. She also climbed their cherry tree to "fetch the bees down in my a pron [*sic*]." A Pennsylvania woman grew kidney beans, potatoes, peas, beans, asparagus, radishes, greens, raspberries, strawberries, and pears. Gardening became more important as the profits in staple crops declined, and urban markets expanded. Some women turned the sale of garden crops into a thriving business, providing cash for the family.[11]

Women tended poultry to provide eggs and meat for the table and feathers for mattresses and pillows. Women, including slaves and servants, sold surplus hens and eggs at local markets or to their neighbors. Urban women bartered tea and coffee for these farm products.[12] In Charleston, South Carolina, slave women ran the Lower Market, where poultry, eggs, and garden produce was sold. They often purchased the goods from other slaves in the countryside.[13]

Although some wealthier white women bought their fowl from slaves on their own plantation, many considered poultry-care their responsibility. The tutor of a prominent Virginia family in the 1770s discovered the mistress of the household checking her hens by candlelight. A simple transaction illustrates the pervasiveness of poultry in the lives of women of all classes: In 1772 the mother of one of Virginia's most aristocratic families bought three old hens from a woman and girl hawking them door-to-door. She then partially repaid a debt owed to her young daughter with the hens.[14]

By mid-century, butter and cheese molds and churns became common in estate inventories. On some southern plantations an overseer's wife might be expected to supervise or run the dairy.[15] Cheese served as a form of cash. As late as the 1790s many Connecticut families paid the local minister in cheese.[16] Dairying became a major source of income for families on farms within carting range of growing market towns. By 1740, Connecticut, for example, had four major market towns, 25 regional market towns, and 43 country towns all serving as centers for local farm products. As herds grew larger, men cared for them while women milked and ran the dairy. The work was seasonal since cows often went dry during the winter, when fodder became scarce.[17]

Women also managed farms and plantations. Widows, such as Elizabeth Porter, regularly ran farms to support themselves and their minor children, although they had to share estate administration duties with other executors more often later in the century, or if the estate were large. A widow's dower life interest left her in charge of the land, even if she could not sell it. As the number of widows rose after 1750, so did the number of women managing estates. In one Maryland county in 1758 nearly half the 46 women listed as heads of plantations were running those farms without adult white male help. By 1790, single women headed 16 percent of the large plantations in Charles County, Maryland. Not all women had to wait until they were widowed to run farms, however. The teenage Eliza Lucas managed three South Carolina holdings when her father took an officer's post out of the colony. She continued to manage the farms during her marriage to Charles Pinckney, and then when she was widowed.[18]

Agriculture was a major means of sustenance for Indian nations east of the Mississippi. While men helped prepare the fields, women raised the crops of corn, beans, peas, roots, and squash. Women also gathered wild rice, fruits, fungi, berries, honey, and nuts, and collected maple sugar. They processed sunflower seeds for oil. Women often owned the fields and the crops collectively. Indian women sold corn to travelers and traders, a fact that led the garrison at Fort Loudoun to employ a woman as purchasing agent for Cherokee corn in the 1750s. The Mohawk chose a leading clan matron each year to oversee women's agricultural work, and she distributed food at councils and festivals. Religious rituals in many groups connected fertility and corn to female images or deities.[19]

As European settlement encroached and game was depleted, eastern Indians extended searches for game, and villages dispersed. Some Indians sold land in order to buy meat, thus reducing their hunting and farming resources. Settlers' livestock, and that introduced into Indian communities to replace game, destroyed women's fields. Some villages began to fence fields. The Mohawk were not the only group to replace women's communal agriculture with individual households and plots.[20]

Increased pressure to farm in the European style displaced women. Mohawk women eagerly adopted iron hoes in the first half of the century to ease cultivation. The introduction of the plow and harrow in the middle of the century involved men in farming. Missionaries encouraged Indian males to farm, since they thought men should grow the grain crops. Many Indians resisted the reversal of gender roles, and others blended old and new ways. The Brants, for example, adopted many European customs. Joseph Brant advocated individual plot farming with the plow, and had servants to help. But his wife Catherine continued to go to the spring sugar camps to help with maple sugaring. After 1774, widowed Molly Brant apparently also adopted European farming methods. She had a barn and owned slaves to help with chores.[21]

American Indian women were not alone in being affected by a social construction of womanhood assigning women to the private, domestic sphere. Although many women still managed farms after 1750, men increasingly limited women's control of family businesses and farms. Free women tended to withdraw from fieldwork, even as they continued to garden and tend dairies. Agricultural wages for women fell as gender distinctions increased. This withdrawal from fieldwork extended to free African Americans in Virginia, when the assembly exempted free black women from the tithe in the 1760s. Seemingly it was more important to the Virginia elite to see all free women as dependent nurturers than it was to squeeze a little tax income from a politically powerless group.[22]

As mistress of a working plantation, Elizabeth Porter was not only responsible for household management, but for much of family production, supervising the labor of children and slaves, including Amy and Peg. The women of the Porter household made featherbeds from the down of the large flock of geese they kept; carded, spun, and wove wool and linen cloth; and rendered lard for candles and soap. Such production was not trivial. A featherbed was worth as much as an ordinary horse. Elizabeth, Peg, and the other women in the household made enough beds to ensure that each of the Porter children received a bed in their "portions."[23]

For Elizabeth, and others of her generation, this work was their contribution to a household enterprise, not a measure of independence. Thomas's will, after all, gave away four of the featherbeds she had made. Amy's and Peg's work was part of their servitude, not a mark of independence. When the household is the production unit, and when male heads of household work at home and seldom receive cash for their work, no easy distinction exists between work and home, production and nurture.

Household production was hardly static during the last half of the century. As stores and credit grew, many families (like the Porters) focused on producing a few items and bought the rest. Stores accepted in-kind payment, allowing families to exchange items made at home for those made elsewhere. Home producers were thus encouraged to specialize (in dairying, for example) in response to growing consumer demand. As orchards expanded, women began making hard cider rather than brewing small beer. Indian women turned to making and selling baskets, table mats, moccasins, and pottery to support themselves. By 1772, Catawba women traveled door-to-door selling pots. Shoemaking responded to growing consumer demand. By 1780, Massachusetts shoemakers had recruited wives and daughters to stitch soles to the uppers. Women worked in their kitchens, squeezing the work in among other household tasks.[24]

Making cloth and clothing was the most widespread and economically important kind of home production. The colonies had a nearly insatiable demand for cloth. Indian women sought ready-made cloth and blankets; in exchange they scraped, tanned, and worked leather to make moccasins, shirts, and other items to sell to traders. Rising standards of living during the eighteenth century allowed many white women to purchase cloth while others bought the tools to produce it (often with slave help). Unlike in other trades, women weavers made nearly the same wage as men. Massachusetts families consumed nearly three-quarters of the 170,000 yards of cloth produced at home from 1751 to 1760. Cloth and sewing materials made up three-quarters of all imports by Philadelphia merchants. Thus the demand of women of all races for manufactured cloth was one of the major engines driving eighteenth-century American trade.[25]

The spindle and flax and wool spinning wheels were common in all areas of European settlement by 1750. Elizabeth Porter owned the tools for making both linen and wool thread in 1767. Five years later she had added cotton cards. Her daughter-in-law Magdalene Porter's household did the family weaving.[26] A woman could make £40 a year (plus room and board) by 1776 as a weaver in Virginia, enough to live in modest comfort. Women often exchanged skills in dyeing, weaving, spinning, carding, knitting, and sewing with one another.[27] Both rural and urban elite women purchased British manufactured cloth for their immediate families, but continued to supervise free and slave women in making cloth for slaves and servants. For others, spinning was a social activity, done only at frolics in other women's homes.[28]

When the Stamp Act boycotts cut off imports, many women returned to cloth production. During the boycotts of the 1760s Debo-

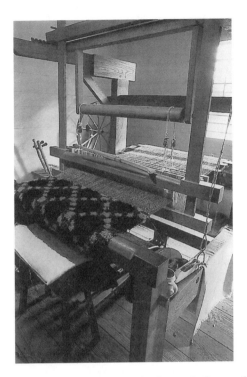

The women of the Porter household used a loom similar to the one shown here. *Courtesy of the Colonial Williamsburg Foundation.*

rah Franklin made all the cloth for her family, as she had done when first married. Others hired skilled women to teach their slaves or supervise plantation manufactories. Home work could be elegant. Women periodically produced silk and finer cloth, including cambric and duroys and serges. Hanah Adams supported herself with sewing and knitting before the war, then turned to more profitable bobbin lace until the market collapsed after peace returned.[29]

Many urban women had no access to the raw materials or tools for making cloth. As the wars and periodic depressions of the second half of the century swelled the poor rolls in many cities, officials and philanthropists employed women and children to make cloth. Many had to be taught to spin. George Whitfield hired women to teach spinning to poor Savannah girls, for example. Although Boston, New York, Philadelphia, and Charleston all set up spinning and weaving projects, these succeeded only when British cloth was unavailable or demand exceeded imports and home production. Furthermore, women resisted efforts to locate this work in large supervised halls, preferring Philadelphia and Boston projects that allowed women to spin at home and bring in the finished thread. In 1775, 400 women were employed by the United Company in Philadelphia in spinning and weaving, and a woolen company there employed nearly as many.[30]

The movement for independence politicized women's sewing and cloth production. The purchase of imported cloth added to colonial indebtedness and dependence on Britain. Spinning bees became public rituals demonstrating colonial self-sufficiency and firmness as boycotts of imported goods became the main form of resistance to imperial taxation. Used earlier to publicize efforts to set up manufactories to employ the poor, the ritual of a public spinning now merged with Revolutionary fervor. Elite women and girls demonstrated their patriotism by participating in public spinning bees. Urban public spinnings could involve 40–100 young women at a time and attract 600 spectators. From 1768 to 1770 there were at least 46 such bees (30 in 1769 alone), involving 1,644 women. Nearly three-quarters were held at ministers' homes. Such public events were less about production (often the work was donated to clergy or charities) than about demonstrating solidarity. The women arrived wearing homespun, and had colonial-grown refreshments and herbal (not imported) tea. Home spinning gained new meaning. Women imagined themselves as "a fighting army of amazones [*sic*]" or felt "Nationaly" as they worked at home.[31]

All clothing and linens had to be stitched by hand, most of it by women working in groups or alone. Many carried needlework on social calls. Middle-class women made over clothes as well as sewing new items. Slaves and servants made their own clothes and sewed for the household, contributing to the intricate needlework gracing the beds of elite families. Needlework continued to be a part of elite women's lives. By age five, Sally Franklin was "industrious with her needle." Many elite young women at boarding schools learned to make shirts. Some clothes could be ordered from professional seamstresses or tailors either in the colonies or in England, or bought ready-made. Women in the household provided the rest, with occasional help from itinerant sewers who might stay overnight while working.[32] Women also knit stockings and made hats. Sometimes boys would help with the knitting in winter. Stockings, after all, needed replacing frequently. Hats might be made from fabric, knitted wool, or braided straw.[33]

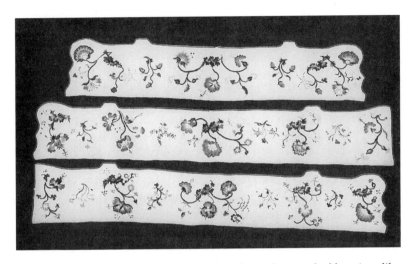

Throughout America, women used their needles to decorate bed hangings like these. *Courtesy of the Colonial Williamsburg Foundation.*

There was greater market demand for cloth than for clothing, and wages for women who sewed were half of a man's. For many women, however, sewing was the only option for support. Philadelphia women produced shirts for the Indian trade during the 1760s in a well organized putting-out system. During the colonial wars, government officials depended on women to supply the troops.[34]

During the Revolution the Commissary General of Military Stores hired women to make cartridges and clothes for soldiers. Connecticut set quotas on its towns, proportionate to their size, for clothes for soldiers. Hartford's quote was 1,000 coats and vests and 1,600 shirts in mid 1776. Committee of Safety members gathered and paid for items as women completed them. Over the next 12 months the state set levies for canteens, wood bowls, tents, iron pots, shirts, woolen overalls, stockings, and shoes. Throughout the war, demand continued despite growing reluctance of women to produce the needed items. Since armies relied on home manufacturing, it is not surprising that George Washington requested that Philadelphia women turn a cash collection they had raised for soldiers into shirts.[35]

On one level the new nation assumed women were part of the labor force. Enslaved women were obviously workers. Cloth manufacture was defined as work for women and children by 1780. A sail-cloth factory opened in Boston, for example, on land owned by a woman, with at least

14 girls employed as spinners, and a matron to oversee the work. Younger children turned the wheels for the girls. Alexander Hamilton, Tench Coxe, and others promoting economic development assumed manufacturing in the new nation would use a female labor supply.[36] On another level, however, by 1800, women's economic contributions were repackaged by the middle- and upper-classes as family nurture and support. The emphasis on patriotism as a motive for women's production may have helped divorce women's work from its economic roots. Needlework could be viewed as ornamental, spinning and weaving as something done by lower-class workers in the household. This ideology began to emerge before independence, but the Revolution speeded its triumph.

Increased consumption affected housework. All women expended much of their energy on household care—cooking, cleaning, washing, mending, and ironing. Even elite women recorded getting up at 4:00 A.M. to iron all day.[37] Washing and cleaning remained seasonal (not weekly) tasks because they were so exhausting. As more families acquired small luxury items such as tea sets, linens, pewter, and nice furniture, these items needed to be maintained. This consumer revolution affected even the distant French communities in Illinois.[38] Slaves or women too poor to own these items cleaned them for others. Thus the consumer revolution affected nearly all women, whether they bought items or not.

Of all the household tasks, food preparation and cooking changed the most in the late eighteenth century. Women slaughtered livestock, dried fruits, and cured meats in order to do their cooking. The expansion of gardens and wheat production and the spread of crops such as the potato and the peanut brought greater variety to tables. New food-preservation methods ensured a more varied diet throughout the year. Rather than serve from a simple stockpot all day, women prepared a variety of dishes. These required new cooking techniques and equipment.[39]

Women sought help with household work from daughters, servants, slaves, or women who came as occasional hired labor. Although hired day labor was most common in urban areas, plantation mistresses also hired free women. In Philadelphia in 1775 about one-quarter of all adult women were in service—hired, indentured, or enslaved. Women's work paid much less than men's, about one-third to one-half less, despite the demand for their services.[40]

Because women moved back and forth between maintenance, production, and farming in their daily tasks, it is hard to determine the proportion of household tasks performed by purchased labor. The fact that female redemptioners and servants clustered in urban areas, and that their purchasers were often merchants, shopkeepers, and innkeepers, suggests female contract labor was valued most for its use in household production and maintenance.[41] Newspaper advertisements for female slaves often listed household skills. African cooks helped spread the use of such foods as the peanut, black-eyed peas, and eggplant in the late eighteenth century. Between 1760 and 1800 the percentage of enslaved women assigned to house service more than doubled, going from 15 percent to 33.[42] Household maintenance was a double burden to many enslaved women, since at the end of the day they still had their own cooking, washing, and cleaning to do.

The household labor market reorganized during the last quarter of the eighteenth century as wage and slave labor displaced indentured servants. By the 1770s the sale of female servants did not always cover the cost incurred in importing them. The colonial wars and the growing number of urban poor from 1750 to 1775 pushed many women to compete as wage workers, thus driving down wages.[43] Wage labor included live-in servants and daily workers. In the 1760s in Philadelphia, women's wages ranged from £4 to £10 a year, barely a subsistence wage.[44] The Revolutionary War disrupted the supply of immigrant servants, but after the war, many women of African descent entered the household labor market as indentured or day servants due to gradual emancipation in the middle and northern states. Wages kept pace with inflation, rising to about £23 by 1795, but the number of women seeking work kept wages down.[45]

Live-in and day laborers created a floating pool of help that came and went in a household. These workers were the underside of the newly emerging domestic ideology. The only way middle- and upper-class women could maintain the image that they did not "work" was by hiring others to do the work for and with them. Live-in workers, often young girls, received room and board plus a wage. Although contracts were often for a year, turnover was very high. Day workers (or local occasional labor) were often older women supporting families. Widowed daughter Ann Porter Sampson added to her income during the Revolution by occasionally sewing for other families.[46] Rural female day laborers remained a mix of free blacks, local whites, and American Indians whose lands had been overrun by settlement. Sometimes they worked for room and board alone.[47]

Even shared tasks and a generally rising standard of living did not ensure that women experienced these changes similarly. There was no guarantee that a hired or enslaved cook's family ate any of the new variety of foods she cooked. More than one woman complained of hunger while in indentured service.[48] Women—free and unfree—washed, ironed, and mended clothing more elegant than any they would ever own. The elite's standard of living rose faster than that of other groups, creating a greater disparity of wealth.[49]

Poor and unfree women were not the only workers. In Philadelphia in 1775 almost half of women 15 years or older were not mistresses of a household with a male present. About 15 percent of these were unmarried women living at home. The rest were self-supporting or bound labor.[50] Marriage could offer entry to a trade, since women often worked with their artisan husbands and carried on the business in their absence. Men sometimes used their wives as a way to pursue occupations otherwise closed to them. The wives of Anglican clergy sometimes ran glebe farms, as canon law barred clergy from manual labor; Pennsylvania magistrates were not to sell liquor, but one magistrate drew up the bills while his wife collected the money. Benjamin Franklin hired another woman to help Deborah in his shop and thought girls should learn accounting to help their husbands, but he drew the line at learning trades. Women's earning power served as the family's reserves. Franklin's sister, for example, assumed she might have to go into business with her daughter if her son-in-law's business continued to fail.[51]

Deborah Read Franklin was a model tradesman's wife. Before marrying Deborah, Benjamin's money quickly disappeared. Although he occasionally charged her with extravagance, evidence suggests she was a better manager than he. The Franklins built their printing enterprise on lots originally owned by Deborah's family. Deborah managed the accounts, folded and stitched pamphlets, tended shop, purchased rags for paper making. Under her management the print shop expanded beyond stationery to general merchandise. After Benjamin's appointment as postmaster general for the colonies, Deborah oversaw that operation as well, even when pregnant with Sally. In 1748 Benjamin retired from active involvement in his businesses on an income of £2,000 a year, his partners ran the print shop, and Deborah continued to manage the post office. In the decade before her death in 1774, Deborah managed their businesses, built a new house, and had full power of attorney, while Benjamin spent those years in Britain.[52]

Although Benjamin and Deborah Franklin were very successful, Deborah's role as shopkeeper was hardly extraordinary. Almost 15 percent of women in Philadelphia in 1775 were in retail trades or property management. A similar number worked as artisans (mostly mantua-makers and glovers) or laborers (especially washerwomen), took in boarders, or kept school. In any given year in Philadelphia about one-fifth of the tavern-keepers and one-third of the shopkeepers were women, in addition to those with day-to-day oversight of a family concern (like Deborah Franklin). The men most likely to leave their whole estates to their wives were middle-level craftsmen. Their wives were probably silent partners in their businesses.[53]

Women throughout the colonies used strategies similar to those in Philadelphia to support themselves. In less urban North Carolina, women were about one-fifth of the tavern-keepers. Boston women worked as saddlers, iron mongers, cutlers, brew masters, soap-makers, bakers, milliners, and purveyors of cheese, bacon, seeds, and spices. Eighteen shop owners, 10 boarding-house operators, five tavern-keepers and innkeepers, four milliners, two mantua-makers, two prostitutes, a midwife, a seamstress, a coffeehouse owner, a teacher, and a printer were among the women filing loyalist claims with the British. One of the major ferry sites in Pennsylvania was run by an African-American woman for 40 years. Southern women worked as upholsterers, shoe-makers, gunsmiths, blacksmiths, shipwrights, tanners, millers, and fullers.[54]

Taking in an occasional paying lodger could quietly expand into a formal business. Women moved in and out of the boarding business as space and family finances required. About 8 percent of Philadelphia's women heads of household kept boarders in 1775. Churchwardens paid families for homecare of the elderly, sick, or orphaned. Taking in boarders was one of the few options open to middle-class and gentry women supporting families, especially in a college town or capital city, where "respectable" men might require lodging for some time. Benjamin Franklin met Deborah Read while boarding with her family. President James Madison met his wife the same way.[55] As the home became a private space, boarding homes remained private spaces contrasted with the more public arena of inns, hotels, and taverns. Thus an important business strategy became invisible as "work."

Shopkeeping and tavern-keeping were by far the most common businesses for women. They required minimum capital and could be run as extensions of a home. Since women regularly sold small quantities of home brewed beverages or goods, they could move into larger scale trade by degrees, often ignoring licensing rules. In fact, opposition by women marketers and customers defeated attempts to license vend-

Christiana Campbell's Tavern was one of the many operated by women in the late eighteenth century. *Courtesy of the Colonial Williamsburg Foundation.*

ing in Boston in the 1730s. Women boycotted the markets and continued to buy from street vendors. In many southern ports black women dominated local markets. American Indian women often sold baskets in local markets. Many small retailers lived close to the edge. Philadelphia women charged with running unlicensed tippling houses often escaped fines by pleading poverty. Frontier women entered the same businesses. Before Margaret married Brant Canagaraduncka she sold liquor and ginseng to support herself. Indian women controlled the liquor trade in many hide- and fur-trade areas by mid-century.[56]

Women's businesses tended to be small because they had less access to the developing credit markets necessary for expansion and less opportunity to make trading voyages to establish credit, connections, and sources. In addition, many business women were uncomfortable with too public a stance. This was especially the case for wealthier women operating from their homes. The new idea of the home as private conflicted with the reality of the home as business. Although Jane Vobe's Williamsburg tavern appeared in the *Virginia Gazette* as the site of meetings, or a place to pick up mail and play tickets, she never advertised. A gentlewoman running a place catering to the elite, she operated on the borders between public and private.[57]

Local governments closely regulated taverns, often setting prices and requiring licenses. Taverns and inns provided accommodations and meals for travelers, meeting rooms, and served as the local pub and postal station. In New Jersey there was one tavern for every 400 people. In the less settled rural countryside and frontier, families sometimes found themselves running taverns because travelers had nowhere else to stay and eat. The image of taverns as "male" space ignores the many women who operated and worked in them. While elite women might not frequent taverns except when traveling, women from the lower classes frequently joined local men in these spaces.[58]

Some women shopkeepers were quite successful, maintaining separate businesses even if married. Elizabeth Murray Smith carried an inventory of more than £700 through three marriages. She returned to England at one point to learn bookkeeping, and helped other women enter business. Margaret Hutchinson's store gave her an income of £78 a year before she fled as a loyalist. Millinery stores, selling imported small luxury items such as combs, pins, buttons, and buckles, were usually run by women importers who maintained credit lines in England. By the Revolution such stores were found in most market towns. Some women found a special niche by catering to the trade of other women. At least one African emigrated to Georgia after having been a "considerable" trader in Gambia for many years. Women in shopkeeping often worked with a network of other female small traders in short-term partnerships. They also hired other women to help with the household.[59]

At the time of the Revolution women were especially prominent as printers. Women held the contracts for state printing in several states, including Maryland and Pennsylvania, and a woman printed the first official copy of the Declaration of Independence. Women did not serve formal apprenticeships in printing; they learned from family members. Mary Katherine Goddard ran the *Maryland Journal* from 1774 to 1784 for her brother while he served as surveyor of the post roads. Clementina Rind, publisher of the *Virginia Gazette*, and Anne Catherine Green, who ran the *Maryland Gazette*, both inherited their papers from their husbands. In some cases the women ran the business but left the printing to male employees.[60]

Middle-class women supported themselves as teachers. Because teaching could be interpreted as an extension of women's socializing of the young, the rising ideology of domestication did not prevent women from opening schools. Married women and widows were common among teachers. New England's famous school laws did not cover girls, and Massachusetts excluded girls and schoolmistresses from the school census until 1789. The towns that did provide girls' education often hired women to teach them.[61] Women taught very young children and slaves, for example, in the slave schools British philanthropists supported at mid-century in Williamsburg, Virginia, and Philadelphia.[62]

Female entrepreneurs exploited the growing interest in education and absence of systematic education in most colonies. By the 1730s women were advertising schools in the larger towns. Women could find work as teachers in many small schools by the 1740s. Although historians have often considered women's "adventure" schools as having little academic content, the number of such schools multiplied over the century, providing decent livings for the women who ran them. Sarah Osborn's school in Newport operated for 30 years and at its peak had as many as 70 students. In contrast, a plantation schoolmistress in Virginia might earn only £6.12.0 and board. After the Revolution, increased attention to women's education also expanded women's teaching opportunities.[63]

Like teaching, medicine provided a number of opportunities for women since there were no powerful medical associations or licensing laws to bar women or those not trained as physicians or surgeons. Several women had general medical practices. Margaret Hill Morris, for example, practiced medicine in Pennsylvania during the last quarter of the century. She owned medical books, kept a recipe book including medicinal cures, and treated patients during both the 1793 and 1797 yellow fever epidemics in Philadelphia. Another practitioner, Constant Woodson, advertised one of her cures in the *Virginia Gazette*.[64]

The most common medical practice for women was midwifery. There was a steady call for obstetrics services in every community. Loyalist Janet Cumming, formerly a Charleston, South Carolina, midwife, claimed that her practice brought in £400 a year, but she charged up to £40 for a delivery, more than 20 times the standard fee. Several eighteenth-century midwives attended 3,000 or more deliveries. Midwives had low mortality rates. Martha Ballard of Maine attended nearly 1,000 births from 1778 to 1812 with only five maternal deaths, 14 stillbirths, and five deaths of infants within a few hours of birth. In general, midwives had survival rates for infants comparable or better than physicians.[65] Midwives might be experienced older women who had assisted at other births, or women who had sought training. Mary Rose of Williamsburg, Virginia, studied midwifery with local doctors before opening her practice in 1771. A South Carolina woman advertised that she had anatomy certificates from Edinburgh. Some midwives were skilled slaves who attended both black and white women. Midwives were not passive observers at a birth. Records indicate that they cleared obstructions from the birth canal and manipulated the fetus to aid in delivery.[66]

In the last half of the eighteenth century, medical doctors, claiming superior anatomical knowledge and using technical advancements (opium and forceps to ease pain and speed delivery), began attending women at childbirth. Midwives and doctors practiced in the same town, but the choice gradually was cast as knowledge (doctors) vs. experience (midwives). Simultaneously, those present at the birth began to be more exclusively family, with neighboring women calling after, not during, labor. None of this happened overnight. By 1790 traditional childbirth and midwives were still flourishing, but forces were set in motion that would marginalize midwives by 1900 and eliminate many of the social supports for women in childbirth.[67]

Much of women's economic participation was affected by a changing credit system in late eighteenth-century America. Colonists had long participated in a form of book credit, where transactions were recorded and kept without expectation of interest. In a cash-poor economy using barter, this made sense. Often the account remained open until one party died. Women participated freely in this small-scale world of credit, often with transactions credited to their husbands' names.[68]

After 1740 a formal credit market with signed bonds and notes became more common. The sums were larger, and the notes bore interest. In this market, gender mattered. Men more often sought this type of credit to expand business operations. It increased the risk of bankruptcy and foreclosure, thus threatening the security of wives and children. One woman recorded her "hearte is burnt with anger and discontent, want of every necessary thing in life and in constant feare of gapeing creditors" who were trying to collect her husband's debts in 1769. More than one woman began a business venture in order to pay off interest-bearing debts accumulated by her husband. After the Revolution, legal changes gave creditors access even to women's separate estates and dower.[69]

Women, however, were not totally absent from this growing sector of the market. Women, especially widows, invested in interest-bearing notes as a form of income. In eighteenth-century South Carolina, women were a major source of funds. Many men and women considered such investments more secure than the risks of doing business.

Benjamin Franklin, however, was displeased to find that Deborah Franklin had invested money in notes without his prior consent. The commercial credit market, like many other trends in the Revolutionary era, thus had a double edge: It both excluded women from acquiring capital necessary to be major participants in the economy (while placing their estates at greater risk), and it allowed women to withdraw from active business or farming participation, supported by the income from invested money that fueled the commercial expansion.[70]

The Revolution thus traded economic roles for domesticity. Home manufacturing became more important during boycotts and the years of disrupted trade. Women's ability to manage shops, trades, and farms helped to free men to participate in war and politics. Opportunities for teaching expanded. Commercial and ideological changes, however, placed these activities in new patriotic and nurturing contexts. As the home privatized, some forms of women's economic enterprise slipped from view. Women running home businesses increasingly walked a fine line between the visibility necessary for business and an unseemly public light on a supposedly private place. Women's investments funded a credit expansion that they could not tap, while their property became ever more vulnerable to creditors. Without physically moving a single farm, and without removing all women from the fields, the popular consciousness nonetheless separated the family farm or plantation into two spheres, one of work and the other of nurture. Women whose lives did not match these new domestic models, especially African Americans, American Indians, and poor women, were simply rendered invisible or considered less than "real" women.

CHAPTER FIVE

Dutiful Daughters and Independent Minds

At the age of five, Sarah Franklin had already learned much about the role and skills her doting parents expected from her. She was "industrious" in sewing, delighted with books, and "perfectly dutiful and obliging, to her parents and to all." Already enrolled in a dancing school, she would soon start harpsichord and French lessons. In eighteenth-century America, a girl's education began early and was eminently vocational. Sally's education combined practical knowledge of housewifery with academic basics and the skills designed to show her polish and grace in Philadelphia society.[1] Eighteenth-century Americans prepared their daughters for adult life through formal and informal education. Opportunities varied greatly by class and race, and families never depended solely on formal institutions. Socialization and education blended, as playing children mimicked adult roles and tasks. Daughters mixed lessons from books, stories, and songs with work alongside adults in family production. Women's education was practical, but the definition of practical changed as families more frequently included literacy as part of women's education. By 1790 a recognizable market of women readers and writers existed.

The particular mix of literacy and other skills taught to any daughter depended on her race and class. Education was expected to reinforce class and gender differences. The poor received less "book" learning and spent more time on economic skills. Education was intended to make an elite woman more competitive in a marriage market increasingly valuing gentility. As part of the consumer culture, education was both a commodity to consume and a tool for consumption of books and other items. It was certainly useful for everyday business in the growing commercial economy. In a highly competitive religious world, literacy became a means of conversion, and of maintaining loyalty among the faithful.

One clear goal of all parents was to have their children survive. Not surprisingly, wealth increased the odds of survival; so did living in the less crowded countryside. The odds that an infant would survive to adulthood improved slightly in the first half of the century, although there were great variations. About 70 percent of Germantown families lost no children, but over one-quarter of white Philadelphia infants died in the first year, and half died by age 15. The Porters did better, losing only three of 10 before age 21. The Franklins lost one of two. Mortality for children of slaves ran well over 50 percent. Amy was one of only two slave infants born on the Porter plantation between 1740 and 1753 to reach adulthood. Disease and famine took many Indian infants. Margaret Brant lost at least two. Child mortality increased for all groups during the War for Independence. After the war the rates dropped for middle- and upper-class families, but not for the poor.[2]

Education literally began at the mother's breast. Infants remained with mothers until weaned, among whites, usually shortly after they were a year old. Women of the middle- and upper-classes sometimes combined weaning with a trip away from home. Estate inventories often treated slave mothers and infants as a single unit. Women in Africa often nursed infants for several years. Although pressured to follow the customs of the white community, many enslaved women still extended the nursing period by several months, thus delaying any possible separation by work assignment or transfer of ownership. A high rate of lactose intolerance among Africans made breast-feeding crucial for infant survival. American Indian women had more extended times of nursing and often let the child wean itself.[3]

Teaching children to behave began almost immediately. In European communities, a seven-month-old infant might scoot around in a small cart, following her mother as she worked. Enslaved mothers also took infants to the fields, stopping periodically to care for them. American Indian mothers confined infants to a cradle board, which could be hung or propped near their work, although some Indians adopted more European customs. Infants either learned how to stay out of open fires and away from hot pots or did not survive. Indian mothers tended to teach by example, to use praise or reward, but if necessary they might spray water on a child's face, dunk it in water, or frighten it with threats of evil spirits. White mothers used praise and physical punishment. One mother noted that her 10-month-old daughter had received her first whipping, and since then "When she has done any thing that she suspects is wrong, will look with concern to see what Mama says."[4]

The Revolutionary era considered childhood a time of transition and learning about adult roles. White children's clothing was adapted from adult styles, while infants wore long flowing dresses. After toilet training, girls wore simply cut dresses. Indian girls wore little frocks as soon as they could walk to help prepare them for short skirts later. Slave children might go naked or wear simple shifts. Parents who dressed children too formally or expected adult behavior were criticized. Anne Blair of Virginia noted unfavorably that a visiting family had left their little girl "stuck up in a Chair all day long with a Coller on."[5]

Children combined play and helping with family chores. Girls on the New England frontier played with sleds and took care of orphaned animals. Children of all races might help grind corn for a family meal while listening to stories. Both Indian and white children enjoyed helping with the maple sugaring. Childhood was less secure and shorter for slaves. Owners might consider young children a burden, and sell or give them away. Scattered evidence suggests that slave children began regular work between age five and eight. Children tended tobacco plants with their mothers, or they watched the infants. Some slave children served as companions to white children on a plantation.[6]

From about age eight to adulthood, daughters in free families (white or black) learned skills as they helped in the household. Many families, including upper-class ones, sent their daughters to live with relatives or neighbors as part of their education. Because mothers loved their children, they sent them where they could learn household skills such as making seats for chairs. Child-rearing was a cooperative venture of the household, relatives, and friends. One woman noted in her journal that the 12-year-old girl staying with her "grows quite Womanly lately—I shall be very proud if I can make a Clever Girl of her, for she was realy [*sic*] a Baby when she came here."[7]

Poor girls or orphans as young as age eight might be apprenticed or bound out to learn the skills of housewifery. Some apprentice agreements specified learning skills such as carding and spinning. Deborah Sampson, for example, orphaned at five, was bound out at 10 as a farm hand until age 18. Occasionally girls were bound to trades such as dressmaking or millinery. The work was challenging. The mortality rate for South Carolina girls between ages 10 and 14 was higher than that of the adult women they worked alongside.[8]

Moravian communities separated children from parents at an even earlier age, and gave them more extensive educations, until the new ideology of domesticity changed their practices. At five the children were separated by sex. The girls lived together in special "choirs," receiving academic, vocational, and religious education until joining the Single Sisters' Choir at 19. After infancy, parents had no role in their children's lives, nor did they attend to the child if it were dying. By the 1760s, Moravians began emphasizing nuclear families and built single family homes. By 1771 over half the children were living with their parents, and by the 1780s only a handful of girls still lived in the dormitories. Thus, by the Revolution most Moravian mothers and daughters were working together as Moravians adopted domesticity.[9]

Guardianship law reveals much about the coming of age for girls. English and colonial law presumed the mother was guardian, unless a man designated someone else in his will. Most men named no guardians, or specified the mother. Few parents named guardians for children over 10; some declared their teenage children of age. At age 14, orphaned boys and girls could choose their own guardian. Colonies set the legal age of majority for girls between 16 and 18. Boys had to wait longer. In some places, if an underage female orphan married, she was declared of age. Virginia was not such a colony. Seventeen-year-old Ann Porter thus chose her betrothed as her guardian when her father died a few months before her wedding.[10]

Girls' opportunity for formal education and literacy grew during the eighteenth century. New England town schools had achieved a 90 percent basic literacy rate for men by 1700. Girls, however, were not included or attended only in short summer sessions. Over the course of the eighteenth century, girls' education improved, and by the Revolution most New England girls learned to read and write. In Windsor, Connecticut, for example, 90 percent of the girls born in the 1740s could read and write. A girl's literacy depended on her father's attitudes and his own literacy. Lacking New England's system of public schools, areas outside New England lagged in both men's and women's literacy. But evidence shows that by 1750 a majority of adult women everywhere could sign their names. Their daughters had an even higher rate of basic literacy. Three-quarters of women who had to sign legal documents in Goochland County in 1775 could do so without aid. The critical "take-off" period for women's literacy precedes independence and is more likely tied to the general economic and social changes of the period than to Revolutionary ideology.[11]

Literacy, however, is more complicated than just signing one's name. Since writing was a skill taught after reading, many women learned to read but not to write. Records for such women are scarce. Margaret Brant and the Porters fell into this category. None could sign their names, yet the Porters owned 28 books, and Margaret owned a prayer book. Even those who could write had different levels of skill. Deborah Franklin and most literate women of her generation were not polished writers. They could write a letter and keep accounts. Sally's generation, however, felt comfortable enough to write frequently and for pleasure. Thus, they left more documentation of their lives in letters and journals than their mothers did. The fruits of full literacy would be reaped by Deborah's and Elizabeth's granddaughters.[12]

Wills, court orders, and charity projects illustrate what the Revolutionary generations considered adequate education for most girls. When in the 1750s Mary Smith of Virginia endowed a free school in her parish, she specified that boys would get three years of schooling and girls two. Both were to learn reading and writing, but only boys needed to learn arithmetic. The New York Charity School had a similar arrangement, limiting girls' education to reading, religion, and needlework, while boys also learned writing, spelling, and ciphering. Thus, schooling for many girls consisted of a little reading and recitation of the catechism. Such education began early. Families sent children as young as three and four to learn to read.[13]

Gender segregation was a frequent part of colonial education. In Connecticut, girls often only attended school during summer terms, when women teachers taught basic literacy to younger children. Schools as diverse as Union Academy in Germantown, the Bethesda Orphan House in Georgia, and the Moravian school at Bethlehem all segregated boys and girls. Only the Moravians offered more than a few hours a day of academic training to girls. Many of the segregated classes served women from laboring classes. The elites who sponsored education for the laboring classes favored gender segregation since the schools were supposed to socialize children to economically productive roles. For women, that meant household production and marriage; thus, much of the school day for girls was spent spinning, sewing, or knitting.[14]

Although many parents might be satisfied if their daughters learned "to Read, Write, Sow & Mark" (as a 1772 contract specified), other families expected more both academically and vocationally. Sally Franklin was among the many girls from more well-to-do families who studied French. Typical was the young woman who studied French for three months in 1781. She had progressed from reading fables to reading Telemachus. Her tutor wanted her to continue, but "it is as much as I can spare," although she hoped to learn more on her own. Others became fluent in languages. More complete educations for girls in the last half of the century included grammar, geography, history, music, drawing, and dancing. Sewing was absolutely necessary. Families that could afford it hired teachers for more advanced needlework, or sent girls to private sewing schools. In families where religion did not prohibit it, both boys and girls learned dancing. Dancing was among the important ways of demonstrating one's gentility and social standing in Revolutionary America.[15]

A girl's education clearly depended on the initiative and persistence of the family. Elite families might bring their daughters home from school in the middle of a quarter to help at home. Women of the Revolutionary era often apologized for the holes in their education. Some families chose to send children to live with relatives who could oversee their education and might have better access to teachers. Thus Mary Blair Braxton sent her young daughter Betsy to live with Mary's mother and sister Anne in Williamsburg, Virginia. The family hired teachers for dancing and writing. The sisters supervised her reading and sewing. Betsy's studies, however, were often interrupted for social occasions. After all, these, too, were part of her education in the manners of her class.[16]

A small number of women throughout the British empire, usually from families with highly educated fathers, had long had access to good educations. As the number of well-educated fathers grew, and as mothers gained enough literacy to encourage their daughters' educations, the number of well-educated women rose. Susanna Wright, educated in England, migrated with her family to Pennsylvania. She knew French, Latin, and Italian, and studied philosophy, natural science, and agriculture on her own. Several home-educated women knew enough classics to teach their sons. Abigail Smith Adams and her sisters were introduced to a systematic study of literature and poetry by her brother-in-law Richard Cranch. Hanah Adams, a noted scholar after the Revolution, acquired her education by reading the books in her father's bookstore and library. The young men who boarded with her family taught her Latin, Greek, geography, and logic. Eliza Lucas read Plutarch, Virgil, Locke, Malbranch, and law, much to the chagrin of a neighboring woman who was afraid Eliza would wear herself out and not marry.[17]

Between 1740 and the War for Independence, small academies and schools sprang up throughout the colonies. Some were coeducational; others were for girls alone. They catered to elite families who aspired to the gentility of the ruling classes in the mother country. Parents set up and ran some schools. Others were "adventure" schools, opened by a particular teacher, for profit. Husbands and wives sometimes ran such a school together or hired outside teachers for specific subjects. In some cases girls attended more than one school simultaneously (in much the same way that parents today may send children to private music schools or sports camps, after the regular school day). Students could board or live at home. At £5 for a year at a day school and £24–30 for a year boarding, parents were investing heavily in their daughters. Only the well-to-do could afford such options. Although adventure schools lacked adequate endowment and fluctuated in attendance, the best, such as those run by Anthony Benezet (where Sally Franklin may have attended), offered a broad curriculum and competent teaching.[18]

Sarah Osborn's school in Newport, Rhode Island, was a very successful "adventure" school from 1744 to 1774. She provided a rigorous, religious-centered education with attention to reading, writing, and arithmetic using hymns, prayers, and the Bible as texts. She referred families more interested in having their daughters learn manners to a school taught by another woman in town. At its peak Osborn's school had 70 students, both day and boarding. Osborn let poorer neighbors pay for their daughters' education by doing washing, ironing, or sewing.[19] Thus mothers provided the in-kind services that educated their daughters.

Another measure of the interest in schools is the efforts expended to found schools for young blacks. Both Quakers and Anglicans set up formal schools. The Associates of Dr. Bray soon provided financing and books for Anglican efforts in Virginia, New York, and Pennsylvania. After Deborah Franklin visited the new school in Philadelphia, she decided to enroll their slave boy, and wrote to Benjamin describing the school. Benjamin published her letter in England and *he* was promptly elected to membership in the Bray's Associates. All the Bray's Associates schools closed by the Revolution, although the one in Williamsburg lasted until its teacher, the widow Anne Wager, died in 1774. Anthony Benezet began evening classes for slaves in his Pennsylvania home beginning in 1750. In 1770 Benezet convinced the Philadelphia Monthly Meeting to begin an African school. Opening with 22 boys and girls, the school eventually served adults, too. About 250 students had attended by 1775. Other slaves learned in the same informal ways that whites did. Some plantation mistresses also taught their slaves how to read and write. Fugitive slave advertisements suggest that one out of seven escaped Massachusetts slaves could read.[20]

All efforts to educate slaves shared certain features. The schools taught very young boys and girls (ages three to eight) reading, spelling, good pronunciation, religion, cleanliness, and morals. Many of the schools hired women as teachers. Student turnover was high. The owners removed children from school to help with chores. Slave schools resembled the charity schools for whites in length of time children spent there, curriculum, and gender distinctions. They reserved arithmetic for boys, and taught girls knitting and sewing. In other words, this was education shaped for women who would be part of dependent laboring classes. It was designed to inculcate values of modesty, deference, and piety. Household skills mattered at least as much as literacy.[21]

The religious awakenings renewed efforts to found schools for Indians. Here, too, boys had precedence. Virginia began efforts early in the century, but the Brafferton at the College of William and Mary was for boys only. Between 1730 and 1760 all the Middle Colonies and Massachusetts experimented with Indian schools. These mid-century attempts insisted on complete adoption of Euro-American culture. Mission Indians often lived in special villages, assumed Christian names, and avoided alcohol and native dances and festivals. The Brant family came into direct contact with these missionary efforts. Margaret had responded to Anglican missionary efforts between 1730 and 1750, having each of her children baptized. In 1754 she was admitted to communion, and soon both a church and school adjoined her home.[22]

Missionaries discovered that since Indian women had such important control of families and children, they needed to educate girls. Women's support was crucial to missionary efforts. Margaret Brant hosted the Fort Ontario minister Theophilus Chamberlain from 1766 to 1767, when he ran a school at Canajoharie. The mother of a noted Mohegan Presbyterian minister not only led her son to church, but personally inspected the school he wanted to attend to learn English. John Brainerd considered Delaware women better subjects than men

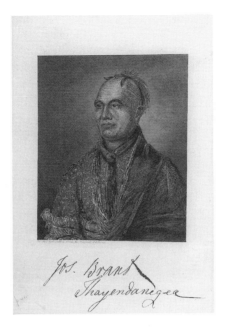

Joseph Brant was the member of Margaret Brant's family most often portrayed in nineteenth-century texts. This portrait is from an 1886 biography. *Reproduced by permission of the Huntington Library, San Marino, California.*

for education, acculturation, and Christianization. Because Brainerd insisted men do the farming, Indian women had been reduced to making brooms and baskets to support themselves. He suggested a school to teach women to spin and knit. It offered an alternative to Indian women displaced from their traditional agricultural duties. Brainerd's suggestion hit what became the main theme of education for Indian girls—they were to be trained to be good housewives. Literacy was secondary.[23]

Margaret's son Joseph Brant attended Moor's Indian Charity School in Lebanon, Connecticut. From 1761 to 1769, the school also accepted Indian girls. Founder Eleazar Wheelock suggested admitting girls in order to curb running away, drunkenness, and misbehavior among the male students, and to provide suitable spouses and helpmeets for the boys. The 16 girls were about one-quarter of the school's enrollment. Drawn from a number of nations, including the Delaware, Mohawk, Oneida, and several of the New England Algonkian groups, all were familiar with Christianity, spoke some English, and may have already had some schooling. The girls attended class only one day a week. Wheelock placed them as servants with local families so the girls could learn household skills such as sewing, dairying, and spinning. Some families treated the girls as slaves. Although these women were to be mates to missionaries, they were not educated as gentlewomen (as whites might have been), but as laboring-class women.[24]

What education the women Wheelock called "amiable black savages" received was of questionable benefit to them. Each Sunday as they sat in the back of the woman's side of the church, the girls learned anew that they were doubly subordinate. Arriving when they were between 12 and 16, they missed the usual time for courtship in their communities. Their education was too scanty to make a living at sewing among the whites, and they no longer fit comfortably in their own communities. The most successful of the 16 was Hannah Garrett, a Pequot who grew up in a Narragansett village with its own mission church and school. Despite her "education" at Moor's and the mission school, she never learned to write. Hannah used her housewifery skills as the wife of David Fowler, a Mohegan who taught school at Montauk. After the Revolution they resettled on Oneida land.[25]

Most interesting is the exaggerated version of gender-specific education that Indian girls learned at these schools. As already noted, charity schools for whites and blacks often taught girls sewing or knitting rather than arithmetic. However, the proportion of vocational education to literacy education for Indian girls was weighted much more toward vocational time. Most never learned to write. The girls attending the Indian schools were much older than those attending Bray's Associates schools, or charity schools for whites. For Indians this was their second education. As young children they had been educated in their Indian communities. Now they were to replace that experience with the lessons of Moor's School. It is no wonder that most lived uneasily between two worlds once they left the school.

The level of literacy among the Mohawk elite, however, suggests broader access to schools than might first be assumed. Whether Molly could write or not, she owned music books, and her daughters were thoroughly literate, having studied with tutors and in Canada. Joseph's third wife, Catherine Adonwentishon, the daughter of Indian trader George Croghan, also had basic literacy skills and could sign her name. Margaret Brant clearly thought literacy important. She not only hosted the English schoolteacher, she used physical force to prevent him from closing his school. She may have seen education as essential for

Mohawk survival. The teacher's stay was troubled due to his ethnocentrism, but the Mohawks literally could see the writing on the wall. Book learning was necessary to survive in a world with powerful whites.[26]

The growth in women's literacy raised concern about women's proper role. Those promoting women's education thought it prepared women for their roles. Others were concerned about the liberating elements inherent in literacy. This discussion focused on the education of elite women, since the education of others was heavily vocational. There is plenty of evidence that Americans both valued formal education for women, and feared it. As women's roles changed and educational opportunities grew, so did the number of negative comments. Satires of intelligent or educated women circulated widely in the colonies. The visibility of women's formal education threatened those who linked book education to male roles and independence. Women, long considered "lesser" men, challenged male superiority by showing their intellect. Women defended their intelligence and education when challenged. It could hardly have eased the fears of a young Princeton student when the wife of the college president "talked him quite silent" after he advocated restricting women's education and writing to appropriate topics.[27]

Families supporting women's education saw it as an investment. Obituaries in colonial newspapers included such lines as "her only fortune was an extraordinary education," or noted a woman was known "for embellishments of her mind, the brilliancy of her conversation, and the sanctity of her manners." These passages illustrate the ways a family assimilated an expanded book education for women into their goals of social advancement and piety.[28]

English novels and advice manuals circulating in America just before the Revolution also assumed a level of women's education, or argued for it. *Six Sketches on the History of Man, containing the Progress of Men as Individuals*, by Henry Home (Lord Kaims), for example, included a letter on the "Progress of the Female Sex." Home argued that a woman's education would allow her to maintain influence over men as she aged, and that "Married women, in particular, destined by nature to take the lead in educating their children, would no longer be the greatest obstruction to good education, by their ignorance, frivolity, and disorderly manner of living." This argument echoed the growing domestic ideology, and would become a major theme in discussions of women's education after independence.[29]

After the Revolution, American educational reformers extended the defense of women's education by linking it to the development of the new nation. Educated mothers were needed to raise children who could be good citizens in the new republic. These children needed self-control, virtue, and to contribute to the national good. Some women reformers argued that women needed education to be independent, or that women deserved education because they had intellects to develop. In the end, Americans accepted the idea that education prepared women for motherhood. Unlike males, who would choose their vocation and whose higher education was preparation for professions, all women had the same domestic vocation. Even former slaves needed to be responsible mothers in the new republic, thus Philadelphia abolitionists opened a school for black women in 1792. Eleanor Harris, an African who had taught in England, served as the teacher.[30]

The emphasis given to women's education in the aftermath of the Revolution was thus double-edged. Women's education needed to expand, but it was to serve a different purpose than men's education. Massachusetts first included schoolmistresses in its laws in 1789, and towns began including girls in the school census, but girls attended the short summer sessions. Although the Boston Act of 1789 required girls and boys to study the same subjects, it left girls attending school for fewer hours and fewer days. Women's more advanced education usually did not include classical education or extended training in logic, rhetoric, and speculative thought. Those subjects trained men for public occupations. Women needed an education that protected their innocence and virtue. While Benjamin Rush, Judith Sargent Murray, and Susanna Rowson all argued that women's education needed to foster self-reliance, they linked this to skills needed as a mother in the new republic. Women needed reading, grammar, penmanship, figures and bookkeeping, natural philosophy, geography, vocal music, and to run their household and start their children's education. History, philosophy, poetry, and moral essays would help women teach their sons to value liberty and maintain the republic.[31]

Thus the academies that opened after the Revolution might acknowledge that women's intellects were equal to men's, but as the Reverend Penuel Bowen argued, women's destined role in life did not require they be learned; it did require they be virtuous. The academy he opened in Savannah in 1786 for young women offered a "practical" education for women. The Young Ladies Academy that opened the next year in Philadelphia taught grammar, geography, arithmetic, oratory, chemistry, rhetoric, composition, spelling, and natural philosophy. The Moravians opened their academy to other girls in 1785 with a curriculum including German, English, French, arithmetic, needle-crafts, history, geography, music, Bible, and astronomy. The academy's real draw, however, was its reputation for teaching the values of modesty, simplicity, and good manners. The founding of the first Roman Catholic convent in Maryland allowed Catholic families to educate their daughters in America in a context of virtue and piety. By excluding the classics and stressing the special suitability of the education they offered women, these academies reinforced gender as the essential determinant of women's lives.[32]

The heightened interest in women's education brought solid support for some of the academies. The Young Ladies Academy in Philadelphia, which attracted elite women from as far away as Maine, incorporated in 1792. Even academies in small towns had permanent physical plants, multi-teacher staffs, and community financial support.[33] Many of the attributes of post-Revolutionary education were present before the Revolution, including curriculum, school-size, and financial support, but they were now more common and accepted.

What society intends an institution to do, and what participants absorb from that experience, can vary. No matter how much reformers thought they were creating an education for mothers in the new republic, some students responded directly to the educational challenges or had their own motives for learning. Young women attending these new academies saw themselves as pioneers. The student addresses of the first two graduating classes (1792 and 1793) from the Young Ladies Academy in Philadelphia not only defended women's intellect and women's right to speak in public, but claimed that women should have roles in the church, law, and government. Whatever its intent, the academy did not domesticate all of its first charges.[34]

As more women became fully literate in the second half of the eighteenth century, they became consumers and producers of literature. One Revolutionary-era widow, for example, listed access to his library as one of the characteristics of a good husband. Between 1730 and 1790 Americans founded 376 circulating libraries. American publishing also expanded. Printers reprinted English works adapted or edited for American audiences, and published original materials by American authors. Every state passed some form of copyright law by 1786. Four years later Congress passed the Federal Copyright Act, giving authors control over their work for 14 years, renewable for a second 14. Copyright protection encouraged publication.[35]

Women had access to some of the new libraries and shared purchased books as they had long done. Reading aloud became family entertainment. Women read anything they could find, from religious materials and how-to manuals to poetry and novels. Reading offered an opportunity for self-education. Women were reading newspapers before the war, but magazines mixing fiction and nonfiction grew in popularity after the Revolution. Many women published stories with themes supporting the Revolution and challenging partriarchal control. Romantic novels drew strong support from women readers.[36] The range of women's reading suggests a hunger for self-improvement, the growth of leisure time among middle- and upper-class women, and a search for guidance in how to negotiate the shifting sands of gender roles in the Revolutionary era.

Women read widely, and discussed their reading with others. Letters and journals before the Revolution mention such novels as *Pamela, Clarissa, Joseph Andrews,* and classics such as the *Iliad* and works by Milton and Shakespeare. Astute readers, they critiqued works in letters to other women and made literary references to characters in *Candide* and novels by Mrs. Ratcliffe and poetry by Alexander Pope. Publishers geared household manuals, recipe books, and ladies journals toward this growing market of readers. Before the Revolution only household manuals from England circulated in the colonies, but in the new republic, American women published their own.[37]

Women's reading habits provoked warnings that reading would make women neglect their work. Novels, it was feared, would give women unreasonable expectations and excite their passions. If women were going to read, then they should read history, an eminently rational subject thought to ennoble its readers. One measure of the increase in women's reading was the amount of ink spent in trying to direct it appropriately.[38]

Conservatives might have been worried that women would read the "wrong" things, but much of what women read was religious. Southern women's libraries included sermons, prayer books, psalms, Elizabeth Burnet's *A Method of Devotion,* and Elizabeth Singer Rowe's works. Women read all the major and minor devotional books, meditations, and religious poets. Esther Burr was so taken by Rowe's work that Burr fantasized conversing with her. Women also ventured to publish their own ecstatic and poetic visions of death, salvation, and heaven.[39]

More women began writing poetry in the years before the Revolution. Many of their poems were personal (ex. growing old) or occasional (written to comment on or celebrate a specific event). Most were unpublished. Unpublished poems, however, could see wide circulation,

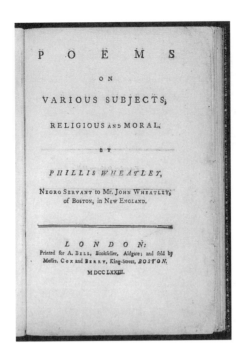

Title page of an early edition (1773) of Phillis Wheatley's poems. *Reproduced by permission of the Huntington Library, San Marino, California.*

passed from friend to friend. Some even circulated as collections. Hanah Adams described such a circle of friends in her *Memoir*—"most of them wrote verses, which were read and admired by the whole little circle." Similarly, Susanna Wright of Chester, Pennsylvania, circulated her poems in manuscript to her male and female correspondents. Only three of her poems have survived, one of which links being unmarried to ideas of independence. Individual poems appeared in newspapers or magazines, often anonymously. Annis Boudinot circulated poems among her friends in Princeton, New Jersey. Her women friends prompted her to write a poem responding to a satire of women's intellect that appeared in the newspaper. She sent it to the paper in reply.[40]

Not all such authors were white. The first identified poem written by an African-American woman described the Indian attack on Deerfield in 1746. Lucy Terry Prince had witnessed the raid while a slave of Ebenezer Wells. It survived as a ballad in Deerfield's oral tradition and was first printed a century after being written. More well-known is Phillis Wheatley. Brought from Africa and purchased as a young slave by the Wheatley family, Phillis was tutored by her mistress. Phillis

Mercy Otis Warren used her pen to participate in the political discussions of the American Revolution. *Bequest of Winslow Warren. Courtesy, Museum of Fine Arts, Boston.*

wrote her first poem at 11, and had her first poem published at 13 in 1767. In an era ambivalent about slavery and the capabilities of African Americans, Phillis became a celebrity. The Countess of Huntington sponsored an English edition of her poems, and the newly emancipated Phillis traveled to England in 1774 to publicize the volume. Phillis Wheatley married John Peters in 1776, bore three children, and published only a few additional poems before her death in 1784. Her manuscript poems disappeared after her death.[41]

Often critiqued by scholars wanting to find an early advocate of race and gender equality, Wheatley's publication was constrained by what her white patrons wished to hear. She made her point in subtle ways. Lines in her poems had clear double meanings pointing out the ironies of race. She used images of light and dark, or bondage, identified herself as African, and used biblical references to Egypt (where Israelites were slaves). She did not defend women's ability to publish, she just demonstrated it to the best of her ability. In her poems liberty, plenty, peace, and fancy are feminine, while death and power appear as male.[42]

As readers, women were interested in the lives of other women. They bought eulogies or memorials lauding women as models of spirituality. Men, often the memorialized woman's husband or minister, wrote or edited most of the autobiographies and memoirs. Embedded within these memoirs, however, are excerpts from the women's own writings—diaries, confessions, meditations. At least one woman, Elizabeth Estaugh, reversed this format by serving as the editor of her husband's work in 1744. Men also chronicled accounts of adventurous women, such as Deborah Sampson Ganett, who served as a soldier, or Mary Jemison, who had chosen to live as an Iroquois throughout her adult life after being captured as a child. Thus men helped refashion women's roles, and appropriated women's voices, while recognizing the growing audience of female readers.[43]

Several women earned reputations in nonfiction genres after the war. Printers frequently pirated Judith Sargent Murray's *Gleaner* essays in the 1790s. Her own edition had 700 subscribers. Murray began publishing in 1784 and often chose to write in support of women's education. Mercy Otis Warren published poems, satirical political tracts in the form of plays, and a serious history of the American Revolution. Her publishing began in the 1770s and continued to the end of her life. Of the 15 histories produced by patriots in the years immediately after the war, Warren's stands out for her understanding of the role of historian as social and political critic, and of historical theory. Hanah Adams gained a reputation as a scholar of the Revolution and religious history. After being cheated by a printer, Adams published and promoted her own second edition and lived comfortably off the sales of her *Alphabetical Compendium of Various Sects* and other works.[44]

Thus the Revolutionary generation reaped both the fruits and the tares of the efforts to educate women that developed throughout the second half of the century. Increasingly literate, and with growing access to academies, schools, books, libraries, and publishing, women became an active part of the reading and writing public in the new republic. At the same time, the rationales for education increased the emphasis on gender, defined a specific nurturing role for women, and tried to force women of varying needs and backgrounds into a single pattern. The growth in women's literacy was not an argument for equality. Throughout the period families decided that women did not need the same education as men. When compounded by ethnocentrism and racism, as it was for American Indian women and African-American women, women's education was even more problematic.

CHAPTER SIX

Sisters of the Spirit

W hen Benjamin Franklin was in England in 1758, he sent Deborah and one of her women friends large-print copies of the Book of Common Prayer "so you will both of you be reprieved from the use of spectacles in church a little longer."[1] Franklin's gift symbolized women's role in religion in the middle of the eighteenth century. The printed word, private devotions, and worship shaped women's religious expression. Not all late eighteenth-century American women belonged to churches, but religion was integral to their societies, shaping everyday custom and providing interpretative frameworks for events and behavior. For many women (and men) religion had a deeper meaning, an expression of deeply-felt spirituality offering comfort and forgiveness for human failings. For others, religion was a rational way to set standards, hold a community together, and elicit benevolence. For still others religion was a deeply contested ground where forces of good and evil struggled for control of persons, society, and culture.

Revolutionary America might have been religious, but it was not homogeneous. By 1776 it was home to more than a dozen religions brought by European immigrants to America. In addition, enslaved Africans practiced a variety of beliefs (including Islam), and each Indian nation had its own spiritual traditions. Despite this diversity, eight of the 13 colonies that voted for independence had given either the Anglican or Congregational Church special legal status. Another made tax-support a local option. Diversity, however, put increasing tension on established or traditionally dominant churches in each colony.[2]

Far from the European centers of each denomination, their colonial variations had more local control. Many denominations imported European clergy or sent candidates to Europe for training and ordination. Pulpits sat vacant in the meantime. In the absence of clergy, family piety and religious education gained importance. The number of Bibles, hymn and psalm collections, prayer books, and other religious writings owned by colonists attests to widespread interest in religion.[3]

The War for Independence provided a context for major religious change. State leaders, who needed the support of every religious group, listened to complaints that established churches had an unfair advantage and were inconsistent with individual liberty. Ministers left congregations to join the army or to serve in legislatures. Others fled as Tory refugees. By 1790 only Massachusetts and Connecticut continued state tax support for particular churches (in both cases, Congregational). Secular officials took over duties such as poor relief formerly handled by parishes. The organization of voluntary national denominational structures began. New sects emerged and old ones tried to establish respectability. Baptists and Methodists especially organized to harvest converts at the revivals that followed the Revolution.[4]

Assessing the meaning of women's participation in these religions during the Revolutionary era has been controversial. Women clearly participated in the revivals called the Great Awakening, read and wrote about religion, performed the daily routines of piety, and attended church. Because of its missionary impulse, Christianity affected some women of every group in America, but other traditions persisted. In general, women had few or no roles in the formal governance or ordained ministries of European religions. Theology mixed empowerment with misogyny.[5] Nonetheless, women were integral to the practice and transmission of religion in ways that transcended official lines of power.

Consider Benjamin's gift to Deborah. On one level it symbolizes male direction of a woman's religious activities. Benjamin chose a book written by men and used in worship services where women followed the lead of men. On another level, the gift acknowledges religion as part of a woman's domain. The *Book of Common Prayer* made Deborah an active participant, reading along in the service and making congregational responses. Laity also used it for private devotions and family prayer not led by clergy. Readers (listeners) have often found messages that the writers (speakers) had not intended. An age stressing both rational thought and personal emotional experience gave women room to "read" religion in unauthorized ways.

In a few denominations, women were leaders. The Society of Friends (Quakers) had developed a parallel system of meetings for men and women. Weekly meetings served as times of worship, but Monthly, Quarterly, and Yearly meetings conducted church business. Meeting Houses developed a separate physical space for women, either with a woman's wing or through a system of sliding partitions that divided one large hall for separate meetings. Quaker Books of Discipline reflected the parallel status by using "he and she," etc., to include both men and women.[6] Women's meetings oversaw women members and kept their own records and treasuries. By mid-century the Philadelphia Yearly Meeting had agreed "that Solid Women Friends should be Appointed to sit in the Meeting of Ministers, & Elders, as well as Men." Men's meetings did not overturn women's decisions. Women leaders originally came from all classes, but after 1750 rural meetings increasingly chose wealthy women with servants to help with household duties. In contrast, about one-third of the women serving as leaders in Philadelphia were of modest means. As the Revolution neared, middle-class women dropped out of leadership.[7]

Although Quakers did not ordain clergy, those men and women who traveled and spoke frequently were viewed as preachers. When a traveling Friend came to town, many non-Quakers attended.[8] Quaker women could inspire other women to leadership or shock those who found it improper. Most women began by speaking in their own meetings. Some had to put aside their own doubts about the propriety of women speaking in public. Eventually those with a strong call might begin to travel.[9] One-third of the traveling Friends memorialized in a 1787 volume were women. Most female traveling Friends had grown children or were widows. They became part of a transatlantic community, testifying throughout the empire. Thus Quakers gave women authority and visibility as leaders, although women made less use of these opportunities in the last part of the century.[10]

The small Moravian settlements in Pennsylvania and North Carolina also had specific roles for women, and a theology with strong feminine imagery. Moravians allowed both men and women to be acolytes and deacons, but only men could be priests or bishops. Moravian communities organized in residential/spiritual units called "choirs." There were choirs for children, single men, single women, married men, married women, widowed men, and widowed women. Women, often the wives of clergy, led the women's choirs, and sometimes the children's choir. In the community near Winston-Salem, North Carolina, women were one-third of the leadership. Over time the women's leadership in the life of the community declined. By 1778 the community at Bethlehem cut its governing council to representatives of the four adult choirs. Women's status as Elders depended on their status as wives of Elders, and women more than men were asked to resign offices upon the death of a spouse.[11]

The churches formed during the eighteenth-century revivals originally gave women a voice. Women in some Baptist and Separatist congregations could vote on church governance and discipline. After the War for Independence, as Separatist and Baptist congregations struggled to regularize, they began limiting women's participation. Some congregations limited the vote or role of Elders to men; others began polling men individually and then asking women to rise jointly to give assent. Although historians have offered group-specific explanations for these changes, the larger pattern suggests a redefinition of church governance as public acts unsuited to women's new private roles. Churches may also have sought order and "respectability" by controlling women and conforming to traditional patriarchy.[12]

No other colonial churches with European origins gave women direct leadership roles by 1776. Women could, however, publicly demonstrate their church support and their piety, and hold certain church positions. As Anglicans, Deborah Franklin, Elizabeth Porter, and Margaret Brant understood women's religious roles to include patron, sexton, teacher, and musician. Women had numerous opportunities to be patrons. Between 1753 and 1774 Elizabeth Stith both endowed a school in Virginia for poor children and provided her local parish with elegant plaques of the 10 commandments, Creed, and Lord's Prayer. William Franklin's wife Elizabeth made equally elegant gifts to a New Jersey church. The roles of musician and sexton went to women with less money. Women occasionally played the organ. As a sexton a woman cleaned pews and escorted parishioners to their pews, kept the church keys, cared for the church linen, and laid out the dead for burial. Sextons had physical control of the building.[13]

The late eighteenth century was not only an era of political upheaval and revolution, but one of continuing religious renewal. Religious renewal touched Americans across the whole spectrum of belief, ranging from a Quaker reformation to prophets and spiritual revival among

American Indians.[14] The religious ferment provided space for women to take new leadership roles. Beginning with the Great Awakening in the late 1730s, and ending with the second Great Awakening after the Revolution, America experienced a series of overlapping, periodic revivals.[15] The revivals emphasized emotion and immediate conviction of sin, repentance, and salvation rather than rational acceptance of salvation and duty. Each region had its own timing for the revivals spread by different denominations. In the South, Presbyterians were followed by Methodists and Baptists in spreading revival after 1740.[16] To the north, waves of revivals split local churches into Old Light, New Light, and Baptists.

The irrational and mystical were an integral part of many religions, and gave women a public voice. In the American Indian communities, such visions were a normal part of religious expression. Ojibway women made powerful use of visions.[17] Christian clergy and laity also paid great attention to signs, dreams, and visions. Many men and women interpreted their dreams as signs from God, and recorded them in letters and journals. Methodists regularly recorded accounts of possession, signs from God, and visions by men and women.[18]

The visions of Mary Reed illustrate the ways in which spiritual experience could alter normal lines of authority in a congregation. Several members of the Durham, New Hampshire, congregation began to have visions in 1742. Reed's minister allowed her to declare her visions publically during the service, and used them as the subject of an exhortation. When she had more visions, Reed moved to the minister's home, where she spent the next week praying, singing, and instructing her minister.[19] The usual roles of minister and congregant had reversed.

Dreams and trances, however, disturbed many laity and clergy who worried that the experiences were delusions. In addition, the reversal of authority inherent in such direct revelations could be threatening to clergy. One unlucky minister divided his congregation by preaching against trances. Women demonstrated their disrespect for the minister by sitting in the broad aisle of the church knitting during services. Both men and women interrupted him and called him names.[20]

By mid-century, women comprised a majority of those (of all races) present at regular worship and a majority of those who made declarations of membership. Studies document this female majority of worshipers across a spectrum of congregations including New York Dutch Reformed, Pennsylvania Moravians, New England Congregationalists, Virginia Baptists, and Methodists.[21] If men had abandoned the churches, women were a majority only by default. But women's active participation in revivals, clergy disputes, and local church disputes suggests that churches attracted women because they found religion empowering.[22] More women than men joined churches during the revivals, thus increasing women's majority status. While New England men joined under the old Half-Way Covenant (membership without communion rights, available to all baptized people), women became full members. As the heat of a revival cooled, men became inactive members faster than women.[23]

The Quakers turned inward rather than to evangelism. As a result of the Quaker reformation, perhaps one-third to one-half of Quakers quietly left the church. Led by an elite of Public and weighty Friends, reforming meetings focused on internal discipline, marriage, education, and family. Meetings enforced discipline against sexual offenders, those who married outsiders, and worldliness.[24] The Quaker reforms certainly created major conflicts for men engaged in politics and business in a way that they did not for women. Women's greatest risk of disownment was at marriage.

African-Americans had to maintain customs far away from the African societies where the religions flourished. In contrast, Indians struggled to maintain indigenous religious traditions against cultural encroachment at home. Slavery made the transference of complete African religions difficult. Many of the slaves were young; they lived in scattered, ethnically mixed groups; and whites opposed many African customs. Muslims could hardly build a mosque, or import a mullah. Other African religions used sacred places or village ceremonies impossible for those enslaved to duplicate. Private prayer, burial and birthing customs, and magic practices often did survive. These were areas in which women often had special authority. Like blacks, Indians faced the disruption of rituals because of lost cultural knowledge, but the reason was demographic—the high death rate and resulting merger of villages threatened tradition.[25]

Sporadic earlier attempts to evangelize the enslaved Africans became more frequent and successful after mid-century. Anglicans, Presbyterians, and Baptists began attracting African-American members in the large slaveholding colonies. The Methodist movement also attracted a following among Africans before and after independence. Since these efforts brought Africans into white congregations, there was little room to blend African and Christian forms until African-Americans formed their own congregations after the American Revolution.[26] Renewed interest in evangelism and humanitarianism drove Anglican efforts to convert slaves. The other churches' efforts were part of their revival activities. All the churches found that African women were more likely to be baptized than men. Among Methodists, 73 percent of the black members were women in the last two decades of the century. Although the evangelical churches have received more publicity, Anglicans mounted more sustained and consistent efforts. The result was a growing body of African-American Christians who worshiped in mixed congregations (with segregated seating).[27]

The records of Christian churches in the colonies suggest that women were a majority of converts among American Indians and African-Americans, as well as among whites. In New London, Connecticut, for example, from 1739 until 1783, 14 Indian women and seven men were admitted as members. Similarly, the years of the Great Awakening changed the patterns of membership among Natick so that women members outnumbered men two to one. There is some evidence that women were the majority of the members of Indian Christian communities outside New England. It was Margaret Brant's attachment to the Anglican church (and thus her appearance in its records), in fact, that has made it possible to trace her life.[28]

No single factor explains why there were more women than men in white, black, and Indian Christian communities. Because most black women seeking membership were of childbearing age, historians have thought they hoped to claim spiritual status for themselves and their children in a community that denied them other forms of status. However, women of all races were more likely to join churches as young adults of childbearing age, making it hard assign a unique motive to enslaved women's actions. The numerical majority of women among Indian members of Christian congregations may simply be a result of women's majority status in the Indian's population in settled areas. However, since white and black women were also a majority in church, but a minority in the population, other factors must have been at work.[29] Any explanation for a women's majority in church membership must consider that church membership was an individual, autonomous choice for women by 1750. Deborah Franklin, her daughter, and her niece faithfully attended Sunday services in Philadelphia, but Benjamin was not a member and attended very irregularly. Deborah's experience was common. By the middle of the century, husbands and wives did not usually join churches together. Young women who became members of churches during revivals expressed both their faith and their independence from their families.[30]

Many women joined churches about the time they married. Both marriage and church membership may be interpreted as acts of submission—in marriage submission to coverture and male headship of families, and in religion to church authority and male clergy. But given the independence women exercised in becoming members, they may have taken the step as a sign of their adult status. Women's independent choice of membership suggests a demonstration of their adult status, separate from their husbands. Religion often divided couples rather than uniting them. Since husbands may not have been church members or were members of another church, women could not use them as spiritual guides. The revivals of the Great Awakening contributed to women's freedom of choice by increasing their options and emphasizing personal conversion.[31] Some women even left their families and joined small religious celibate communities like Ephrata near Lancaster, Pennsylvania. Ephrata attracted enough married women to arouse local hostility.[32] Late eighteenth-century Americans could tolerate a woman declaring religious independence by attending a different church from her husband, but they could not tolerate a woman also declaring independence from male authority over the family.

Women's religious autonomy made them agents of religious change or forces for stability in their families. In Elizabeth Porter's community of Manakin in the 1770s, Baptists, Anglicans, and Methodists competed for members. Baptist conversion spread along lines of female kinship. Elizabeth Dutoy and Thomas Porter were devout Anglicans. Thirty years of activity by evangelicals in the area had not shaken the Porters' church loyalty. Sarah Watkins Porter, wife of Elizabeth's son John, however, breached the Porters' religious unity. Sarah's kin were early Baptist converts; she and two brothers converted by 1775. She brought both John and his brother Isaac (who lived with them after Elizabeth's death in 1772) into the Baptist fold by 1780. They were the only children of Elizabeth and Thomas to convert before 1780.[33]

As hostess and mistress of a household, a woman could extend hospitality to visiting clergy and thus open her home to their preaching. Susanna Wheatley of Newport, Rhode Island, considered herself "greatly honour'd" to shelter visiting clergy sent by the Countess of Huntington. Women's hospitality in the face of opposition from their husbands became a recurring theme in early Baptist literature. In one early account, a Mrs. Pearce invited a Baptist preacher to her son-in-law's house while he was away. She died soon after, and her husband granted her deathbed plea that he open his house to Baptist preaching.[34]

Her deathbed request suggests that Mrs. Pearce had originally used her daughter's house and her authority as mother to do what her husband would not allow her to do in her own home.

At times men acted as surrogates in church offices for their wives. Deborah Read Franklin was a lifelong devoted Anglican. Her husband Benjamin was one of America's most noted Deists. Yet Deborah's involvement with Christ Church and St. Paul's in Philadelphia pulled Benjamin into church circles. Deborah Read's family were active leaders at Christ Church. Benjamin helped with the Church's business affairs and was one of the managers for the lottery used to raise money for a steeple and bells in 1752-53.[35] Similarly, when the husband of Deborah's niece sought Anglican orders, Benjamin Franklin found himself enmeshed in church politics.[36] Thomas Porter inherited his vestry duties in much the same way. Porter was one of three men of English background appointed to the vestry of King William Parish (the church for Huguenot refugees in Virginia) between 1748 and 1750. In each case the men were married to women whose families were traditional parish leaders. Such surrogate actions remained common on the American frontier well into the next century.[37]

Women's ethnic loyalties affected church membership and reinforced women's autonomy in their choice of denomination. In the pluralistic society of eighteenth-century America, religious loyalty seemed to matter more to women than to men, especially when religion reinforced ethnic identity. When men of Dutch Reformed background began joining Anglican Trinity Parish in New York, their wives did not. They chose instead to remain tied to the Dutch congregation.[38] In some cases women seem to have joined the Dutch congregation in response to their husbands' actions in leaving it.

Most communities in Revolutionary America offered residents a choice of churches. Although denominational structures grew stronger throughout the century, individuals crossed denominational lines to hear preachers, even if they were deeply committed to one church. One Long Island woman's diaries, for example, document that she attended other services besides her own and frequently heard itinerant preachers, including Quakers. On at least one occasion, members of her family went to three different denominations' services on the same Sunday.[39] A good preacher of any denomination could draw a crowd. As Alice Colden reported on a trip to her Anglican Church in New York, "there were a vast many more people than our little Church cou'd [sic] hold, whither any converts were made I know not but many desenters [sic] were there."[40]

One of the paradoxes of early mission work among Indians is that female converts outnumbered male, but women also offered stronger resistance to missionary efforts. Women had cause to resist missionaries who insisted they adopt European gender roles that barred women from formal leadership and undercut their work and family patterns. Contact over 150 years had created a "middle ground" between white and Indian culture. One result of the middle ground was the incorporation of some Christian elements into Indian religion, including some written prayers. Trans-Appalachian Indians had a respite from missionary pressure after the British expelled the Jesuits from the area, since Protestant missionary work there did not begin until after the American Revolution. Changes in women's religious roles in these areas during the late eighteenth century were more a result of renewal movements among Indian religions than of missionary incursions.[41]

Indian women had important roles in planting and healing ceremonies. Indian beliefs linked women with fertility and creation. Customs of menstrual seclusion reinforced these links. During menses a woman's spiritual power could prevent a man from having a successful hunt. Seclusion recognized women's power, gave them a break from tasks, and sometimes brought women together. In the eighteenth century, Ojibwa women joined medicine lodges called Midewiwin that connected women of different small bands while preserving traditional beliefs.[42]

Indians east of the Mississippi mixed resistance with religious renewal movements after 1736. These revivals, despite occasional female leaders, often had a negative impact on women. For example, although women joined Midewiwin societies, only males served as priests. Renewal movements usually formed around a prophet who preached a return to traditional ways. Ironically, since women had maintained more of the traditional religious practices, the renewal movements focused on returning men to the old ways. In the process, religious leaders shifted participation to emphasize male rituals and roles. Since trade goods helped make women's lives easier, and because they were often engaged in trade, the demands that followers reject these items were hard on women. At times the revivals seemed aimed at women who were cultural mediators or controlled the liquor trade.[43]

If Indian women were most resistant to Christianity, they also became the majority of converts, continuing their roles as cultural mediators.[44] Resistance was possible among groups further from white settlement, but Indian women like Margaret who felt pressure from white culture on a nearly daily basis adopted mediation. Although most Mohawk were nominally Christian, Margaret went further by becoming a communicant. Not all churches approached evangelism among Indian tribes in the same way. The Moravians encouraged Indian converts to form separate villages, where they could continue to hunt, farm, fish, and practice traditional crafts. Other churches more closely mixed conversion and assimilation. Moor's Indian School, set up by Eleazar Wheelock (where Margaret's son Joseph Brant was educated), clearly had an assimilationist agenda for both boys and girls.[45]

Religion was not limited to acts of public worship on Sunday. The practice of religion was deeply embedded in everyday life. The revivals drew attention to the dailiness of religion by emphasizing "worldly" attitudes and actions that drew one away from a godly path. It did not matter whether one were American Indian or of European or African descent, religion regulated sexual relationships, marriage, childbirth, death, coming of age, and diet.[46] Behavioral codes varied depending on the dominant culture in each area. Hence Anglican Virginia enjoyed theater and dancing, while such amusements received a chilly reception in Pennsylvania or New England. Similarly, during Indian revivals communities might reject the very trade goods another Indian village still eagerly sought. The increase in religious pluralism by the time of the Revolution created internal challenges in each community. These were especially clear in the areas of European settlement.

Dancing and the music that accompanied it, drinking liquor, playing cards, and fashionable dress all became symbols in a struggle between two religious cultures. When an Anglican husband tried to physically force his Quaker-convert wife to dance, they were really fighting over her spiritual identity.[47] Barbara Heck helped organize Methodist classes in New York in 1765 after being shocked by card playing among her friends. The classes were to provide a shield against such worldly temptations. In Virginia, dancing and gaming were part of the competition by which male gentry achieved status in society. Baptist revivals challenged the gentry's authority and the social order by rejecting gentry culture. Since the majority of Baptists were women, this struggle also had gender implications, as women rejected a male-centered culture. There was a similar edge to women's attempts to have Quakers adopt total abstinence rather than a moderate use of alcohol.[48]

Women participated in family worship, rituals, and religious education. Women and men were responsible for the religious education of the children, servants, and slaves within their household. Anglican missionary tracts urging slaveholders to evangelize their slaves were always addressed to both masters and mistresses of slaves, for example. American Indian women, both Christian converts and those of traditional Indian religions, taught rituals and beliefs to their children. Because public worship for Roman Catholics was illegal in the British Empire, there were few priests or services. Catholic women filled the void in their families by overseeing devotions, teaching their children, and providing family chapels where priests could conduct private services.[49] Enslaved African-Americans had the most difficulty fulfilling these family roles because of the many disruptions and separations caused by slavery.

Pious women of all denominations took seriously creating a "life of piety" for their family. Literacy helped women with this task. Women read to their family from the Bible at night, listened to their children recite catechisms, psalms, and Bible verses, and organized family prayers. Mothers might have had their young children recite scripture, hymns, or sacred poetry while dressing each morning. Others expected children to memorize prayers and quizzed them on the Sunday sermons. Elizabeth Foote Washington of Virginia held morning and evening prayers for family and slaves on the plantation until 1792. Then the Baptist slaves withdrew because they could not pray with the "unconverted" Anglican Washington. The first Methodist classes were often extensions of family worship, including slaves and servants.[50]

In return, churches identified women with family piety. The Quaker reform movement that began in 1755 put renewed emphasis on the Quaker family. Women's meetings had always been concerned with family issues, and now men also turned their attentions from politics to spirituality and the family. Because Methodism emphasized worship and prayer beyond the Sunday services, the family was an essential location for these actions. The church emphasized that piety was part of feminine nature. Methodist women were expected to be evangelists within the family.[51]

Private devotions by women were also important. As a young teen in 1773, Martha Laurens, daughter of a prominent South Carolina Anglican family, responded to a family crisis by drafting a private spiritual covenant. Then she devoted herself to prayer and the study of religion. Hannah Heaton of Connecticut regularly withdrew for daily prayer, meditation, and readings, and she kept a spiritual journal. She read the lives and journals of clergy as guides to her own behavior, thus seeing herself as a minister, not as a woman submitting to a minister.[52]

A few women transformed their religious devotions into a way of life more rigorous than the practice of ordinary piety. Roman Catholics dared not risk founding convents in the British colonies until after disestablishment. However, pietists experimented with religious communities after mid-century. The monastic community of Ephrata offered both men and women a celibate, ordered life. Both men and women wore distinctive garb and had their hair cut short, with a shaved crown. The Quaker ascetic Phebe Smedley followed a pattern of personal denial that led contemporaries to compare her to a medieval nun. She slept on the floor and abstained from meat, sugar, tea, and coffee. While in Philadelphia in 1781 she attracted a small company of women who shared her lifestyle.[53]

Women's religious roles in the family increased as the new domestic ideology took root. In mid-century New England, clergy were nearly as likely to use a woman's life as a man's for the subject of a sermon. Over time they focused more on women's piety and linked it to domesticity. By 1787 a new model of feminine piety was in full force, a model that separated women from the world and linked them to family nurture. James Maury Fontaine's sermon eulogizing Frances Page of Virginia exemplifies the new emphasis. According to Fontaine, Page had no enemies because she had "no competitions with the world, but that laudable one,—*who* should *outdo* in *kindness*, and *good offices.*" Fontaine further equated her excellence as a mother with her Christian virtues.[54]

Clergy felt more direct supervision was necessary when women organized midweek prayer groups than when women led family devotions. All major denominations had traditions of midweek prayer meetings in the homes of laity. Methodism actually began as an outgrowth of such prayer meetings by Anglicans, but turned these into the unique Methodist "classes."[55] The advent in the 1740s of the revivals (usually referred to as the Great Awakening) revitalized private prayer groups as a part of religious guidance and evangelism. Baptist, Congregational, and Presbyterian prayer groups both provided the core for a revival and sustained the harvest afterwards.

Sarah Osborn was one of the best-known of these lay group leaders. She began by overseeing the spiritual growth of the girls who attended her Newport school. In 1741 a group of women began meeting at her home to sing hymns, read scripture, and discuss spiritual matters. Through written rules of order, the women created a group supportive of, but independent from, any Newport congregation. In the 1760s the number of groups at Osborn's house grew until nearly a tenth of Newport attended her meetings. Osborn watched boundaries carefully: Her husband read prayers to mixed or men's groups, but she led the discussion. Osborn extended her reach beyond the usually approved subjects for female evangelizing. By 1773 a nearly blind and aged Sarah Osborn had relinquished leadership of most groups to the Reverend Samuel Hopkins, but she continued with the original women's group until her death.[56]

A similar revival in central New York in 1779 was initiated by a prayer meeting of women. Although supervised by a minister, one of the women conducted the meetings. In another case, meetings at the Long Island home of Mary Cooper helped sustain a revival. Mary Cooper, a devout Baptist, occasionally exhorted (a form of preaching) at Friday meetings and hosted meetings at her home. In each case, clergy supported women's leadership but kept it under a watchful eye.[57]

Anglican evangelicals built the Methodist movement upon small group classes. There were opportunities for women to lead sex-segregated classes. For example, one of New York's first two Methodist classes was a women's group led by Barbara Heck. Mary Thorm and Mary Wilmer led Methodist classes in Philadelphia. Many Methodist classes formed around households, thus reemphasizing the familial nature of the classes. The number of women leading classes dropped rapidly after the Revolution. In the 1790s Methodists recast class leadership as a public ministry suitable for men. Some male class leaders sought ordination, an option not open to women. At the same time they began segregating classes by race. By shifting the education of servants and slaves to a public venue, Methodists distinguished family prayer (still often led by women) from classes (now led by men).[58] The new saints of the Methodist church became heroic male circuit riders.

Clergy worried that women might challenge male leadership. A woman in Middleton, Connecticut, was censured by the church for "wanting to govern," after she gathered a group of followers. New England Separatist congregations censured several women after the Revolution for trying to participate in church decisions, or for raising questions about church discipline. Criticism and self-doubt led Sarah Osborn to write a long defense of her actions in a 1769 letter to an out-of-town minister who supported her actions. Thus while Osborn's leadership may have threatened some local clergy, she was able to seek and find outside clerical approval. One year later Osborn's group of women succeeded in calling Samuel Hopkins as minister of the Second Church in Newport, despite opposition from the other congregational minister in town. Other women exercised similar influence in church politics. Mary Cooper's Separatist congregation, for example, divided in 1773 over accepting tax support. Mary's sister was among the most vocal women in opposition. The minister she opposed was her own son-in-law. Even in Anglican Virginia in 1770, two women played key roles in a controversy concerning a minister's orthodoxy.[59]

If women could lead classes, judge the orthodoxy of clergy theology, and instruct clergy through dreams and visions, it was only a small step to preaching or exhorting in more public arenas. Public familiarity with Quaker women as preachers created some space for women. New England Separatist congregations, Methodists, and Baptists had women lay preachers and exhorters. Mary Cooper's sister served as a lay preacher for their Separatist Congregation on Long Island, for example.[60] The Free Will Baptist movement in the 1770s accepted women as preachers after other Baptist organizations and Methodists limited these offices to men. In the years after the Revolution, many new sects emerged, and clergy struggled to maintain authority in the face of vocal church members.[61] In such an atmosphere, one way to reassert control was to enlist men in efforts to control women.

Two women of Quaker background founded religious movements during the 1770s. Both movements attracted a high percentage of women followers, emphasized celibacy as a spiritual good, and created controversy by emphasizing pacifism during an era of war. Community acceptance of women as Quaker preachers and revival leaders let them build movements based on their charismatic personalities. One of the movements would make the difficult transition from spiritual movement to institutionalized church. Both give a glimpse of an alternative outcome to the domestic piety that became the norm for women by 1800.

Born a Quaker, Jemina Wilkinson converted during a Baptist revival in 1774. After a bout with typhus, she believed she had died and been reanimated by Christ. Wilkinson was a striking woman who attracted followers throughout Pennsylvania, New York, and Rhode Island. Calling herself Universal Friend, she preached universal salvation, free will, rejection of war and slavery, and belief in direct revelation. Her movement stalled when Wilkinson found herself trapped in litigation after the failure in 1790 of a plan to create a settlement in western New York with about 200 to 250 of her followers. The movement collapsed after her death in 1819.[62]

Ann Lee also began as a Quaker, joining a breakaway English sect in 1758 that emphasized the androgyny of God and expected the imminent arrival of a female messiah to balance Christ's earlier appearance in male form. In 1774 Lee and a small group of followers immigrated to the colonies. By 1776 Lee had concluded that she was Christ's female successor. She began traveling, preaching a message of celibacy and pacifism. She and her followers (called Shakers) were jailed in 1780 as suspected Tories. Hostile crowds stopped meetings and beat Ann so severely that she died from the injuries in 1784. Her followers gathered in 1787 to create a religious community based on separate but equal roles for men and women, celibacy, and a simple life. Shaker communities spread in the nineteenth century, and one small community remains today.[63]

In both Ann Lee's and Jemina Wilkinson's theology, the emphasis on celibacy and a female parallel to Christ struck responsive chords among women during an era of changing sexuality. Society increasingly emphasized women's morality and motherhood. Celibacy not only ended childbearing and motherhood, it transformed sexuality into a spiritual gift given to God rather than to another person. Wilkinson added celibacy to her message in the 1780s. Visions in 1770 convinced Lee that intercourse was the reason for the expulsion of Adam and Eve from paradise, and that as Christ's successor she had atoned for the sin of Eve and thus all women. Other small sects that successfully attracted a high proportion of women, such as the Ephrata Cloister, also advocated celibacy and an androgynous God. New London, Connecticut, had a similar group led by a woman about mid-century. They united with the Moravians, who endorsed celibacy as an option and provided single women a spiritual space of their own.[64]

Public and private blended in another arena, causing some tension between clergy and women. The Anglican clergy built their ministry around public ceremonies and parish visits. To be a good pastor was to preach, catechize, baptize, and provide religious rituals as defined by the *Book of Common Prayer*. Birth, marriage, and death were marked by such rituals, but they were also milestones in family life. Colonial customs had made the home the usual site for these rituals, and women acted as mistresses of ceremonies. The result was a quiet tug-of-war between clergy and women over the location of the ceremony.[65] If the ceremonies were held at home, then family custom had the upper hand. If they were held at the church, then the authority of the clergyman held sway. Baptism was the most crucial to clergy because it was the entrance into church membership. Symbolically, the location mattered. It was important that this rite not be a private family affair, but rather witnessed by the congregation. Anglican clergy found resistance to church baptism throughout the century. Religious competition weakened the minister's position, for families could simply have the child baptized by a different minister. As late as 1774, clergy were still meeting resistance in Virginia when Philip Vickers Fithian recorded the following exchange: "Yesterday the Inspector . . . desired the Parson to wait on them in his family and christen his child—Is the child sick? No Sir—Why then today? It is the Mother's desire, Sir—Why was it not brought to Church? The Mother is unwell, Sir." Eventually, Parson Thomas Smith agreed to do the home baptism.[66] Here a mother's wishes overrode the desire of a minister.

The growing separation of public and private by mid-century made it more important for clergy to assert the public nature of baptism. Between 1732 and 1760 Anglican ministers reported resistance and threats when they baptized black and white children at a public baptism during worship. In these protests racism may have mixed with resentment that baptism was not done at home. Heightened sensitivity to the role of baptism in church membership conflicted with gentry families' construction of a private family life.[67]

For the church, death symbolized the passage of a believer to judgement and salvation, but clergy in America shared control of funerals with laity. English customs mixed home funerals, a church ceremony, and a procession to the grave and internment.[68] The reformation shortened this set of rituals, but out of necessity women continued to prepare the bodies of the dead at home. Eighteenth-century families often chose to bury an individual right away and at home. Funerals followed at the convenience of the clergy and with enough advance notice to invite guests. Clergy had no reason and little leverage to challenge women's control of such occasions. One minister even admitted his wife was taking care of the arrangements for *his* father's funeral. The body was already buried, so clergy could not use burial in consecrated ground as a way to gain control of the funeral rituals. By refusing to preach, they simply lost an opportunity to reach a good crowd.[69]

Marriage was more problematic. The formation of a new family unit was regulated by statute and brought contractual rights. In England, church courts handled divorce and punished fornication and adultery. Church of England clergy were required to register marriages and make public announcements of an upcoming marriage (publishing the banns). However, marriage was already out of the control of the clergy since there were alternative ways to marry and since many colonists ignored the legal niceties. Missionaries had to either forgo evangelizing among those enslaved or accept individuals in relationships without a church ceremony. Under such conditions clerical power over marriage began as compromised and ambiguous.[70]

The privatization of the family, changing concepts of marriage, and a desire to maintain group loyalty through family ties led to a new emphasis by clergy on marriage. In New England, clergy began to officiate at weddings as a response to social disorder caused by the revivals and the increasing number of women joining without their husbands. After 1750 marriage by clergy became the norm in Connecticut. For example, in Preston, from 1750 to 1800 clergy presided at 235 marriages. Only 51 couples chose to go to magistrates, most early in the period. Churches also emphasized marriage by seating congregants in family pews, with husbands and wives sitting together, instead of by sex.[71]

In the Society of Friends, where there were no ordained clergy, it was the responsibility of the women of the church to regulate marriage. Quakers put the basic fabric of women's lives—children, marriage, birth, and neighborliness—under a religious discipline that gave women's actions authority. Both Quaker men and women had to secure the permission of the women's meeting to marry. The Quaker reforms beginning in the 1750s emphasized marriage regulation. Not all meetings responded immediately to the reform movement, but when they did, they might review as many cases in three months as they had in the previous 75 years. While this enhanced the power women exercised through Quaker meetings, it also identified women with marriage.[72]

Appearance at church after a marriage became an occasion of note further tying together religion and marriage. When William Nelson Jr. and his new bride attended Sunday service at Stratton Major Parish in 1771, The Reverend William Dunlap responded with a sermon using the biblical story of Jacob and Rachel to make pointed comments on marriage. Similarly, the attendance at meeting of a newly married couple who were friends of Deborah Norris was the subject of a special letter to another friend, marking the occasion. The bride had dressed in her wedding clothes for her first appearance as a married woman in meeting.[73]

Moravians also reordered their approach to marriage. When the Moravian communities moved from communal groups to conjugal family units, women's spiritual responsibility dwindled. Women derived some of their authority from men, but had represented women.

Now men represented each family and had responsibility for all children. Moravian religious imagery also changed to reflect domesticity. Spiritual biographies of men and women, which had been essentially genderless during the communal years, began to show gender differences. Women's lives were described in connection to the domesticized Christ and to kin. Men's accounts emphasized the community.[74] Thus even Moravian theology identified women with the family and men with the community by the early nineteenth century.

Sarah Bache and the other women of her generation had to find religious space and meaning for themselves and their children in a changing setting. By the end of the century, some forms of religious leadership for women were muted, while American society recognized special claims by women as leaders of religious education in the family and collective benevolent actions, especially for other women and children. Missionaries increasingly emphasized domestic roles as essential to Christianity, and Indian renewal movements among the Iroquois and others emphasized male leadership. Missionaries thus became instrumental in increasing patriarchy among Indians. The heightened tension between the role of private faith and public worship/polity thus changed women's roles without clearly placing religion in either the public or private sphere. The tension within the new, more confining roles would eventually provide its own escape hatch. Women expanded their domestic roles until they incorporated most of parish life. Meanwhile, men created a political structure and public domain of church governance where women had little or no direct voice. In 1790, the exclusions from participation caused by gender segregation were real, the empowerment still only potential.[75]

CHAPTER SEVEN

"An Injurious and Ill Judging World"

From 1752 to 1754 Margaret was caught up in a set of rituals that brought her face-to-face with what another eighteenth-century woman called "an injurious and ill judging world."[1] Widowed Margaret gave birth to a son in the winter of 1752 to 1753. She identified the father as Brant Canagaraduncka in March 1753, when the local Anglican missionary baptized Jacob. She upset both the European and Mohawk communities since Brant had only recently become a widower, and Jacob had been conceived before Brant's wife died. Margaret and Brant married in an Anglican ceremony that fall, scandalizing the Mohawk. They thought he had married with undue haste and should have married his dead wife's sister. Five months later Margaret made a public confession at church for the sin of adultery and was admitted to communion. The rituals Margaret used to legitimize her behavior in her adopted European church were the very acts that brought her the greatest criticism in the Mohawk community.[2]

Margaret was caught on the boundaries between two societies with shifting cultural norms. The shifts allowed her (and other women) to deviate from social norms, but they also made it difficult to know what the norms were. War blurred social boundaries, making things even more fluid. American society spelled out its norms in a series of laws, institutional orders, and customs. What America chose to define as deviancy for women and the means it used to enforce conformity reveal much about its values. In Margaret's case, rules of church membership and social reputation were tools of enforcement. Law provided the most formal tool. All women in America were affected by the actions of those identified as wayward. Social strategies and definitions illustrate late eighteenth-century Americans' uneasiness with shifting gender roles, and the efforts of the male elite to regain control by gendering disorder.

The double standard for men and women widened during the Revolutionary era in ways that served the interests of a male elite. By conflating public and private virtue, Revolutionary ideology required that women participate in building a virtuous republic by controlling their sexuality. Revolutionary ideology gave women ways to resist norms, but it also made them more vulnerable to charges of individual responsibility. Women's restrictions and vulnerability eventually outweighed any opportunities.

Just a few years after Margaret's "transgression," Molly Brant faced a very different reaction when she bore Sir William Johnson a child conceived before Johnson's wife had died. Context and class mattered. Both the Mohawk and the British saw this relationship as within fur-trade norms. What is most interesting is the double standard applied by the church. Margaret and Brant were being "tutored" in the ways of civilization, and thus faced censure for violating behavioral norms. No Anglican missionary was in a position to suggest Sir William Johnson (and thus Molly Brant) needed civilizing.

Margaret's case, like those of most women who crossed social boundaries, involved issues of sexuality. Sexual norms were matters of public policy. Every colony had laws making adultery a criminal act. Except for prosecution of bastardy, fornication, adultery, and infanticide, women appear in most criminal records as victims. Women accounted for only 10 to 20 percent of all criminal charges, including sexual offenses. However, changing patterns of courtship and economics and the separation of public and private helped redefine criminal activity. After 1775 the courts showed much more interest in crimes against property. Although about a third of the charges against women were for theft and similar crimes, women's rates of prosecution dropped by the end of the century.[3] The new focus on property affected even sexual regulation as women's reputations became a form of property.

Men firmly controlled the formal insitutions of society used to enforce social norms. All judges, juries, and lawyers were men. Male legislators passed the laws and were elected by men (except in New Jersey, where some propertied women voted after 1780). The clergy and church conferences that enforced church discipline were largely male (or became so), except for Moravian, Shaker, and Society of Friends congregations. Nonetheless, women held their own in these forums as long as they were present or not silenced. Conviction rates for women were similar or less than those for men. Women brought complaints to court (and were complained against), testified, sued, and regularly used the courts to settle probates and guardianship or register property transactions.[4]

Women participated in the legal enforcement of community standards by filing complaints on their own behalf, or on behalf of others. Courts also turned to midwives or juries of matrons to investigate when women's special knowledge of reproduction, childbirth, or care of infants was an issue.[5]

However, after 1750 women literally were seen less at court and heard less at church. Women had men represent them in court and gave depositions from home. Since the courts also heard fewer prosecutions of women, fewer women attended court. These changes, positive in many ways, also had a cost—less familiarity with the law and court procedures. Women's withdrawal from church governance was less voluntary. Individual women protested decisions of New England congregations to limit votes to male members. Such women were then disciplined as disorderly. Thus in law and religion, men controlled the formal venues for defining deviance and punishing those who transgressed.[6]

It would be foolish to expect those who enforced social norms to rise above them. Sentencing trends reflect social perceptions of race, class, and gender. White women convicted of capital offenses were more likely than blacks or Indians to escape death through reduced sentences or pardons. Ideas of women's dependence and obedience provided legal loopholes. Some women escaped prosecution by claiming men had ordered them to participate in illegal actions. Once women began to withdraw physically from the courts, they might have their husbands stand as proxy when charged with a crime. Convicted women petitioned the courts for leniency, emphasizing their dependence and weakness, friendlessness and need of protection. Women were more likely to receive corporal punishment or fines and less likely to be shamed or forced into service than men.[7]

One form of pardon available to men and women before the Revolution was benefit of clergy. This one-time-only pardon of a capital offense required that the person so pardoned be branded on the thumb and transported as a convict servant. Originating out of the right of clergy to answer only to church courts, it had been extended to women over the course of the seventeenth and early eighteenth centuries. In Virginia benefit of clergy became available to women following the case of an enslaved African woman who claimed the pardon. Women did not enjoy this right for long. During the Revolution, states eliminated benefit of clergy as a feudal holdover inappropriate to a republic.[8]

Early Americans of European descent were not sexual prudes. They assumed both men and women could and should find sexual pleasure, but also punished acts (not sexual identities) that fell outside community norms. Colonies (and later states) had laws against fornication (sex outside marriage), adultery (sex with a married woman), bastardy (bearing a child out of wedlock), bigamy (marriage to more than one individual simultaneously), prostitution (sex for pay), incest (sexual acts among family), rape (forced sex), sodomy (non-vaginal sexual acts), and bestiality. Only men were prosecuted for the latter two offenses. Lesbianism went nearly unnoticed.[9]

A single flow of events could easily include several potential "crimes." For example, committing bastardy required prior commission of fornication. Communities could choose to interpret an act as fornication or as rape, incest, or adultery, and thus respond differently. During the Revolutionary era communities reinterpreted specific sexual offenses. These changes increasingly focused community censure on women, defined male responsibility as economic, and distinguished between public concerns and private behavior.[10]

Race affected how societal norms applied more than class. Although vulnerable to sexual abuse, female indentured servants were held to society's sexual norms and prosecuted for sexual misconduct. In most areas, slave communities simply existed outside of white societal norms and their enforcement. Owners decided on any punishment for a slave's conduct. The few New England states that prosecuted blacks for sexual misconduct also recognized slave marriages as legal. Church enforcement of moral codes for all members, including African Americans, increased after 1750 as more African Americans joined churches after the Great Awakening.

The many Africans in the slave population influenced sexual standards. Slave communities adapted African traditions to fit local conditions and their owners' expectations. The skewed sex ratios led to instances of polyandry. African traditions of premarital sex persisted, with many enslaved teenageers bearing a child well before they established long-term relationships.[11]

Exclusion of slaves from the codes of conduct reinforced the patriarchal power of white males. White men could have sexual access to black women without fear of prosecution for fornication, adultery, or rape. Since in most areas blacks could not testify against whites, free African-American women were also without legal recourse. A man could have sexual relations with a black woman with no risk to his reputation. In contrast, the state could and did intervene when a white woman had consensual relations with a black man. Women risked prosecution, with punishment often being sale into service. In the eighteenth century, however, such prosecutions were rare and followed the same trends as prosecution for other forms of fornication. Married white women who had relations with black men risked adultery charges. When the Virginia and Maryland legislatures finally granted divorces by legislative act after the Revolution, it was to white men whose wives bore mulatto children. Prosecution was thus asymmetrical. If only a few cases involving white women and black men came to the courts, none came involving white men and black women.[12]

Sexual customs varied among eastern American Indians, but differed even more from practices in European-descended communities. Premarital sex, polygamy, homosexuality, and cross-dressing were all widely accepted. Indians coupled marital fidelity with easy separation and divorce. Rape and prostitution were uncommon in Indian society until introduced as a response to European behavior.[13] Cultural misinterpretations arose easily between those of European descent and Indians. Whites often missed the constraints in Indian society entirely and interpreted Indian behavior, especially women's, as wanton or promiscuous. When Indian women offered traders intercourse as part of hospitality rituals including gift giving and barter, the traders saw prostitution. Whites often treated all Indian women as prostitutes, even while missionaries spent much of their time convincing Indians (like Margaret) to conform to European standards of sexual behavior.[14] Thus European sexual norms and assumptions directly affected Indian women.

Churches more frequently assumed responsibility for maintaining sexual standards later in the century. Margaret Brant, for example, faced church discipline. Some churches developed formal hearing processes to handle misconduct charges. Many congregations emphasized punishment of moral offenders over maintenance of internal harmony. Men controlled a hearing process that increasingly assumed women were naturally sinful. Some refused to baptize children conceived outside of (or before) marriage. Parents delayed baptism or had the child baptized elsewhere to direct attention away from the facts of conception. Women or couples disciplined by a church rarely faced legal prosecution for the same offenses.[15]

In many ways, British America was like a small town. Even the largest city in British America was under 40,000 at the time of the Revolution. Whole counties might have only 5,000 inhabitants. People interacted face-to-face, and reputation mattered greatly. Men and women had to protect their good names if they hoped to prosper. For women that meant their sexual reputation; for men it was integrity. Single women were particularly at risk. In the eighteenth century slander became a civil matter. Slander suits pitted the credibility of the litigants against each other since truth was a defense. Thus the most vulnerable women were least likely to sue. After 1763 even civil suits declined. Women brought 43 percent of slander suits before 1763; after that date, only 12 percent. As women withdrew from the courts into a private sphere, they no longer used a public courtroom to defend their honor.[16]

Changing courtship customs and the privatization of morality shook the white community's strictures against fornication. Before 1750 many couples cohabited without a marriage ceremony. Government or church officials sometimes chose to bring proceedings against the couple, but enforcement was spotty and social standing could protect couples. Shifts in marriage and divorce law made such unions more risky after 1750, especially in terms of inheritance. Church officials increased their oversight of such couples. Thus, although prosecutions of such long-term couples declined, the social stigma and rules of inheritance increased leverage against such unions.[17]

Sanctions against fornication changed greatly in the last half of the eighteenth century. Originally officials charged couples with fornication who conceived a child before the wedding, although the couple often received a lesser penalty than those who did not wed. Premarital pregnancy rates rose throughout the century until eventually one-third of all couples conceived a child before marriage. As the rates peaked, criminal prosecution for fornication of couples who married after conceiving a child nearly ceased. By marrying, these couples had restored social order and had identified a father to provide support for the child. Any sanctions were left to the churches, as Margaret Brant found out.[18]

Illegitimacy rates also rose in the late eighteenth century. Pregnancy was usually the way that fornication came to public notice. Prosecution was erratic. Some areas prosecuted only the women. Women who escaped prosecution often came from elite and skilled craft families, or were widows choosing to live with a man rather than remarry and lose control of property. Some areas focused on prosecuting bastardy rather than fornication. In Lancaster County, Pennsylvania, after 1779 only reputed fathers were prosecuted. Another Pennsylvania study showed that only the reputed father was prosecuted in 40 percent of the cases.[19]

The local officials' main concern was securing financial responsibility for a child born out of wedlock. Where fathers were prosecuted, women started filing the charges as a way of securing support. Where women were prosecuted, judges often dropped charges or reduced penalties if a father was named and held responsible for support. In Connecticut many women short-circuited the legal process by naming the father in court and then asking for support. By 1720 they could file paternity suits with little risk of prosecution, and by 1740 such suits were common. Originally the woman's word was the only proof needed. Connecticut eventually required prosecution to ensure that reputed fathers had procedural rights. Since the issue was financial responsibility, courts had no need to prosecute couples who married, and could ignore women from families with obvious economic resources.[20]

Communities thus enforced a double standard. Men either denied paternity or fornication charges or posted bond. Women prosecuted for fornication faced punishment in addition to posting bond to support the child. Thus women were held accountable for their sexuality in a way white men were not. In New Haven, Connecticut, for example, from 1750 to 1780 more than 60 women were charged with fornication and only one man (a black slave). The community shifted concern from morals to financial support, while resting increasing responsibility for morality on women.[21]

Church sanctions for sexual offenses increased as legal sanctions decreased. However, such control was uneven because not everyone was a church member and because some churches emphasized forgiveness over proscription. After the Revolution, the Episcopal Church in Philadelphia for the first time restricted infant baptism to children born in a legal marriage. The Presbyterian Church required the mother (but not the father) to publicly confess wrongdoing to the congregation. The Quakers disowned any male or female member who had either an illegitimate child or a premarital pregnancy. The German churches continued to baptize children regardless of their parents' status.[22]

Adultery provided a greater threat to patriarchy, since its traditional definition was sexual relations of a married woman with a man not her husband. Over the course of the eighteenth century, popular definitions of adultery shifted to include men's violations of wedding vows. Growing ideas of marriage as a contract and of mutuality in marriage shaped the informal definition. Criminal statutes still reflected traditional law. Most adulterers faced fines or whipping. Unable to pay fines, women more often were whipped. Although Massachusetts law allowed judges to require a woman to wear a letter "A" on her clothing, only once did a judge order this after 1740. Women's indictments were much more elaborate than men's, emphasizing that society found adultery a more serious offense for the woman.[23] As in fornication, courts saw women as responsible for the sexual actions of a couple and as needing control.

Actual prosecutions for adultery, however, were few and far between. In states without divorce laws, couples who separated and remarried or who married after being deserted committed adultery or bigamy. It did not serve the community to prosecute couples like the Franklins who fell into this category. Connecticut filed criminal charges against only six couples and three additional women for adultery from 1710 to 1770. There is plenty of evidence that eighteenth-century Americans committed adultery with some frequency, but society chose to enforce its disapproval in other ways.[24]

Rather than criminally prosecute adulterers, society expressed its disapproval by making adultery the most widely recognized grounds for divorce. Adultery was accepted as grounds for divorce in all of the colonies or states granting divorces. The first divorce laws in both New York and Rhode Island granted absolute divorces only for adultery. When the Massachusetts governor and council refused to grant divorces from 1754 to 1757, the General Court passed private laws granting six divorces—all for adultery. Legal papers show that Virginia lawyers were also convinced adultery was grounds for divorce.[25]

Courts originally held women to stricter standards of sexual responsibility in divorce suits claiming adultery. Courts saw men as having property rights in exclusive sexual access to their wives, and granted divorces to men more readily. In Massachusetts, before 1774 only men filed for divorce based solely on adultery. Courts granted a divorce in about 70 percent of cases. Husbands adding another cause to adultery were even more successful. Even when women combined adultery and other charges, only a little over half were granted divorces. After 1774 the number of women's suits on grounds of adultery rose, as did their success rate. Connecticut and Rhode Island cases followed a similar pattern. Granting divorces equally in adultery cases put a small dent in the double standard, but it remained in effect in other ways.[26]

Women were more hesitant to bring their husband's adultery to notice, often waiting years before asking for a divorce. Many put up with flagrant behavior, including incest, before filing for divorce. Men often filed for divorce as soon as they had any evidence of adultery.[27] Women may have feared the courts would only listen if they had demonstrated unusual suffering. Or they may have feared financial loss. Men could bring cases immediately because women were expected to exercise sexual control. The rise in women's success in securing divorce may have been because they waited until their cases were so compelling.

Both bigamy and incest were criminal offenses seldom prosecuted.[28] In both cases, the state was more concerned with practical matters than morality, choosing to leave the family behind a growing veil of privacy. The state responded when charges appeared as part of divorce proceedings or in suits for control of property. Rather than prosecute, they used civil remedies. Given the difficulty women had in supporting themselves, many abandoned women (like Deborah Franklin) simply remarried, thus committing technical bigamy. It was not in the interest of governments concerned about growing poor rolls to prosecute such cases.[29] Incest prosecutions were equally rare. Connecticut had only two prosecutions from 1725 until after the Revolution.[30] White communities defined incest to cover a broad range of relationships, including relations between step-siblings and stepparents, cousins, and brothers- or sisters-in-law. Both men and women were held responsible for incest. For example, in a case involving a father and his 20-year-old daughter in 1769, he was whipped and the daughter was assessed a £5 fine. In Massachusetts in the 1750s two women were sentenced to wear an "I" on their clothes, one for relations with a brother-in-law and the other for relations with her stepfather.[31]

Race and class affected issues of adultery, bigamy, and incest. Enslaved women were positively encouraged to take new spouses when separated from the old. White men's sexual access to enslaved women often violated incest taboos of both black and white communities, especially when white males did not acknowledge paternity of slave offspring. Indian communities had strict rules of consanguinity. Since adoptees were literally accepted into the family, communities treated them as blood relations. Thus Indians might see kinship where whites did not. However, Iroquois and Algonquian customs required that if a spouse died without issue, the survivor was to marry a sibling of the dead spouse, or a surrogate chosen by the dead person's family. Margaret and Brant Canagaraduncka violated this norm when they married. If Brant had followed this custom, the Reverend Ogilvie, who performed the marriage ceremony for Brant and Margaret, would have been more scandalized than he was by their adultery.[32]

There was little prostitution in the colonies until the colonial wars, urbanization, and increasing poverty helped encourage the emergence of a formal trade. The trade was clearly gendered—women ran brothels and practiced prostitution, while men were the customers. Prostitutes often solicited in unlicensed tippling houses run by women. Liquor sales were also tied to prostitution in the Indian trade. Leaders in both communities thus tried to control the sale of liquor in order to control prostitution.[33]

Americans, already uneasy about changing courtship customs and growing rates of illegitimacy, focused their concern about disorderly women on prostitutes. Women walking alone in New York were harassed by young men who saw all unescorted women as loose. Americans increasingly categorized women as either "good" or "fallen." That white women might have black clients only increased concern. As the double standard focused attention on women's sexuality, the fact that prostitution involved both buyer and seller disappeared from view. By 1753 New Yorkers targeted brothels for court-ordered raids after which the convicted prostitutes were whipped or branded. Philadelphia also began prosecution by 1764. With willing army customers and a growing number of women forced into the economic margins, prostitution grew during the Revolutionary War. Prostitutes came to symbolize social disorder and moral decay in the supposedly virtuous republic. Newspapers demanded action, citizens petitioned for suppression of the trade, and mobs attacked brothels in New York and Boston.[34]

Despite the periodic outbursts, the gendered nature of the trade also protected prostitution, for some men quietly supported it. For example, the loyalist claims of a mother and daughter who had been prostitutes in Boston were strongly supported by high-ranking British officers and male Bostonians.[35] By the end of the century prostitution was a fixture in most cities, but the women who practiced the trade were vulnerable to periodic harassment and ostracism, while their male clientele went unnoticed.

Rape trials scrutinized the victim more than the accused. Women were not passive in rape cases. Outraged female relatives filed many of the complaints when children were raped, and they filled courtrooms during rape trials. Typically, rape had to be reported in a timely manner (in some colonies within 40 days) and was defined as carnal knowledge of a girl under 10 years old or of a woman against her will. Forcible rape was a capital offense without benefit of clergy. In Massachusetts, there had to be evidence beyond the testimony of the victim to convict on capital charges. Matrons' juries conducted physical exams of victims. Judges instructed Connecticut juries to be skeptical of victims and look for malicious intent. Trials hinged on the reputations of those involved and on the issue of consent. The victim became the focus—did she resist vigorously? Had she talked to or encouraged him in any way?[36]

Class and racial considerations shaped rape prosecutions. Enslaved women had no legal recourse if raped. Women were taught to be pleasing to men and especially men of higher status. Thus when a woman was raped by a man of higher social status, juries could almost always find something to suggest implied consent: She had offered him a drink, or spoken politely to him first, or not resisted enough. Women often did not file charges in such cases because they saw the coerced sex as seduction, or knew that a jury would not believe her word against that of a gentleman. Some women who chose not to report rape later used it as a defense when prosecuted for fornication. Men convicted of rape tended to be outsiders, transients, blacks, servants, or others of low status. The only two Connecticut men executed for rape were black. After 1769 hanging was mandatory for a black convicted of rape or attempted rape of a white woman in Virginia.[37]

There were few rape convictions because many cases went uncharged and because many men were charged with lesser offenses. With no units to investigate crimes, there was little hope of finding rapists such as three sailors who raped a Charleston woman in an alley in 1788. Two of the three men convicted of rape in Virginia in the eighteenth century were pardoned. The Massachusetts Superior Court heard only 12 cases of rape in the eighteenth century. In Connecticut the conviction rate for rape in the eighteenth century was 35 percent. Conviction on lesser charges was more common. In both Massachusetts and Connecticut men were charged with or convicted of assault and lascivious carriage rather than rape.[38] By mid-century, Massachusetts courts even had second thoughts about the death penalty when the defendant was black. From 1765 to 1779 Massachusetts grand juries regularly returned two indictments in rape cases, to give juries an optional lesser charge on which to convict if they balked at the death penalty. After 1779 grand juries refused to indict for rape at all. The double standard and reluctance to charge men with a capital offense robbed women of legal recourse when raped.[39]

During the War for Independence, rape had political implications. Soldiers treated sexual assault as an extension of war, and both sides committed atrocities. There are documented rapes in Connecticut, Staten Island, and New Jersey. Many of the women were gang raped. Although there are mentions in American records of soldiers being whipped for rape, the better documented cases involve the British forces, with Hessian troops earning themselves an especially notorious reputation. Some women signed affidavits, but American officials had no control over British troops. The British sometimes disciplined their own troops. The message to women, however, was that they were defenseless and dependent on men for protection during war.[40]

Family violence did concern the community. Neighbors sometimes intervened to restore peace within the family, shelter a wife, or use vigilante action against the husband. In one New Jersey town at mid-century, men dressed in women's clothes, painted their faces, and whipped suspected wife beaters. Balancing family privacy against community order, magistrates intervened in ways designed to preserve family units. Since women tended to verbal violence and men to physical force, most cases reaching the courts were of wife abuse. Courts tried to reform men's behavior through court orders, fines, or whipping. Many husbands ignored court orders. Thus the most common reason for desertion by women was flight from abuse. By 1740 judges were aware that it was unfair to grant a man a divorce on grounds of desertion when he had driven the wife away through abuse. That left a woman legally entangled with her abusive husband. Then as now, the violence could result in death, with women more often the victims than the perpetrators.[41]

Court records document both the existence of abuse and women's limited options. In Massachusetts 42 women and two men cited cruelty in their pleas for divorces. Women filed three-quarters of all Rhode Island divorce proceedings that claimed cruelty as the reason for divorce. Most states did not grant divorces on grounds of cruelty, and those claiming cruelty were rarely granted a divorce before the Revolution. In the South, local courts were willing to grant separations based on cruelty upon request. No matter how Virginians might be scandalized by a minister who tied his wife to their bed and cut her with knives, no official intervened. Ideas of companionate marriage helped lawmakers see wife abuse as evidence of a nonviable marriage. New York's 1787 divorce law, for example, allowed full divorce only on grounds of adultery, but legal separations were available for cruelty and desertions. In 1798 Rhode Island added extreme cruelty to the list of grounds for divorce, making official what judges were already doing. Unfortunately, the growing privacy of the family also made it more difficult for magistrates or neighbors to intervene when the wife did not seek divorce or separation.[42]

Assault was the most common crime committed by married women in Pennsylvania, and mostly against members of her household. When a woman assaulted an adult, she did so in support of a male family member, and often after drinking. Newspapers applied a double standard by reserving special scorn for intoxicated women, and using alcohol-related deaths of women to editorialize against drink in a way they did not when men were the victims.[43] New England churches applied a similar double standard. Men's actions were seen as responses to particular circumstances, women's as flowing from their nature.[44]

Women had ample opportunity to abuse children, especially apprentices or servants. Whites could inflict high levels of violence on African-American children and adults without facing legal charges. For example, Elizabeth Bishop of Berks County, Pennsylvania, never stood trial for killing her black female servant. The evidence of abuse of family members is less clear. Eighteenth-century parents increasingly focused on childhood as a unique time for learning, but they may have actually increased corporal punishment in their efforts to shape a child.[45] Child abuse by Indian and African Americans is harder to document. Indians tended to use community displeasure rather than punish children physically, so abuse was less of an issue in these communities. As in all periods, some women (and men) killed their children in anger or deep depression. The slave mother who drowned her four-year-old daughter and the poor woman who killed her eight-year-old son rather than see him live in service may have fallen into this category.[46]

The most serious form of family violence women committed was infanticide. It was first-degree murder, punishable by death. During the colonial period in Massachusetts, a child was the victim of 84 percent of homicides committed by women. Infanticide accounted for 74 percent of Pennsylvania women's murder charges. Nevertheless, the number of such cases was small—34 in Pennsylvania, 12 in Virginia. To be acquitted, women charged with infanticide needed to prove that the baby had been born dead or had died of natural causes. Officials suspected women were trying to avoid fornication or bastardy charges by killing the infant after concealing their pregnancies. Thus concealing a birth was both a crime and evidence used against women in infanticide cases. The testimony of other women often played a major role in these cases. Even when prosecution for fornication and bastardy declined, women remained at risk of investigation should an illegitimate child die at birth or shortly thereafter.

Over time, the death penalty made juries more reluctant to convict women of a crime often committed without witnesses and with a real possibility that the infant died naturally. Some prosecutors stopped bringing charges. Juries sometimes reduced the charges to concealment. Massachusetts changed its law in 1784 to make concealment of a death a crime. They hoped that juries unwilling to convict on a capital offense would be willing to send a woman to jail for a year and face a fine. Other women claimed benefit of clergy or were pardoned. A few women appealed to the wives of the judges for clemency. Thus as in the case of rape, the state had to define a lesser crime and penalty in order to continue regulation in this area.[47]

In 1754 Elizabeth Porter and her daughter Elizabeth Branch were shocked to learn that neighbors Mary and Obediah Smith had been poisoned by two slaves and a free mulatto. It is hard to prove that African arrivals used poison to resist their enslavement, but of the 180 Virginia slaves tried for poisoning in the eighteenth century, two-thirds were from the Piedmont, where a high percentage of newly arrived slaves lived after 1730. Because women were thought to have special knowledge of herbs and plants, folk medicine and conjuring, they were at greater risk of being accused of poisoning. Two slave women, each named Phillis, one from Boston, Massachusetts, and the other from South Carolina, stood trial for poisoning whites in their household during the 1750s, for example.[48]

When the courts stopped regulating morality closely, they turned to protection of property. Courts were already helping property owners benefiting from the commercial revolution to collect their debts. From 1700 to 1800 about one-third of all of women's crimes were against property. In Massachusetts after 1760, it was a majority of all women's crimes. Much of women's theft was concentrated in the commercial, urban centers of America where there was a concentration of the poor. A frustrated Pennsylvania court sentenced Mary Winter, then pregnant with her third child, to 117 lashes in 1779 for three counts of theft. She had several prior convictions. If a convicted woman could not pay a fine, she went to prison or was sold as a servant. Slaves may have seen theft as a way to take back some of the fruits of their own labor, but they risked severe penalties for theft. Virginia's slave code, for example, made theft of goods over 20 shillings punishable by death, and women were convicted and sentenced to death under that law.[49]

Runaways were a constant concern in eighteenth-century America. In every case the runaway, whether wife, apprentice, servant, or slave, had committed a form of theft by denying the head of the household their services. Husbands deserted, but wives were technically runaways, and men could legally require them to return. Most preferred simply to announce they would no longer be responsible for the woman's debts. The courts seldom punished wives, but rather mediated between the couple or granted separations for good cause. Courts enforced the return of servants and apprentices, often adding additional time to the contract for service. Punishments for runaway slaves were physical (often maiming), since it was impossible to add to a life term of service. Some groups of runaways became outlaws, living on the frontier or in swamps, and risked death if caught. The frontier was risky. Indians sometimes killed runaways, returned them for rewards, or enslaved them. Others welcomed runaways into the community.[50]

Enslaved women, however, were less likely to run away than men. In all areas less than 20 percent of runaways were women. Men had access to jobs involving travel, and had fewer concerns about children left behind. Newly-arrived Africans tended to run toward the frontier or to try to return to Africa. Others sought to visit family or blend into the small free populations in cities. Overall, runaways tended to be young adults, to avoid winter flight in bad weather, and to go alone. About one-quarter of women left with children and/or their spouses.[51]

Some forms of unruliness and dissent by women were uneasily tolerated by the community, such as disorder resulting from personal expressions of faith. (See Chapter Six for a full discussion of women's religious roles.) Such occasional excesses confirmed fears that uncontained religious enthusiasm threatened the social fabric. Both men and women took part in disturbing incidents, but the prominence of women in them made the events even more threatening.[52] Religious revelation occasionally led to violence. In 1742, South Carolinians were shocked by the death of Anne La Brasseur, a widow of substantial means who had been attracted by the revivals to a "Third Communion." She shot herself in order to dwell in heavenly mansions sooner. The frontier South Carolinian followers of Jacob Weber believed that he personified Christ, his wife the Virgin Mary, and their slave the Holy Spirit. Seven members of the sect were tried (and four) convicted for murdering two men whom they thought personified Satan.[53] These atypical but widely publicized events allowed critics of the Great Awakening to paint the whole movement as chaotic. New England churches may have responded by reworking church governance to make it more orderly (by disenfranchising women) and by overseeing the lives of their members to ensure order. In this process women came under renewed scrutiny.[54]

American Indian revivals could also lead to violence. Communities under cultural stress sometimes blamed misfortune on witches. They then searched for the man or woman they deemed the malevolent witch and the person was flayed alive. Women's strong involvement in traditional medicine lodges meant that they sometimes acted as the executioners for their accused husbands.[55] Missionaries condemned the medicine lodges in general and especially those with strong women participants, citing these witchcraft hunts as further proof of the need to "civilize" Indians.

The reason that women such as Anne La Brasseur were at home is that madness was treated as a periodic happening, and individuals were cared for at home or by guardians in the community. Supernatural forces were often seen as the cause of being "distracted." By mid-century, a new understanding of madness as a disease gathered support and left the "sick" individual responsible for causing the disease. Less tolerant of disruptive behavior, the Revolutionary generation founded mental hospitals to remove the mentally ill from the community. The definition of madness also may have enlarged. Women found themselves in these new institutions under different circumstances than men. Assertive behavior, sexual promiscuity, and challenging men were treated as signs of madness in women.[56]

Another group of women came to be defined as deviant based on their economic status. Eighteenth-century Americans were troubled by the growth of a class of dependent poor. A majority were women and girls, many widows or single women with families to support, others elderly with no family resources. Out of 1,200 widows in Boston in 1742, 1,000 were considered poor. Charleston relief applicants from

1751 to 1774 included 618 children, 180 women (half of whom were heads of families with 157 children), 84 men, and 20 married couples. These women did nothing wrong except find themselves dependent upon the state and not upon a male.[57]

Economic recessions tied to the periodic wars of the eighteenth century created many of the poor. By the 1760s one-quarter of Charleston's white population was among the poor. Exceptionally cold winters in the mid 1760s forced Philadelphia families unable to afford firewood to request aid. As the numbers of poor increased, cost-conscious officials tried to distinguish between the "deserving" poor and the "disorderly" poor, who may have brought on their own poverty through immorality or idleness. Women who turned to prostitution to support themselves thus were no longer "deserving." The economic protests, port closings, and years of war necessary to achieve independence threw even more women into poverty.[58]

Traditionally, communities provided small stipends for the deserving poor, or housed those unable to care for themselves with others. Orphans and poor children were apprenticed, the boys to learn a skilled trade and the girls to learn housewifery. However, girls were less likely to leave home than boys. They were placed as day workers or left with their mothers to help in their own households. When in the 1730s cities built almshouses to care for the poor, poor women resisted leaving their homes to reside in institutions where they were closely regulated. Officials used a variety of strategies to take care of a growing number of poor children. In Charleston, for example, from 1750 to 1775 officials placed 109 children at a free school, paid women to care for 70 children, gave clothing to 110 children, bound out 22, put 46 in the workhouse, six in the hospital, and paid for 30 more to leave Charleston with their parents.[59] By placing more poor in institutions where they would supposedly learn the habits of industry that they "lacked," eighteenth-century Americans moved toward defining poverty as a personal failing, another form of immorality and disorder.

One way cities tried to limit responsibility for the poor was to reduce eligibility. The South Carolina Assembly raised the residence requirement for eligibility of aid from three months to a year when they built a new poor house and hospital in 1768.[60] Massachusetts tightened its laws in 1767 so that communities would enforce "warning out" more stringently. "Warning out" was a process by which a town forced new arrivals who might go on relief to leave. The town was only responsible for those born there or those who had established legal residence.

Boston warned out about 25 people a year before 1745, then the average rose to 65, with major a increase in 1755 to 222. For even smaller communities poverty had a female face. About 58 percent of the poor received in Wrentham from 1732 to 1769 were female. Since by law married women were required to reside where their husbands chose, poor women could not return to their towns of birth to seek aid, while "warning out" laws kept their husbands (unless a foreigner) from following the wife to her home town.[61] A mobile population of poor, warned out from community to community, was another mark of social disorder troubling late eighteenth-century governments.

By the 1760s cities were trying to shift part of the burden to private philanthropy, and make the poor support themselves. Quaker merchants in Philadelphia founded a private investment group to set up an almshouse for people with disabilities and the elderly, and a workhouse for all others. This "Bettering House" was supposed to have economies of scale for food and clothing, and put the poor to productive work. It received enthusiastic support from Benjamin Franklin, who was known for his advocacy of hard work and thrift. When it opened, the city forced all but 15 percent of the poor on aid to live there, where they were segregated by age and sex, thus splitting families. The house operated at a loss every year, as artisans, the poor, and the officials who administered more traditional aid resisted the change. In 1775 women in the "Bettering House" begged an English doctor to get them out. There were numerous runaways from the institution, and people refused public relief to stay out of the house.[62]

The growth of a class of female dependent poor was significant during an age that valued its independence. The new arrangements for poor relief increased supervision and intervention in women's lives without helping them regain their economic self-sufficiency. Those dismissed from the poor house often had to leave their children behind, and thus risk losing custody entirely. For these women, the Revolution hardly brought independence.[63] By separating families and treating poverty as a moral failure, Revolutionary America labeled poor women as deviant.

By 1790 women who fell outside social norms were increasingly treated as dependent, helpless, and yet somehow individually responsible for their own fates. As the state reduced its direct intervention in the regulation of morality (except where it intersected with economic issues), a growing double standard put the responsibility for maintaining standards on women's shoulders. A second racial double standard meant that Indian and African-American women received neither the protections nor the visibility that white women had. The economic dislocations of a half-century of war and urbanization produced a growing class of female dependent poor, and increased focus on property crimes by women. Officials responded to the feminization of poverty by creating institutions that deepened that dependency. Thus women were both watched less and watched more. Those who stayed within social norms might find greater independence; for others, the result was increased dependence and scrutiny.

CHAPTER EIGHT

The Garden Within

Despite separate tasks in the household, men and women at the beginning of the eighteenth century lived in a gender-integrated world. Women were expected to fill in for their husbands on the farm or at the business, as a parent, and sometimes even in court. The household was a place of business and community. Neighbors walked in unannounced; visitors shared family beds and meals. Rooms in a home were multipurpose. People slept, ate, and worked in the same spaces. There were public places in a community, such as the church, courthouse, tavern, market, or capitol, but women visited these as well as men. The home was not separate from public life. Men had some public positions that women could not hold, but women could participate by assuming certain roles.[1]

By 1790 middle- and upper-class families made the home a place of retreat and nurture. They decided which visitors to receive, and had formal spaces set aside for visiting. Individuals linked work to public spaces in order to separate it from the domestic duties of women. Men developed a public life and world, while women cultivated a network of female friends in the private garden of the home. This separation had profound effects for all women and men, whether they lived their lives according to the new social rules or not. Fused with political rhetoric from the Revolution, the split between public and private provided a new role for women: the republican mother.

Many spaces—social, economic, emotional, and political—took on new shapes in the last half of the century. Women withdrew from the courthouse, for example. As discussed in earlier chapters, prosecution patterns changed so that proportionately fewer women were defendants in criminal cases, and their appearances for civil matters also diminished. Probate issues had brought many women to court at the beginning of the century. When there was no will, widows had first rights to administer their husbands' estates; in wills men often named their widows as sole administrators. Women also reported on management of the property given to underage children. Although some women went out of their way to settle out of court, most took care of their business. By the middle of the century, men used their wills to surround widows with other executors, or to exclude her. In Amelia County, Virginia, the percentage of widows named as executors dropped from 65 percent when the county was new to 43 percent in 1775. Additionally, men changed the kinds of bequests they left their wives to life interests or income and the right to use a portion of a house. Sons received direct control of the land. Not surprisingly, the share of wealth held by women dropped. In Boston, women's share of taxes (a measure of personal property) went from 7.1 percent in 1687 to 5.3 percent in 1771, although the percentage of single women in the population was similar. Thus women managed less property and had less control over it (although life interests could be sold) than they had earlier, and had less reason to come to court.[2]

By the middle of the century colonial debt included a number of interest-bearing and time-certain forms of borrowing. Courts moved to more formal and technical pleas, a process certainly helped by the development of a legal profession. Uncontested debt collection swelled court dockets. Women seldom appeared in these cases. Connecticut women appeared in about 19 percent of civil suits in the early decades of the century, about 10 percent at mid-century, and only 4 to 5 percent by 1775. Women's names appeared mainly with their husbands' and usually as collectors of debts, rather than as debtors. In other words, women made little use of new credit opportunities. Although women were involved in a higher number of civil suits, the percentage of suits involving women dropped. In the last half of the century almost all men in Connecticut appeared in court for some reason, but less than one in 10 women did.[3]

Changing land-sale practices also affected women. Under English law, married women had an undivided third interest in all the couple's real property. A woman had to give up this dower interest for a land sale to be final. England used a complicated series of documents followed by a private interview of the wife by a judge to ensure she had not been coerced. Virginia and Maryland were the first colonies to develop a simpler procedure whereby both the husband and wife signed a joint deed. Because courts recognized that women might be coerced, many colonies eventually required wives to appear in court to confirm the deed. Colonial court decisions in the 1740s reinforced the interview requirement. New York and Pennsylvania added the interview requirement shortly before the War for Independence.[4] These interviews brought many women to court. However, in 1748 Virginia passed a law allowing a justice to interview the woman at home, making her appearance in court unnecessary. Women in Elizabeth Porter's neighborhood in the 1770s still attended court 70 percent of the time to relinquish dower. Elizabeth Porter herself made several appearances to relinquish dower rights. In Lancaster County, however, only 35 percent of land transfers included a physical appearance in court by the woman. The rest used the interview at home.[5]

Just as women's withdrawal converted the courtroom into a male space, changes in household work gendered the home in new ways. The time and labor commitment to housewifery expanded as women adapted to changes in cooking, the consumer revolution, and a rising standard of living. For Abigail Adams, housewifery was so much a part of her identity that when she finally traveled to England after the Revolution, she insisted that her servant and crew scrub the cabin floors to her satisfaction.[6]

As families adopted the newer standards and lifestyles, women spent less time helping men in farming or trade. In families without purchased labor, women made smaller adjustments to their time. Slaves and servants first freed plantation mistresses and daughters from the fields, but a growing proportion of female slave and servant labor went to household duties. Men appointed other men as coexecutors or administrators of estates because many women were less familiar with farm or business management than they had once been. Women filing loyalist claims in the 1780s could list in detail the contents of a house, but knew only parts of the family business. Men, conversely, often lumped household things together, but knew in detail the family financial arrangements.[7]

Despite the shift of some African-American women to household tasks, the majority remained in fieldwork. Household slaves may have been girls considered too weak for the fields or a few women with special training. A succession of young girls could only help with the less skilled parts of housework, such as fetching water and wood. On small plantations women did both field- and housework. However, gender differences also affected farming assignments. As the Chesapeake shifted to wheat farming, men did the plowing and new tasks, but women and children continued tending tobacco fields. Men and women still worked together, but male slaves had more opportunity to learn skilled or semiskilled work, while women were assigned to hoe or collect and spread manure. While men cut and shaped fence posts, women might be leveling a ditch.[8]

Middle- and upper-class adults were able to free themselves from some forms of physical labor. Although elite women still did exhausting work such as ironing, both men and women had more time to devote to children and social activities.[9] Leisure activities grew for men and women as colonists supported orchestras, lectures, theater, assemblies, and balls. Men, however, also developed a club life apart from women—ranging from philosophical and literary clubs to masonic orders.

Colonists began to define special spaces for leisure. Theaters, taverns, and club rooms provided special rooms for activities. The wealthy began dedicating certain rooms of their homes to specific activities, thus creating public and private spaces within the home. When Deborah and Benjamin Franklin built a new home in the 1760s, they placed the kitchen in the basement. The other nine rooms, three to a floor, gave members of the household their own rooms and separate space for a dining room, a library, and a parlor. Another Pennsylvanian proudly described their new house as having a "little Hall with a Parlour on each side & a Kitchen behind." The house also had three upstairs chambers and three garret rooms. Although the house had less specialized space than the Franklins' home, "public" activities were all zoned to the first floor.[10]

Differentiation of space and privacy remained rudimentary, however. Most Philadelphians lived in narrow two-and-a-half-story buildings with two rooms per floor. The bottom served as a shop, sitting room, and kitchen, while the family slept upstairs. Even a wealthy Philadelphia family closed part of their house in the winter and squeezed a minimum of 11 people (including five servants) into the front two chambers. In the countryside, one- or two-room homes were common. Half the slaveholding families in Halifax County, Virginia, lived in one- or two-room houses in 1785. Estate evidence suggests the Porter house probably had two rooms connected by a passage and lofts above. At its peak, the Porter household contained three generations, with at least 11 whites. Amy, Peg, and the 17 other slaves slept in the lofts (along with some of the Porter children), or on the floor, in the separate kitchen, or in small cabins about 12' square.[11]

By 1784 the upper and middle classes had adopted the new standard of privacy, but others had not. Elizabeth Trist, an upper-middle-class traveler, found the one-room cabins and shared beds of the frontier a shock. Her hostesses thought her stuck up and one pointedly told Trist "that she thought a Woman must be very inceure [*sic*] in her self that was afraid to sleep in the room with a strange man." Trist expected the privacy of a separate chamber for women, if not for herself. Most of the families she stayed with couldn't even see the advantage of separate rooms.[12]

Moravians also responded to privatization, by replacing their single-sex living and working units with privatized, domestic family units. Bethlehem began in the 1760s, Salem 10 years later. In the process, child-rearing and domestic labor became the duties of all married women as opposed to those of a few specialists. Men continued to farm and practice trades, although they had to cope with a privatized economy. Women continued to be identified by choir through their clothing, but distinctions for men disappeared. Moravian women had always done different work than men, but the move to private households reordered women's work more radically than men's.[13]

Missionary efforts also centered around privatizing Indian households and domesticizing women. As long as furs or deerskins were the center of Indian-European relations, Europeans had little reason to challenge Indian gender assignments. Even the introduction of black slaves did not disturb the division of labor. By the eighteenth century, land cessions and depleted supplies of game had greatly reduced the resources of eastern Indians. Missionary efforts became more assimilationist, insisting that men become farmers, asserting male headship of families, and teaching Indian women domestic duties. Education for Indian girls emphasized domesticity over academics. While Indian men might resist being feminized, women also resisted losing their traditional authority and roles.[14]

Eighteenth-century whites struggled to fit Indian women's behavior into terms whites could understand. For example, they interpreted occasions when Indian women signed deeds and land treaties as relinquishing of dower (rather than transferring land that they traditionally controlled), or emphasized women's household roles (over the obvious planting roles) in creation myths. Moravian missionaries created separate villages for converted Delaware, where women did much of the farming and men hunted. Although the missionaries acknowledged that women tended fields, they saw the women as tending to the domestic duties of cooking, tending the fire, and dressing game.[15]

By the middle of the century, missionary efforts had changed a number of Indian communities. The Natick Indians in New England adopted European farming in the 1720s and 1730s, and women shifted to household tasks. By the late 1750s Natick widows had to petition to sell land because they only knew "Household business" and could not farm. Although mostly poor, Natick estate inventories from the last half of the century show that the Indians owned linens, earthenware, and forks at about the same rate as white families. When Mary Thomas died in 1778, her inventory (the last recorded in the village) reflected her domestic life. She had delftware, a mirror, and tea- and coffeepots.[16]

Margaret Brant, her daughter, and her daughters-in-law were directly affected by similar pressures on the Mohawk. By mid-century the Mohawk had moved into individual cabins, and women's work changed from communal agriculture to household management. By the 1760s Mohawk hired whites to plow and fence their cornfields. Women no longer had to haul firewood, for there were horses to do that. By 1775, cabins at Canajoharie and Fort Hunter had glass windows and substantial farm implements and household goods. Margaret and Molly had houses well-stocked with kitchenware and sewing goods. While Molly and Margaret served meals combining traditional crops and game with domesticated ones, their household tasks would have been familiar to most European-descended women. Not all women adopted domestic duties with such speed. Mary Jemison, who had lived with the Iroquois since she was a young girl, did not learn to sew until after the Revolution, when she was middle-aged.[17]

In the wake of the American Revolution, missionaries extended their efforts at assimilation with the endorsement of national leaders. Women were an afterthought; the emphasis was on creating male heads of families who would own property and farm. Indian women tried to accommodate and adapt rather than totally assimilate. Catawba women, for example, resisted efforts to change their names after marriage and insisted on separate control of land. In the 1780s the headsmen deeded the entire reservation to the women. In the 1790s many Cherokee women eagerly accepted the gifts of looms and spinning wheels from the government (and training to use them). Rather than give up farming, however, some cultivated cotton to use with their cards, wheels, and looms.[18] Thus the growth of efforts toward Indian assimilation, and the required "domestication" of Indian women, paralleled the rise of domesticity as an ideal for white women. Both were results of the same trends in religion, ideology, and economics, but the impact was different for each group of women.

Naming patterns reflected the growing gender differentiation and greater emphasis on individualism for males. A handful of names— somewhere between four and 14, depending on the region—account for a majority of all men's first names in early America. An even smaller handful—four to eight—were shared by over half the white women in America. The Porters followed traditional patterns, naming sons and daughters for themselves and their parents, and repeating names when children died. Children's names were visible signs of family connectedness. Elizabeth and Thomas used all of the most common names for girls, and two of those for boys. Elizabeth, like second-generation immigrants in other areas, chose to use the English version of her family's names.[19]

The children of Elizabeth and Thomas continued family tradition with multiple uses of Elizabeth, Thomas, Dutoy, and other family names, but they drew on 16 different children's names including Phebe, Archibald, and Chastain, all less common names unique in the family. In general, families drew from a larger pool of names in the late eighteenth century, chose fewer biblical names, broke family patterns more often, assigned middle names, and used nicknames (such as the Franklins using "Sally" for their daughter Sarah). Branching out was more pronounced in choosing boy's names, and the use of nicknames was more common for girls. If the family had a pet name for a boy, it was dropped as he reached adulthood. Women continued to be called by these diminutives. Nicknames—Billie, Dick, Nannie, Sallie—were often assigned to slaves. Thus boys received more individualistic names, while girls' names suggested permanent childhood and subordination.[20]

While women, black and white, may have shared certain names, Amy learned a different lesson from her name. By the Revolution enslaved African-American parents were asserting some control in naming their children. The names were ones familiar to their white masters and mistresses, and yet with some ties to Africa. English names that sounded like African names were popular even if stripped of

African meaning. The most obvious development was parents' insistence on naming some children for kin, despite the confusion created when two or more slaves had the same name. Thomas Porter's 19 slaves bore 15 names. Hampton, Jude, and Frank each repeated. Families usually named children for fathers and paternal kin. Girls repeated the name of a grandmother. Families thus linked their children to a broader kin network, repeating the names of those who might be most easily separated from the family by sale, residence, or work assignment.[21]

Developing surname conventions helped to further mask a woman's individuality. English traditions required that the woman assume her husband's surname. Records often refer to women only by title and surname, thus emphasizing their relationship to men. Huguenots, Dutch, Scots, Germans, and Indians all had surname conventions that did not require married women assume the name of the husband, but by the middle of the century social pressure for women to assume her husband's last name was overwhelming. The Manakin French did not continue the separate surname tradition beyond the immigrant generation. Missionaries put pressure on Indians to use paternal surnames, despite matrifocal kin patterns. The Mohawk Margaret and her children acquired a last name linking them to her last husband, Brant Canagaraduncka. Molly thus became identified with a stepfather who, by Mohawk thinking, had no kin ties to her. In contrast, enslaved African Americans almost never had last names, for that would suggest an "owner" other than the master or mistress. Most of the handful of slaves who received last names were boys, thus giving greater individuality to boys than to girls.[22]

Shared work and life-cycle events, such as childbearing, had long provided women with a special tie to other women, usually kin and neighbors. Visiting, both during the day and for extended stays, helped maintain networks for both men and women. Close friendships could cross gender lines, both among kin and acquaintances. Family and neighborhood ties cut across class lines. The Franklins continued to correspond with kin who remained in trade. The extended Porter family included both justices of the peace and small farmers. The tangled web of intermarriages in Manakin made it hard for Elizabeth's daughters to distinguish neighbor from relation. Molly Brant considered William's white children part of her family. Although some widows, the poor, and servants were excluded from these networks or became part of a mobile population, poor relief assumed they had connections—by sending them back to their "home" community.[23]

Mobility did not necessarily destroy a kin network. When Manakin families moved to frontier areas, they settled near friends and family. They returned to visit Manakin kin frequently, continuing to appear in court and church records long after their move. As those enslaved found partners, they, too, built kin networks. These networks stretched but did not break when the owner's estate divided slaves among heirs, or when plantation owners sent young adults to a new frontier quarter. One measure of kin networks among slaves was the high number of runaways who were sought or found visiting family in another area. In both settled rural and urban areas, the growing density of the community cut distances for trips to neighbors, the county courts, and church.[24]

Neighbors witnessed wills and deeds, appraised estates, testified in court, and stood bond for one another. They gossiped, shared tasks, and provided mutual aid. Neighbors also shared games and amusements, meeting at social occasions such as funerals and weddings. Although it might appear that women led more isolated lives than men since infant care and domestic duties limited travel and visiting, women visited in spite (or because) of these impediments. The lower density of population in rural areas increased the distances women traveled, but did not prevent visits. Childbearing caused women to travel. Women returned to their birth families to be at "home" for childbirth, or women in their families came to them. Nursing women did take "a sucking child" with them on social visits. They also used a trip to begin weaning. Illiteracy promoted local travel for women, since they needed to find someone who could write to compose a letter or draw up a deed. There is evidence to suggest that illiterate women attended court days specifically for this purpose.[25]

For many eighteenth-century women, visiting was "the heardest work" they did. Part of visiting was "business" with her neighbors, buying and selling home and garden products.[26] Such visits cut across class lines. Other visits maintained social status within the community, or extended kin and friendship ties outside the local neighborhood. Shifts in the relative importance of these three kinds of friendships mark the development of a separate women's sphere.

Both women's increased literacy and better systems of communication allowed women to build long-distance networks of friends. By 1750 enough middle- and upper-class women had achieved the practical literacy to sustain networks by correspondence. Women wrote letters to fill gaps between visits, and to extend neighborhood patterns of visiting. They requested small favors—the purchase of sewing supplies, the sending of preserved foods—and exchanged gossip. Letters sent advice and emotional support, and discussed religion. Such extended networks found a home for an orphan, and a publisher for works of poetry. Women began patterning their friendships on models they read, and let model form-books shape their written "conversation" with friends.[27]

Franklin's position as postmaster general for the colonies meant that he contributed directly to the development of communications. Consumers invested in horses and vehicles to travel the new post roads and other colonial roads. When it was necessary, women drove the wagons or chairs (a two-wheeled open carriage) themselves, and could fix a broken hitch with their ribbons and garters. Rural women visited less during weather extremes and harvests, and when sickness peaked. Where a town was nearby, women's travel was more evenly scattered throughout the year, but weather and sickness interfered at times. As one New York woman noted after delaying a sleigh trip in January 1747, "all convayances by Water are shut up & the weather has been so extreem hard that there was hardly any travelling any way for a week past . . . ."[28]

Family ties reinforced women's friendships. Sisters and cousins called each other "Friend." Women also turned to their peers, whether related or not, to find a "Sister of my heart." Women brought together by religion, especially during revivals, called each other sister and shared deep emotion as they met in small groups or corresponded. Literature brought others together. Such bonds could "cement a union . . . which was interrupted only by the removal of parties to distant places, and disolved [sic] only by their death." As men created a competitive culture for themselves (separate from women) in politics, taverns, and clubs, women sought each other's support and comfort. They certainly began to rely on each other more as witnesses to legal documents, and they began showing a preference for other women in their wills. Thus collectively these factors helped create a climate that nurtured the growth of women's networks.[29]

An elaborate set of social events provided the excuses for visiting and travel for middle- and upper-class women like Sally Franklin. Young women went to housewarmings, christenings, boat races, horse races, and balls. They went on daily visits and took chariot rides, alone or with adults. Young girls got into scrapes together, such as smashing the new family carriage when a horse bolted. Dancing school, rowing on the river, walks, riding, or skating in the winter brought young people together. When in town they went to tea and to the theater. At night family and friends might sing or play music, sometimes sitting informally on the front steps.[30]

Even women from modest middle-class farm families could expect constant comings and goings. Quiltings and sewing and spinning frolics happened several times a year. In 1769 one woman of a Long Island farm recorded 28 sets of women visitors, most of whom stayed at least one night. She went to town frequently for church and visiting, although not as often as her daughter, who caught smallpox with three young friends while on a visit. The diarist also sailed to New England for 11 days at the beginning of August, and packed in at least three tea visits among the family business that caused the trip.[31]

Many of these social events also involved men. Without the records men kept we would know much less about women's visiting, but their records are partial, for men missed much of what women did together. The diaries also document the extent to which men had lives separate from women. One married man's diary from the 1740s, for example, mentions no women for the first month and a half of entries. Few entries include his wife, even when she was with him on visits. Since they sometimes met on the road and came home together, it is clear she had an independent round of visits. His diary thus documents both shared and separate social lives for them as a married couple.[32]

These "Custamary invitations of the Season" provided occasions for women to meet but did not guarantee friendship. Women built upon these beginnings by writing letters or journals where they could have a "Free interchange of Sentiments." Women's letters and diaries are much more available from the second half of the eighteenth century. This reflects not only the higher level of literacy among women, but their deliberate use of writing to maintain ties with other women, "whose mind was tun'd in unison with my own." Women celebrated friendship with other women in their poems and letters.[33] The earliest-known journal by an American woman is actually a series of long letters, mailed periodically by Esther Edwards Burr to her friend Sarah Prince in the 1750s. The two women discussed literature and ideas. When Burr died in 1758, Sarah recorded the loss of her "Beloved of my heart." Women understood that such writings occupied a semipublic space, for most were shared with others. Esther left her journal open for her husband to read.[34]

Women and men constructed these new social patterns in an era of contested gender roles. The subtle shifts in law, household duties, naming patterns, and social customs both challenged and constructed Americans' understanding of gender. Americans still saw women as essentially like men, only lesser. Intended as helpmeets, consorts, and mothers, women assumed public and private roles as family needs dictated. Men talked of "my" family, but women used "our." Women's sexuality made them loving consorts and seductive sinners. A mother's tenderness nurtured children and drove her to selfishly put the interest of her child above the public good. Public arenas such as government and diplomacy belonged to rational men, but women could intrude as family agents or patrons.[35]

Differences between Indian and Euro-American gender perceptions pressured Indians in many ways to eliminate "public" roles for women. In the eighteenth century, English policy encouraged matrilineal tribes to choose leaders based not on matrilineal customs, but through inheritance from father to son. British also complained on multiple occasions that Indian delegations created unnecessary expense by bringing women and children to treaty negotiations. They did not understand that women were *part* of the delegation. In 1758, Sir William Johnson lectured the Iroquois for disobeying his orders and bringing women to negotiations about the return of white captives, despite women's direct interest in the subject. Johnson had called "none but those who were . . . Authorized to proceed on business" (i.e., men), and while recognizing women's "Zeal & Desire to promote a good work," he wished they had all stayed home. Even his connection to Molly Brant did not let him see that the Iroquois thought women were necessary for the "business on Which they were Summoned." By the end of the American Revolution most eastern Indian groups had yielded to pressures to send male delegations to diplomatic negotiations. In 1791 Molly Brant challenged such a delegation of Stockbridge Indians, asking how it could be a peace delegation without including women.[36] Her challenge, however, was a voice from the past. As white Americans placed women in a private sphere, it became unthinkable to see even women from other cultures as public beings.

The second and third quarters of the eighteenth century show many signs of shifting gender constructs. Newspapers and their readers treated women as private individuals defined by special gender roles and characteristics. Articles acknowledged women's bravery in defense of others and in endurance of troubles, but seldom praised their independence. Stories showed women as victims or as subject to irrationality and passion. Many women appeared as unnamed background figures, part of the social landscape. Negative notices were more common than positive ones. Most positive notices were of deceased women, praised for their private virtues, piety, and domesticity.[37] The focus on deviancy helped define social boundaries in a period where women's behavior was changing. When the *New York Weekly Journal* in 1740 and 1741 carried a satire series suggesting women would readily accept guardianship in order to be thought eternally young, it played to its readers' discomfort with women's status.[38]

The underlying text of these newspaper articles was that women were getting out of control, that they did have power, that passionate women might rule rational men. Editors warned about extravagant dress and published poems showing women's faults.[39] British writers took up the same themes, and American printers reprinted their works. In an essay widely read in the colonies, Henry Home, Lord Kaimes characterized women as destined to be mates for men, more sedentary and disposed to obedience, gentler, and less patriotic because their only connection to the state was through men. If treated with humanity and introduced to morality gradually, women would become trustworthy, "delicious companions, and uncorruptible friends." He granted women intellectual powers, but argued that they should not be educated to rival men. The ambivalence here is striking. Home advocated a level of equality necessary between friends and companions, yet saw equality as a threat since women might challenge men.[40]

Women were, of course, getting more education. These discussions about women's roles proliferated as literacy became widespread among women. Women were also asserting themselves in evangelical religion, exercising more choice in courtship, and investing their mothering with new meaning. The shifting roles shaped women's activism during the Revolution. Women heard the political rhetoric about liberty and bondage resonate with religious overtones. Liberty was as much spiritual as political. The "yoke of Bondage" meant both sin and unjust British policies, such as the Stamp Act. Women's spinning bees demonstrated women's benevolence and piety as well as their patriotism.[41] Women made virtue and piety their version of civic support.

Another subtext appearing in women's conversations was a valuing of youth and its image of a compliant and innocent, yet sexual, woman. Youth as a virtue for women was emphasized in several ways by mid-century. After 1730 women's portraits portrayed them as younger versions of themselves with their hair down. In contrast, men were made to look older and shown with symbols of their work. In general,

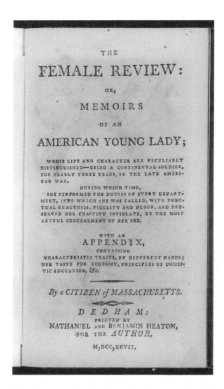

THE

FEMALE REVIEW:

OR,

MEMOIRS

OF AN

AMERICAN YOUNG LADY;

WHOSE LIFE AND CHARACTER ARE PECULIARLY
DISTINGUISHED—BEING A CONTINENTAL SOLDIER,
FOR NEARLY THREE YEARS, IN THE LATE AMERI-
CAN WAR.
DURING WHICH TIME,
SHE PERFORMED THE DUTIES OF EVERY DEPART-
MENT, INTO WHICH SHE WAS CALLED, WITH PUNC-
TUAL EXACTNESS, FIDELITY AND HONOR, AND PRE-
SERVED HER CHASTITY INVIOLATE, BY THE MOST
ARTFUL CONCEALMENT OF HER SEX.

WITH AN
APPENDIX,
CONTAINING
CHARACTERISTIC TRAITS, BY DIFFERENT HANDS;
HER TASTE FOR ECONOMY, PRINCIPLES OF DOMES-
TIC EDUCATION, &c.

By a CITIZEN of MASSACHUSETTS.

DEDHAM:

PRINTED BY
NATHANIEL AND BENJAMIN HEATON,
FOR THE AUTHOR,

M,DCC,XCVII.

Title page of a 1797 edition of *The Female Review*. *The Female Review* was a highly sentimentalized account of Deborah Sampson Gannett's experiences as a soldier during the revolution. *Reproduced by permission of the Huntington Library, San Marino, California.*

women's clothes in portraits tended to resemble those of children. Novels had young women heroines, while older women often appeared as contributing villains. Americans began expecting older women to withdraw from amusements like dancing, and to dress somberly and slightly out of fashion.[42]

Because the Euro-American society in the eighteenth century defined things by role and not identity, dress located individuals within the community. Criticism of women's extravagant dress thus was a lightly veiled critique of female pretentions to be what they were not. The Revolutionary generation's response to cross-dressing illustrates how gender, role, and clothes intersected. More than one colonial mob disguised themselves as women, who, after all, could not be held responsible for political actions. Women sometimes wore men's clothing to ride or work in the fields, assuming male garb when performing male activities. Cross-dressing in the theater, in ballad traditions, and at masquerades was well established.[43] As society voiced more anxiety about women, female cross-dressing appeared more threatening. During the Revolution Deborah Sampson Gannett enlisted under her brother's name, bringing the ballad tradition to life. By the time her romanticized biography appeared in 1790s, however, women had a new identity. To dress as a man was unwomanly, thus the text and title (*The Female Review*) are defensive, stressing Deborah's femininity, marriage, and motherhood. So are the documents in Deborah Gannett's application for a war pension.[44]

In the mid–eighteenth century the world had not yet divided sharply into either sacred and secular or into public and private spheres. By the end of the century, clear lines of demarcation had appeared for both. Shifting understandings of gender were both partial cause and partial effect of religious change. Religion uncomfortably straddled the fence, with piety and faith firmly tied to the private home, and the institutional church defined as public. Women's growing identification with the private and domestic cemented the connection between femininity and piety.

Conservatives, troubled by some of women's actions, found comfort in giving motherhood a religious purpose. It is hard to oppose the idea that mothers should have a positive influence on their children. It did not challenge men's authority or contact with children. Formulaic phrases appearing in wills after 1770, however, refer to fathers as "honored" and mothers as "beloved," "tender," and "affectionate." Eulogies emphasized motherhood more. Evangelical religion and sentimental novels insisted a mother's influence was special. By 1800 those writing memoirs of their childhoods considered it obligatory to include scenes describing their mother's role in their religious education. Women's letters and journals include concerns about child development and their delight in things their small children did. By the end of the century, the role of mother would subsume activities previously seen as economic.[45] Eliza Lucas Pinckney, who had managed rice and indigo plantations, saw child-rearing as her "Business." The woman who once contributed to family income by sewing a child's shirt, now saw that same action as nurture.

Several threads of thought shaped a new image of women. The religious revivals validated emotion and emphasized women's piety and virtue. According to the Scots Common Sense philosophers then teaching and writing, women served as the transmitters of customs and morals upon which government depended; Adam Smith even argued that family love was the model for government. Literary sentimental-ism emphasized domestic personal happiness, and gave women the larger share of sensibility and chastity. Women's withdrawal from some public arenas, their increased household duties, and the emphasis on the emotional support provided in companionate marriage all helped identify women with virtue and economic and legal dependence, and define the public sphere as male. Political rhetoric gave independence and dependence gender overtones.[46]

By the 1770s, women began to stake out a claim that they were at least the moral equals of men. Deborah Norris in 1778 seemed less than impressed by young "Lords of the Universe" who ruled over all forms of creation, including women who had "equal if not superior Qualities with themselves," especially since men were "the slaves of vice," and urged women to look to "the native standard of the female mind" for models of virtue. By 1790, virtue, compassion, imagination, and modesty appeared in clear female form, usually linked to women occupying domestic private space. In 1784 Elizabeth Willing Powel summed up the new understanding of sex roles. Women occupied the "more endearing & private & Man for the more active & busy Walks of Life."[47]

Although women claimed virtue as a special female gift, the Revolu-tion provided them with no distinctive versions of public virtue demon-strating their patriotism. Men and women participated in public actions. Only in the sacrifice of their sons for the cause and as helpless victims did women claim roles not also claimed by men. The Revolu-tionary generation defined citizenship in a series of polarities involving independence (citizenship) and dependence (slavery). In these pairings, each negative represented "female" qualities. Women were thus a form of "other" in the definitions of citizenship.[48]

Discussions of marriage and motherhood answered the question of how women would share in the new republic. Marriage as a freely entered, and sometimes broken, contract illustrated relations between people and government. If marriage was political, so were women's lives. Private virtue became a public good. Political theory merged pub-lic virtue (the ability to do what was good for the society as a whole) with private virtue. Chastity became a symbol of national honor; seduc-tion tales were metaphors for how republics could survive a corrupt world through innocence and virtue. The religious imagery women used for the Revolution made the new metaphor easy to adopt. By modeling and teaching virtue, women could influence their sons and husbands to be good public citizens. Since the new republic granted mothers the major share in child-rearing, they could participate in the new republic as republican mothers.[49] It was the perfect answer to those who had argued women were less patriotic and put private interest above civic good.

The new ideology claimed these traits were natural to women; that is, rather than roles, they were inherent in women's nature. To see women as naturally domestic, however, required a selective set of class and race lenses. The ideal was not attainable or even desired by many white women who had to contribute to a family income. Out of the daughters in the Franklin, Porter, and Brant households, only Sarah Franklin Bache was able to fully embrace the new ideals. The various Indian cultures and communities of enslaved African Americans continued to provide alternative visions of women's roles. Indian women resisted attempts to force them into patrilineal nuclear families, to give up traditional leadership roles, or remove them from agriculture. African Americans developed their own versions of a good woman— worker, mother, and wife—adapted to slavery. Upper- and middle-class whites looking through their cultural lenses found Indians lacking. "Lazy" Indian men let "their" women do the farming.[50] Indian women appeared "unwomanly." Similarly, an ideology emphasizing motherhood and virtue seemed designed to exclude slave women, who could neither protect their own virtue nor prevent a separation from their children.

The Revolutionary generation thus restructured women's roles. Changing courtship patterns, companionate marriage, rising literacy, and a growing sense that women were different from men opened the way to reshaping norms for women by destabilizing relations with men.[51] Religious and philosophical trends emphasized emotion, sentiment, and virtue in ways that made men and women seem different. Spending more time on domestic housewifery, child care, and female friendship, women abandoned commercial credit transactions and withdrew from public forums, retreating to a private domestic world. Many of the same forces were at work in Europe, but the American Revolution gave a special twist to the articulation of roles. Revolutionary rhetoric emphasized women's dependence. Middle- and upper-class white women created republican motherhood as a means of participating in nation-building. In the process they ignored the realities of life for poor women, and reinforced ideas of Indian women and enslaved African Americans as "other."

CHAPTER NINE

Daughters of Liberty

The active participation of women in the Revolutionary War was effectively masked by the new domestic ideology. For some young women, the war had little effect on their daily routines except to provide opportunities to meet interesting young men in uniform, or to limit social life due to absent young men. However, epidemics, food shortages, mob actions, and military actions along the coast and interior ensured that at some point most women faced direct interruption of their lives due to the war.[1] While Americans could reconcile such effects of war with the new domestic ideology, they would have to work harder to reinterpret women's active roles and political mobilization during the war.

Mass political mobilization was a trademark of the protest leading to independence. Women's roles in church, market, and family ensured their participation in this mobilization. While men could be overtly and explicitly political, women often fused politics with religion. During the boycotts of the 1760s and 1770s, women's home production took on political significance. Women often used overtly political language, calling themselves "Daughters of Liberty" when participating in large public spinning events. However, the spinning matches often began with a church service, and clergy often received the results of the spinning. Of the more than 46 spinning events in New England between 1768 and 1770, involving 1,644 women, ministers hosted 30 and attracted 94 percent of all participants. Leaders characterized the boy-cotts as examples of virtuous denial, a discipline of piety familiar to women. As preachers theologically interpreted the struggle against the British each Sunday, women constituted the majority of congregants.[2]

Because the leaders of American protest in the 1760s and 1770s chose economic boycotts as a major weapon, the market decisions of ordinary women and men became political acts. A woman shopkeeper selling imported goods took a political stand simply by remaining open. Protest leaders could not afford to ignore women. Leaders put pressure on women merchants to sign the Associations (public documents promising to support the boycotts) if they did not volunteer. Those who refused, such as Anne and Betsy Cummings of Boston, found their names published in the local papers. Bostonians who opposed the protests pointedly began shopping at the Cummings' store. Their cus-tomers thus further politicized their business.[3]

The American leadership sought women's support for the boycotts both through publicity and rituals of political inclusion. Protest leaders appealed to husbands to inform their wives that boycotts were neces-sary for protection of home and family from slavery. Both supporters and opponents of the protest sought the authority that came from being the voice of the whole people. Women, servants, and apprentices par-ticipated in the mass meetings of the "Body of the People" that Boston used to ratify various boycotts from 1768 to 1774. New York merchants who wanted to end boycotts, following repeal of all the Townsend Duties except the one on tea, conducted a poll showing that 794 people of all ranks and sexes wanted to end the boycott. In at least three cases women signed their own forms of Associations, promising as consumers not to use boycotted products, especially tea. In 1770, 536 Boston women signed a women's document. In 1774, women of Edenton, North Carolina, and Charleston, South Carolina, signed similar women's Associations. Because of women's roles in the economy, their support was essential, but these public political acts were extraordinary enough to allow the British to satirize the women as mannish.[4]

Enforcement of the boycotts depended on women in several ways. Women's home production had to compensate for the lost goods. Even wealthy Deborah Franklin made homespun clothes for her family dur-ing the boycotts. As consumers of goods, women's everyday actions became politically charged. The Boston Committee of Safety appointed three prominent women to search suspected female smugglers of boy-cotted goods in 1776. The tea boycotts after 1768 meant that Elizabeth

Porter and her daughter-in-law Magadelene Porter could not serve tea to visitors without committing a political act. When a Long Island farm woman drank tea with company in 1769, she knew her husband would be upset. Some women switched to coffee or only served tea on very special occasions. Even children understood the significance. Nine-year-old Susan Boudinot politely took a cup of tea on a visit to New Jersey Governor William Franklin's home, curtsied, and threw the contents out the window.[5]

When the colonial protests began in 1765, William was the royal governor of New Jersey and Benjamin was acting as agent in Britain for Pennsylvanians trying to replace their colony's proprietary government with a royal charter. Removed from the colonial scene, Benjamin underestimated the colonial reaction to the Stamp Act and gave his political enemies an opportunity to paint him as a supporter of royal government. In mid-September 1765, William warned Deborah and Sarah that a mob intended to march on their house. William evacuated his sister to his home in New Jersey, but Deborah boarded up her house and loaded a gun to wait for the mob. Political allies of the Franklins patrolled the streets of Philadelphia and headed off any bloodshed. Deborah faced the turmoil of the decade with only William and Sarah's help, for Benjamin did not return from England until after she died of a stroke in 1774. In the same period, William, Sally, and Benjamin made choices that would put them on opposite sides of the revolution. In 1767 Sarah married Richard Bache, a recent immigrant whose import business had been ruined by the boycotts. Richard borrowed money to start again, but continuing protests and high risks prevented recovery. Richard and Sarah chose to support a cause that brought them close to financial ruin. Throughout 1776, as the Continental Congress met in Philadelphia to conduct a war and debate independence, Sarah acted as hostess for her father, and Richard took over the postal system of the new nation from his father-in-law. In contrast, William was arrested as a Loyalist in June 1776 and spent two years in prison.[6]

Although some women and men tried to ignore politics, many women's diaries and letters include comments on elections, political events, and pamphlets. Young men and women discussed politics over tea. Mothers added political poems to the daily family devotions. Daughters forwarded copies of Congressional resolutions to their parents. Women took political stands by marching in the crowds and making uniforms, cartridges, and powder wallets as armed conflict seemed

more likely. They politicized their social lives by shunning both neighbors who took a different political stance and enemy troops stationed in
their areas. Mecklenberg, North Carolina, women were among those
who signed a voluntary Association pledging to only allow men who
had not avoided military service to court them. Others purchased bonds
to help finance the war. As one woman later argued, "if She did not
fight she threw in all her mite which bought ye Sogers food & Clothing
& Let Them have Blankets. . . . "[7]

Politically aware women tried to help other women understand the
political and military situation. In letters and poems, women stated the
political case. Mercy Warren admonished a female correspondent that
they could not "embrace the hand that holds out the chain to us and our
children." Her comment linked politics and domesticity while calling
forth images of the bondage of sin and slavery. Politics had long been
Warren's family's business, and thus she saw no conflict between her
domestic roles and political argument.[8]

Others, however, did see a conflict in direct political statements, so
many women's comments have a defensive edge. "Don't think I am
engaging in politics," warned one woman who was, of course, being
political. Mercy Warren thought John Adams had questioned her right
to speak about politics in 1776, and she let him know her displeasure.
Adams quickly assured her that she was mistaken: "I never thought
either Politicks or War, or any other Art or Science beyond the line of
her sex." Many women who lived through the Revolution thought of
themselves as political.[9] What is amazing is how quickly after the war
that perception was translated into domesticity and stripped of political
meaning.

Warren was among the women who chose to publish their views.
Women were active as printers and publishers of newspapers during the
war. Women who feared criticism for meddling too directly in politics
published their poems and letters in the newspaper anonymously. In
1772 Mercy Warren chose anonymous publication for her biting satire
of Royal Governor Thomas Hutchinson, *The Adulator*. First appearing
in two installments in the *Massachusetts Spy*, the play ended with a warning that the people might take up arms. She wrote two more plays on
political themes by 1774 (*The Defeat* and *The Group*) and pamphlets, all
appearing anonymously, although close friends and family knew she
was the author. Males supported Warren's efforts because they recognized she clearly had an extraordinary gift.[10]

Women's political mobilization continued after independence. Abigail Adams gently reminded her husband John to "Remember the Ladies" as Continental Congress fashioned new laws for a new nation. Her concern was separate property rights for women, which would have limited the marital dependence of coverture. John Adams not only treated her request as a joke, he urged that Massachusetts retain the property restrictions for male voters since women had as good a claim to vote as propertyless men. Unable to vote, Abigail nonetheless campaigned for candidates of her choice during the war.[11]

Some propertied women raised the question of political participation directly. Mary Willing Byrd, a wealthy widow, protested in 1781 that the state of Virginia had forced her to pay taxes without representation. Three years earlier Hannah Lee Corbin had questioned her brother Richard Henry Lee in the same vein. She had hoped that a new law authorizing "freeholders and housekeepers" to elect tax commissioners superseded Virginia law limiting the franchise to men. Her extensive property holdings clearly made her a freeholder. Lee agreed that propertied women should vote, and that he would "at any time give my consent to establish their right to vote." However, Lee tried to discourage his sister by pointing out that elections were "tumultuous assemblies" inappropriate for women, and women could depend on male property owners to protect the interests of all propertied people. All people whether they voted or not needed to pay the costs of the government that served them.[12] Thus Richard Henry Lee acknowledged that propertied women were independent and had a right to vote, but as women they neither needed to nor should exercise that right.

What Mary Byrd and Hannah Corbin requested became reality in New Jersey. The New Jersey state constitution adopted in 1776 granted the vote to all free inhabitants worth £50. The possibility of women voting does not seem to have crossed legislators' minds until 1780 when a few women voted. In 1790 Quaker Federalists explicitly used "he or she" in a revision of the voting laws for the seven counties with the largest Quaker and Federalist populations. When the Democratic-Republican Party gained control seven years later, they extended the language to the remaining counties (their areas of strong support) and included married women. In 1800, New Jersey rejected as redundant a state constitutional amendment that would have explicitly qualified women as voters in congressional elections. Partisan politics led both parties to recruit ineligible voters, and, in 1807, the Democratic-

Republican majority changed the law to exclude all women and blacks from voting while including all free adult white males.[13]

꞊ For most women, however, war mobilization was a matter of survival. As troops maneuvered and fought, women inevitably found themselves in war zones. Troops terrorized and plundered as they traveled. Rachel Wells of Borden Town, New Jersey, petitioned Congress in 1786 for compensation because she had been robbed by soldiers of both sides. In 1779 Tory raiders plundered homes of prominent Connecticut rebels, taking some prisoners. In South Carolina they roughed up and wounded refugee women and children. Southern campaigns left behind a swath of burned homes, furnishings, and crops. Soldiers systematically looted plantations of boats, carts, tools, animals, doors, and shutters, and confiscated slaves. Soldiers of both sides stripped women of their clothes. An all too common occurrence was the South Carolina incident where British soldiers stripped women of wedding rings, earrings, shoe buckles, and even their hatpins.[14]

Bombardments and fires were life-threatening and left women and their families homeless. When the French shelled Newport, Rhode Island, in 1778, women and children ran through the zone of fire to reach shelter. Eliza Farmer and her husband lived for the better part of a year in a free fire zone in Pennsylvania between the lines of opposing troops in order to keep their house from being burnt or torn down. Women and children in Burlington, New Jersey, huddled in cellars during a bombardment by Revolutionary troops driving out Hessian occupiers.[15]

Women who gave direct aid to combatants risked reprisals by the other side. The British offered a $2,000 reward for the capture of New York City resident Elizabeth Burgin, who helped up to 200 American prisoners of war escape in 1779. After hiding in the city for two weeks, she reached rebel lines. Washington helped her get a pension. Ideas of women's benevolent nature protected women who eased the suffering of the wounded or of prisoners. New Yorkers in 1784, for example, provided a testimonial to the "generous, charitable, and benevolent" conduct and "warm attachment to their Country, during the late war" of three women who had aided Revolutionary prisoners of war during the British occupation. Similarly, American prisoners of war in Philadelphia signed a certificate commending Martha Gray for her help. The women, and the prisoners they helped, understood their help to be political, even if the British did not. Other women proclaimed their neutrality by aiding prisoners of both sides.[16]

A number of women took great risks to aid the British. Twenty-six women who filed for compensation as loyalists claimed that they had directly aided British prisoners of war or soldiers, carried dispatches, or acted as spies. Scattered records suggest that in every state some women (such as the 32 accused in Albany County, New York, in 1780) risked their lives aiding the British. Revolutionary troops burned one New York woman's foot severely with hot coals after she helped loyalists reach British lines. New Jersey eventually set the penalty for treason as death. Men convicted of treason could escape death by serving in the army; women had to serve a year in prison and pay a £300 fine. Women convicted a second time faced death with no reprieve. Mobs threatened some women suspected of loyalism, ransacked their homes, stripped them, or forced them to flee. Women who remained in their homes in areas under rebel control while their husbands served with the British were especially suspect. Such women might have to prove their support for the Revolution or that they were harmless. Writing to their husbands was treason.[17]

The Brants, Porters, and Franklins all faced the impact of these maneuvers and reprisals directly. Molly and Joseph Brant worked to make the Iroquois British allies. Following the defeat of the St. Leger expedition, Molly and Margaret fled deeper into Indian country. Molly left behind most of her silver, jewels, clothes, and furniture, which were quickly plundered by the chair of the Tryon County Committee of Safety and others. An Oneida Indian claimed her house. Sarah Franklin Bache had to flee Philadelphia twice in order to avoid capture by the British. She first left in 1776, and again in September 1777, just after giving birth to a daughter. Her seven-year-old son Benjamin accompanied his grandfather abroad in 1776 and did not come home until 1785. As the daughter of a signer of the Declaration of Independence and wife of the U.S. postmaster, she was a prime target, despite her brother William's support for the British. In 1780 the war came to the Porters as British troops raided Chesterfield County, confiscated livestock and supplies, and burned the county courthouse. The Porters knew many left homeless by the raids. Amy chose not to risk death from disease, separation from family, and punishment if captured to escape to the British lines, but many other slaves in the area responded to a chance for freedom.[18]

Women also risked rape. Attacks in Connecticut and New Jersey are particularly well-documented through legal depositions. The first group of raiding British or Hessian soldiers beat Christiana Gatter's husband, but the second group broke in at 2:30 a.m. and gang raped her in her Connecticut home. The pattern was similar in New Jersey, where 13-year-old Abigail Palmer was raped by passing soldiers in 1777 four nights in a row, despite attempts by her grandfather and aunt to protect her. They also raped the aunt and a friend who came to comfort her. Finally an officer rescued Abigail and her friend following another rape in the British camp. In another Huntington County case, Rebekah Christopher fought off a rape attack and then stopped the rape of her 10-year-old daughter in the barn.[19] Although the rapes by Hessians are better documented, American soldiers also raped. The Sullivan Clinton expedition of 1779 to Iroquois lands raped the Onandaga women they captured despite orders not to do so. The armies used rape as a symbol of power. Women's bodies were literally territory claimed by victorious soldiers.[20]

Given the risks of remaining in an area when troops passed through, many women joined Sarah Bache in flight. Every rumor of movement or appearance of ships off the coast touched off a flurry of refugees, mostly women and children. In December 1776 (just before the battle of Trenton), Eliza Farmer fled her Pennsylvania home. Piling bedding in a wagon, she took prepared chicken and bread, and "a couple of bottles of wine." There were so many refugees that they had to beg for permission to throw their bedding on the floor of an inn, sharing the room with the innkeeper's family. Many women echoed the sentiments of the Virginia woman who wrote

> —Families flying from the habitations, etc., etc., & what is still worse, slaughter & Death to close up the rear. Oh shocking! Oh Horrible! surely any spot of Earth on this Globe, where Freedom & Peace can be enjoy'd, would now be more desirable than living here.

Women, loyalist or Revolutionary, of all races, refugee or stay-at-home, understood these feelings. When Revolutionary forces retook Wilmington, North Carolina, in 1782, Anne Hooper (who had been expelled from her home during the British occupation) led a petition effort requesting that the state not enforce an order expelling loyalist wives and children.[21]

If the war in the east brought terror to many women, the war in the west was even harsher. The frontier war mixed conflicts over land with the War for Independence. By 1777 white settlers were indiscriminately killing women and children, Indian allies, and friendly Indians trying to warn communities or serve as guides. Frontier mobs even killed Delaware who were officers in the Continental Army. Indian women were killed in exceptionally brutal ways, with mutilation such as ripping out their wombs. Women's bodies became a medium for denial of basic humanity.[22] The most brutal frontier slaughter came in 1782 when militia stumbled upon Moravian Indians at Gnadenhutten. The European goods used by these assimilated, pacifist Indians were taken as proof that they had participated in raids on whites. Condemned to death, the 96 men, women, and children prayed through the night and were slaughtered in small groups one after another.

Indian attacks put frontier whites and Indian allies at risk, but Indians generally left alone those from their own side. Loyalist Katy Shankland of Cherry Valley, New York, was so sure Indian and Tory raiders would not harm her that she was calmly sitting and spinning when Joseph Brant burst into her house. He protected her and her five children from angry Seneca who, for once, lost control, killing and plundering friend and foe in the 1778 raid. Although protective of allies, Indians at war recognized no noncombatants. Indians killed women and children during attacks and those unsuitable as prisoners or those who could not keep up with the raiding party. By 1782, as war in Kentucky grew ever more bitter, the Shawnee killed prisoners, but Creek and other groups continued to take prisoners as the fighting dragged on into the 1790s on the frontier.[23]

Captive-taking once again shaped frontier warfare, and women were the majority of such prisoners. Former neighbors of the Porters were among the 170 Kentucky women and children taken to Canada in 1780 in the largest single raid of the frontier war. In raids on Georgia, South Carolina, and Florida, Creek forces captured and kept as slaves a number of blacks. Anna Oosterhout Myers, who had been an Indian captive as a little girl, faced a nightmarish repeat in 1778. On April 17, 1778, Indians took Anna, her husband, and four children captive. Anna and her husband managed to convince raiders to release all but the husband and three-year-old son. Her husband returned in 1779, but not until peace in 1783 did Anna get her son back.[24]

The war on the frontier included widespread destruction of crops, homes, and belongings. Both British and American troops sent repeated expeditions to Indian villages to burn crops and foodstuffs. This waged war directly on the Indian women who planted and tended these crops. The Sullivan expedition against the loyalist Mohawk in 1779 destroyed 40 villages, killed cattle and horses, cut down fruit trees, and burned cornfields and stores of corn. George Rogers Clark burned five Shawnee villages in 1782, leaving similar destruction behind. Kentucky militia continued such actions even after the villages signed a peace treaty in 1785. The British punished the Catawbas for helping the Americans by burning villages and taking their animals in 1780 and 1781. Indian women and children were left to starve or become refugees. It is likely that Margaret Brant was a casualty of the food shortages in the later years of the war.[25]

Food shortages plagued women periodically throughout the war, and Indian communities faced the worst shortages. The fear of famine was all too real for the urban poor when prices rose faster than pay, and troops bought or took the few surpluses. From 1776 to 1779 women took part in at least 37 actions in five states protesting merchants selling goods above a fair price. In one-third of the cases women were a majority and led the action. In the earliest actions women often confiscated the goods, sometimes leaving a "fair" payment behind. The early food riots often supported Committee of Safety positions, or enforced price controls. Later, as the shortages made poor families more desperate, the rioters sometimes targeted Committees of Safety withholding goods. In 1778 and 1779 Connecticut was so short on provisions that Yale College had to send its students home. A broadside by a "Daughter of Liberty" in 1779 articulates women's problems in a period of runaway inflation and shortages:

> It's hard and cruel time to live,
> Takes thirty dollars to buy a sieve.
> To buy sieves and other things too
> To go thro' the world how can we do
> For times they sure grow worse and worse
> I'm sure it sinks our scanty purse. . . .
> We must go up and down the Bay
> to get a fish a-days to fry,
> We can't get fat were to die.

Sieves, fat, fish, coffee, and tea were all necessary supplies for cooking, household manufacture, or barter with rural housewives willing to trade coffee and tea for market produce.[26]

The British, with supply lines stretching across the Atlantic, also had shortages. British officers considered foraging a punishment for rebel families, and did little to prevent troops who set stock loose, cut fences and trees, and raided vegetable cellars. Hessian troops had an even worse reputation. The rebels cut off supplies during the British occupations of Newport in the winter of 1776. Hungry and desperate for firewood, the British tore down over 480 buildings and cut all the island's trees except for fruit trees to provide firewood. During the British occupation of Philadelphia in 1777 and 1778, soldiers went door-to-door asking for blankets. When one woman refused, the soldier helped himself.[27]

Epidemics and disease struck without regard for politics or combatant status. Dysentery and respiratory diseases such as pneumonia, smallpox, and tuberculosis played havoc among refugees, soldiers, and prisoners camped in close and unsanitary quarters, and swept through communities taking especially the young and old. The Moravian community at Bethlehem was greatly disrupted by a typhus epidemic in 1778 which began in one of their buildings being used as an army hospital. Women, exhausted by nursing others in the family, or with lowered resistance from pregnancy and childbirth, died. Women serving as paid nurses in military hospitals were at greater risk of dying than soldiers in combat. Diseases killed many of the African Americans who fled slavery to fight for the British in exchange for freedom.[28]

Housing for soldiers and prisoners was a problem throughout the war. The Revolutionary forces paid women to board British prisoners and billeted soldiers with families when encamped in a town. Suspected loyalists might find their homes seized for use as a hospital or prison. The British quartered troops with those they considered disloyal, including neutralist Quaker families. Women alone were special prey. Officers occupied the largest or most public rooms, denying women access to front doors or kitchens and disrupting the house with gaming and drinking. The actions of British occupying forces convinced some loyalist women to support the Revolution or be neutral.[29]

Desperate women petitioned those in authority for help. Women emphasized their dependency and poverty while using an emotional, pleading tone depreciating their status as women. After 1780 the widows and orphans of officers of the Continental line received half-pay pensions, but widows of enlisted men, those in state units, or those in the navy had no help. Congress was more likely to grant the petitions of men injured during the war than they were the petitions of widows of men killed in the war. Only 5 percent of petitions sent to Congress came from women, perhaps because Congress was unresponsive. Women sent more petitions to states, pressing for "Something to keep me from starving." State legislatures singled out specific women for aid rather than pass general bills. In the nineteenth century Congress finally authorized pensions for needy veterans and their wives.[30]

Loyalist women also spent much of the war as petitioners. Seven states passed laws confiscating loyalist property. Living first on the charity of the military and then as exiles in Britain or elsewhere, loyalists petitioned for compensation. Molly Brant, who had been a valuable ally for the British among the Mohawks, received a £100 pension and over £1,000 compensation for the items she had lost when she abandoned her home. Some exiles went to England. Women claimants had more difficulty documenting their loss, made more errors in their petitions, and were less successful than men. They had a higher rate of refusal and a lower rate of compensation. Less able to work to supplement small pensions, women in exile often sold or pawned their clothes to buy food.[31]

The loyalist exiles included African Americans who had been promised freedom if they left their owners and helped the British. At the end of the war, there were thousands of blacks behind British lines, hoping for removal. The British could not afford to resettle them all. White loyalists claimed many of the blacks as servants. "Sequestered" blacks (those confiscated as property) were sold to raise funds, given to white loyalists as compensation for losses, or claimed by the army for work details. The rest were largely resettled. Approximately 2,800 went to Nova Scotia in 1783. Of these almost half were women or girls. Others went to New Brunswick or the Caribbean. Their travels were not over. In the 1790s many moved to Sierra Leone.[32]

Many women remained in their homes when their husbands fled to British protection or joined British loyalist units. A married woman could join her husband behind British lines without committing treason, but many women remained at home to try to save family property. Neither Elizabeth Graeme Fergusson nor Grace Galloway were able to prevent confiscation of their properties as part of their loyalist husbands' estates. Fergusson, however, supported the Revolution and refused to join her husband after the war. Galloway criticized the government at every chance. She never understood why Pennsylvania compensated other women but not her, despite her refusal to file for a dower compensation. She wanted full control of property. In contrast, Mary Willing Byrd did preserve her land in Virginia through family connections and astute lobbying.[33]

The reluctance of Revolutionary leaders to consider married women independent actors created a problem for officials when husband and wife chose different sides in the Revolution. The women who stayed behind acted separately from their husbands. Women could be punished if they supported the British, so why did not the states recognize those supporting the rebel cause? Hungry for revenue from confiscated estates, and eager to punish notorious loyalists, states found their excuse in coverture. Under English common law, the husband clearly owned the couple's personal property. Thus wives had no recourse when the state seized furnishings, carriages, jewels, and clothes. Grace Growden Galloway vented her humiliation and anger in her diary when she saw others driving "her" carriage around Philadelphia while she was walking "like a common woman."[34]

Women's dower rights complicated land confiscations, since wives owned a one-third life interest in all real estate the state wanted to seize. Husbands had a life interest in property owned by the wife before marriage (or held in trust for her). States confiscated the husbands' rights to these lands as well as the property jointly owned. Seizure deprived women obeying the Revolutionary governments of a home and income, but states granted monetary compensation for dower rights rather than recognizing women's independent property rights. Grace Galloway fought throughout the war to regain confiscated property she had inherited from her father. She died uncompensated, but her daughter later recovered the property.[35]

Quaker pacifism led many Friends to be neutral throughout the war, which irritated zealots on both sides. The Pennsylvania government sent prominent male neutrals among Philadelphia Quakers to custody near Winchester, Virginia. Meeting in groups to draft petitions, women in their families lobbied throughout 1778 to bring them home or to visit. One delegation drove to Valley Forge to present a petition to George Washington. Martha Washington served as a buffer between the general and petitioning women. General Washington gave the women a pass through the lines and a letter to the Pennsylvania governor. Embarrassed by the death of one of the men, the government used the petitions as an excuse to send the survivors home.[36]

Throughout the war women struggled to maintain businesses and plant crops while hoping for their absent husbands' return. Political leaders, diplomats, and those enlisting in state or Continental units spent years away from home. Weakened by a stroke in 1769, Deborah died in 1774 from a second stroke, possibly brought on by years of stress as she waited for Benjamin to finish his service as an agent of Colonial governments. Militia service drew others away at crucial times. Elizabeth Porter's daughters carried on at home while their sons and husbands served, perhaps in the unit led by Elizabeth's brother, Captain Isaac Porter. Some women enjoyed the challenge, gaining confidence in their business decisions over time. More than one woman began the war writing to a husband about "your" farm, then called it "ours," and finally "my" farm. Many men began the war leaving detailed instructions for their wives, and ended the war asking their advice or with the wives independently running things. For other women, the war brought only failure and dependency.[37]

During the war some women moved their household skills to the public arena. The country lacked the infrastructure necessary to convert a generally comfortable lifestyle into liquid assets and mobile supplies necessary to feed, clothe, and pay an army. Women's home manufacture and farming activities provided many of the supplies for the army. Some women, however, decided to organize efforts on a larger scale. During the bitter winter of 1777 and 1778, Mary Fraier of Chester County solicited clothes daily from her neighbors, then cleaned and patched them before delivering them to the troops.[38]

In 1780 Sarah Franklin Bache helped organize a more public effort by women after the fall of Charleston. Esther DeBerdt Reed sparked the effort by publishing a pamphlet listing historical heroines and urging women to donate funds for the troops. Sarah Bache was one of the 36 women who met three days later to organize a women's fund drive. They emphasized the public nature of their meeting by publishing its proceedings in the *Pennsylvania Gazette*. From the beginning they had national plans. The women hoped to encourage other women in the country to do similar projects. While Esther Reed wrote to the wives of the state governors, Sarah Bache handled correspondence with Bethlehem and Lancaster, Pennsylvania.[39]

In order to raise the funds, the original group of women divided Philadelphia into 10 areas and assigned teams of prominent women to canvas every woman in that area. Sarah Franklin Bache worked with Ann Willing Francis in district five. According to Anna Rawle Clifford (who did not support the Revolution), Sarah and the others

> paraded about the streets . . . some carrying ink stands; nor did they let the meanest ale house escape. The gentlemen were also honoured

with their visits. Bob Wharton declares he was never so teased in his life. They reminded him of the extreme rudeness of refusing anything to the fair sex; but he was inexorable and pleaded want of money, and the heavy taxes, so at length they left him, after threatening to hand his name down to posterity with infamy.[40]

The women originally hoped to award each soldier a cash gift of $2 specie. The drive successfully raised $300,000 in paper money (or about $7,500 specie) from 1,600 contributors. However, George Washington feared the soldiers would spend cash on drink or that the money would feed discontent among soldiers paid in nearly worthless paper. He wanted the women to give the money to the government. The women refused so Washington suggested the women provide shirts. Esther Reed died before the project was done, and Sarah Bache was among the five women who found the linen and supervised the sewing and distribution of 2,200 shirts to the soldiers in Washington's command before the end of 1780.

Although the women did not succeed in mobilizing women in every Pennsylvania town, they inspired efforts in Maryland, New Jersey, and Virginia. Efforts in New Jersey and Maryland raised about $32,000 more in paper. Martha Washington encouraged efforts in Virginia by writing to the wife of Governor Thomas Jefferson. Martha Wales Jefferson was too ill to coordinate efforts, so she forwarded the request to Eleanor Madison, wife of the President of the College of William and Mary, who circulated the letter to prominent Virginia women. Virginia county treasurers reported contributions ranging from $1,560 to $7,506. The funds from these efforts bought shirts and stockings, which, of course, had to be sewn and knit by women.[41]

Sarah Bache and the other project leaders demonstrated that women had studied well the methods of political mobilization used by their husbands. They organized a committee of correspondence, used newspapers for publicity, and tapped interstate social networks. Their system of treasurers made use of existing male political boundaries and assumed that wives of state leaders themselves had leadership duties. Although blocked in their original intent to distribute funds, the women thwarted attempts to absorb their money into the male-controlled federal treasury. Instead, women organized a second effort converting their funds into goods produced by women's labor. The whole process illustrates women's familiarity with politics, economic participation, and networking.

Somewhere between 100,000 and 232,000 Americans served in a state, Continental, or local unit at some time during the war. About 20,000 women served in regularly recognized positions with the army; a few hundred more enlisted and served in units, and a much larger number took part in the defense of their communities. A few later received pensions based on their services. Women's participation, except for those who enlisted as regular soldiers, maintained gender and role differences.[42]

It is difficult to reconcile a belief that women are naturally dependent, gentle, and domestic with the reality of women who took up arms during the Revolution. Thus Americans later had to reinterpret women's actions into appropriate supportive roles, or dismiss them as disorderly. Women served both in formally organized regiments and in local units raised for defense. A few women's names appear on lists drawn up by local officials to identify those who could serve in militia or on guard. Irregular local defense groups included some independent women's units. For example, after Lexington in 1775, 30 to 40 women formed a unit, elected officers from their ranks, and dressed in men's clothes to guard a bridge where British troops might cross. Similarly, a South Carolina woman, her daughters, and a son-in-law defended an ammunition dump threatened by the British.[43] Such women acted as deputy husbands, or by assuming male garb temporarily took on the roles that went with the clothing. These efforts, if not forgotten, were remembered as women "helping" men or protecting the domestic sphere.

Many women informally joined the fighting on the frontier. All were at risk, and women fought in self-defense. One Kentucky woman beat off an Indian attack on her home, killing or wounding six Indians who tried to enter. Women molded bullets; wrapped cartridges; carried water, powder, and shot; and dressed in men's clothes to convince attackers there were more men present. The exploits of a 16-year-old girl, running from Fort Henry's stockade to nearby a blockhouse and back under fire to fetch powder, became legendary. Indian women also participated in fighting, defending homes when attacked and accompanying warriors on expeditions. At the battle of Oriskany in 1777, the Oneida leader Honyery Doxtater was wounded. His wife then kept his weapon loaded as well as firing her own. Other Indian women helped despoil the homes of those defeated. To do this they had to accompany the war parties.[44]

An unknown number of women enlisted as soldiers in the army, often with a husband or brother. Some women disguised themselves to enlist, a tradition well-established in balladry familiar to the lower classes who provided most of the enlisted soldiers. Other women joined openly, and their names appear on pay records and muster rolls. Women dressed according to their role, so such women wore men's clothing. Margaret Corbin, for example, enlisted under her own name with her husband. Both were wounded while serving with the artillery at Fort Washington in 1776. Her husband died, but a disabled Margaret was taken captive, released, and assigned to the Corps of Invalids. Posted at West Point, she served to the end of the war and is the only Revolutionary War veteran buried there.[45]

Deborah Sampson Gannett, who enlisted as Robert Shurtlef, is the best-known enlisted woman. She served at White Plains, Yorktown (where she helped storm a redoubt), was wounded twice, and was finally discharged in 1783. Because her family needed money, she later agreed to a biography and went on a speaking tour where she appeared in uniform. She successfully petitioned Massachusetts for pay due her as a soldier, and petitioned Congress for a veteran's pension. Her husband eventually received a pension as the spouse of a soldier.[46]

Both the British and American military had specific positions for women. Army women (or women of the regiment) held regular support positions, drew army rations for themselves and their children, and were subject to military law. A military court sentenced Mary Johnson to 100 lashes and dismissal from the army after convicting her of plotting with other men and women to desert from Valley Forge. Most army women were related to soldiers, but some were widows. In the units of former slaves raised by the British, African-American women served as regimental women. Some British bought enslaved women to serve as cooks and washers. All army women were expected to be of good character; the army drummed out of service those who were lewd or promiscuous. Since these women were doing a recognized woman's job, they wore skirts. The American army recruited women from among the many refugees accompanying the army. Women slowed an army's march, but General Washington did not suggest sending them away because some women were "absolutely necessary." They were necessary enough that one group attached to Anthony Wayne's regiment could go on strike for adequate pay.[47]

European armies had a set proportion of such women, usually five per company. Enlisted men's wives coveted the paid positions and filled empty slots quickly. During the Revolution, the British army used about one woman for every 10 men, but added to the number during

the war. About 2,000 women accompanied the 7,200 men of Burgoyne's army when he invaded New York in 1777. The Americans had
fewer women per unit. Units stationed near West Point and New
Windsor in early 1783 had 21 regiments with 10,380 officers and rank
and file. The ration reports also list 405 women and 302 children. The
Secretary of War wanted to set a ratio of one woman for 15 men, but
Washington was afraid a quota would encourage refugee women to
leave. That, in turn, would result in higher male desertions. Part of the
reason the American army appeared so ragged was that they had too
few regimental women. Not until 1802 did the army set a quota. Only
hospital units could exceed four per company.[48]

Some of the women sewed, cooked, or did laundry, but since enlisted
soldiers were supposed to do these things themselves, most women did
these tasks for hospitals or for those who could pay. Sarah Osborn (not
related to the Connecticut teacher) joined the army with her commissary husband in 1780, and at Yorktown the next year "took her stand
just back of the American tents . . . and busied herself washing, mending, and cooking for the soldiers, in which she was assisted by the other
females." She later claimed in a deposition that she carried beef, bread,
and coffee "in a gallon pot" to the men in the entrenchments during
bombardments for "it would not do for the men to fight and starve,
too." Others served as support for medical units and the artillery. Army
women carried the water necessary to cool guns down after repeated
firing. When members of a gun crew were killed or hurt, the women
carrying water might be pressed into service. There are several documented cases of this happening, including the case of Mary Hayes of
Carlisle, Pennsylvania, who joined her husband's gun crew during the
battle of Monmouth. Her action may be the origins of the Molly
Pitcher story. She wintered at Valley Forge with the army and
remained with the army until the war was over. In 1832, Pennsylvania
recognized her status as a veteran and awarded her a pension.[49]

Women who served with medical units did more than wash and
cook. The military considered women superior to men as nurses, and
hired them from the beginning. Nurses dispensed medicine in the
absence of a surgeon, cleaned, emptied pots, and bathed the patients.
The hospital in Williamsburg advertised for women to be nurses in July
1776. Under a new organizational structure in 1777, the Continental
Army Medical Corp required one matron and 10 female nurses for
every 100 wounded. The matron supervised the hospital and gave non-
medical direction to nurses for twice the pay of an army sergeant. At a

single ration and 24 cents a day, pay was too low to attract enough nurses, especially since they sometimes had to provide their own soap and brooms. Many nurses had children. At the hospital in Albany in 1780, the matron and three of the seven nurses had children with them. Given risks from epidemic, the nurses were at greater risk of death than men on the battlefield.[50]

Not all women served in hospitals run by the Continental Army. States sometimes paid women tavern-keepers to care for the wounded. Other women volunteered. In Philadelphia in 1777 the churches, State House, and theater all became hospitals for American soldiers, and women brought coffee and whey to the wounded. Margaret Morris cared for sick and wounded of both sides in New Jersey in the winter of 1776 and 1777, and in the spring she treated American soldiers and their wives for "itch fever." The soldiers were grateful enough to smuggle messages and supplies through the lines to Margaret's sister.[51]

Numerous women traveled unofficially with armies. Washington was unable to enforce orders requiring women to travel with the supply wagons and baggage (but not ride in the wagons) rather than with the marching troops. Wives of high-ranking officers, refugee women, and wives of enlisted men all accompanied armies. One of the best journals describing the Burgoyne invasion was written by Baroness von Riedesel who accompanied her officer husband on the campaign. When John Sullivan led his troops into Iroquois lands in 1779 on a punitive expedition, the troops left 1,200 civilians, mostly families of the soldiers, at Fort Sullivan. The women and children had marched to the fort from Pennsylvania with the troops. Women and children could be found among prisoners of war as well.[52] Large numbers of African-American civilians also traveled with the British. Having escaped to British lines, or having been confiscated by British troops, they eked out a precarious existence. At Yorktown, for example, the British drove away all African Americans not performing army duties. They huddled in the woods starving and ill, unwilling to face angry owners at home and unwelcome among the besieged British.[53]

Although war mobilized women politically and forced others to recognize the political consequences of their actions, the Revolution did not create a feminist consciousness. However, it led individual women to analyze the status of women. The process of creating separate spheres and demarking public and private were too incomplete to facilitate extended analysis of gender. Women acted together publicly in support of their families. They increasingly relied on networks of women for support and guidance. The Revolution was an intrinsic part of their lives, and they viewed it through domestic, family, and theological lenses. For some women the traditional deputy husband role explained their political actions. They had to preserve property for the family, or sign petitions in the absence of a husband. Women assumed that they, too, held an office when their husbands did. Abigail Adams liked to think of herself in 1775 as "Mrs. Delegate."[54]

Ideas of women's natural dependency increased during the war, fed by Revolutionary rhetoric and experience. Although some women's petitions politely requested male leaders to rethink policies, most reinforced the idea that women were dependent upon men. Exile reduced successful women to dependency. Male politicians found it difficult to see female voters in New Jersey as independent. They linked women's suffrage to partisan attempts to control voting. The women who successfully managed stores, homes, and farms were merely acting as good deputy husbands. The postwar public soon blurred the distinctions among women who enlisted as soldiers, army women, and the many wives who traveled with the army without status. The Revolutionary generation honored women as patriots. Because women participated in the war through ordinary actions, they did not have to separate family, religion, child-rearing, or their daily chores from political action. When the nineteenth-century Americans reinvented the home as a private space infused with piety and nurture, and separate from politics and the market, they also lost the ability to see the public nature of women's lives during the Revolution.

CHAPTER TEN

Mothers of the Republic

In 1807 Abigail Adams wrote to Mercy Warren that they had witnessed so many rapid changes that their minds had "been outstripped by them, and we are left like statues gaping at what we can neither fathom, or comprehend." Certainly change, in all its forms, had been a constant for Americans in the last half of the eighteenth century. The signing of a peace treaty in 1783 with major European powers did not end the American Revolution. Americans continued to work out the implications of events for at least another decade. For women in the new nation, change brought a series of trade-offs. The material and cultural conditions that shaped Deborah Franklin's, Elizabeth Porter's, Margaret Brant's and Peg's lives no longer held true for their granddaughters. Class, race, and particular circumstances would determine how individual women viewed the fruits of the Revolution. Collectively, however, women found no great improvement in their status. The Revolution brought both promise and new restraints into women's lives.[1]

The political rhetoric of the Revolution provided both a language with which to claim rights and the ways in which dependent groups could be ignored. Revolutionary rhetoric argued that to be dependent was to be reduced to a slave. Liberty required independence. Before the Revolution everyone was a subject, and both men and women might be dependent on a patron, a relative, or an employer. As the use of the independence/dependence dichotomy spread, men increasingly claimed independence, even if they did not own property or vote. Women, African Americans, and Indians became symbols of a natural dependency that overlooked exceptions (such as single women or free blacks). Women, however, were more likely to see particular women or roles as either independent or dependent and apply both halves of the dichotomy to themselves.[2]

Some women applied Revolutionary ideas of independence to their own lives. Women's poetry and family letters often made a parallel between single women and liberty. A father gently inquiring whether his widowed daughter had suitors might ask if she were still a "Daughter of Liberty." Even before independence, Susanna Wright could praise staying single in a poem, noting that for such women "He only rules those who of choice obey." This application distinguished among women by role (married or single) but reinforced the idea of married women as dependent.[3]

If independence and liberty were synonyms, how could married women such as Sarah Franklin Bache or Marie Porter Guerrand think of themselves as free? The Revolutionary generation often voiced the idea that women were born as free as men. As a Pennsylvania woman put it "there is no sex in soul." Mercy Warren used similar language in an essay published in 1779. Some women of the Revolutionary generation emphasized psychological independence or self-respect. Others equated liberty with its theological meaning of freedom from the yoke of sin. Marie Porter Guerrant had heard about the yoke of sin and free will at church in King William Parish. Sarah Bache would have heard similar references from the pulpit of Christ Church and St. Paul's in Philadelphia. By relying on a theoretical equality and freedom, Judith Sergant Murray was free to acknowledge sex differences in her 1779 essay called "On the Equality of the Sexes" (finally published in 1790) and explain them as a result of men's and women's education. Women thus converted liberty and equality into qualities attainable regardless of political or economic dependence.[4]

Women needed to sever the link between economic independence and liberty to see themselves as free. The new nation's legal reforms reemphasized coverture and married women's dependence. True, some states eliminated the preference for sons in intestate laws and reduced a husband's claim on a wife's separate estate. However, men increased their use of wills to devise land to sons and personal property to daughters. Pressure from creditors seeking access to family assets eroded protections of dower, paraphernalia, and separate estates under equity. In some states women lost the right to make wills for property held in trust. Following an English decision in 1769, the courts ruled husbands were implicit passive trustees in separate estates without named trustees. Women increasingly made their husbands active trustees as well. Virginia and South Carolina legislatures ended dower rights in slaves, thus making them the absolute property of a husband.[5]

The legal changes put Sarah Franklin Bache's inheritance at risk. When Benjamin Franklin died in 1790, Sarah was a principal heir, receiving a separate estate to compensate for the marriage jointure never made. Pennsylvania recognized women's separate estates but protected claims based on debts contracted before the separate estate was created. Richard Bache's business ventures had gone sour several times and he had numerous creditors. Luckily he had settled most claims before Sarah received her inheritance, or Sarah's estate could have been at great risk.[6]

Coverture remained the issue. It affected not only women's economic status, but their citizenship. By not recognizing marital independence and eliminating coverture, the Revolutionary generation chose a conservative course limiting political and social transformation. It also created problems for women as citizens. The concept of coverture confused attempts to hold married women to a definition of citizenship based on independent, voluntary actions. For example, the Pennsylvania courts ruled that a woman who left to be with her loyalist husband did not commit treason unless she refused to return after the peace in 1783, thus implying women had no choice. Yet many women did make active choices to side with the Revolution, and states recognized them.[7] Coverture explained how women could be born equal and yet not need to be consulted in the formation of governments. The women voting in New Jersey or those who asked for the right in Virginia had independent estates. The erosion of separate estates thus reduced the one way married women could be independent property owners, given the continuation of coverture.

The new domestic ideology and changing market conditions muted women's economic status. Married women did not stop making clothes, candles, or butter, but the meaning of these tasks changed. They were now symbols of women's domesticity, nurturing, and virtue. Women's production was no longer defined as "work." Women were seen as dependent consumers in a market economy. Like most other women, Ann Porter Sampson could continue to sew shirts for pay, but she lacked access to credit to hire others to sew for her. Much of Ann's inheritance had been in slaves and personal property, which passed to her husband immediately. Her small share of her father's land reduced the resources available to her mother. Testamentary trends thus ensured that women would hold less property than their husbands. These economic changes all increased women's dependency and made the world of business a space for males.[8]

The war years had issued many calls for women to demonstrate consumer restraint and virtue and thus show patriotism. At the beginning of the Revolution, Americans personified virtue and power as masculine and luxury and liberty as female. Women could corrupt and undercut the Revolution unless called to a new standard of virtue. Mercy Warren wrote her poetry to inspire women to that new standard. The Revolutionary rhetoric enhanced women's tendency to blend religion and politics. After all, virtue and industry were both the roads to victory and to salvation. By the end of the war, virtue had been domesticated. Public virtue (civic responsibility) had been merged with private virtue. If virtue was to check power, women would have to civilize men and teach them virtue. For women the way to serve the public was to purify their lives and pray for the community.[9]

When the war ended, women had to find a new way to demonstrate their patriotism through less heroic measures. Women's political activity made the new republic uneasy. Some women turned to a traditional outlet by writing about politics, publishing pamphlets, poetry, and books on political issues and history. But, as Mercy Warren discovered in 1804 when she published her history of the Revolution, writing about politics was now outside the "road of female life." Many Americans read Mary Wollstonecraft's *Vindication of the Rights of Women*, but found parts of it unwomanly or "too independent." Some women even found it embarrassing to read out loud. Americans assumed that an unwomanly female would be unattractive and lacking in virtue. It was only a small step to assuming that such women were sexually loose.[10]

One route to political participation lay through the family. The only distinctly female form of patriotism available when the War for Independence began was a mother giving her son to the cause. Writers, however, were busy focusing on motherhood. Philosophers, novelists, and poets sentimentalized a mother's influence over a child and invested it with the power to shape morals and patriotism. Love of family was the model for loving one's country. As women took this message to heart, they embraced Republican Motherhood. Mothers would shape good citizens for the new republic. Offers of public offices could not corrupt their patriotism. Thus women would model ultimate disinterested public virtue for their sons. Women fused the public and private to create a new patriotic role.[11]

A less political, more private vision shaped the idea of evangelical motherhood. Women would shape their families into committed Christians. The home was an island of purity separate from a corrupt world. Republican motherhood, in contrast, was based on the assumption that the home served a public purpose. Because separate sphere ideology was still evolving and because both versions emphasized motherhood as influential and women as domestic, few Americans noted the contrasting assumptions about public and private. Domesticity, however, reigned supreme. By 1787, when Hanah Adams published a pamphlet called *Women Invited to War*, the enemy was spiritual and the goal was to create a virtuous home.[12]

Women were also to be republican/evangelical wives. British political thought for almost two centuries had used the metaphor of the family to explain the relationship of individuals to government. Americans adopted the metaphor, shifting the emphasis from parent/child to husband/wife. Society was still a family headed by men, but women would gently lead men and children toward the virtue necessary in a republic. Since families worked together for the common good, not for a selfish individual, a republican wife was a disinterested patriot, above the power brokering and selfish realities of elective politics. Women's virtue now stood for that of the nation. Just as women could be seduced by men without a conscience, so could a citizenry. Only through marriage (republican government) could seduction be thwarted and virtue and innocence maintained. If women did not remain pure, what hope was there for men?[13]

The republican metaphor had several implications for marriage. Women were encouraged to stay single until they were sure of their choice. Liberty was not to be confused with license, however. Young women would be held responsible for their virtue, their beau's virtue, and the virtue of the nation. Premarital pregnancy gained new stigmas. If contracts between governments and citizens could be broken, then so could a marriage contract. Revolutionaries had extended John Locke's paralleling divorce with breaking an unjust "contract" between a ruler and subjects to support their rebellions, and then found that republican theory made it hard to oppose actual divorce. Thus it is not surprising that both the possibilities for divorce and the number of petitions increased.[14]

The ideas of republican and evangelical wife/motherhood shaped post-Revolutionary discussions about women's education. Some reformers, such as Judith Sargent Murray, tried to convince parents that education would give women the self-sufficiency and independence necessary to make better marriage choices. The idea that an education would prepare women to be good mothers appealed to more parents. Mothers could not instruct their sons in morals, liberty, and republicanism without the appropriate tools. Women's education could no longer focus on "graces"—music, dancing, drawing, and needlework (although these remained subjects)—but rather on the practical subjects they needed to share with sons—grammar, history, geography, and arithmetic. Reformers disagreed on subjects such as philosophy and politics. Clearly women needed to read materials that stressed virtue, morality, and industry. In fact, widespread literacy among the upper- and middle-classes helped to spread the ideas of domesticity, separate spheres, and republican motherhood.[15]

The expansion of women's education was part of a larger trend. Men's opportunities expanded with the founding of new colleges and academies, including state universities. But women's education drew strength from the domestic ideology, and it ensured women's inclusion in the expansion of education. The Boston School Act of 1789 stipulated that boys and girls receive instruction in the same subjects. Massachusetts began to count girls in its school census, and included schoolmistresses in the laws that dealt with schoolmasters. Academies for women offered their own courses but offered a wider range of courses than before. The Young Ladies Academy (which opened in Philadelphia in 1787), Pennuel Bowen's English Academy in Savannah (opened in 1786), and Sarah Pierce's Litchfield Academy were models of the new school. Reform did not mean equal education for women. Boston girls attended fewer hours and days than boys. Many New England towns reserved the summer session for girls and small children. Older boys attended sessions during the long winter term. Thus women had greater, but unequal, opportunities designed to fit them to a role defined more by the mind and heart than by skills or labor.[16]

Religion acquired a split personality. It was both public (worship) and private (piety), rational (theology) and emotional (conversion). Men dominated its official leadership and polity. The few religions where women had exercized these roles were marginalized, or women silenced. Thus the process of creating national and local church structures—synods, dioceses, circuits, etc.—excluded women just as the constitutional ratification processes had. In turn, women claimed the practical elements of religious belief—traditional customs, piety, benevolence, and community. Women were thus left to model virtue, benevolence, and piety for a male audience that increasingly saw such concerns as irrelevant to their lives.

For many women, however, ideas of republican wife/motherhood and marriage had no application to their lives. Independent single women could only participate in the republican family metaphor as surrogate mothers. Teaching allowed single women to shape young republicans. Unless she stepped in to assume the duties of a mother for relatives, a single woman's only family role was as a dependent daughter. Poor women could not afford the luxury of education or domesticity. At times they could not even retain control of their children as relief officials sent children to different institutions or bound them out. Many poor women worked for women who did accept the new roles. Thus they became invested in helping others achieve domesticity by denying it to themselves.

African Americans and Indians could not easily don the garb of republican motherhood. The status of slave was by definition the opposite of an independent republican. White society granted neither blacks nor Indians the virtue necessary to be republican (or evangelical) mothers. Whites interpreted the sexual vulnerability and irregular marriages of enslaved women as proof of their moral bankruptcy. Most free black women were too poor to afford domesticity. Indian women's marriage and work customs did not fit the republican/evangelical model. No matter how important or wealthy Mary Brant became, white New Yorkers saw only an Indian concubine who had prostituted herself for luxurious living and monarchy. Whites saw Indian women's farming as proof that Indian males were lazy and unvirtuous, and that Indian women were mannish, another sign of a lack of virtue. Even if Indian and black women did demonstrate the requisite virtue, they were still disqualified. Indian males did not belong to the republic, but to their tribes (excluding those fully assimilated). Only a few free black males could vote. Thus republican motherhood had no purpose. Black and Indian women could be mothers, but not of the republic.

To participate in the evangelical version of motherhood and marriage required nearly complete assimilation. Thus even Mary Brant's lifelong association with the Anglican Church did not meet the standard. Evangelical assumptions of modesty, virtue, and piety were so tied to European culture and customs that no woman who blended Indian and European customs could qualify. Mary Brant's daughters, educated in Canada and married to whites, came closer, but they paid a high price—the loss of their native culture.[17]

Although the construction of domesticity excluded blacks, Revolutionary-era ideas brought substantive change. The rhetoric of independence and religious equality of souls led some to question the institution of slavery. Most eighteenth-century white Americans had not fully accepted the increasingly common idea that blacks were less than human. By mid-century Quaker meetings discussed whether owning slaves was morally wrong. By the 1770s, Quaker testimony condemned any buying or selling of blacks. Friends began privately emancipating the slaves they held. The Philadelphia meeting moved to disown any members who still held slaves in 1776; other meetings followed suit the next year. In 1784 the Methodists agreed to expel those who held slaves, and held to that position for over a decade despite a growing number of white members in the South. Some Baptist congregations also opposed slavery.[18]

Other individuals recognized the contradiction inherent in struggling against British forced dependence while holding others in that state. As one of the Porters' neighbors explained when freeing his slaves by will, "all mankind has an Equal claim to freedom." Loyalists critics had pointed out the absurdidty of slaveholders declaring that all men were created equal. Revolutionaries, troubled by the contradiction and by British offers of freedon to slaves, showed an interest in emancipation. In 1770 perhaps 5 percent of the African-American population was free, but the war brought new opportunities for freedom through flight and military service. Between 1780 and 1804 all states north of Maryland moved toward full emancipation, usually through gradual emancipation laws.[19]

In Massachusetts, the courts used the rhetoric of liberty, equality, and freedom to end slavery. Two suits by African Americans in Massachusetts provided the legal opportunities for this ruling. According to tradition, Elizabeth Freeman (sometimes called Mum Bett) learned that the Massachusetts state constitution incorporated the famous "All men are created equal" phrase from the Declaration of Independence. Elizabeth fled her master after he hit her with a shovel. He sued to make her return, and she filed a countersuit claiming her freedom. Another slave joined in her suit, and the Great Barrington court ruled both were free in 1781. Elizabeth (a widow) and her young daughter then worked for wages for many years for the family that sheltered her. Her case was a precedent for the more famous Quok Walker case, which extended the ruling to all enslaved people in Massachusetts.[20]

Before the Revolution some states had passed laws barring manumission. Intended to prevent owners from dumping elderly slaves or slaves with disabilities, the laws prevented the freeing of young, able-bodied slaves as well. During the war, the upper South allowed owners to free slaves so they could serve as soldiers in place of the drafted owner. Virginia repealed its prohibition on private manumission in 1782, provided the slave was under 45 years old. Delaware, Maryland, and Kentucky followed Virginia's lead by 1792. South of Virginia, the legislatures refused to legalize private manumission. A frustrated legislature twice reenacted its law forbidding private manumission as citizens ignored the law. By the 1830s southern states had once again reinstated or enforced laws forbidding the private freeing of slaves.[21]

Southern courts, especially in the Chesapeake, also accepted suits for freedom based on claims of descent from a white woman. State laws and racial theory had not yet insisted that "one drop" of African background made a person black. According to law, children of a black father and white mother were supposed to be bound as servants until age 31. Then they were free; however, many whites tried to quietly "convert" such servants to slaves. In 1771 Mary and William Butler successfully sued for freedom claiming a free grandmother. An appeals court overturned the decision, but their daughter Mary sued in 1787. Her successful suit set a precedent for other cases. Southern courts allowed hearsay evidence about ancestors with light skin and straight hair as evidence of freedom. Like private manumission, this avenue closed by the 1830s.[22]

By 1790 there were 3,894 free black male heads of households and 513 free black women heading households in the United States. Free black women congregated in urban areas where employment opportunities were better. The black population in Philadelphia grew at a rate two and a half times that of the white population in the 1780s. In Virginia the free population grew from 2,000 in 1782 to 12,000 a decade later. Most free blacks continued to work for wages in the households of others. Amy, however, was not among those freed. Daniel Branch's will gave Amy and three other slaves to his four sons if the sons paid each daughter £30. Thus Amy died serving a grandchild of Elizabeth Dutoy Porter. But slaves on at least five neighboring plantations benefited when their owners used their wills to grant them freedom.[23]

While revolutionary rhetoric led some to question slavery, for many others in the new nation the rhetoric of independence simply highlighted the differences between men and women, and the differences between whites and other races. When the rhetoric about independence and dependence combined with the definitions of *who* was dependent, white males stood in stark contrast to all other groups in society. Revolutionary rhetoric made the dependent status of slaves more obvious. Since the Revolution emphasized rationality, defenses of slavery were increasingly based on scientific "proof" of racial inferiority.[24]

Indian groups east of the Mississippi, battered by the long frontier war, signed peace treaties in the 1790s ceding much of their land. Many found themselves on reserves too small for self-sufficiency. At Fort Stanwix in 1784 Indian commissioners told the gathered Indian leaders that they were mistaken to think of themselves as free or independent. They were "subdued" nations whose land had been conquered.[25] Four decades later the U.S. Supreme Court made it official by ruling that Indians belonged to dependent nations. Indian women and enslaved women were thus doubly dependent.

The war itself highlighted women's dependence as petitioners and refugees. The new governments, state and national, left married women in coverture and thus legally dependent on their husbands. The discussion of male political rights pushed many to argue that any male head of a family should be able to vote as the independent head of a family. By implication such arguments made all women in the family dependent. New Jersey finally carried this logic to its conclusion, disenfranchising propertied women and enfranchising propertyless men in 1807.

Freedom was fragile for African Americans. Although some black women acquired property and flourished, others found dependency just a meal away. Many blacks lived as dependents in the homes of others, or turned to public relief. For several years after emancipation, Philadelphia Quaker women provided assistance to those freed through the Committee to Inquire into the Condition of Freed Slaves. Children bound as servants until age 28 accounted for one-quarter of all blacks living in white Philadelphia households. Many had been bound when their impoverished parents had sought relief. In slave states, men were more likely to be able to earn enough to redeem multiple members from slavery. Women struggled to free even one. There was always the risk of kidnap and sale as a slave, even with the protection of special committees formed by prominent whites in Philadelphia and New York. Despite such hardships, African Americans began to build their own cultural institutions and communities in cities, but the marginal lives of many made it hard to counter views of African Americans as naturally dependent.[26]

When Sarah Franklin Bache helped organize the efforts of Philadelphia women to raise money and sew shirts for the soldiers, she was following in the footsteps of her mother. Deborah Franklin had participated in efforts to support charitable organizations when Sarah was a child. The renewed emphasis on piety, virtue, and charity provided a rationale for expanding women's efforts after the war. The opportunities were many, as churches had to seek voluntary contributions to survive. Women responded by forming groups to raise funds and provide support. As recession followed war, the numbers of elderly, poor, orphans, and sick seeking help increased. Women funded orphanages and hospitals, and provided aid to meet the need, especially for women and girls.[27] Society interpreted these efforts not as demonstrations of women's economic power, but as illustrations of female charity and dependence.

Eighteenth-century Americans worried about the many signs of the breakdown of social order—the decline of deference, the challenge of new religious groups to established churches, the rise of a transient class of poor. Social disorder troubled a society beginning to link political self-rule to a virtuous republic. As enlightenment philanthropy merged with religious moral perfectionism, Americans became more aware of their faults, their poor, and violence in their society. The rise of newspapers helped publicize violent events throughout the Americas, thus magnifying social disorder.

The enforcement of gender roles was one way society could confront this chaos, but gender roles themselves were changing. By 1790 the two main elements of the new norm—woman as dependent nurturer and moral guardian—were widely accepted. Ideas of female piety converged with an understanding of virtue as a moral (emotional) sense and the sentimentalization of domestic relations. As early as 1750, Americans had begun reinforcing domesticity through social policy and law. Ideas of women's liberty at first coexisted with the growing acceptance of separate spheres for men and women. It was not that women were incapable of acting in the public sphere, but rather that it was not their job.[28] Over time, the new nation obliterated the traditional flexibility allowing women to assume a wide variety of roles by converting domesticity from a role into a biological trait. Memories of women's participation in the American Revolution were ignored or the actions reinterpreted to fit the new expectations for women.

White settlers made constant demands for land cessions from Indians after the war. Through resurveying, converting leases to freeholds, and new treaties, Indians lost their lands. Between 1775 and 1790, more than 80,000 non-Indian settlers poured into the Kentucky and Ohio lands claimed by the Shawnee, despite continued frontier warfare. Cherokee and Creek ceded lands. Divided by the war, the Iroquois could not resist settlers. In 1784 the British granted the loyalist Mohawk the first of several reserves in Ontario. Mary moved to Cataraqui (Kingston) on Lake Ontario and died there in 1796. The Iroquois nations in the United States were soon tricked or forced to cede most of their homeland to New York. The Treaty of Greenville in 1795 set up an annuity system to pay for ceded lands. Indian nations entered a downward spiral where each cession made it harder to survive and thus led to new land sales.[29]

Women's influence in tribes declined under constant pressure, as war leaders gained greater power and missionaries continued their efforts. In 1785, Nancy Ward, the Beloved Woman of Chota, took part in the negotiations at Hopewell, the last time Cherokee women had an official role at such negotiations. Women continued to speak in council for many years, with waning effect. Missionaries insisted on treating men as heads of households and expecting them to do the farming. Women were to learn domestic skills such as weaving and spinning. Some Cherokee men purchased slaves to help in the cultivation. Since Cherokee law awarded land ownership to the person who cultivated it, land passed into male hands. By 1808 the Cherokee had recognized inheritance of land based on paternity and reduced women's claim to a widow's share. Reorganization of Cherokee governance in 1826 created a centralized system that disenfranchised women.[30]

If it were not bad enough that Indian women lost their traditional economic roles, a series of spiritual revivals also displaced women. The revivals emphasized a return to tradition, but an altered tradition. Intermarriage was discouraged, and women were subordinated to men. New medicine lodges barred women. By emphasizing dress and hairstyles that were different, men set themselves apart. Among the Ojibwa, a new sacred lodge called the Wahbino forbade women from touching anything sacred. Women had been active in the other medicine lodges for years. Reform efforts led by the Seneca leader Handsome Lake similarly excluded women from leadership among the Iroquois.[31]

By 1790 the fortunes of the Franklin, Porter, and Brant households were in the hands of a new generation. Peg, Deborah Franklin, and

Elizabeth Dutoy Porter had all died before independence. Margaret Brant was a casualty of the war. Many of the next generation were also gone. Deborah Croker Dunlap died one year after her aunt. Elizabeth Porter's children had an especially hard time during the war years. Isaac, an officer during the Revolution, never married. Death claimed Marie, Elizabeth, John, and William; three of the four died during the war. Ann was a widow. Sarah Porter Hatcher and her husband Thomas had joined their neighbors in moving west.

The future diverged for the descendants still living in 1790. Amy was still a slave serving in the Branch household, her prospects dimmed as cotton culture revived slavery. Elizabeth Branch's children would never achieve the wealth of their parents, but they survived as small planters. Sarah Franklin Bache became her father's hostess until his death in 1790. Mother of eight, Sarah Bache was a model of the new domesticity until her death from cancer in 1807. Mary Brant spent her last years making sure that her daughters would inherit her confiscated property. Mary lived with one foot firmly planted in Mohawk traditions and the other in assimilation. Her daughters carried assimilation farther by marrying whites. Only her son married and remained in the tribe. When Mary died in 1796, her homeland was gone, she was dependent upon a pension from the government, and she was under constant pressure to conform to the new gender ideology.

Women were active participants in the American Revolution, and yet the Revolution proved strangely unrevolutionary when it came to women's legal status. The conditions of women's lives changed dramatically during the war and after it, yet for each new door that opened another closed. Sarah Hatcher's family shared in the economic opportunities of the opening frontier. They did so at great cost to the Indian women whose land it had been, and to African-American women like Amy, who were torn from their families to clear and plant that frontier land. If Sarah Bache ended the war in comfort as her father's hostess in Philadelphia, Mary Brant died in exile.

The trade-offs also came in less material, but longer-lasting forms. If married women were not independent, they had new importance as republican or evangelical mothers. Republican and evangelical models of the family, however, left the poor, Indians, and African Americans more firmly outside the social norms than ever before. For Indian women, those models were powerful engines of assimilation that helped strip them of customary power. The new gender distinctions both excluded women from public roles in church and state and obscured the actual public roles women held. They also strengthened women's claims to informal leadership in religion, and to participation in benevolent work for church, home, and community. If women found it harder to participate in the market economy, they had new options for education. Instead of being the junior partners in an economic partnership, wives were nurturing companions leading their husbands and children to virtue. The Revolution changed the lives of all, but its fruits came unevenly and the price was high.

Throughout it all, women continued to create meaningful lives for themselves and to find ways to be useful to their world. However, Mary Brant's daughter Margaret, Deborah Bache, and Elizabeth Branch and the women on her plantation would travel different roads than the ones taken by the grandmothers whose names they bore. Their memories of the American Revolution and women's participation in it would be distorted by the lenses of domesticity through which their generation and later ones would see the world.

Through that lens, women's active participation in the Revolution was transformed. Mary Hayes, the regimental woman paid to bring water to cool artillery, became Molly Pitcher, risking death to bring water to her thirsty husband. The female nurses so necessary to military hospitals disappeared from view so thoroughly that women would have to struggle to be allowed to nurse in the Civil War. Women's gentleness and domesticity had unsuited them for places as shocking as a battlefront hospital. The patriotic spinning bees and women's associations pledged to boycott British goods were quickly stripped of their political overtones and became simple domestic acts in support of families. The domestic lens ensured that African-American women, American Indians, and poor working women were invisible, not only during the Revolution, but from the category "woman." When in the 1840s Elizabeth Ellet published the first history of women in the American Revolution, the many forms of activism resurfaced as momentary acts of heroism motivated by appropriate domestic and patriotic concerns.

When the great-granddaughters of Margaret Brant, Deborah Franklin, Elizabeth Porter, and Peg came of age, so did a new women's movement. That movement brought to fruition the promise inherent in companionate marriage, greater education, the ideology of independence, and the association of women with benevolence, piety, and morality. Women had acquired a sense of themselves as different from men and formed their own organizations in church and community. These became the levers with which they would challenge women's exclusion from the public sphere, and the institution of slavery. But their version of history carried no hint that women had ever lived in a world where public and private merged and women had roles in both. The domestic revolution had been more thorough than its political contemporary, the American Revolution.

NOTES

Preface

1. In all cases where I used a dissertation that has since appeared in print, I have kept my citation to the original dissertation. In the essay on sources, I have cited the published version since it is more available to interested readers.

Chapter 1

1. The information on the Dutoy and Porter households comes from a larger study under way on the Manakin community. For basic information on the French at Manakin see R. A. Brock, *Documents, Chiefly Unpublished Relating to the Huguenot Emigration to Virginia and to the Settlement at Manakin Town* (Richmond: Collections of the Virginia Historical Society, vol. V, 1886); Pierre Dutoy will, Henrico County Deeds and Wills, October 3, 1726, Virginia State Library. Future references to Virginia county records will use the following abbreviations: VSL=Virginia State Library, D/W=Deeds/Wills, HCR=Henrico County Records, CCR=Cumberland County Records, GCR=Goochland County Records, CHCR=Chesterfield County Records, PCR=Powhatan County Records.

2. The Vestry Book of King William Parish, tithe lists for 1719, 1720, 1723, 1724, Virginia Historical Society MSS.

3. The information on the Porter family is pieced together from scattered church and legal records as part of my research efforts to trace the French community at Manakin, Virginia. See the will of Pierre Dutoy, in HCR, D/W, 1726, and of Isaac Dutoy, Thomas Porter, and Elizabeth Porter in CCR, W/D, 1752, 1767, and 1772. For other information, see Priscilla Harriss Cabell, *Turff & Twigg*, Vol. 1, Richmond, VA, 1988, 73, 117–19. See also the tithe lists for 1726–1738 in King William Vestry Book, Virginia Historical Society, and the King William Parish Register in Brock, *Documents Chiefly Unpublished*.

4. Barbara appears as head of the household on the King William Parish tithe lists for 1726, 1729, 1730, and 1731 (King William Parish Vestry Book, Virginia Historical Society). Her relationship to Anthony Benin is noted in Pierre Dutoy's will, HCR, D/W, October 3, 1726. Barbara's date of death is unknown, but she was still alive when Martha Dupuy Chastain wrote her will in 1740, leaving Barbara a £5 bequest. Martha Dupuy Chastian will, GCR, D/W, May 20, 1742.

5. King William Parish tithe lists 1726–1740, King William Parish Vestry Book, Virginia Historical Society. The evidence for the marriage of Marianne Dutoy and John Lucadou is from Thomas Porter deeds where Lucadou is described as owning land that Marianne had patented in 1732. He died by 1739, when she married James Goss (Cabell, *Turff & Twigg*, 73).

6. This sketch is pieced together from fragments of county and church records. It appears that Thomas Porter acquired after marriage all the land he sold during his lifetime or bequeathed in his will. Pierre Dutoy will, 3 October 1726, HCR, D/W, VSL; Thomas Porter will, signed 15 April 1765, recorded 27 April 1767, CCR, W/D, VSL; King William Parish Vestry Book, *passim*, Virginia Historical Society; Cabell, *Turff & Twigg*, 117–20.

7. King William Parish Register, in Brock, *Documents, Chiefly Unpublished*, *passim*. For discussions of naming and child-rearing in general, see Daniel Scott Smith, "Child-Naming Practices, Kinship Ties, and Change in Family Attitudes in Hingham, Massachusetts, 1641 to 1880," *Journal of Social History*, XVIII (Summer, 1985): 541–66; John J. Waters, "Naming and Kinship in New England: Guilford Patterns and Usage, 1693–1759," *New England Historical and Genealogical Register*, CXXXIX (July, 1984): 161–81.

8. The inventory Elizabeth Porter and her son John filed in 1767 when Thomas died provides much information on household activity. Other inventories from the same area in the 1740s have similar contents. Thomas Porter inventory, 27 July 1767, CCR, W, VSL. See, for example, the estate of Gideon Chambon, another King William Parish resident about the same age as Elizabeth. He also owned three slaves, was married, and had a young family. Gideon Chambon inventory, 21 August 1739, GCR, D/W, VSL.

9. See Lorena Walsh, "Community networks in the Early Chesapeake," in Lois Green Carr, Philip D. Morgan, and Jean B. Russo, eds., *Colonial Chesapeake Society* (Chapel Hill: University of North Carolina Press for the Institute of Early American History and Culture, 1988); for the vestry service of the Dutoys and Porters, see The King William Parish Vestry Book, Virginia Historical Society MSS; for Barbara's illiteracy see her signature by mark on the deed of Jacob Capon to Stephen Chastain, 14 March 1728/9, GCR, D, VSL. The evidence on Elizabeth's literacy is less clear. Elizabeth signed by mark as a witness on a deed in 1738/9. Thirty years later Elizabeth signed the inventory of her husband's estate. Five years later she signed her own will by mark. If she learned to write, it was apparently after age 30, and the skill was seldom used.

See Deed, Stephen Chastain to Ed and William Hampton, 20 February 1738/9, GCR, D/W; Thomas Porter inventory, 22 July 1767, CCR, W; and Elizabeth Porter will, 22 June 1722, CCR, W, VSL.

10. When Thomas Porter died more than 20 years later, the household had acquired only a few luxury items of furnishings, although his slaveholdings would place him in the upper third of all slave-owners. Other inventories for comparable Manakin families from 1735 to 1745 reinforce my description of the Porter living quarters. See the Thomas Porter inventory, 27 July 1767, CCR, W; Gideon Chambon inventory, 21 August 1739, GCR, D/W; and Anthony Trabue inventory, 21 August 1744, GCR, D/W, VSL. For comparative slaveholding, see Allan Kulikoff, *Tobacco and Slaves: The Development of Southern Cultures in the Chesapeake, 1680–1800* (Chapel Hill: University of North Carolina Press for the Institute of Early American History and Culture, 1986), 338.

11. Philip D. Morgan, "Slave Life in Piedmont Virginia, 1720–1800," in Carr et al., eds., *Colonial Chesapeake Society*, 444.

12. See the tithe lists for King William Parish for 1723 through 1734 found in the King William Vestry Book, Virginia Historical Society.

13. Mechal Sobel, *The World They Made Together: Black and White Values in in Eighteenth-Century Virginia* (Princeton: Princeton University Press, 1987); Kulikoff, *Tobacco and Slaves.*

14. For marriage to Indians, see Morgan, "Slave Life," in Carr, et al., eds. *Colonial Chesapeake Society*, 464. The births of Amy and Dick appear in the King William Parish Register for September 1, 1740, and May 16, 1742. In 1740 Porter's only female slave seems to be Peg. However, according to the 1744 tithe list (the next surviving after 1738), Thomas Porter owned five slaves including Hampton and Jude, who seem to be a couple. They are both willed to Elizabeth and appear in close proximity on the Thomas's inventory. The child, Dick, on the inventory appears to be their son. Thomas Porter will, 15 April 1767, CCR, D/W; the Thomas Porter inventory, 27 July 1767, CCR, D/W; Elizabeth Porter will, 22 June 1772, CCR, D/W, VSL.

15. Joan R. Gundersen, "The Double Bonds of Race and Sex: Black and White Women in a Colonial Virginia Parish," *Journal of Southern History*, LII (August 1986). Using the records of large plantations in the piedmont, Philip Morgan found evidence that women on those plantations bore children very regularly 28 months apart. My records for small plantations in the first half of the century show a less regular pattern. In either case, the birth interval is still slightly longer than the average for white women in the eighteenth-century Chesapeake, thus resulting in a lower completed family size for black women.

16. Historians have found slaves more eager to name sons for male members of the family. Fathers were often separated from families, and naming children for them emphasized the tie. The Porter slaves did repeat male names, but they also repeated female names, something less common in general. See the

Thomas Porter inventory, 27 July 1767, CCR, W, VSL. For naming patterns in general see Morgan, "Slave Life," in Carr, et al., eds., *Colonial Chesapeake Society*, 445.

17. Gary Nash, *The Urban Crucible: The Northern Seaports and the Origins of the American Revolution* (Cambridge, MA: Harvard University Press, 1986), abridged ed. 110.

18. Carl Van Doren, *Benjamin Franklin*, (New York: Viking Press, 1938), 125; Mary D. Turnbull, "William Dunlap, Colonial Printer, Journalist and Minister," *Pennsylvania Magazine of History and Biography*, CIII (April 1979): 143–44.

19. Mary Beth Norton described the general differences between life for urban and rural women in the mid-eighteenth century. Mary Beth Norton, *Liberty's Daughters: The Revolutionary Experiences of American Women, 1750–1800* (Boston: Little, Brown and Company, 1980), 21–28.

20. David Freeman Hawke, *Franklin* (New York: Harper and Row, 1976), 23–39.

21. Marylynn Salmon, *Women and the Law of Property in Early America* (Chapel Hill: University of North Carolina Press, 1986), 61.

22. For the Connecticut discussion, see Cornelia Hughes Dayton, "Women, Before the Bar: Gender, Law and Society in Connecticut, 1710–1790" (Ph.D. diss., Princeton University, October, 1986), 304–6.

23. Hawke, *Franklin*, 23–27, 38–39; Van Doren, *Franklin*, 70–71, 90–93. Van Doren raises the possiblity that William was Deborah's child, but comes to no conclusion. As William approached majority, surviving accounts suggest that his relationship with Deborah was strained and that Deborah feared Benjamin would leave all his property to William, thus slighting Deborah and their daughter Sarah. On this point, see Daniel Fisher, "Diary," Mrs. Conway Robinson Howard, ed., *Pennsylvania Magazine of History and Biography*, XVII (1893): 271–72, 276.

24. Franklin was not the only member of the colonial elite to live in a common-law marriage. Charles Carroll Sr. did not marry Elizabeth Brooke until 1757, when their son, Charles Carroll (later a signer of the Declaration of Independence) was 20. Unlike Deborah Read Franklin, Elizabeth Brooke continued to use her birth name until a ceremony was performed. Sally D. Mason, "Mama, Rachel, and Molly: Three Generations of Carroll Women," in Ronald Hoffman and Peter J. Albert, *Women in the Age of the American Revolution* (Charlottesville, VA: University of Virginia Press, 1989): 251–57.

25. Hawke, *Franklin*, 38–39, 64; Turnbull, "Dunlap," 146–47; Van Doren, *Franklin*, 125; Gary Baker, "He That Would Thrive Must Ask His Wife: Franklin's Anthony Afterwit Letter," *Pennsylvania Magazine of History and Biography*, CVIV (January 1985): 27–42.

26. Van Doren, *Franklin*, 125; Mary D. Turnbull, "William Dunlap, Colonial Printer, Journalist and Minister," *Pennsylvania Magazine of History and Biography*, CIII (April 1979): 144.

27. Van Doren, *Franklin*, 81.

28. For general background on eastern Indians in this period, see Gary B. Nash, *Red, White, and Black: The Peoples of Early America* (Englewood, NJ: Prentice-Hall, 2nd ed., 1982); James H. Merrell, *The Indian's New World: Catawbas and Their Neighbors from European Contact through the Era of Removal* (Chapel Hill: University of North Carolina Press, 1989); Theda Perdue, *Slavery and the Evolution of Cherokee Society, 1540–1866* (Knoxville: University of Tennessee Press, 1979); Isabel Thompson Kelsay, *Joseph Brant, 1743–1807: Man of Two Worlds* (Syracuse: Syracuse University Press, 1984); and David B. Guldenzopf, "The Colonial Transformation of Mohawk Iroquois Society" (Ph.D. diss., Anthropology, SUNY Albany, 1986).

29. Richard White, *The Middle Ground: Indians, Empires, and Republics in the Great Lakes Region, 1650–1815* (New York: Cambridge University Press, 1991), 198–204; Gregory Evans Dowd, "Paths of Resistance: American Indian Religion and the Quest for Unity 1748–1815" (Ph.D. diss., Princeton University, 1986), 183; Merrell, *The Indian's New World*, 136–37.

30. Kelsay is adamant that Margaret was a Mohawk commoner and that Joseph Brant had to later rely on marriage to bring him the connections that made him a chief. Barbara Graymont, however, notes that Molly Brant, Margaret's daughter, did serve as a clan matron. Kelsay, *Joseph Brant*, 7, 32; Barbara Graymont, *The Iroquois in the American Revolution* (Syracuse: Syracuse University Press, 1972), 30; Guldenzopf, "Mohawk," 32–38.

31. Guldenzopf, "Mohawk," 43–55. Canajorie had approximately 180 residents in 1713. Kelsay estimates a population in the 1740s as 250–300 people. Kelsay, *Joseph Brant*, 46–47.

32. Guldenzopf, "Mohawk," 30–32.

33. Material on Margaret Brant is included in the biography of her son Joseph. Kelsay, *Joseph Brant*, 7, 39–52. Some sources suggest only two marriages for Margaret, but Kelsay's research indicates four.

34. Graymont, *The Iroquois in the American Revolution*, 10–11.

35. Kelsay, *Joseph Brant*, 41–44.

36. Guldenzopf, "Mohawk," 71–72.

37. Kelsay, *Joseph Brant*, 44–52.

38. Nash, *Red, White, and Black*, 229, 232–34, 249–50; Merrell, *The Indian's New World*, 136–37.

39. Kelsay, *Joseph Brant*, 39–40.

Chapter 2

1. A. G. Roeber, *Palatines, Liberty, and Property: German Lutherans in Colonial British America* (London and Baltimore: Johns Hopkins University Press, 1993), 151–53; Daniel Scott Smith, "Behind and Beyond the Law of the Household," *WMQ*, LII (January 1995): 149.

2. The information on the women of the Porter household is inferred from their presence (or absence) in county records, deeds, wills, and inventories. See the records of Powhatan, Chesterfield, Goochland, and Cumberland Counties, VSL.

3. For brief biographies of Sarah Franklin Bache and Mary Brant, see Whitfield J. Bell Jr., "Sarah Franklin Bache," in Edward T. James, Janet Wilson James, Paul S. Boyer, eds., *Notable American Women: A Biographical Dictionary* (Cambridge: Belknap Press of Harvard University, 1971), and Milton W. Hamilton, "Mary Brant," *ibid.* For Deborah Croker Dunlap, see Turnbull, "William Dunlap"; for Margaret and Mary Brant see Kelsay, *Joseph Brant.*

4. Cabell, *Turff & Twigg*, 118. County records have only tiny glimpsesof Barbara Dutoy, thus suggesting she rarely left her French community. On the two occasions she witnessed a legal document, she signed by mark. Deed of Capon to Chastain, 14 March 1728/9 and 17 June 1729, GCR, D, VSL.

5. Virginia common law gave a husband absolute ownership of all moveable property a woman brought to or acquired during marriage, except for a small reservation of personal clothing, jewels, or tools called paraphernalia. Unless the couple had a prenuptial agreement or her family created a trust, the woman's rights to real estate were limited to dower, a one-third life interest in all property brought to or acquired during marriage. French and German immigrants were used to Roman law traditions. Under community property rules, the husband and wife each retained control of property brought to the marriage. They jointly owned what was acquired during marriage. G. Roeber, *Palatines, Liberty, and Property*, 50–54; Joan R. Gundersen and Gwen Victor Gampel, "Married Women's Legal Status in Eighteenth-Century New York and Virginia," *William and Mary Quarterly*, 3rd ser., XXXIX (January 1982).

6. Beverly Prior Smaby, *The Transformation of Moravian Bethlehem: From Communal Mission to Family Economy* (Philadelphia: University of Pennsylvania Press, 1988); Daniel B. Thorp, *The Moravian Community in Colonial North Carolina: Pluralism on the Southern Frontier* (Knoxville: University of Tennessee Press, 1989).

7. Bernard Bailyn, *Voyagers to the West: A Passage in the Peopling of America on the Eve of the Revolution* (New York: Vintage Books, 1986), 3–7, 26, 54–55, 451–60; Bernard Bailyn, *The Peopling of British North America: An Introduction* (New York: Vintage Books, 1988), 9–11; Nash, *Red, White, and Black*, 290.

8. Bernard Bailyn, *Peopling of North America*, 9–14; Bailyn, *Voyagers to the West*, 129–40, 173; Daniel B. Shea, ed., "Some Account of the Fore Part of the Life of Elizabeth Ashbridge," in William L. Andrews, ed., *Journeys in New Worlds: Early American Women's Narratives* (Madison: University of Wisconsin Press, 1990), 150; Farley Grubb, "Morbidity and Mortality on the North Atlantic Passage: Eighteenth-Century German Immigration," *Journal of Interdisciplinary History*, XVII (Winter 1987): 565–72; Gundersen, "The Double Bonds

of Race and Sex"; Philip D. Morgan and Michael L. Nicholls, "Slaves in Piedmont Virginia, 1720–1790," *William and Mary Quarterly*, 3rd ser., XLVI (April 1989): 221; Donald Wright, *African Americans in the Colonial Era: From African Origins Through the American Revolution* (Arlington Heights, IL: Harlan Davidson, 1990), 22–33; Debra L. Newman, "Black Women in the Era of the American Revolution in Pennsylvania," *Journal of Negro History*, LXI (July 1976): 277.

9. The Scots group had to turn back. Organizer James Hogg found himself involved in a morass of claims and counterclaims. Bailyn, *Voyagers to the West*, 135–40, 507–15; Bailyn, *The Peopling of North America*, 13–14. For mortality of German women, see Grubb, "Morbidity and Mortality on the North Atlantic Passage."

10. Bailyn, *Peopling of North America*, 9–11.

11. Grubb, "Morbidity and Mortality on the North Atlantic Passage," 565–85.

12. Kaylene Hughes, "Populating the Back Country: the Demographic and Social Characteristics of the Colonial South Carolina Frontier, 1730–1760" (Ph.D. diss., Florida State University, December 1985), 72.

13. Farley Grubb, "Immigrant Servant Labor: Their Occupational and Geographic Distribution in the Late Eighteenth-Century Mid-Atlantic Economy," *Social Science History*, IX (Summer 1985): 251–55; Sharon Salinger, " 'Send No More Women': Female Servants in Eighteenth-Century Philadelphia," *Pennsylvania Magazine of History and Biography*, CVII (January 1983): 30–33, 40.

14. Bailyn, *Voyagers*, 332–38, 565–66; Margaret M. R. Kellow, "Indentured Servitude in Eighteenth-Century Maryland," *Histoire Sociale-Social History*, XVII (November 1984): 239–40.

15. Both young men and women negotiated contracts lasting until they were of age. Since more of the men were younger, the average length of their contracts was longer than for women.

16. Kellow, "Indentured Servitude in Eighteenth-Century Maryland," 239–40; Salinger, " 'Send No More Women,' " 51–52. Jacqueline Jones, "Race, Sex, and Self-Evident Truths: The Status of Slave Women During the Era of the American Revolution," in Hoffman and Albert, eds., *Women in the Age of the American Revolution*, 311. Jones argues that slaves replaced women in domestic service, but that seems to depend greatly on the colony involved.

17. It is difficult to arrive at a figure of the percentage of immigrant women in the late eighteenth century who were married. Most female white immigrants came in family groups. Families, however, included daughters not yet married, and widowed female relatives. A majority of female servants were unmarried, except among redemptioners. It is impossible to determine what percent of slaves had been married in Africa, but none arrived in an intact family group. If slaves are considered part of the migrant population, then a majority of female migrants were single on arrival.

18. Bailyn, *Voyagers*, 258–60, 303, 332–38, 565–66; Kellow, "Indentured Servitude in Eighteenth-Century Maryland," 239–40; Grubb, "Servant," 251–57; Salinger, " 'Send No More Women,' " 38. The estimate of 140 married servants is extrapolated from Grubb.

19. Kellow, "Indentured Servitude in Eighteenth-Century Maryland," 235–39. For examples of runaway female convict servants, see the *Virginia Gazette*, 29 July 1737, 4, and 18 November 1737, 4.

20. Bailyn, *Voyagers*, 325–30; Kellow, "Indentured Servitude in Eighteenth-Century Maryland," 235–39.

21. Salinger, " 'Send No More Women,' " 40; Sharon Ann Burnston, "Babies in the Well: An Underground Insight Into Deviant Behavior in Eighteenth-Century Philadelphia," *Pennsylvania Magazine of History and Biography*, CVI (April 1982): 151–86; Julia Cherry Spruill, *Women's Life and Work in the Southern Colonies* (New York: W.W. Norton & Co., 1972 [paperback ed.]); Shea, ed., "Life of Elizabeth Ashbridge," in Andrews, ed., *Journeys in New Worlds*, 150–51; Kellow, "Indentured Servitude in Eighteenth-Century Maryland," 249–50. See Chapter Seven for a discussion of infanticide.

22. Jean Butenhoff Lee, "The Social Order of a Revolutionary People: Charles County Maryland, 1733–1786" (Ph.D. diss., University of Virginia, 1984); Kellow, "Indentured Servitude in Eighteenth-Century Maryland," 231, 239–40. See the Peter Louis Soblet estate inventory, 26 September 1757, Cumberland County, Will Book, VSL and the Joseph Trabue estate inventory, 1757, Chesterfield County, Will Book, *ibid.*

23. Morgan and Nicholls, "Slaves in Piedmont Virginia, 1720–1790," 218; Wright, *African Americans*, 18; Gundersen, "The Double Bonds of Race and Sex."

24. Wright, *African Americans*, 9–11, 22–36, 40–43; Deborah Gray White, *Ar'n't I a Woman?: Female Slaves in the Plantation South* (New York and London: W.W. Norton & Co., 1985), 63.

25. Philip D. Morgan, "Slave Life in Piedmont, Virginia, 1720–1800," in Carr, et al., eds., *Colonial Chesapeake Society*, 433–37; Walter Minchton, Celia King, and Peter Waite, *Virginia Slave-Trade Statistics, 1698–1775* (Richmond: VSL, 1984); Donald M. Sweig, "The Importation of African Slaves to the Potomac River, 1732–1772," *William and Mary Quarterly*, 3rd ser., XLII (October 1985): 509–11; Kulikoff, *Tobacco and Slaves*, 65, 336.

26. King William Parish was originally in Henrico County, but the creation of new counties put it on the border, split between Cumberland, Goochland, and Chesterfield when they were created from Henrico. After the Revolution the creation of Powhatan County placed most of the parish within a single county. The figures I am using are based on a study of Chesterfield County slave imports done by Philip Morgan and Michael Nicholls. Morgan and Nicholls, "Slaves in Piedmont Virginia, 1720–1790," 218–19, 221, 236. For the sex ratios, see Gundersen, "The Double Bonds of Race and Sex," 353–56,

and Morgan, "Slave Life in Piedmont, Virginia, 1720–1800," in Carr, et al., eds., *Colonial Chesapeake Society*, 433–37. The outlines of the slave trade and its economic impacts are in Kulikoff, *Tobacco and Slaves*, 65, 336; Minchinton, et al., *Virginia Slave-Trade Statistics, 1698–1775*, xv; Donald M. Sweig, "The Importation of African Slaves," 514.

27. Russell Menard, "Slavery, Economic Growth, and Revolutionary Ideology in the South Carolina Lowcountry," in Ronald Hoffman, John J. McCusker, and Russell Menard, *The Economy of Early America: The Revolutionary Period, 1763–1790* (Charlottesville, VA: University Press of Virginia for the United States Capitol Historical Society, 1988), 260; Jones, "Race, Sex, and Self-Evident Truths," 309; Daniel C. Littlefield, *Rice and Slaves: Ethnicity and the Slave Trade in Colonial South Carolina* (Urbana and Chicago: University of Illinois Press, 1991), 145–56; Peter Wood, *Black Majority: Negroes in Colonial South Carolina from 1670 through the Stono Rebellion* (New York: W.W. Norton & Co., 1974), 35–62.

28. Wright, *African Americans*, 70–73; Vivienne L. Kruger, "Born to Run: The Slave Family in Early New York, 1626–1827" (Ph.D. diss., Columbia University, 1985), 80, 131–55.

29. Charles W. Akers, " 'Our Modern Egyptians': Phillis Wheatley and the Whig Campaign Against Slavery in Revolutionary Boston," *Journal of Negro History*, LX (July 1975): 397–99; R. Lynn Matson, "Phillis Wheatley—Soul Sister?," *Phylon*, XXXIII (Fall 1972): 222–30; Sidney Kaplan, *The Black Presence in the American Revolution* (Boston: University of Massachusetts Press, rev. ed. 1989), 170–82; David Grimsted, "Anglo-American Racism and Phillis Wheatley's 'Sabel Veil,' 'Length'n Chain,' and 'Knitted Heart' " in Hoffman and Albert, eds., *Women in the Age of the American Revolution*, 340–41, 344–51, 365, 370.

30. Nash, *Urban Crucible*, 68–70, 206; Gary B. Nash, *Forging Freedom: The Formation of Philadelphia's Black Community, 1720–1840* (Cambridge: Harvard University Press, 1988), 143; Soderlund, "Black Women," 51–52; Newman, "Black Women," 277–78; Joan Jensen, *Loosening the Bonds: Mid-Atlantic Farm Women, 1750–1850* (New Haven: Yale University Press, 1986), *passim*.

31. Gundersen, "The Double Bonds of Race and Sex," 363–65.

32. For inheritance studies see Lisa Wilson Waciega, "A 'Man of Business': The Widow of Means in Southeastern Pennsylvania, 1750–1830," *William and Mary Quarterly*, 3rd ser., XLIV (January 1987): 45–54; Lisa Wilson Waciega, "Widowhood and Womanhood in Early America: The Experience of Women in Philadelphia and Chester Counties, 1750–1850" (Ph.D. diss., Temple University, 1986), 194–204; Toby Lee Ditz, "Ownership and Obligation: Family and Inheritance in Five Connecticut Towns, 1750–1820" (Ph.D. diss., Columbia University, 1982), 243–51; Jean Butenhoff Lee, "Land and Labor: Parental

Bequest Practices in Charles County, Maryland, 1732–1783," in Carr, et al., eds., *Colonial Chesapeake Society*, 311–31; Lee, "Social Order," 175–85, 191; Linda Speth and Alison Duncan Hirsch, *Women, Family and Community in Colonial America: Two Perspectives*, Women and History, Number 4 (Haworth Press, Inc. for the Institute for Research in History, 1982), 15–16; Lois Green Carr, "Inheritance in the Colonial Chesapeake," in Hoffman and Albert, *Women in the Age of the American Revolution*, 166–77; Carol Shamus, "Early American Women and Control Over Capital," in ibid., 138–43; David E. Narrett, "Men's Wills and Women's Property Rights in Colonial New York," in ibid., 113–32; Gloria L. Main, "Widows in Rural Massachusetts on the Eve of the Revolution," in ibid., 78–84; Gundersen and Gampel, "Married Women's Legal Status in Eighteenth-Century New York and Virginia"; Carole Shammas, Marylynn Salmon, Michel Dahlin, *Inheritance in America From Colonial Times to the Present* (New Brunswick and London: Rutgers University Press, 1987); David E. Narrett, *Inheritance and Family Life in Colonial New York City* (Ithaca and London: Cornell University Press, 1992), 41–108.

33. Hughes, "Back Country," 57. The French settlement moved across the Mississippi River in order to avoid coming under British control. Some French settlements in Illinois, however, became British following the Seven Years' War and then found themselves in the United States at the conclusion of the War for Independence. Susan C. Boyle, "Did She Generally Decide? Women in Ste. Genevieve, 1750–1805," *William and Mary Quarterly*, 3rd ser., XLIV (October 1987), 775–89. For the experience of one woman long separated from her husband see Annette Kolodny, ed., "The Travel Diary of Elizabeth House Trist: Philadelphia to Natchez, 1782–1784," in Andrews, ed., *Journeys in New Worlds*, 183–232.

34. Wright, *African Americans*, 141.

35. Cabell, *Turff & Twigg*, 16, 73, 117–19; Will of Pierre Dutoy, Henrico County Deeds and Wills, October 10, 1726, Virginia State Archives.

36. Elizabeth Porter will, 22 June 1772, CCR, W, VSL; land purchases for the Porters are recorded on 17 February 1731/2, GCR, D/W and 27 November 1752, 22 May 1749, and 15 January 1744/5, CCR, D, VSL; Gundersen and Gampel, "Married Women's Legal Status," 120–27.

37. Daniel Branch will, 1782, PCR, W, VSL. Dutoy Branch received payments from the estate of Samuel Flournoy and Benjamin Harris for schooling children between 1779 and 1783. Estate account of Samuel Flournoy, 16 July 1795, PCR, W, and Benjamin Harris estate, [1786] CHCR, W, VSL.

38. Darret B. and Anita H. Rutman, *A Place in Time: Middlesex County, Virginia, 1650–1750* (New York: W.W. Norton & Co., 1984), 236. Maryanne Dutoy Lucadou Goss and her then-husband James Goss sold their holdings in the area between 1743 and 1752. Deed of James and Mary Anne Goss to Matthew Bingley, 20 March 1743/4 GCR, D/W, and deed of James and Mary Anne Goss to Mathew Bingley, 20 March 1743/4 GCR, D/W, and deed of James and Mary Anne Goss to Thomas Porter, 27 November 1752, CCR, D, VSL.

39. Hughes, "Back Country," 45–53; Lucy Watson's Account of New Settlers, 1762 (recollections being taken down by her son), Historical Society of Pennsylvania MSS. Bailyn, *Voyagers*, 10, 54–55, 478; Richard Morris, "Urban Population Migration in Revolutionary America: The Case of Salem, Massachusetts, 1759–1799," *The Journal of Urban History*, IX (November 1982): 18.

40. Bailyn, *Voyagers*, 12–14, 55–56.

41. Daniel Guerrant's mother was a Trabue by birth. Trabue was in Kentucky by 1774 scouting land for himself and others. Chester Raymond Young, *Westward into Kentucky: the Narrative of Daniel Trabue* (Lexington: University Press of Kentucky, 1981); Kulikoff, *Tobacco and Slaves*, 77, 145–55; Bailyn, *Voyagers*, 537.

42. Richard White, *The Middle Ground: Indians, Empire, and Republics in the Great Lakes Region, 1650–1815* (New York: Cambridge University Press, 1991), 323–24.

43. Guldenzopf, "Mohawk," 47, 55, 61–71, 69, 166; Kelsay, *Joseph Brant*.

44. Guldenzopf, "Mohawk," 71–72, 96–97, 137, 166; Kelsay, *Joseph Brant*, 614–15; Graymont, *The Iroquois in the American Revolution*, 10–11, 290–91.

45. Kelsay says that Margaret and Joseph lived in a small house built by Margaret's husband Brant and that Molly Brant built a new house next to theirs after William Johnson's death. Guldenzopf's archaeological excavations showed two structures and a barn. He identified the smaller structure as a summer kitchen, but noted that Molly Brant called it a second house. This is probably Margaret's cabin. Molly listed her belongings when she had to leave many of them behind during the Revolution. Kelsay, *Joseph Brant*, 39–52, 68, 114, 140; Guldenzopf, "Mohawk," 103–7.

46. Merrell, *Indian's New World*, 106; Marshall J. Becker, "Hannah Freeman: an Eighteenth-Century Lenape Living and Working Among Colonial Farmers," *Pennsylvania Magazine of History and Biography*, CXIV (April 1990): 249–53, 259. Becker sees Hannah's family as cut off from traditional ways, but the map he provides showing the summering places of the Lenape and the moves he describes for Hannah's family suggest an adaptation of traditional seasonal moves.

47. Merrell, *The Indian's New World*, 24, 95–108, 112, 125, 195–98; Nash, *Red, White, and Black*, 241–42; Hughes, "Back Country," 63.

48. White, *The Middle Ground*, 187–88, 329; Daniel Usner, *Indians, Settlers, and Slaves in a Frontier Exchange Economy: the Lower Mississippi Valley before 1783* (Chapel Hill: University of North Carolina Press for the Institute of Early American History and Culture, 1992).

49. Kathryn E. Holland Braund, "The Creek Indians, Blacks and Slavery," *Journal of Southern History*, LVII (November 1991): 619–20; Merrell, *Indian's New World*, 31; Usner, *Exchange Economy*.

50. Merrell, *Indian's New World*, 31; Usner, *Exchange Economy*; Graymont, *Iroquois in the Revolution*, 30.

51. White, *The Middle Ground*, 333.

52. Spruill, *Women's Life and Work in the Southern Colonies*, 242–43; Margaret Connell Szasz, *Indian Education in the American Colonies, 1607–1783* (Albuquerque: University of New Mexico Press, 1988), 156–58, 165; Merrell, *Indian's New World*, 24, 87, 123; White, *The Middle Ground*, 189, 213; Usner, *Exchange Economy*.

53. Perdue, *Slavery and Cherokee Society*, 29.

54. Gregory Evans Dowd, "Paths of Resistance: American Indian Religion and the Quest for Unity, 1745–1815, Vols. 1 & 2" (Ph.D diss., Princeton University, 1986), 84.

55. Perdue, *Slavery and Cherokee Society*, 11; John C. Dann, *The Revolution Remembered: Eyewitness Accounts of the War for Independence* (Chicago: University of Chicago Press, 1980), 269; Graymont, *Iroquois*, 189; Seaver, *Jemison*, 24–31; "Martin's Station," *The Huguenot*, XXX (1983–1985).

56. Graymont, *Iroquois*, 18; Seaver, *A Narrative of the Life of Mrs. Mary Jemison* , 37–40; Dann, *Revolution Remembered*, 269.

57. Axtell, *Indian Peoples*, 154.

58. White, *The Middle Ground*, 243, 301–4; Nash, *Red, White, and Black*, 252–54.

59. Dowd, "Paths of Resistance," 159, 162, 196–211, 256–63; Nash, *Red, White, and Black*, 232–55; White, *The Middle Ground*, 344–48.

60. Dowd, "Paths of Resistance," 159, 249–56; Guldenzopf, "Mohawk," 67–69.

61. Kelsay, *Joseph Brant*, 54–68; Graymont, *Iroquois*, 30.

62. Smaby, *Moravian*, 99; Becker, "Hannah Freeman," 259–60.

63. Hughes, "Back Country," 33; Eliza Lucas Pinckney, *The Letterbook of Eliza Lucas Pinckney*, edited by Elise Pinckney with assistance by Marvin R. Zahniser and an introduction by Walter Muir Whitehill (Chapel Hill: University of North Carolina Press, 1972), 146–49.

64. Nash, *The Urban Crucible*, 113–14, 149–55.

65. Kelsay, *Joseph Brant*, 203–8; Hamilton, "Mary Brant," 230; Graymont, *The Iroquois*, 147–59.

66. Kelsay, *Joseph Brant*, 149–50, 225–72; Hamilton, "Mary Brant," 230; Graymont, *The Iroquois*, 147–61.

67. White, *The Middle Ground*, 358.

68. Dowd, "Paths of Resistance," 357–70; Graymont, *Iroquois*, 253; White, *The Middle Ground*, 384–89; Colin Calloway, "The Shawnees' Revolution" (paper presented at the Annual Meeting of the Organization of American Historians, Washington, D.C., 1990), 6.

69. Linda K. Kerber, *Women of the Republic: Intellect and Ideology in Revolutionary America* (Chapel Hill: University of North Carolina Press for the Institute of Early American History and Culture, 1980), 48; Braund, "The Creek Indians, Blacks and Slavery," 618–19.

70. Graymont, *Iroquois*, 190; Braund, "The Creek Indians, Blacks and Slavery," 618–19, 621; Perdue, *Slavery and the Evolution of Cherokee Society*, 9–11, 629.

71. Frederic R. Kirkland, ed., "Three Mecom-Franklin Letters," *Pennsylvania Magazine of History and Biography*, LXXII (July 1948): 267n; Whitfield J. Bell Jr., "Sarah Franklin Bache," 76.

72. Norton, *Liberty's Daughters*, 157; also Norton, "A Cherished Spirit of Independence: The Life of an Eighteenth-Century Boston Businesswoman," in Carol Berkin and Mary Beth Norton, *Women of America: A History* (Boston: Houghton Mifflin, 1979), 55; and Norton, "Eighteenth-Century American Women in Peace and War: The Case of the Loyalists," *William and Mary Quarterly*, 3rd ser., XXXIII (January 1976): 400–401.

73. George C. Chalou, "Women in the American Revolution: Vignettes or Profiles," in Deutrich and Purdy, *Clio Was a Woman*, 58–59; Chester W. Gregory, "Black Women in Pre-Federal America," in ibid., 58–59; Kruger, "Born to Run," 636, 659–68; Ira Berlin, *Slaves Without Masters: The Free Negro in the Antebellum South* (New York, Vintage Books, 1976), 16–19; Mary Beth Norton, *Liberty's Daughters*, 209–11; Sylvia R. Frey, *Water From the Rock: Black Resistance in a Revolutionary Age* (Princeton, NJ: Princeton University Press, 1991), 193.

Chapter 3

1. The phrase appears in a letter of E[lizabeth] Fergusson to Mrs. Smith, 21 April 1792, Society Collections, Historical Society of Pennsylvania.

2. For wedding customs see Spruill, *Women's Life and Work in the Southern Colonies*, 86–87, 111; Mary Maples Dunn, "Women of Light," in Carol Berkin and Mary Beth Norton, eds., *Women of America: A History*, 124–28; Joan R. Gundersen, "The Non-Institutional Church: The Religious Roles of Women in Eighteenth-Century Virginia," *Historical Magazine* of the Protestant Episcopal Church, LI (December 1982): 349–50. Contemporary accounts include Mary Cooper Diary, 24 April 1771, Field Horne, ed., *The Diary of Mary Cooper: Life on a Long Island Farm 1768–1773* (Oyster Bay, NY: Oyster Bay Historical Society, 1981), 31; Sally Fisher to Sally Fisher, 16 December 1781, John A. H. Sweeney, ed., "The Norris-Fisher Correspondence: A Circle of Friends, 1779–1782," *Delaware History*, VI (1954–1955): 224–26; Jeffry Watson Diary, 30 January 1757, Edward M. Cook Jr., "Jeffry Watson's Diary, 1740–1784: Family, Community, Religion and Politics in Colonial Rhode Island," *Rhode Island History*, XLIII (August 1984): 100. For a warning against "immoderate feasting" at weddings, see Philadelphia Yearly Meeting Decisions, 1747, Book of Discipline, [Westbury, Long Island] Society of Friends, New York Historical Society MSS.

3. Most of the marriages and births are recorded in William Douglass, *The Douglass Register*, edited by W. Macfarlane Jones (Richmond: J.W. Ferguson & Sons, 1928). Underage Anne chose her husband as her guardian just

before they married. See 26 October 1767, CCR Order Book, VSL. There is no record of Elizabeth's marriage to Daniel Branch, but she was married by 1752 when her uncle, Isaac Dutoy, left her a bequest in his will. Isaac Dutoy will, March 1752, CCR, W, VSL.

4. Kulikoff, *Tobacco and Slaves*, 46–47, 55–56, 213; James Gallman, "Relative Ages of Colonial Marriages," *Journal of Interdisciplinary History*, XIV (Winter, 1984): 611–12, 615; Susan Edith Klepp, "Philadelphia in Transition: A Demographic History of the City and Its Occupational Groups, 1720–1830," (Ph.D. dissertation, University of Pennsylvania, 1980) 79–80; Robert V. Wells, "Marriage Seasonals in Early America: Comparisons and Comments," *Journal of Interdisciplinary History*, XVIII (Autumn, 1987): 302–7.

5. Turnbull, "William Dunlap" 143–49, 157.

6. Hawke, *Franklin*, 255; Van Doren, *Benjamin Franklin*, 359; Marylynn Salmon, "Equality or Submersion? Feme Covert Status in Early Pennsylvania," in Berkin and Norton, *Women of America: A History*, 95–96; Turnbull, "William Dunlap" 143–46; Eugenia W. Herbert, "A Note on Richard Bache (1737–1811)," *Pennsylvania Magazine of History and Biography*, C (January 1976): 85.

7. Klepp, "Philadelphia in Transition," 65–75; Kruger, "Born to Run," 404. Studies of slaves in plantation areas suggest that enslaved women in those areas had a child or two in their teens, and then settled into a marriage in their 20s.

8. Kelsay, *Joseph Brant*, 68, 77, 105, 140; Hamilton, "Mary Brant," 229–30.

9. For descriptions of the role of matrons and families in Indian marriages and for courtship customs see Kelsay, *Joseph Brant*, 108; James Axtell, ed., *The Indian People of Eastern America: A Documentary History of the Sexes* (New York: Oxford University Press, 1981), 81, 90–91; Mary E. Young, "Women, Civilization, and the Indian Question," in Deutrich and Purdy, *Clio Was a Woman*, 106–7. What Catherine Weissenberg and Mary Brant thought of each other is not recorded.

10. For a discussion of the factors inhibiting family formation among blacks see Lee, "Social Order," 181, 343–55. In the Virginia Piedmont the sex ratios were more balanced or had a surplus of women because more girls than boys were among the younger slaves most often purchased by Piedmont planters. In addition, larger planters often shifted their women and children to plantations in the Piedmont where the soil was fresher and better able to support tobacco. Adult males stayed on the older tidewater plantations to grow grain crops. Morgan and Nicholls, "Slaves in Piedmont Virginia, 1720–1790," 221–24; Gregory, "Black Women in Pre-Federal America," 56; Kruger, "Born to Run," 305; Frey, *Water From the Rock*, 33–34.

11. The white population also did not provide Amy with marriage options. Marriage between a black and white was illegal. While an unsanctioned relationship was possible, the evidence for racial mixing in the eighteenth-century Piedmont is limited. Few mulattos appear on inventories. Even *if* evidence

existed for Amy (such as a mulatto child), it would not prove that Amy had entered a voluntary relationship.

12. Gregory, "Black Women in Pre-Federal America," 56; Morgan and Nicholls, "Slaves in Piedmont Virginia, 1720–1790," 221–24; Lee, "Social Order," 294–98; Cheryll Ann Cody, "There Was No 'Absalom' on the Ball Plantations: Slave-Naming Practices in the South Carolina Low Country, 1720–1865," *American Historical Review*, XCII (June 1987): 576; Jean R. Soderlund, "Black Women in Colonial Pennsylvania," *The Pennsylvania Magazine of History and Biography*, CVII (January 1983): 54; Gundersen, "The Double Bonds of Race and Sex," 355–57.

13. See, for example, the short courtships of Esther Edwards and Aaron Burr and of Mary Fish and John Noyes. Carol F. Karlsen and Laurie Crumpacker, *The Journal of Esther Edwards Burr, 1754–1757* (New Haven: Yale University Press, 1984), 6–18; Joy Day Buel and Richard Buel, Jr., *The Way of Duty: A Woman and Her Family in Revolutionary America* (New York: W.W. Norton & Co., 1984), 22.

14. Rutman and Rutman, *A Place in Time*; Daniel Blake Smith, *Inside the Great House: Planter Family Life in Eighteenth-Century Chesapeake Society* (Ithaca and London: Cornell University Press, 1980), 140–51; for family urging a visit see Jemima Condict Harrison diary in Elizabeth Evans, *Weathering the Storm: Women of the American Revolution* (New York: Charles Scribner's Sons, 1975), 38. For examples of family negotiations on a widow's remarriage, see Buel and Buel, *The Way of Duty*, 66, and the negotiations of Mary and Catherine Alexander with Walter Rutherford in Paula D. Christenson, "The Colonial Family in New York: A Study of Middle and Upper Class Interpersonal and Insitutional Relationships" (Ph.D. diss., SUNY Albany, 1984), 22.

15. Smaby, *The Transformation of Moravian Bethlehem*, 159–60; Thorp, *The Moravian Community in Colonial North Carolina*, 20, 65–67; Mary Maples Dunn, "Women of Light," in Berkin and Norton, eds., *Women of America*, 128–29; Barry Levy, *Quakers and the American Family: British Settlement in the Delaware Valley* (New York: Oxford University Press, 1988), 132–34, 195, 238–39, 253. For a Quaker woman who left her church for marrying out of meeting see Evans, *Weathering the Storm*, 248.

16. For examples of family delaying tactics see Buel and Buel, *The Way of Duty*, 34–36; J. A. Leo Lemay, ed., *Robert Bolling Woos Anne Miller: Love and Courtship in Colonial Virginia, 1760* (Charlottesville: University Press of Virginia, 1990), 10–13; Charles W. Akers, *Abigail Adams: An American Woman* (Boston: Little, Brown and Company, 1980), 78–79.

17. Klepp, "Philadelphia in Transition," 97–98.

18. Gregory, "Black Women in Pre-Federal America," 56; Morgan and Nicholls, "Slaves in Piedmont Virginia, 1720–1790," 221–24; Lee, "Social Order," 294–98; Cody, "There Was No 'Absalom' on the Ball Plantations,"

576; Soderlund, "Black Women," 54; Gundersen, "The Double Bonds of Race and Sex," 355–57.

19. Elizabeth Ashbridge married a man in New York, for example, who fell in love with her for her dancing. Shea, ed., "Life of Elizabeth Ashbridge," 153–54; John D'Emilio and Estelle B. Freedman, *Intimate Matters: A History of Sexuality in America* (New York: Harper & Row, 1988), 21, 42; Laurel Thatcher Ulrich, *Good Wives: Image and Reality in the Lives of Women in Northern New England, 1650–1750* (New York: Alfred A. Knopf, 1982), 122–23; Deborah Norris to Sarah Wister, [December 26, 1778], Kathryn Zabelle Derounian, " 'A Dear Dear Friend': Six Letters from Deborah Norris to Sarah Wister, 1778–1779," *Pennsylvania Magazine of History and Biography*, CVIII (October 1984): 506; Esther Edwards Burr Journal, 21 June, 1757, Karlsen and Crumpacker, eds., *The Journal of Esther Edwards Burr*, 265; Lemay, *Robert Bolling Woos Anne Miller*, 2–7, 52–56.

20. See, for example, Dayton, "Women Before the Bar," 91–92; Burnston, "Babies in the Well," 183–84.

21. For a detailed study of one tragic abortion case involving prominent families in Connecticut see Cornelia Dayton, " 'Taking the Trade': Abortion and Gender Relations in an Eighteenth-Century New England Village," *William and Mary Quarterly*, 3rd ser., XLVIII (January 1991): 19–49. For a classic example of a couple circumventing family objections, see Robert Gross, *The Minutemen and Their World* (New York: Hill and Wang, 1976), 99–101. D'Emilio and Freedman, *Intimate Matters*, 5, 41–47; Stephanie Grauman Wolf, *Urban Village: Population, Community, and Family Structure in Germantown, Pennsylvania, 1683–1800* (Princeton: Princeton University Press, 1976), 222; Klepp, "Philadelphia in Transition," 93. Klepp's figures may be high due to her method of figuring premarital pregnancy.

22. Klepp, "Philadelphia in Transition," 87–95; Wolf, *Urban Village*, 258; D'Emilio and Freedman, *Intimate Matters*, 43, 72.

23. D'Emilio and Freedman, *Intimate Matters*, 43–47, 72; Ulrich, *Good Wives*; Jan Lewis argues that the Revolutionary rhetoric eventually turned a woman's sexual powers into a virtue, for a virtuous woman could use that sexuality to seduce men into virtuous lives and actions. The reverse of this was also possible. If men were completely immune to a woman's virtue, she was helpless and would be seduced. A woman's power only worked if the man had a conscience. Jan Lewis, "The Republican Wife: Virtue and Seduction in the Early Republic," *William and Mary Quarterly*, 3rd ser., XLIV (October 1987): 700–702, 715. Mary Beth Norton argued that women were restrained during courtship in order to preserve their purity and thus their value in the marriage market. Her evidence, however, is heavily from the 1780s, by which time the new internal controls were beginning to emerge. Evidence suggests less restraint before the final quarter of the century. Norton, *Liberty's Daughters*, 50–53.

24. Peter Hoffer, *Law and People in Colonial America* (Baltimore and London: Johns Hopkins University Press, 1992), 76.

25. Margaret was disciplined by the Anglican Church for adultery with Brant Canagaraduncka. They married in an Anglican ceremony on September 9, 1753, six months after the baptism of their son Joseph. Kelsay, *Joseph Brant*, 30–31, 52, 68.

26. For evidence on the conducting of ceremonies after cohabitation and on couples ignoring church and legal forms see S. Charles Bolton, *Southern Anglicanism: The Church of England in Colonial South Carolina* (Westport, CT: Greenwood Press, 1982), 122; Helena M. Wall, *Fierce Communion: Family and Community in Early America* (Cambridge: Harvard University Press, 1990), 136. Kaylene Hughes argued that frontier couples in South Carolina eagerly sought to formalize their marriages. Her evidence, however, is of couples seeking marriage who had lived together a long time. I would argue that such couples saw formal ceremonies as a convenience but not a necessity. Hughes, *Populating the Back Country*, 124.

27. It is not technically correct to say that slaves could not marry. The records of the Anglican churches in Philadelphia include 29 marriages from 1727 to 1780 involving a slave. In New England slaves could and did marry. The special report of John Garzia, who served as an Anglican missionary in Virginia, reported marrying a slave couple in 1724. Most clergy, however, were reluctant to celebrate marriages for those who could be separated against their will. Soderlund, "Black Women," 54; Joan R. Gundersen, *The Anglican Ministry in Virginia, 1723–1766: A Study of a Social Class* (New York: Garland Press, 1989), 110–11.

28. For a discussion of marriage ceremonies among blacks, see Frey, *Water From the Rock*, 32–33.

29. The patterns of relationships and marriage have been studied more thoroughly for the Canadian fur trade. See Sylvia Van Kirk, *Many Tender Ties: Women in Fur Trade Society, 1670–1870* (Norman and London: University of Oklahoma Press, 1983), 9–122.

30. Smaby, *The Transformation of Moravian Bethlehem*, 55–57, 159–60; Thorp, *The Moravian Community in Colonial North Carolina*, 20, 44–45, 65–67.

31. Klepp, "Philadelphia in Transition," 119–21; Alexander Keyssar, "Widowhood in Eighteenth-Century Massachusetts: A Problem in the History of the Family," *Perspectives in American History*, VIII (1974): 88–90; Lisa Wilson Waciega, "Widowhood and Womanhood in Early America," xii-xiv; Kulikoff, *Tobacco and Slaves*, 172. For two women who turned down such offers see Eliza Lucas Pinckney to Mrs. King, 27 February 1762, in Pinckney, ed., *The Letterbook of Eliza Lucas Pinckney*, 175–76 and Buel and Buel, *The Way of Duty*, 60–66, 85.

32. Lee Chambers-Schiller dates the shift in values slightly later, the 1780s, crediting the American Revolution with a language of liberty that some women

applied to their status. The evidence here suggests an earlier date, but one still tied to political theories of liberty that undergirded the War for Independence. Lee Virginia Chambers-Schiller, *Liberty, a Better Husband, Single Women in America: The Generations of 1780–1840* (New Haven: Yale University Press, 1984), 10–15.

33. Mary Beth Norton discusses this rhetoric in her study of women in the Revolution, but treats it as an effect of the Revolution. However, the rhetorical tie of liberty to singleness and marriage to bondage appears in writings before independence (see the examples cited in this note). Norton, *Liberty's Daughters*, 240–42; Pattie Cowell, ed., " 'Womankind Call Reason to Their Aid': Susanna Wright's Verse Epistle on the Status of Women in Eighteenth-Century America," in *Signs: Journal of Women in Culture and Society*, VI (Summer 1981): 799–800; Buel and Buel, *The Way of Duty*, 88; Esther Burr, Journal Entry, 21 June 1757, Karlsen and Crumpacker, eds., *The Journal of Esther Edwards Burr*, 265.

34. Joan R. Gundersen, "Independence, Citizenship, and the American Revolution," *Signs: Journal of Women in Culture and Society*, XIII (1987): 59–77.

35. Gundersen and Gampel, "Married Women's Legal Status in Eighteenth-Century New York and Virginia," 114–34; Salmon, *Women and the Law of Property in Early America*. Salmon's study demonstrates that the actual terms of dower varied from colony to colony and that paraphernalia was not claimed in all states. In Connecticut women could not make postnuptial agreements with their husbands, and the "jointure" was the major property claim available to women. Jointures could be claimed only upon the death of a husband.

36. Elizabeth Dabney Coleman, "Two Lees, Revolutionary Suffragists," *Virginia Cavalcade*, III (Autumn 1953); Gundersen, "Independence, Citizenship, and the American Revolution," 74–75.

37. Gundersen, "Independence, Citizenship, and the American Revolution," 75; Norton, *Liberty's Daughters*, 136; Salmon, *Women and the Law of Property*, 94–95, 112–15, 123–28, 133–34, 149. Salmon and I interpret her evidence differently. She sees the net effect of the changes as improving women's status by emphasizing the increased sense of companionship with a husband. I find a loss of control.

38. Hawke, *Franklin*, 38. See the negotiations as reported in Spruill between Bernard Moore and Thomas Walker. In this case John Walker's courtship of Elizabeth Moore proved successful. Spruill, *Women's Life and Work in the Southern Colonies*, 146–47.

39. See, for example, the wills of Peter David and Elizabeth Moracet. Peter David will, signed 21 December 1781, recorded [1785] Henry County Will Book 1; Elizabeth Moracet will, signed 7 December 1746, recorded 2 March 1750/1, CHCR, W, VSL.

40. Marylynn Salmon, "Women and Property in South Carolina: The Evidence from Marriage Settlements, 1730–1830," *William and Mary Quarterly*,

3rd ser., XXXIX (October 1982): 655–722; Salmon, "Equality or Submersion? Feme Covert Status in Early Pennsylvania," in Berkin and Norton, *Women of America*, 98–101.

41. Axtell, ed., *The Indian Peoples of Eastern America*, 80; Carol A. Devens, "Separate Confrontations: Indian Women and Christian Missions, 1630–1900" (Ph.D. diss., Rutgers University, 1986), 28.

42. Salmon, *Women and the Law of Property in Early America*, 60–61.

43. Klepp, "Philadelphia in Transition," 113–16; Spruill, *Women's Life and Work in the Southern Colonies*, 183. For an example of a woman who remarried following her husband's desertion and later sought a Revolutionary war pension based on the service of both men, see Dann, *The Revolution Remembered*, 248–50.

44. Nancy Cott, "Divorce and the Changing Status of Women in Eighteenth-Century Massachusetts," *William and Mary Quarterly*, 3rd ser., XXXIII (October 1976): 587–91; Salmon, *Women and the Law of Property*, 61–62; Frank L. Dewey, "Thomas Jefferson's Notes on Divorce," *William and Mary Quarterly*, 3rd ser., XXXIX (January 1982): fn214.

45. Sheldon S. Cohen, "The Broken Bond: Divorce in Providence County, 1749–1809," *Rhode Island History*, XLIV (August 1985): 68–70; Kerber, *Women of the Republic*, 161; Dayton, "Women Before the Bar," 285, 292–96, 304–6; Cott, "Divorce and Changing Status," 606.

46. Cott, "Divorce and Changing Status," 587–91, 599–606; Nancy Cott, "Eighteenth-Century Family and Social Life Revealed in Massachusetts Divorce Records," in Nancy F. Cott and Elizabeth H. Pleck, *A Heritage of Her Own* (New York: Simon and Schuster, 1979), 123–24; Frank L. Dewey, "Thomas Jefferson and a Williamsburg Scandal: The Case of Blair v. Blair," *Virginia Magazine of History and Biography*, LXXXIX (January 1981): 44–63.

47. Salmon ties the English instructions on divorce received by colonial governors to the disallowance of the Pennsylvania law. Cott links it to actions in Massachusetts, New Hampshire, and New Jersey, as well. I would add the furor over Blair v. Blair in Virginia to the provocations.

48. Kerber, *Women of the Republic*, 181; Salmon, *Women and the Law of Property*, 63–67.

49. Salmon, *Women and the Law of Property*, 63–83.

50. Sarah Cantwell's advertisement March 27, 1776, as cited in Spruill, *Women's Life and Labor*, 180–82; Dayton, "Women Before the Bar," 285–306; Kerber, *Women of the Republic*, 178–79; Cott, "Divorce and Changing Status," 592, 599–606.

51. See Mary Cooper's diary entries for 13 July 1769, 16 July 1769, 17 August 1769, 23 August 1772, 24 August 1772, 31 August 1772, 11 January 1773, in Horne, ed., *The Diary of Mary Cooper*, 15, 17, 38, 48.

52. Ann Taves, ed., *Religion and Domestic Violence in Early New England: The Memoirs of Abigail Abbot Bailey* (Bloomington: Indiana University Press, 1989),

76–89. Taves does not connect the incidents of adultery and incest to Abigail's pregnancy. That connection is mine, after correlation of information on the birth of her children with times she noted Asa's sexual advances toward other women.

53. Salmon, *Women and the Law of Property*, 53–54.

54. Kerber, *Women of the Republic*, 170–80; Cohen, "The Broken Bond," 77.

55. Dayton, "Women Before the Bar," 323; Cott, "Divorce and Changing Status," 611.

56. Journal Entry, 21 June 1757, Karlsen and Crumpacker, eds., *The Journal of Esther Edwards Burr*, 265. For a similar comment by Mary Fish, see Buel and Buel, *The Way of Duty*, 37, 80.

57. For the Franklin poem, see Van Doren, *Franklin*, 148. The full inscription reads "Violate by sale slave of Amos Fortune by Marriage his wife by her fidelity his friend and [ ] she died his widow." Sidney Kaplan, *The Black Presence in the Era of the American Revolution*, 262. For another example of a woman who expected marriage to be friendship, see Taves, ed., *Religion and Domestic Violence in Early New England*, 56.

58. Frances Bland to Frances Bland Randolph, ca. 1770–1771, Tucker-Coleman Papers, Swem Library, College of William and Mary. Jeffry Watson Journal entry, 2 April 1756, in Cook, "Jeffry Watson's Diary, 1740–1784," 99.

59. Ulrich, *Good Wives*, 238; D'Emilio and Freedman, *Intimate Matters*, 43.

60. Cohen, "The Broken Bond: Divorce in Providence," 77.

61. Deborah Norris to Sarah Wister, [18 April 1778] in Derounian, " 'A Dear Dear Friend,' " 501–2.

62. D'Emilio and Freedman, *Intimate Matters*, 40–43.

63. Lewis, "The Republican Wife," 704; Kerber, *Women of the Repbulic*, 269–83; Akers, *Abigail Adams*, 115.

64. Dewey, "Thomas Jefferson and a Williamsburg Scandal," 44–63; Dewey, "Thomas Jefferson's Notes on Divorce," 212–23.

65. C.B. [Kitty Eustace Blair] to [Anne Blair Bannister] 18 July 1772, Tucker-Coleman Papers, Earl Gregg Swem Library, College of William and Mary. Kitty and James Blair's suit for divorce pulled in many of Virginia's leading families.

66. There is a very revealing set of letters on Blair v. Blair in the Tucker-Coleman Papers. St. George Tucker was a friend of Dr. James Blair. See C.B. [Kitty Eustace Blair] to [Anne Blair] 18 July 1772; [St. George Tucker] to Mrs. [Kitty Eustace] Blair, 23 September 1772; St. George Tucker to Doct[o]r [James] Blair, 21 September 1772; [Dr.] James Blair to St. George Tucker, 16 September 1772; [St. George Tucker to Dr. James Blair] 20 September 1772, in Tucker-Coleman Papers, College of William and Mary.

67. The information on the Porters is pieced together from wills and church records in Cumberland and Powhatan counties. Marie Porter married Daniel Guerrant in 1770. The last date she appears in records is 1775, when she

and Daniel witnessed a neighbor's will. Daniel's will names five children and a wife Elizabeth. The children include a son named Thomas Porter. Given family naming patterns two other children may have been Marie's, but it seems likely she was dead by 1780. Sara Porter Hatcher registered births of three children born in 1764, 1767, and 1777 in St. James Northam records. Her father willed her land in Buckingham County, and other children may have been recorded there. Elizabeth Porter Branch had her last child in 1768. She was alive in 1772 when her mother died, but she died before her husband in 1782. Magdalene Chastain Porter had children born in 1765, 1767, 1770, 1772, and 1774. Her husband died in 1775. Ann Porter Sampson had her first child in 1768, had one other child, and was pregnant with a third when her husband died in 1776. Sarah Watkins Porter and her husband John had nine children before he died in 1784 at age 50. The youngest child was about four. See John Porter will, 16 September 1784, PCR, W; Charles Sampson will, 19 February 1775, GCR, D/W; Thomas Porter will, 27 April 1787, CCR, W; Elizabeth Porter will, 22 June 1772, CCR, W; Daniel Branch will, 15 August 1782, PCR, W; Peter Harris will, 28 August 1775, CCR, W; William Porter will, 28 August 1775, CCR, W; Daniel Guerrant will, 1802, CCR, W, VSL. For Deborah Dunlap, see Turnbull, "William Dunlap, Colonial Printer, Journalist and Minister," 161–63. For Molly Brant see Kelsay, *Joseph Brant*, 140. For Sarah Bache, a convenient source of information is Bell, "Sarah Franklin Bache," 75–76.

68. For examples of these patterns and the variations due to infant mortality and the Revolution, see Buel and Buel, *The Way of Duty*, 34, 42, 133, 144; Judith Leavitt, *Brought to Bed: Childbearing in America, 1750–1950* (New York and London: Oxford University Press, 1986), 14–15; Barbara E. Lacey, "The World of Hannah Heaton: The Autobiography of an Eighteenth-Century Connecticut Farm Woman," *William and Mary Quarterly*, 3rd ser., XLV (April 1988): 296; Sally D. Mason, "Mama, Rachel, and Molly: Three Generations of Carroll Women," in Hoffman and Albert, *Women in the Age of the American Revolution*, 281–84. Susan Klepp computed completed family sizes for three generations of women in Philadelphia (pre-Revolutionary, Revolutionary, and post-Revolutionary). For the upper class these numbers were 7.7, 5.9, and 6.9, respectively. For the middle class they were 4.9, 5.4, 6.5; for the lower middle class, 6.2, 5.5, 4.6. Only the lower class showed an increase during the war, from 4.2 to 5.1. The size returned to 4.3 for the post-Revolutionary generation. Klepp, "Philadelphia in Transition," 206. Stephanie Grauman Wolf also reported a rise in fertility after the war. Wolf, *Urban Village*, 263–69. For Prince George County, see Kulikoff, *Tobacco and Slaves*, 58–59. There is some evidence for a mini-baby boom after the war. See J. Louge, "The Case for Birth Control before 1850: Nantucket Reexamined," *Journal of Interdisciplinary History*, XV (Winter 1985): 378. The study by Jan Lewis and Kenneth Lockridge of Virginia gentry women born 1710–1759 and 1760–1799 showed little variation, with both groups bearing on average about eight children. However, the

break points for this study mask any short-term changes during the Revolution. Jan Lewis and Kenneth A. Lockridge, " 'Sally Has Been Sick': Pregnancy and Family Limitation Among Virginia Gentry Women 1780–1830," *Journal of Social History*, XXII (Fall 1988): 5.

69. Sarah Porter Hatcher appears to have had an interrupted cycle of child-births. There was a 10-year interval between the births of daughters Sarah and Elizabeth Porter. *The Douglass Register*, 209. For interrupted patterns of child-birth, see Elaine F. Crane, "The World of Elizabeth Drinker," *The Pennsylvania Magazine of History and Biography*, CVII (January 1983): 27; Akers, *Abigail Adams*, 52; Klepp, "Philadelphia in Transition," 176–77; Constance B. Schulz, "Daughter of Liberty: The History of Women in the Revolutionary War Pension Records," *Prologue*, XVI (Fall 1984), 151.

70. Robert V. Wells, "Women's Lives Transformed: Demographic and Family Patterns in America, 1800–1970," in Berkin and Norton, *Women of America*, 27. For evidence on birth controls see Crane, "The World of Elizabeth Drinker," 11, 27; Akers, *Abigail Adams*, 26, 52; Lewis and Lockridge, " 'Sally Has Been Sick,' " 9–11; Smaby, *The Transformation of Moravian Bethlehem*, 73–75; Klepp, "Philadelphia in Transition," 176–77, 195; Norton, *Liberty's Daughters*, 233. For a fascinating and nuanced study of the social context of one particular fatal abortion, see Dayton, " 'Taking the Trade,' " 19–49.

71. Mason, "Mama, Rachel and Molly," in Hoffman and Albert, *Women in the Age of the American Revolution*, 281–84.

72. Esther Burr Journal, 7 August 1755, Karlsen and Crumpacker, eds., *The Journal of Esther Edwards Burr*, 142. For Mary Cooper's attendance at her neighbor's labor, see Mary Cooper Diary, 1 August 1772, 23 January 1773, 24 February 1773, 30 August 1773, in Horne, ed., *The Diary of Mary Cooper*, 39, 49, 66; see also Jeffry Watson Diary, 12 August 1743, Cook, ed., "Jeffry Watson's Diary," 96; Levitt, *Brought to Bed*, 89; Norton, *Liberty's Daughters*, 78–79; Laurel Thatcher Ulrich, " 'The Living Mother of a Living Child': Midwifery and Mortality in Post-Revolutionary New England," *William and Mary Quarterly*, 3rd ser., XLVI (January 1989): 30; Ulrich, *Good Wives*, 127–31; Buel and Buel, *The Way of Duty*, 159. For Indian birthing customs, see Axtell, ed., *The Indian Peoples of Eastern America*, 15, 18, 21, and Devens, "Separate Confrontations," 113.

73. Ulrich, " 'The Living Mother of a Living Child,' " 32–33. Four out of 37 women who married in Woburn, Massachusetts, between 1700 and 1710 died of illness associated with childbirth. Similarly, the causes of death for six out of 62 female deaths in Orangeburg and Amelia, South Carolina, between 1750 and 1761 were childbirth-related. Alexander Keyssar, "Widowhood in Eighteenth-Century Massachusetts: A Problem in the History of the Family," *Perspectives in American History*, VIII (1974): 89; Hughes, "Populating the Back Country," 91, 93.

74. Women's historians do not all agree on the causes of the shifts in birthing practice. Some focus on the benefits to physicians of capturing this

part of medical practice, others continue to grant women agency in the shift. See Levitt, *Brought to Bed*, 4–83; Ulrich, " 'The Living Mother of a Living Child,' " 27–48.

75. Deborah and Benjamin Franklin lost their son Francis in an epidemic. Three of Thomas and Elizabeth Porter's 10 children died before age 21. Margaret Brant lost at least a son and daughter. John and Sarah Watkins Porter also lost at least one child. The birth records for Peg are incomplete. Both children recorded in the Parish Register seem to have survived.

Chapter 4

1. On economic changes, see Thomas Doerflinger, "Farmers and Dry Goods in the Philadelphia Market Area, 1750–1800," in Hoffman, et al., eds., *The Economy of Early America*, 181; Russell B. Menard, "Slavery, Economic Growth and Revolutionary Ideology in the South Carolina Low Country," in ibid., 258–59; Bruce Mann, *Neighbors and Strangers: Law and Community in Early Connecticut* (Chapel Hill: University of North Carolina Press, 1987), 36–54.

2. Norton, "Eighteenth-Century American Women in Peace and War," 387–93. Elizabeth Drinker was one such woman who vocalized her insecurity while demonstrating extensive economic knowledge and activity; Elaine F. Crane, "The World of Elizabeth Drinker," *The Pennsylvania Magazine of History and Biography*, CVII (January 1983): 6–8. Lord Kaims, for example, commented that commerce was an area "which women are capable of as well as men." Henry Home, Lord Kaims, *Six Sketches on the History of Man, containing the Progress of Men as Individuals* (Philadelphia: R. Bell and R. Aitken, 1776). For women's participation see Ulrich, *Good Wives*, 38–39, 44–46; Boyle, "Did She Generally Decide?," 783–87; Taves, ed., *Religion and Domestic Violence in Early New England*, 65. For contrasting views of women's participation in shopping, see Kulikoff, *Tobacco and Slaves*, 225, and the Mary Coats Account Book, 1760–1770, Historical Society of Pennsylvania.

3. Dayton, "Women Before the Bar," 61–63,73–78; Toby Ditz, "Ownership and Obligation: Family and Inheritance in Five Connecticut Towns, 1750–1820" (Ph.D. diss., Columbia University, 1982), 337, 359–60; Gundersen and Gampel, "Married Women's Legal Status in Eighteenth-Century New York and Virginia," 116–33. On a widow managing estates, see Buel and Buel, *The Way of Duty*. On *feme sole* status, see Salmon, *Women and the Law of Property in Early America*, 46–47.

4. Norton, "Eighteenth-Century American Women in Peace and War," 391–92.

5. Kulikoff, *Tobacco and Slaves*, 399; Marvin L. Michael Kay and Lorin Lee Cary, "Slave Runaways in Colonial North Carolina, 1748–1775," *North Carolina Historical Review*, LXIII (January 1986): 14–17.

6. Tithe records suggest Peg apparently was hired out by Barbara Dutoy from 1726 to 1729 and in 1733 before Thomas and Elizabeth Porter took over the family farm for Barbara. King William Parish tithe lists, The Vestry Book of King William Parish; Gundersen, "The Double Bonds of Race and Sex," 363–67.

7. Jean Russo, "A Model Planter: Edward Lloyd of Maryland, 1770–1796," *William and Mary Quarterly*, 3rd ser., XLIX (January 1992): 81; Morgan and Nicholls, "Slaves in Piedmont Virginia, 1720–1790," 230–33; Wood, *Black Majority*, 35–62; Littlefield, *Rice and Slaves*, 145–56; Wright, *African Americans*, 103–12.

8. Lee, "Social Order," 46; Horne, ed., *The Diary of Mary Cooper*, 1; Pinckney, ed., *The Letterbook of Eliza Lucas Pinckney*, xix; John J. McCusker and Russell R. Menard, *The Economy of British America* (Chapel Hill: University of North Carolina Press for the Institute of Early American History and Culture, 1985), 187. For the seasonality of slaughtering, see Sarah F. McMahon, "A Comfortable Subsistence: The Changing Composition of diet in Rural New England, 1620–1840," *William and Mary Quarterly*, 3rd ser., XLII (January 1985), 26–65.

9. Linda Speth and Alison Duncan Hirsch, *Women, Family, and Community in Colonial America: Two Perspectives* (Institute for Research in History and the Haworth Press, Inc., 1982), 14; Norton, *Liberty's Daughters*, 12–13.

10. Schulz, "Daughter of Liberty," 146; Kellow, "Indentured Servitude in Eighteenth-Century Maryland," 229–54; Salinger, " 'Send No More Women,' " 30–33.

11. Mrs. Harnett of Hilton, South Carolina, in 1775 supplied the town with vegetables, pies, tarts, cheesecake, biscuits, eggs, poultry, and butter. Spruill, *Women's Life and Work in the Southern Colonies*, 64; Mary Cooper Diary, 20 August 1772, 5 October 1772, 3 November 1772, 13 June 1773, in Horne ed., *The Diary of Mary Cooper: Life on a Long Island Farm 1768–1773*, 38–43, 60; Letters of Eliza Farmer to Jack, 16 May 1774 and 19 September 1774, Eliza Farmer Letterbook, 1774–1777, 1783–1789, Historical Society of Pennsylvania.

12. This market crossed racial lines. See Norton, *Liberty's Daughters*, 32; Barbara Clark Smith, "Food Rioters and the American Revolution," *William and Mary Quarterly*, 3rd ser., LI (January 1994), 26.

13. For other evidence on women's role in the poultry and egg market, see Carole Shammas, "Black Women's Work and the Evolution of Plantation Society in Virginia," *Labor History*, XXVI (Winter 1985): 16; Jones, "Race, Sex, and Self-Evident Truths," in Hoffman and Albert, *Women in the Age of the American Revolution*, 312; [H. Mann], *The Female Review: or, Memoirs of an American Young Lady; Whose Life and Character are Peculiarly Distinguished—Being a Continental Soldier for Nearly three years, ...* (Dedham: Nathaniel and Benjamin Heaton, 1797), 60–61.

14. Spruill, *Women's Life and Work in the Southern Colonies*, 65–66; Sally Cary Fairfax Diary, 16 January 1772, [Sally Cary Fairfax], "Diary of a Little Colonial Girl," *Virginia Magazine of History and Biography*, XI (1903–1904): 212–14.

15. McMahon, "A Comfortable Subsistence," 38; when the Washingtons contracted with Edward Violett as overseer in 1762, the contract expressly provided that his wife would tend a dairy in exchange for one-quarter of the butter produced. Spruill, *Women's Life and Work in the Southern Colonies*, 64–77.

16. In 18 months the Rev. Medad Rogers traded more than 450 pounds of cheese paid to him as salary. James Henretta, "The War for Independence and American Economic Development," in Hoffman, et al., ed., *The Economy of Early America*, 79.

17. Mary Beth Norton, "The Evolution of White Women's Experience in Early America," *American Historical Review*, LXXXIX (June 1984): 604–5. For evidence of women milking as well as making cheese and butter see Lacey, "The World of Hannah Heaton," 295. On the growth of markets see Mann, *Neighbors and Strangers*, 47–52.

18. Pinckney, ed., *The Letterbook of Eliza Lucas Pinckney, 1739–1762*, xx–xxi, and letters 2 May 1740 and 20 September 1741. Lee, "Social Order," 92, 344; Ditz, "Ownership and Obligation," 184; Waciega, "A 'Man of Business,' " 47–48; Gundersen and Gampel, "Married Women's Property Rights in Eighteenth-Century Virginia and New York," 116–18, 130–31.

19. Perdue, *Slavery and the Evolution of Cherokee Society*, 16; Guldenzopf, "Mohawk," 20; Merrell, *The Indian's New World*, 37, 126; Graymont, *The Iroquois in the American Revolution*, 10–11.

20. Nash, *Red, White, and Black*, 237; Merrell, *The Indian's New World*, 126; White, *The Middle Ground*, 493; Graymont, *The Iroquois in the American Revolution*, 290–91; Becker, "Hannah Freeman," 251.

21. Dowd, *Paths of Resistance*, 171; Guldenzopf, "Mohawk," 77–81, 107, 166; Kelsay, *Joseph Brant*, 528–31.

22. For the tithe exemption, see William Waller Hening, *Statutes at Large*, 1767; Gloria Main, "Gender, Work and Wages in Colonial New England," *William and Mary Quarterly*, 3rd ser., LI (January 1994): 39–66.

23. Thomas Porter estate inventory, 28 May 1767; Elizabeth Porter estate inventory, 18 August 1772; William Porter estate inventory, 18 October 1775; Thomas Porter will, 27 April 1767; William Porter will, 28 August 1775; Elizabeth Porter will, 22 June 1772, all in CCR, W, VSL.

24. Eric G. Nellis, "Misreading the Signs: Industrial Imitation, Poverty, and the Social Order in Colonial Boston," *New England Quarterly*, XLIX (December 1986): 503–4; Doerflinger, "Farmers and Dry Goods in the Philadelphia Market Area," in Hoffman, et al., eds., *The Economy of Early America*, 177; Lee, "Social Order," 51; Merrell, *The Indian's New World*, 210; Mary

H. Blewett, "Work, Gender and the Artisan Tradition in New England Shoe-making, 1780–1860," *The Journal of Social History*, 224.

25. White, *The Middle Ground*, 132–40; Guldenzopf, "Mohawk," 78–81; Lee, "Social Order," 51; Main, "Gender, Work and Wages in Colonial New England," 39–66.

26. Thomas Porter inventory, 27 July 1767, CCR, W, VSL; Elizabeth Porter inventory, 26 April 1773, ibid.; and William Porter inventory, 23 October 1775, ibid.

27. For the exchange of skills, see Norton, *Liberty's Daughters* (1980), 15–18; Lee, "Social Order," 50; Mason, "Mama, Rachel and Molly," in Hoffman and Albert, *Women in the Age of the American Revolution*, 280; E. Feilde to [Mrs. Maria Carter Armistead], 3 [January] 1776, Armistead-Cocke Papers, Earl Gregg Swem Library, College of William and Mary.

28. Shammas, "Black Women's Work," 13, 23; Wolf, *Urban Village*, 117–18; A. J. Williams-Myers, "Hands That Picked No Cotton: An Exploratory Examination of African Slave Labor in the Colonial Economy of the Hudson River Valley to 1800," *Afro-Americans in New York Life and History*, XI (July 1987): 37. Esther Burr, for example, spun only at frolics; Karlsen and Crumpacker, eds., *The Journal of Esther Edwards Burr*, 27. Spruill, *Women's Life and Work in the Southern Colonies*, 16–17, 75, 80; Sobel, *The World They Made Together*, 49.

29. James Henretta, "The War for Independence and American Economic Development," in Hoffman, et al., eds., *The Economy of Early America*, 53, 59, 66–67; Norton, *Liberty's Daughters*, 164; Russo, "A Model Planter," 76; Jean Blair to Mrs. [Mary Blair] Braxton, 14 October 1769, Blair, Banister, Braxton papers, Earl Gregg Swem Library, College of William and Mary. Thomas Randolph gives the wages for a woman weaver. Thomas Randoph to Mrs. [Frances Bland] Randolph, 16 November 1776, Tucker-Coleman Papers, ibid. For production of finer cloth, see Lucy Watson's Account of New Settlers, 1762, 13, Historical Society of Pennsylvania; Hanah Adams, *A Memoir of Miss Hanah Adams, Written By Herself With Additional Notices by a Friend* (Boston: Gray and Bowen, 1832), 11.

30. Anne Marie Filiaci, "Raising the Republic: American Women in the Public Sphere, 1750–1800" (Ph.D. diss., SUNY Buffalo, 1982), 26, 61–77, 80–90, 179; Nash, *The Urban Crucible*, 117–19, 160, 210, 214–16; Nellis, "Misreading the Signs," 486–89, 500–4.

31. For a description of the public spinning used to launch Boston's philanthropic efforts, see Filiaci, "Raising the Republic," 179. For the political nature of spinning, see Carl Van Doren, *Benjamin Franklin*, 354; Norton, *Liberty's Daughters*, 166–69; Laurel Thatcher Ulrich, " 'Daughters of Liberty': Religious Women in Revolutionary New England," in Hoffman and Albert, *Women in the Age of the American Revolution*, 215–21; James Henretta, "The War for Independence and American Economic Development," in Hoffman, et al., eds., *The*

Economy of Early America, 72–73. Ulrich emphasizes the religious aspect of these events as a means of helping to domesticate political action.

32. Hawke, *Franklin*, 81–82; Fairfax diary, "Diary of a Little Colonial Girl," 212–14; Esther Burr Journal, 10–11 November 1755 and 19 October 1756, Karlsen and Crumpacker, eds., *The Journal of Esther Edwards Burr*, 165, 231; Buel and Buel, *The Way of Duty*, 42, 187, 192.

33. Lucy Watson's Account of New Settlers, 1762, Historical Society of Pennsylvania, MSS. 13. For an example of hatmaking, see Esther Burr Journal, 15 December 1754, Karlsen and Crumpacker, eds., *The Journal of Esther Edwards Burr*, 74.

34. Speth and Hirsch, *Women, Family, and Community in Colonial America*, 50; Main, "Gender, Work and Wages in Colonial New England," 39–66.

35. Henretta, "The War for Independence and American Economic Development," in Hoffman, et al., eds., *The Economy of Early America*, 71–73. See Chapter Nine for a more detailed discussion of the Philadelphia women's efforts. Kerber, *Women of the Republic*, 99–102; Norton, *Liberty's Daughters*, 178–87; Chalou, "Women in the American Revolution," in Deutrich and Purdy, *Clio Was a Woman*, 86.

36. Marie Filiaci, "Raising the Republic," 207; Elaine Forman Crane, "Dependence in the Era of Independence: The Role of Women in a Republican Society," in Jack Greene, ed., *The American Revolution: Its Character and Limits* (New York: New York University Press, 1987), 255.

37. Modern observers often exclude unpaid housework from the category "work." This makes no sense in an agricultural society where much of men's work (such as cleaning the barn) also generated no direct income. For references to ironing, see Mrs. William Willett to Katharine Colden, 25 June 1754, Colden Papers, IX, 137–39; Alexander Colden to Katharine Colden, 16 April 1755, IX, 151–52; Sarah Wister diary, 18 June 1778, in Evans, *Weathering the Storm*, 147.

38. When Thomas Porter died in 1767, the household included walnut tables, 19 knives and forks, coffee- and teapots, 6 punch bowls, and coffee cups. After distribution of goods to adult children, Elizabeth still had plates, cups, and half a dozen knives and forks. Thomas Porter inventory 26 April 1773, and Elizabeth Porter inventory, 27 July 1767, CCR, W, VSL. For growing prosperity, see Doerflinger, "Farmers and Dry Goods in the Philadelphia Market Area, 1750–1800," in Hoffman, et al., eds., *The Economy of Early America*, 176–81; Nash, *The Urban Crucible*, 76; Winstanley Briggs, "Le Pays Des Illinois," *William and Mary Quarterly*, 3rd ser., XLVII (January 1990): 52; Rutman and Rutman, *A Place in Time*, 194.

39. For evidence of women slaughtering animals and drying fruits, see Mary Cooper diary 13 October 1768, 20 July 1769, 23 November 1769, 5 October 1772, 3 November 1772, in Horne, ed., *The Diary of Mary Cooper*, 1–43. On cooking, see Stacy Gibbons Moore, " 'Established and Well Cultivated': Afro-

American Foodways in Early Virginia," *Virginia Cavalcade*, XXXIX (Fall 1989): 80–81; McMahon, "A Comfortable Subsistence," 29–50; Spruill, *Women's Life and Work in the Southern Colonies*, 211.

40. Kulikoff, *Tobacco and Slaves*, 405; Main, "Gender, Work and Wages in Colonial New England," 39–66; for a day laborer doing ironing, see Esther Burr journal, 1 March 1755, in Karlsen and Crumpacker, eds., *The Journal of Esther Edwards Burr*, 95. The figures are based on data in Shammas. I combined the returns for both Chester and Mulberry Wards and refiguring the percentage. Carole Shammas, "The Female Social Structure of Philadelphia in 1775," *The Pennsylvania Magazine of History and Biography*, CVII (January 1983): 71–73.

41. Grubb, "Servant," 257–59, 271.

42. Soderlund, "Black Women," 59; Susan Dion, "Women in the *Boston Gazette*, 1755–1775," *Historical Journal of Massachusetts*, XIV (June 1986): 95–96; Moore, " 'Established and Well Cultivated,' " 80–81; Kruger, "Born to Run"; Shammas, "Black Women's Work and the Evolution of Plantation Society in Virginia," 5–19.

43. Although regional variations in the labor supply must be considered, a court case from 1748 in Connecticut makes clear that even unskilled young girls earned wages higher than skilled women did later in the century in Philadelphia. Arbitration of a lawsuit set the wages for a young, sick girl, Martha Holly, at £26. It is also noteworthy that the contract for labor was between two married women while the husband from the employing family was absent. Dayton, "Women Before the Bar," 78–80.

44. This estimate is based on the wages recorded in the account book of Mary Coats, who kept a store in Philadelphia. Washing for a year and nine months was valued at £7.5.2 1/2. There are several irregular entries for wages. One for £11.8.1 1/2 for Elizabeth Fisher without any length of time specified. Most are between £1 and £2 per quarter, often for only one to two weeks work in that quarter. Mary Coats Account Book, 1760–1770, Historical Society of Pennsylvania; see also Crane, "The World of Elizabeth Drinker," 14, 28; Salinger, " 'Send No More Women,' " 34–35. For a different method of valuation, see Main, "Gender, Work and Wages in Colonial New England," 39–66.

45. Newman, "Black Women," 284; Soderlund, "Black Women," 59.

46. Estate Administration Accounts for Benjamin Harris show payments to "widow Simpson" for making clothes in 1776 and 1778, rec. circa 1786, CHCR, W, VSL; Sally Fairfax noted that "Granny" Carty came to sew. Sally Cary Fairfax diary, 3 January 1772, in "Diary of a Little Colonial Girl," 212–14.

47. Salinger, " 'Send No More Women,' " 30–33; Crane, "The World of Elizabeth Drinker," 18–20; Becker, "Hannah Freeman," 249–69.

48. See, for example, Kellow, "Indentured Servitude in Eighteenth-Century Maryland," 249; Shea, ed., "Life of Elizabeth Ashbridge," in Andrews, ed., *Journeys in New Worlds*, 151; for difference in diet by class see Henry M. Miller,

"An Archeological Perspective on the Evolution of Diet in the Colonial Chesapeake, 1620–1745," in Carr, et al., eds., *Colonial Chesapeake Society*, 191.

49. Nash, *The Urban Crucible*, 162–63; Rutman and Rutman, *A Place in Time*, 194; Lee, "Social Order," 102–4.

50. Shammas, "The Female Social Structure," 71–73.

51. For the clergy actions, see Gundersen, *The Anglican Clergy of Virginia*, 92; for the Pennsylvania incident, see Annette Kolodny, ed., "The Travel Diary of Elizabeth House Trist: Philadelphia to Natchez, 1783–1784," in Andrews, ed., *Journeys in New Worlds*, 205; Kirkland, ed., "Three Mecom-Franklin Letters," 264–72; Patricia Cleary and Peter Thompson, "Commerce and Gender: Women Shopkeepers and Tavernkeepers in Colonial Philadelphia" (unpublished paper, courtesy of the authors, 1991), 18; [Eliza Farmer] to Jackey, 2 February 1775, Eliza Farmer Letterbook, 1774–1777, 1783–1789, Historical Society of Pennsylvania MSS.

52. Van Doren, *Benjamin Franklin*, 38–39, 94, 106, 211; Hawke, *Franklin*, 39, 43, 64, 81, 344; Turnbull, "William Dunlap," 146–47; Baker, "He That Would Thrive Must Ask His Wife," 27–42.

53. I have reworked the information contained in Shammas's charts. Shammas, "The Female Social Structure," 71–75; Cleary and Thompson, "Commerce and Gender," 3; Waciega, "A 'Man of Business,' " 49–51.

54. Dion, "Women in the *Boston Gazette*, 1755–1775," 95–96; Norton, *Liberty's Daughters*, 138; Kirsten Fischer, " 'Disturbing the King's Peace': The Politics of Sexual Misconduct in Colonial North Carolina" (paper presented at the Southern Association of Women Historians, Houston, June 1994), 11; Spruill, *Women's Life and Work in the Southern Colonies*, 288–89: Speth and Hirsch, *Women, Family, and Community in Colonial America*, 29. Alice operated the ferry for her master. Sidney Kaplan, *The Black Presence in the Era of the American Revolution* (Boston: University of Massachusetts Press, rev. ed., 1989), 242.

55. For evidence on boarding, see Dayton, "Women Before the Bar," 72; Speth and Hirsch, *Women, Family, and Community in Colonial America*, 31; Buel and Buel, *The Way of Duty*, 54; Nash, *The Urban Crucible*, 120–22; Edith B. Gelles, "The Threefold Cord: The Elements of Sisterhood" (unpublished paper read at the American Historical Association—Pacific Coast Branch Annual Meeting, Salt Lake City, August 1990), 4, 16; Shammas, "The Female Social Structure," 75.

56. The mean assessment for female shopkeepers and tavern-keepers in 1775 in Chester and Mulberry Wards of Philadelphia was £27. Approximately 70 percent of females headed households in Mulberry Ward and 59 percent of those in Chester were exempted from the tax because of poverty. Shammas, "The Female Social Structure," 74–75; Cleary and Thompson, "Commerce and Gender," 12; White, *The Middle Ground*, 333; Jones, "Race, Sex, and Self-Evident Truths," in Hoffman and Albert, *Women in the Age of the American Revolution*, 312. Abigail Adams's sister Mary Cranch and Mary Fish Noyes Silliman

were among the gentry women who took in boarders. See also Kelsay, *Joseph Brant*, 45.

57. Cleary and Thompson, "Commerce and Gender," 14–24; Spruill, *Women's Life and Work in the Southern Colonies*, 298; Nash, *The Urban Crucible*, 82.

58. Caroline Taylor, "Women and the Vote in Eighteenth Century America," *Humanities*, VIII (July/August 1987): 16; Kirsten Fischer, " 'Disturbing the King's Peace' " (paper presented at the Southern Association of Women Historians, Houston, June 1994), 11–13.

59. Norton, " 'A Cherished Spirit of Independence,' " in Berkin and Norton, eds., *Women of America*, 49–56; Spruill, *Women's Life and Work in the Southern Colonies*, 280–91; Norton, *Liberty's Daughters*, 142; Gregory, "Black Women in Pre-Federal America," in Deutrich and Purdy, *Clio was a Woman*, 54; Mary Coats Account Book, 1760–1770, Historical Society of Pennsylvania.

60. Spruill, *Women's Life and Work in the Southern Colonies*, 264.

61. Kerber, *Women of the Republic*, 200–202; Linda Auwers, "Reading the Marks of the Past: Exploring Female Literacy in Colonial Windsor, Connecticut," *Historical Methods*, XIII (Fall 1980), 204.

62. Thad Thate, Jr., *The Negro in Colonial Williamsburg*, 141–148; Filiaci, "Raising the Republic," 180–81. For another example of women teachers at schools for blacks, see Newman, "Black Women," 287; Liliam Ashcraft Webb, "Black Women and Religion in the Colonial Period," in Rosemary Radford Ruether and Rosemary Skinner Keller, *Women and Religion in America* (San Francisco: Harper and Row, 1983), 239.

63. Mary Beth Norton and Linda Kerber both classify women's schools before the Revolution as "adventure" and find they had little academic content. On the other hand, Julia Spruill and Margaret Szasz are more positive about such schools. Norton, *Liberty's Daughters*, 259; Kerber, *Women of the Republic*, 193–202; Spruill, *Women's Life and Work in the Southern Colonies*, 197–99, 258; Szasz, *Indian Education in the American Colonies*, 37. For examples of women teachers, see Buel and Buel, *The Way of Duty*, 18, 20, 53; Barbara Lacey, "The Bonds of Friendship: Sarah Osborn of Newport and the Reverend Joseph Fish of North Stonington, 1743–1779," *Rhode Island History*, VX (November 1986): 127; Shea, ed., "Life of Elizabeth Ashbridge," in Andrews, ed., *Journeys in New Worlds*, 154–56, 171; contract between Mary Bogie and Robert Hill, December 31, 1772, and receipt December 10, 1773, Charles H. Ryland Collection, Colonial Williamsburg photostat, Virginia State Library.

64. Evans, *Weathering the Storm*, 106; Speth and Hirsch, *Women, Family, and Community in Colonial America*, 30.

65. For successful long midwifery practices in the South, see Spruill, *Women's Life and Work in the Southern Colonies*, 273–74; Ulrich, " 'The Living Mother of a Living Child,' " 28–31; Norton, *Liberty's Daughters*, 139.

66. For trained midwives, see Spruill, *Women's life and Work in the Southern Colonies*, 274; for neighbors attending births, see Lacey, "The World of Hannah

Heaton," 299; Mrs. Chastain, the wife of a Virginia doctor, was paid for atten-
dance at slave births in Chesterfield County, Virginia. For slave midwives, see
Frances Bland to Fanny [Frances Bland Randolph] [1770–1771], Tucker-Cole-
man Papers, College of William and Mary, and Norton, *Liberty's Daughters*, 31.
In the Randolph letter a mother discusses sending Cate to one pregnant daugh-
ter as soon as another daughter has delivered her child. The object is to have
Cate present for the birth, not afterward. For birth intervention, see Ulrich,
" 'The Living Mother of a Living Child,' " 34.

    67. Ulrich, *Good Wives*, 134–35; Levitt, *Brought to Bed*, 4–83.

    68. Dayton, "Women Before the Bar," 34–51; Mary Coats Account Book,
1760–1770, Historical Society of Pennsylvania MSS.

    69. Mary Fish Noyes Silliman and Sarah Osborn both struggled to pay off
debts incurred by their husbands. Buel and Buel, *The Way of Duty*, 199–207;
Lacey, "The Bonds of Friendship: Sarah Osborn," 127; Mary Cooper Diary, 23
August 1769, in Horne, ed., *The Diary of Mary Cooper*, 18. For changes in the
law see Salmon, *Women and the Law of Property in Early America*.

    70. William Alexander to Catherine Alexander, 5 December 1749, in Wil-
iam Alexander Miscellaneous Manuscripts, Box 1, New York Historical Society. Hawke, *Franklin*, 39; Elizabeth M. Pruden, "Widows and *Feme Sole*
Traders: Agents of Change in a Nascent Capitalist Society" (paper read at the
Southern Association of Women Historians, Houston, TX, June 1994).

Chapter 5

    1. Hawke, *Franklin*, 81–82.

    2. Klepp, "Philadelphia in Transition," 152, 162, 253, 261, 279–84; Van
Doren, *Benjamin Franklin*, 125; Kelsay, *Joseph Brant*, 41–44. Two of the Porter
children's deaths can be inferred from the repeat use of names for children. The
third, Dutoy, died by age 20, and a special legacy he had inherited went to other
children. King William Parish Register in Brock, *Documents, Chiefly Unpublished*.

    3. Gundersen, "The Double Bonds of Race and Sex," 361–62; Ulrich, *Good
Wives*, 138–41; Karlsen and Crumpacker, eds., *The Journal of Esther Edwards Burr*,
214, 258; Kruger, "Born to Run," 411; Elizabeth DeLancey to Mrs. Colden, 2
January 1746/7 in Colden, *The Letters and Papers of Cadwallader Colden*, Vol. VIII,
342–43; Smaby, *The Transformation of Moravian Bethlehem*, 145–46. Esther Burr
complained that 14-month-old Aaron cried so hard during weaning that she
couldn't add. She also used a wetnurse to travel before Aaron was weaned. For
lactose intolerance among African Americans, see Moore, " 'Established and
Well Cultivated,' " 77. For an example of infants and mothers listed as a unit, see
the estate inventory of Thomas Porter, 27 July 1767, CCR, W, VSL.

    4. Buel and Buel, *The Way of Duty*, 141; Journal of Esther Burr, 28 Febru-
ary 1755, in Karlsen and Crumpacker, eds., *The Journal of Esther Edwards Burr*,

95; Szasz, *Indian Education in the American Colonies*, 18–23; Axtell, ed., *The Indian Peoples of Eastern America*, 16, 18, 22–25, 34; Morgan, "Slave Life in Piedmont, Virginia, 1720–1800," in Carr, et al., eds., *Colonial Chesapeake Society*, 449.

5. Karin Calvert, "Children in American Family Portraiture, 1670–1810," *William and Mary Quarterly*, 3rd ser., XXXIX (January 1982): 87–113; Buel and Buel, *The Way of Duty*, 161; A[nne] Blair to [Mrs. Mary Blair Braxton], 21 August 1769, Blair, Banister, Braxton, Horner, Whiting Papers, Rare Books and Manuscripts, Earl Gregg Swem Library, College of William and Mary; Axtell, ed., *The Indian Peoples of Eastern America*, 42.

6. Axtell, ed., *The Indian Peoples of Eastern America*, 42; Lucy Watson's Account of New Settlers, 1762, Historical Society of Pennsylvania, 6–12; Kelsay, *Joseph Brant*, 528. For the relative values and evidence of work of slave children see Kruger, "Born to Run," 266, 278–79; Lee, "Social Order," 345; Norton, *Liberty's Daughters*, 29; Soderlund, "Black Women," 57.

7. Norton, *Liberty's Daughters*, 84; Karlsen and Crumpacker, eds., *The Journal of Esther Edwards Burr*, 182; Nancy Schrom Dye and Daniel Blake Smith, "Mother Love and Infant Death, 1750–1920," *Journal of American History*, LXXIII (September 1986): 332–34; Szasz, *Indian Education in the American Colonies*, 32.

8. Norton, *Liberty's Daughters*, 84; Karlsen and Crumpacker, eds., *The Journal of Esther Edwards Burr*, 182; Dye and Smith, "Mother Love and Infant Death, 1750–1920," 332–34; Hughes, *Populating the Back Country*, 85–89; [H. Mann], *The Female Review*, 27–33; Evans, *Weathering the Storm*, 303–4; Szasz, *Indian Education in the American Colonies*, 32, 34; Spruill, *Women's Life and Work in the Southern Colonies*, 189. Kaylene Hughes's mortality figures for the South Carolina backcountry show a slightly higher mortality for girls 10–14 than for women 30–39. My interpretation of that data differs from hers.

9. Smaby, *The Transformation of Moravian Bethlehem*, 107–15, 145–47.

10. Ditz, "Ownership and Obligation," 382–84; Lee, "Social Order," 127–31, 134–49; Klepp, "Philadelphia in Transition," 64; Speth and Hirsch, *Women, Family, and Community in Colonial America*, 21; Gundersen and Gampel, "Married Women's Legal Status in Eighteenth-Century New York and Virginia," 128–29. Susan Klepp says the legal age in Pennsylvania was 12 for girls and 14 for boys, but that would be much lower than in English law. It is more likely that this was the age at which they could choose guardians.

11. Linda Auwers, "Reading the Marks of the Past: Exploring Female Literacy in Colonial Windsor, Connecticut," *Historical Methods*, XIII (Fall 1980): 204–14; Kenneth Lockridge, *Literacy in Colonial New England*; Joseph Perlman and Dennis Shirley, "When Did New England Women Acquire Literacy?" *William and Mary Quarterly*, 3rd ser., XLVIII (January 1991): 50–67; Jack Perlman, "Reply," *William and Mary Quarterly*, 3rd ser., XLVIII (October 1991): 646–48; Joan R. Gundersen, "Kith and Kin: Women's Networks in Eigh-

teenth-Century Virginia" (Citadel Conference on the South, Charleston, SC, 1987), 20; Lee, "Social Order," 237. Linda Kerber, " 'I Have Don . . . much to Carrey on the Warr,': Women and the Shaping of Republican Ideology After the American Revolution," *The Journal of Women's History*, I (Winter 1990). Earlier studies, such as that by Kerber, followed Kenneth Lockridge's lead in dating the literacy transition after the Revolution. However, Lockridge relied on wills, and these provide the lowest measure of literacy since the elderly may be unable to sign even if they were literate earlier, and because wills really trace the level of education afforded 50–80 years earlier. Later studies have been longitudinal and used a wider range of legal documents, enlarging the sample size and pushing the date earlier.

12. Kulikoff, *Tobacco and Slaves*, 196; Mary Beth Norton, "Communications," *William and Mary Quarterly*, 3rd ser., XLVIII (October 1991). Elizabeth Porter, Sr., signed numerous documents with a mark, including her will. Her daughter Marie signed by mark on a document in 1775. Only Elizabeth Porter Sr.'s daughter-in-law, Magadelene Chastain Porter, signed legal documents. Her family had a long tradition of women's literacy. Thomas Porter's inventory includes 10 volumes of Tillotson's sermons, five volumes of Scot, and 13 other books. 23 October 1775, 28 August 1775, and 27 July 1767, CCR, W, VSL.

13. Lee, "Social Order," 234; Spruill, *Women's Life and Work in the Southern Colonies*, 190; Szasz, *Indian Education in the American Colonies*, 39; James E. Seaver, *A Narrative of the Life of Mrs. Mary Jemison* . . . . (London: R. Parken, 1826), 20; Wolf, *Urban Village*, 194. For age of children, see Norton, *Liberty's Daughters*, 258; Russo, "A Model Planter," 77; Crane, "The World of Elizabeth Drinker," 12.

14. Thorp, *The Moravian Community in Colonial North Carolina*, 72; Spruill, *Women's Life and Work in the Southern Colonies*, 190; Wolf, *Urban Village*, 194; Auwers, "Reading the Marks of the Past," 204.

15. Contract between Mary Bogie and Robert Hill, 31 December 1772, in Charles H. Ryland Collection, Colonial Williamsburg photostat from personal papers, Virginia State Library Archives; Evans, *Weathering the Storm*, 290; Crane, "The World of Elizabeth Drinker," 12; Eliza Lucas to George Lucas, 27 October 1741, and in Pinckney, ed., *The Letterbook of Eliza Lucas Pinckney*, 23, 56–57; Spruill, *Women's Life and Work in the Southern Colonies*, 197–202; Szasz, *Indian Education in the American Colonies*, 37; Kulikoff, *Tobacco and Slaves*, 196; Lee, "Social Order," 253–54; Derounian, " 'A Dear Dear Friend,' " 488.

16. Norton, *Liberty's Daughters*, 262; A[nne] Blair to [Mrs. Mary Blair Braxton], 21 August 1762, Blair, Banister, Braxton, Horner, Whiting Papers, Rare Books and Manuscripts, Earl Gregg Swem Library, College of William and Mary; Elizabeth DeLancey to Alice Colden, 4 October 1750, in Colden, *The Letters and Papers of Cadwallader Colden*, Vol. IX, 80–81. Elizabeth DeLancey commented in a letter that son Stephen had brought his sister Nanny to York for the holidays, and that "her Aunt desires she may return to compleat this

quarter, & stay another, but I believe I cant spare her." Elizabeth DeLancey to Mrs. Cadwallader [Alice] Colden, 7 June 1756, in ibid., Vol. IX, 154–56.

17. Cowell, ed., " 'Womankind Call Reason to Their Aid,' " 796–97; Peter Kafer, "The Making of Timothy Dwight: A Connecticut Morality Tale," *William and Mary Quarterly*, 3rd ser., XLVII (April 1990): 191; Akers, *Abigail Adams*, 8–9; Adams, *A Memoir of Miss Hanah Adams*, 1–5, 9–11; Eliza Lucas to Mrs. Pinckney, 1741, Eliza Lucas to Miss B[artlett], March–April 1742 and [June 1742], Eliza Lucas Pinckney to [Mr. Keate] February 1762, in Pinckney, ed., *The Letterbook of Eliza Lucas Pinckney*, 19, 31, 40–41, 180–82; Joanna Bowen Gillespie, "1795: Martha Laurens Ramsay's 'Dark Night of the Soul,' " *William and Mary Quarterly*, 3rd ser., XLVIII (January 1991): 78.

18. Spruill, *Women's Life and Work in the Southern Colonies*, 194–202, 258; Derounian, " 'A Dear Dear Friend,' " 488; Kerber, *Women of the Republic*, 202; Norton, *Liberty's Daughters*, 259. Kerber and Norton are more skeptical of adventure schools, contrasting them unfavorably with post-Revolutionary schools.

19. Grimsted, "Anglo-American Racism," in Hoffman and Albert, *Women in the Age of the American Revolution*, 373; Buel and Buel, *The Way of Duty*, 18, 20; Barbara Ellson Lacey, "Women and the Great Awakening in Connecticut" (Ph.D. diss., Clark University, 1982), 103–4.

20. Tate, *The Negro in Eighteenth-Century Williamsburg*, 135–48; Hawke, *Franklin*, 301; Filiaci, "Raising the Republic," 180–81. Lillian Ashcraft Webb, "Black Women and Religion," in Ruether and Keller, *Women and Religion in America*, 239; Soderlund, "Black Women," 63–64; Norton, *Liberty's Daughters*, 258–59; Cathy N. Davidson, *Revolution and the Word: The Rise of the Novel in America* (New York: Oxford University Press, 1986), 57.

21. Szasz, *Indian Education in the American Colonies*, 72–76.

22. Szasz, *Indian Education in the American Colonies*, 191–203; Kelsay, *Joseph Brant*, 39–52.

23. Kelsay, *Joseph Brant*, 114; Szasz, *Indian Education in the American Colonies*, 196, 221.

24. Szasz, *Indian Education in the American Colonies*, 222–23.

25. Szasz, *Indian Education in the American Colonies*, 191–240.

26. Kelsay, *Joseph Brant*, 114, 140, 225, 274–79.

27. Kerber, *Women of the Republic*, 196–99; the student incident is recorded in Esther Burr's journal, 12 April 1757, in Karlsen and Crumpacker, eds., *The Journal of Esther Edwards Burr*, 38, 257, 279.

28. Obituary of Mary Saunders, wife of John Hyde Saunders, *Virginia Gazette*; Dion, "Women in the *Boston Gazette*, 1755–1775," 89.

29. Henry Home, Lord Kaims, *Six Sketches on the History of Man, Containing the Progress of Men as Individuals* (Philadelphia: R. Bell and R. Aitken, 1776), 252–55.

30. Elizabeth Pleck, *Domestic Tyranny: The Making of American Social Policy against Family Violence from Colonial Times to the Present* (New York: Oxford

University Press, 1987), 47; Norton, *Liberty's Daughters*, 245–49, 271; Kerber, *Women of the Republic*, 203–10; Nash, *Forging Freedom*, 148, 204; Newman, "Black Women," 287. I am not implying that eighteenth-century abolitionists expected African-American women to educate sons for the same roles as whites in the new republic, but abolitionists did think blacks would certainly need tools to be productive members of society.

31. Davidson, *Revolution and the Word*, 63; Kerber, *Women of the Republic*, 200–201, 210, 227–29; Norton, *Liberty's Daughters*, 268; Melvin Yazwa, "Creating a Republican Citizenry," in Jack Greene, ed., *The American Revolution: Its Character and Limits* (New York: New York University Press, 1987), 302–3.

32. Norton, *Liberty's Daughters*, 266, 283–86; Ann D. Gordon, "The Young Ladies Academy of Philadelphia," in Berkin and Norton, eds., *Women of America*, 69–79; Lee, "Social Order," 250; Kerber, *Women of the Republic*, 220–21.

33. Gordon, "The Young Ladies Academy of Philadelphia," in Berkin and Norton, eds., *Women of America*, 69–79; Norton, *Liberty's Daughters*, 272–73.

34. Gordon, "The Young Ladies Academy of Philadelphia," in Berkin and Norton, eds., *Women of America*, 87–91.

35. Davidson, *Revolution and the Word*, 27, 35; Buel and Buel, *The Way of Duty*, 80.

36. Lacey, "The World of Hannah Heaton," 288; Lewis, "The Republican Wife," 692–94; Sarah Wister Journal, 3 June 1778, in Evans, *Weathering the Storm*, 142. Even women who could afford books, such as Elizabeth Drinker, used libraries. Crane, "The World of Elizabeth Drinker," 9–10.

37. Gelles, "The Threefold Cord," 14; Sarah Wister Journal, 24 February 1778 and 3 June 1778, in Evans, *Weathering the Storm*, 136, 142; Agan Blagar [Anne Blair] to Mrs. [Mary Blair] Braxton, 4 September 1769, Blair, Banister, Braxton, Horner, Whiting Papers, Rare Books and Manuscripts, Earl Gregg Swem Library, College of William and Mary; "Warren-Adams Letters," *Massachusetts Historical Society Collections*, LXXIII (1925): 353; Eliza Lucas to Miss Bartlett, n.d., in Pinckney, ed., *The Letterbook of Eliza Lucas Pinckney*; Esther Burr Journal, 12 March 1755, in Karlsen and Crumpacker, eds., *The Journal of Esther Edwards Burr*, 99; Lewis, "The Republican Wife," 692; Spruill, *Women's Life and Work in the Southern Colonies*, 211; Moore, " 'Established and Well Cultivated,' " 80–81.

38. Kerber, *Women of the Republic*, 235–53; Davidson, *Revolution and the Word*, 46–53, 66–78, 73–79.

39. Spruill, *Women's Life and Work in the Southern Colonies*, 208–9; Lacey, "The World of Hanah Heaton," 288; Crane, "The World of Elizabeth Drinker," 9–10; Esther Burr Journal, 13 January 1744, in Karlsen and Crumpacker, eds., *The Journal of Esther Edwards Burr*, 80. Hanah Adams also specifically mentions reading Rowe; Adams, *A Memoir of Miss Hanah Adams*, 9–11; Lacey, "Women and the Great Awakening in Connecticut," 86–89.

40. Terri L. Premo, *Winter Friends: Women Growing Old in the New Republic, 1758–1835* (Urbana and Chicago: University of Illinois Press, 1990), 120; Karlsen and Crumpacker, *The Journal of Esther Edwards Burr*, 38, 248–49; Cowell, ed., " 'Womankind Call Reason to Their Aid,' " 795–98. Adams also noted that she read novels and that the circle was held together by their "mutual love of literature." Adams, *A Memoir of Miss Hanah Adams*, 7–8.

41. Kaplan, *The Black Presence*, 176–82, 238; Gregory, "Black Women in Pre-Federal America," in Deutrich and Purdy, *Clio Was a Woman*, 63; George Shelton, "Negro Slavery in Old Deerfield," *New England Magazine*, VIII (March 1893): 56–57; Grimsted, "Anglo-American Racism" in Hoffman and Albert, *Women in the Age of the American Revolution*, 344–92; Akers, " 'Our Modern Egyptians,' " 397–410.

42. For sympathetic readings of her poetry, see Grimsted, "Anglo-American Racism" in Hoffman and Albert, *Women in the Age of the American Revolution*, 344–70; R. Lynn Matson, "Phillis Wheatley—Soul Sister?," *Phylon*, XXXIII (Fall 1972): 222–30; Akers, " 'Our Modern Egyptians,' " 399–400.

43. Filiaci, "Raising the Republic," 27–29. Evans discusses Gannett's participation in the book by Herman Mann. Evans, *Weathering the Storm*, 303; Seaver, *A Narrative of the Life of Mrs. Mary Jemison* . . . . For a typical religious autobiography edited first by the woman's husband and then by a male scholar, see Shea, ed., "Life of Elizabeth Ashbridge," in Andrews, ed., *Journeys in New Worlds*.

44. Davidson, *Revolution and the Word*, 33, 129–30; Norton, *Liberty's Daughters*, 238; Lester H. Cohen, "Creating a Usable Future: The Revolutionary Historians and the National Past," in Greene, ed., *The American Revolution*, 325; Lester H. Cohen, "Explaining the Revolution: Ideology and Ethics in Mercy Otis Warren's Historical Theory," *William and Mary Quarterly*, 3rd ser., XXXVII (April 1980): 201–7; Filiaci, "Raising the Republic," 32; Adams, *A Memoir of Miss Hanah Adams*, 15; Premo, *Winter Friends*, 115. Premo notes that Adams and Warren were among a group of women who tried to interpret the Revolution to a younger generation.

Chapter 6

1. Hawke, *Franklin*, 172.

2. Denominations present in the colonies included Church of England (Anglican), Church of Scotland (Presbyterian), Congregational, Baptist, Society of Friends, Roman Catholic, Moravian, Huguenot, Dutch Reformed, Swedish and German Lutherans, and Judaism, among others. Many historians have emphasized the ties of Anglicanism to Europe, but the Lutherans, Huguenots, Catholics, Jews, Moravians, and Methodists (before 1786) had the same problems as Anglicans in needing training and/or ordination of clergy available only in Europe. For overviews of colonial religion with differing assessments of peo-

ple's attachment to religion and the range of ways Americans related to spiritual issues, see Patricia U. Bonomi, *Under the Cope of Heaven: Religion, Society, and Politics in Colonial America* (New York: Oxford University Press, 1986); and Jon Butler, *Awash in a Sea of Faith: Christianizing the American People* (Cambridge: Harvard University Press, 1990), 87–127. For Indian religion, see Dowd, "Paths of Resistance". On Africans, see Michael A. Gomez, "Muslims in Early America," *Journal of Southern History*, LX (November 1994), 671–710; Frey, *Water From the Rock*, 240–86.

3. Bonomi, *Under the Cope of Heaven*, 30–119; Butler, *Awash in a Sea of Faith*, 67–128.

4. Thomas J. Curry, *The First Freedoms: Church and State in America to the Passage of the First Amendment* (New York: Oxford University Press, 1986); Frederick V. Mills Sr., *Bishops by Ballot: An Eighteenth-Century Ecclesiastical Revolution* (New York: Oxford University Press, 1978); Thomas E. Buckley, S.J., *Church and State in Revolutionary Virginia, 1776–1787* (Charlottesville, VA: University of Virginia Press, 1977). The establishments in Massachusetts and Connecticut had been altered to allow some people's tax money to go to non-Congregational churches.

5. Jon Butler argues that African religious traditions did not transfer to the British mainland colonies in any meaningful way; however, the evidence of the survival of folk belief, including conjury, and burial traditions (as opposed to ritual), is reasonably strong. Butler, *Awash in a Sea of Faith*, 130–161, 249–50. Muslim practices have been recently documented. Michael A. Gomez, "Muslims in Early America," *Journal of Southern History*, LX (November 1994): 671–710.

6. For example, "Or if he or she Belong to Another Meeting, by Writing to him, or her, Advise them thereof." Book of Discipline, Society of Friends, [Westbury, Long Island] 1719–1777, New York Historical Society MSS, 34. The surviving eighteenth-century Friends Meeting House in Newport, Rhode Island, has sliding partitions.

7. Jean R. Soderlund, "Women's Authority in Pennsylvania and New Jersey Quaker Meetings, 1680–1760," *William and Mary Quarterly*, 3rd ser., XLIV (October, 1987): 722–49; Levy, *Quakers and the American Family*, 214; Mary Maples Dunn, "Women of Light," in Berkin and Norton, *Women of America*, 122–23; Book of discipline, Society of Friends, [Westbury, Long Island], New York Historical Society MSS, 53.

8. See, for example, the autobiography of Elizabeth Ashbridge and the diaries of Jeffry Watson and Mary Cooper for occasions when non-Quakers heard women speak at Quaker meetings. Diary entry, 6 February 1757, in Cook, ed., "Jeffry Watson's Diary," 100; diary entries, 1 June 1769, 27 May 1772, 21 September 1773, Horne, ed., *The Diary of Mary Cooper*, 13, 34, 68.

9. Shea, ed., "Life of Elizabeth Ashbridge," in *Journeys in New Worlds*, 155, 168; Dunn, "Women of Light," in Berkin and Norton, *Women of America*, 119–21; Filiaci, "Raising the Republic," 15–16.

10. See the lives of Susanna Hudson (in Levy) and Sophia Hume (in Spruill) for examples of women whose ministry began after the deaths of their husbands. Shea, ed., "Life of Elizabeth Ashbridge," in *Journeys in New Worlds*, Andrews, ed., 155, 168; Dunn, "Women of Light," in Berkin and Norton, *Women of America*, 119–21; Levy, *Quakers and the Family*, 222; Spruill, *Women's Life and Work in the Southern Colonies*, 252; Filiaci, "Raising the Republic," 15–16.

11. Smaby, *The Transformation of Moravian Bethlehem*, 13, 26–27, 37, 167; Thorp, *The Moravian Community in Colonial North Carolina*, 58–59, 78, 81–83, 93–96; Rosemary Radford Ruether and Catherine B. Prelinger, "Women in Sectarian and Utopian Groups," in Rosemary Ruether and Keller, *Women and Religion in America*, Vol. 2, 264–65.

12. Susan Juster is the one scholar who has pushed this argument the furthest. Juster, *Disorderly Women: Sexual Politics and Evangelism in Revolutionary New England* (Ithaca and New York: Cornell University Press, 1994) 108–44; see also Frey, *Water From the Rock*, 270–71. Nathan Hatch emphasized the democratizing elements in religion in the immediate post-Revolutionary period and dates the search for respectability later. I would suggest that both were present by 1790. Nathan Hatch, *The Democratization of American Christianity* (New Haven and London: Yale University Press, 1989), 83–85, 94–95, 202. For Methodist changes, see Doris Elisabett Andrews, "Popular Religion and the Revolution in the Middle Atlantic Ports: The Role of the Methodists, 1770–1800" (Ph.D. diss., University of Pennsylvania, 1986), 198.

13. Elizabeth Bray Allen Smith Stith endowed the school as Elizabeth Smith through a deed of trust. Her husband died in 1754, and she remarried. Her will is thus recorded under the name Elizabeth Stith. Deed of Trust Joseph Bridger, Miles Cary, Richard Kello, and Richard Baker, 6 January 1753, Isle of Wight County Deed Book 9, 78–83, and Elizabeth Stith will, 22 February 1774, Surry County Wills, Virginia State Library. Speth and Hirsch, *Women, Family, and Community in Colonial America*, 31–32; Spruill, *Women's Life and Work in the Southern Colonies*, 259.

14. Soderlund, "Women's Authority in Pennsylvania and New Jersey Quaker Meetings, 1680–1760," 747; Levy, *Quakers and the American Family*, 16–17.

15. Jon Butler, for example, challenged the use of the term "Great Awakening" as an historical construct that did not adequately describe the diversity of religious experience over the middle of the eighteenth century. Jon Butler, "Enthusiasm Described and Decried: The Great Awakening as Interpretative Fiction," *Journal of American History*, LXIX (September 1982): 305–25. For a classic account of the Great Awakening see Edwin Scott Gaustad, *The Great Awakening in New England* (New York: Harper and Row, 1957).

16. Andrews, "Popular Religion and the Revolution in the Middle Atlantic Ports," 18, 29–30, 49–51; Hatch, *The Democratization of American Christianity*, 83–85.

17. Devens, "Separate Confrontations," 74–75.

18. Lacey, "Women and the Great Awakening in Connecticut," 148; Buel and Buel, *Way of Duty*, 13; Ulrich, *Good Wives*, 224. On visions, mysticism, and dreams, see Taves, ed., *Religion and Domestic Violence in Early New England*, 64; Butler, *Awash in a Sea of Faith*, 221–22; Andrews, "Popular Religion and the Revolution in the Middle Atlantic Ports," 133–38; and Shea, ed., "Life of Elizabeth Ashbridge," in *Journeys in New Worlds*, Andrews, ed., 154–56.

19. Ulrich, *Good Wives*, 224–25.

20. Lacey, "The Bonds of Friendship," 130–32.

21. Joyce Goodfriend, "The Social Dimensions of Congregational Life in Colonial New York City," *William and Mary Quarterly*, 3rd ser., XLVI (April 1989): 257–58; Smaby, *The Transformation of Moravian Bethlehem*, 68; Lacey, "Women and the Great Awakening in Connecticut," 29–31; Wolf, *Urban Village*, 217; Richard Shiels, "The Feminization of American Congregationalism, 1736–1835," *American Quarterly*, III (1981): 46–62; Gerald Moran, "Conditions of Religious Conversion in the First Society of Norwich, Connecticut, 1718–1744," *Journal of Social History*, V (1972): 331–43; William Lumpkin, "The Role of Women in Eighteenth Century Virginia Baptist Life," *Baptist History and Heritage*, VIII (1973): 158–67; Andrews, "Popular Religion and the Revolution in the Middle Atlantic Ports," 89, 170, 188, 231.

22. For the disempowerment thesis, see Bonomi, *Under the Cope of Heaven*, 116. For discussions of women's roles in local church disputes, see Ulrich, *Good Wives*, 66, 216–18; Wolf, *Urban Village*, 225.

23. Lacey, "Women and the Great Awakening in Connecticut," 34–36, 41–42.

24. Butler, *Awash in a Sea of Faith*, 127.

25. For evidence of the survival of African rituals, see Frey, *Water From the Rock*, 32–43; Sobel, *The World They Made Together*, 52–53, 218; Kruger, "Born to Run," 89. On how difficult it was for even an assimilated Indian village to maintain its population, see Daniel Madell, " 'To Live More Like My Christian English Neighbors': Natick Indians in the Eighteenth Century," *William and Mary Quarterly*, 3rd ser., XLVIII (October 1991): 563.

26. Mechal Sobel argues that there were numerous African survivals in Virginia culture and that these influenced the development of white traditions and customs, but the study never demonstrates the full practice of African religion. Jon Butler cites Sobel but elaborates on why systematic practice of African religions did not occur. Sobel, *The World They Made Together*, 52–53, 218; Butler, *Awash in a Sea of Faith*, 153–60. See also Frey, *Water From the Rock*, 32–41. Recent scholarship documents the persistence of Muslim practices; Michael A. Gomez, "Muslims in Early America," *Journal of Southern History*, LX (November 1994): 671–710.

27. Gundersen, "The Non-Institutional Church," 351; Kruger, "Born to Run," 275; Webb, "Black Women and Religion," in Ruether and Keller, eds.,

Women and Religion in America, 237; Andrews, "Popular Religion and the Revolution in the Middle Atlantic Ports," 231; Butler, *Awash in a Sea of Faith*, 161–63. Sylvia Frey considered the Anglicans precursors to the more successful efforts of evangelicals before 1776. However, the numbers and chronology show Anglican efforts continuing and with as much success as in her evangelical evidence. Frey, *Water From the Rock*, 37–44.

28. Daniel Mandell, " 'To Live More Like My Christian English Neighbors': Natick Indians in the Eighteenth Century," *William and Mary Quarterly*, 3rd ser., XLVIII (October 1991): 562; Jacqueline Peterson and Mary Druke, "American Indian Women and Religion," in Ruether and Keller, eds., *Women and Religion in America* (San Francisco: Harper and Row Publishers, 1982), 9; Kelsay, *Joseph Brant*, 39–44, 52, 280; Lacey, "Women and the Great Awakening in Connecticut," 37.

29. Webb, "Black Women and Religion," in Ruether and Keller, eds., *Women and Religion in America*, 237; Peterson and Druke, "American Indian Women and Religion," in ibid., 9; Mandell, " 'To Live More Like My Christian English Neighbors,' " 573.

30. Hawke, *Franklin*, 49; Lacey, "Women and the Great Awakening in Connecticut," 34–36, 131.

31. Ulrich, *Good Wives*, 216–17; Buel and Buel, *The Way of Duty*, 17, 25, 38; Shea, ed., "Life of Elizabeth Ashbridge," in *Journeys in the New Worlds*, Andrews, ed., 166–68; Horne, ed., *The Diary of Mary Cooper*, 24; Lacey, "The World of Hannah Heaton," 280–304; Lacey, "Women and the Great Awakening in Connecticut," 132–37, 150; Norton, "The Evolution of White Women's Experience in Early America," 608; Bonomi, *Under the Cope of Heaven*, 110.

32. Ruether and Prelinger, "Women in Sectarian and Utopian Groups," in Ruether and Skinner, eds., *Women and Religion in America,*, 263.

33. For the baptisms of the children of Thomas and Elizabeth Porter, see "The King William Parish Register," in Brock, *Documents, Chiefly Unpublished*; for the marriages of the children and the baptisms of their children, see Douglas, *The Douglas Register*, edited by Jones; for evidence of Baptist support, see the so-called 10,000 Name Petition, 16 October 1776, and the Powhatan County Petition against religious assessments 28 November 1785, Virginia State Library and Archives. John and Sarah Watkins Porter had nine children, but only the oldest three, all born before 1770, were baptized during William Douglas's ministry. Gundersen, "The Non-Institutional Church," 355–57. The Watkins family had intermarried with the Trabues. Both the Trabues and Watkins became early converts of the Baptists, through Judith Dupuy Trabue's family connections.

34. Susanna Wheatley to the Countess of Huntington, 20 February 1773, in Sara Dunlap Jackson, "Letter of Phyllis Weatley and Susanna Wheatley," *Journal of Negro History*, LVII (April 1972), 212–13; Robert B. Semple, *A His-*

tory of the Rise and Progress of the Baptists in Virginia, Revised and Extended by Rev. G.W. Beale (Richmond: Pitt & Dickinson Publisher, 1894), 174.

35. Van Doren, *Franklin*, 133.

36. Turnbull, "William Dunlap, Colonial Printer, Journalist and Minister," 154.

37. John Harris was elected to the King William vestry in 1748, two months before his daughter married Samuel Flournoy, a King William Parish vestryman. Harris had lived or worked in the parish for 20 years, but not until his daughter made ties with the Flournoys was he invited to sit on the vestry. In 1750 Charles Clarke and Thomas Porter joined the vestry. Clarke had married Marianne Salle, daughter of deceased vestryman Abraham Salle, and Porter had married Elizabeth Dutoy, whose father Pierre had also served on the vestry. Minutes, 26 February 1747/8 and December 28, 1750, The Vestry Book of King William Parish, Virginia Historical Society. The exact date of Clarke's marriage to Salle is uncertain. Marianne Clarke witnessed her mother's will in 1756. Chesterfield County Records, Deeds and Wills, September 1756, Virginia State Library. Samuel Flournoy and Elizabeth Harris took out a marriage bond in Goochland County April 2, 1748. Goochland County Records, ibid. For the nineteenth-century frontier, see Julie Roy Jeffrey, *Frontier Women: The Trans-Mississippi West, 1840–1880* (New York: Hill and Wang, 1979), 98–99; Joan Gundersen, "The Local Parish as a Female Institution: The Experience of All Saints Episcopal Church in Frontier Minnesota," *Church History*, LV (September 1986): 312.

38. Goodfriend, "Social Dimensions of Congregational Life," 267.

39. Diary, 6 November 1768, 30 April, 1769, 1 June, 1769, 5 May 1771, *The Diary of Mary Cooper*, 3–4, 11, 13, 32; Semple, *Rise of Baptists*, 154; Lacey, "Women and the Great Awakening in Connecticut," 135–37. Men also crossed denominational lines. For example, Jeffry Watson periodically attended both Quaker and Baptist meetings. Cook, ed., "Jeffry Watson's Diary," 79–116.

40. Alice Coden to Elizabeth DeLancey, 25 May, 1749, *The Letters and Papers of Cadwallader Colden*, Vol. IX, 8–9.

41. Devens, "Separate Confrontations," 55–59, 68–70; White, *The Middle Ground*, 218, 323–29.

42. Peterson and Druke, "American Indian Women and Religion" in Ruether and Keller, eds. *Women and Religion*, 3–4, 7; Guldenzopf, "Mohawk," 18–19; Dowd, "Paths of Resistance," 64–74, 90; Axtell, ed., *The Indian Peoples of Eastern America*, 55–69, 174–80; Devens, "Separate Confrontations," 74–77. Christian clergy interpreted the customs of menstrual seclusion practiced by many Indian groups as symbolizing women as unclean (linking it to such Judeo-Christian traditions as the ritual bath for Jewish women and Christian traditions of "churching" women to ritually purify themselves after childbirth).

43. Devens, "Separate Confrontations," 74–76; Dowd, "Paths of Resistance," 282–83; Nash, *Red, White, and Black*, 234–235, 261–262; White, *The Middle Ground*, 218, 333.

44. For example, women were 18 of 20 attenders at a service conducted in 1717 by William Andrews at the Mohawk Mission established by the Society for the Propagation of the Gospel. Bonomi, *Under the Cope of Heaven*, 121.

45. Smaby, *Transformation of Moravian Bethlehem*, 99; Szasz, *Indian Education in the American Colonies*, 222–240.

46. Lillian Webb makes this point in her essay on black women, and certainly this is the way American Indian culture is perceived. I would argue that it also applies to Christian traditions. In England, for example, it was church courts that handled questions of marriage, divorce, and sexual offenses. The rite of confirmation is a form of coming of age, the tradition of churching women and baptism are tied to birth. Webb, "Black Women and Religion," in Ruether and Keller, eds., *Women and Religion*, 233; Levy, *Quakers and the American Family*, 78–79.

47. Shea, "Life of Elizabeth Ashbridge," in Andrews, ed., *Journeys Into New Worlds*, 154, 156, 162–63.

48. In Isaac's discussion, Virginia appears as a stage for a company of male actors and male audiences, with women strangely absent. Levy notes the presence of Quaker women in reform without following its implications. The gendered interpretation is mine. Rhys Isaac, *The Transformation of Virginia: 1740–1790* (Chapel Hill: University of North Carolina, 1982), 80–87, 94–104, 161–77; Filiaci, "Raising the Republic," 36–37; Levy, *Quakers and the Family*, 251–53.

49. The original comment was made by John Bossy in a study of English Catholics. Lois Green Carr, "Inheritance in the Colonial Chesapeake," in Hoffman and Albert, *Women in the Age of the American Revolution*, 185; Gundersen, "The Non-Institutional Church," 351–52; Eliza Lucas to George Lucas [n.d.], Pinckney, ed., *The Letterbook of Eliza Lucas Pinckney*, 52. Buel and Buel, *The Way of Duty*, 196; S. Charles Bolton, *Southern Anglicanism: The Church of England in Colonial South Carolina* (Westport, CT: Greenwood Press, 1982), 123, 175–76; Bonomi, *Under the Cope of Heaven*, 105–9; Alice E. Mathews, "The Religious Experience of Southern Women," in Ruether and Keller, eds., *Women and Religion in America*, 226–27.

50. Andrews, "Popular Religion and the Revolution in the Middle Atlantic Ports."

51. Soderlund, "Women's Authority in Pennsylvania and New Jersey Quaker Meetings," 746–47; Andrews, "Popular Religion and the Revolution in the Middle Atlantic Ports," 201; Martha Tomhave Blaufelt and Rosemary Skinner Keller, "Women and Revivalism: The Puritan and Wesleyan Traditions," in Ruether and Keller, eds., *Women and Religion*, 325.

52. Gillespie, "1795—Martha Laurens Ramsay's 'Dark Night of the Soul,'" 73–74; Lacey, "The World of Hannah Heaton," 288.

53. Bonomi, *Under the Cope of Heaven*, 109, fn248; Anna Rawls Clifford diary, 25–29 September 1781, in Evans, *Weathering the Storm*, 292–93.

54. Blaufelt and Keller, "Women and Revivalism," in Ruether and Keller, eds., *Women and Religions in America*, 318–19; James Mary Fontaine, *A Sermon Preached by the Rev. James Maury Fountaine. At the Funeral of Mrs. Francis Page, Wife of John Page, Esq. of Rosewell. On the [ ] day of February 1787* (Richmond: Thomas Nicholson, [1787]), 12–13.

55. Butler, *Awash in a Sea of Faith*, 33.

56. Lacey, "The Bonds of Friendship," 128–36; Lacey, "Women and the Great Awakening in Connecticut," 100–101, 113–14; David Grimsted, "Anglo-American Racism," in Hoffman and Albert, *Women in the Age of the American Revolution*, 377.

57. Diary Entries, 30 November 1769, 25 September 1772, 12 April 1773, 12 August 1773, in Horne, ed., *Diary of Mary Cooper*, 24, 40, 56, 64; Filiaci, "Raising the Republic," 53.

58. Andrews, "Popular Religion and the Revolution in the Middle Atlantic Ports," 21, 166–70, 189–98, 228–29.

59. Juster, *Disorderly Women*, 1–8, 122–31. Lacey, "The Bonds of Friendship," 127–36; Lacey, "Women and the Great Awakening in Connecticut," 100–101, 113–14, 152; Mary Beth Norton, " 'My Resting Reaping Times': Sarah Osborn's Defense of Her 'Unfeminine Activities', 1767," *Signs: A Journal of Women and Culture*, II (Winter 1976): 515–29; Diary Entries, 31 July, 1773—28 August 1773, Horne, ed., *The Diary of Mary Cooper*, 63–64; Gundersen, "The Non-Institutional Church," 352–53.

60. See, for example, diary entry 23 November 1769, Horne, ed., *The Diary of Mary Cooper*, 11.

61. Nathan Hatch's study of religion in the new republic makes this point. However, Hatch seems hardly aware that the majority of members of congregations were female, and focuses his study on the male leadership of these "democratizing" groups. Hatch, *The Democratization of American Christianity*.

62. Ruether and Prelinger, "Women in Sectarian and Utopian Groups," in Ruether and Keller, eds., *Women and Religion in America*, 267–70; Filiaci, "Raising the Republic," 41–45.

63. Ruether and Prelinger, "Women in Sectarian and Utopian Groups," in Ruether and Keller, eds., *Women and Religion in America*, Vol. 2, 266–67; Filiaci, "Raising the Republic," 46–49.

64. Ruether and Prelinger, "Women in Sectarian and Utopian Groups," in Ruether and Keller, eds., *Women and Religion in America: The Colonial Period*, 262–63; Lacey, "Women and the Great Awakening in Connecticut," 27.

65. On the definition of a good minister see Butler, *Awash in a Sea of Faith*, 167. For the battle over baptism, see Gundersen, "The Non-Institutional Church."

66. Bolton, *Southern Anglicanism*, 36; Journal entry, 26 September 1774, Philip Vickers Fithian, *Journal and Letters of Philip Vickers Fithian: A Plantation Tutor of the Old Dominion, 1773–1774*, ed. Hunter Dickinson Farish (Richmond: Dominion Press, 1963), 195.

67. Jon Butler argued that planter resistance to slave baptism had largely disappeared by 1730, but I would argue the records show otherwise. Gundersen, *The Anglican Ministry in Virginia, 1723–1766*, 111–12; Butler, *Awash in a Sea of Faith*, 149. For family changes, see Smith, *Inside the Great House*.

68. Sobel, *The World They Made Together*, 16.

69. William Leigh to St. George Tucker, 3 November 1779, Tucker-Coleman Papers, Box 4, Archives and Manuscripts Division, Earl Gregg Swem Library, College of William and Mary.

70. For a review of the laws of marriage, see Dewey, "Thomas Jefferson and a Williamsburg Scandal," 44–63. For marriage in New England, see Wall, *Fierce Communion*, 49. For slave marriages, see Soderlund, "Black Women," 54.

71. Lacey, "Women and the Great Awakening in Connecticut," 50–51, 61–63, 66–68.

72. Levy, *Quakers and the American Family*, 78–79; Soderlund, "Women's Authority in Pennsylvania and New Jersey Quaker Meetings," 739.

73. *Virginia Gazette*, Purdie and Dixon, 17 January, 1771, 2–3; Deborah Norris to Sarah Wister, 2 August 1779, in Derounian, " 'A Dear Dear Friend,' " 511.

74. Smaby, *The Transformation of Moravian Bethlehem*, 208, 217; Thorp, *The Moravian Community in Colonial North Carolina*, 58–59.

75. For an exploration of this expansion see the essays by Joan Gundersen, Mary Donovan, Elizabeth Turner, and Mary Sicilia in Catherine Prelinger, ed., *Episcopal Women: Gender and Spirituality in a Mainline Denomination* (New York: Oxford University Press, 1993).

Chapter 7

1. The phrase appears in a letter from C. B. [Kitty Eustace Blair] to Anne Blair, 10 July 1772, in Tucker-Coleman Papers, Box 4, Rare Books and Manuscripts, Earl Gregg Swem Library, College of William and Mary.

2. Kelsay, *Joseph Brant*, 52.

3. N. E. Hull, *Female Felons: Women and Serious Crime in Colonial Massachusetts* (Urbana and Chicago: University of Illinois Press, 1987), 44, 48, 60–67; G. S. Rowe, "The Role of Courthouses in the Lives of Eighteenth-Century Pennsylvania Women," *The Western Pennsylvania Historical Magazine*, LXVIII (January 1985): 8–9; G. S. Rowe, "Women's Crime and Criminal Administration in Pennsylvania, 1763–1790," *Pennsylvania Magazine of History and Biography*, CIX (July 1985): 346–54; Michael Stephen Hindus, *Prison and Plantation: Crime, Justice, and Authority in Massachusetts and South Carolina, 1767–1878*

(Chapel Hill: University of North Carolina Press, 1980), 48–50, 64; Rankin, *Criminal Trial Proceedings* (Williamsburg, VA: Colonial Williamsburg, 1965), 205–6; Linda Kealey, "Patterns of Punishment: Massachusetts in the Eighteenth Century," *American Journal of Legal History*, XXX (April 1986).

4. Hull, *Female Felons,* 65–67, 73, 115; Rowe, "The Role of Courthouses in the Lives of Eighteenth-Century Pennsylvania Women," 5–9.

5. Buel and Buel, *The Way of Duty,* 55; Rowe, "The Role of Courthouses in the Lives of Eighteenth-Century Pennsylvania Women," 11; Burnston, "Babies in the Well," 151–86; Dayton, "Women Before the Bar," 134–37; Ulrich, *A Midwife's Tale: the Life of Martha Ballard, Based on Her Diary, 1785–1812* (New York: Knopf, 1990).

6. For reduced court participation by women, see Gundersen, "Kith and Kin," 18–22, and Dayton, "Women Before the Bar," 1, 36–38, 57, 83–85; Rowe, "Women's Crime and Criminal Administration in Pennsylvania," 338, 354–57. On the internal shift in disciplines of New England churches and reduced participation, see Juster, *Disorderly Women,* 75–143.

7. Hull, *Female Felons,* 35, 114–15; Rowe, "The Role of Courthouses in the Lives of Eighteenth-Century Pennsylvania Women," 7–16; Rowe, "Women's Crime and Criminal Administration in Pennsylvania, 1763–1790," 360–66.

8. Rankin, *Criminal Trial Proceedings,* 157; George W. Dalzell, *Benefit of Clergy in America* (Winston Salem: John F. Blair, 1955), 233–71.

9. The best general discussions of changing views of sexuality and public morals are D'Emilio and Freedman, *Intimate Matters,* 1–49, and Pleck, *Domestic Tyranny,* 7–33.

10. For vulnerability, see D'Emilio and Freedman, *Intimate Matters,* 44–45. Mann, *Neighbors and Strangers,* 142–45, and Pleck, *Domestic Tyranny,* 33, discuss the private/public shift.

11. Rutman and Rutman, *A Place in Time,* 176. D'Emilio and Freedman, *Intimate Matters,* 13; Frey, *Water From the Rock,* 34–35.

12. Jones, "Race, Sex, and Self-Evident Truths," in Hoffman and Albert, *Women in the Age of the American Revolution,* 316; Fischer, " 'Disturbing the King's Peace,' " 3; Webb, "Black Women and Religion," in Ruether and Keller, *Women and Religion in America,* 236; Salmon, *Women and the Law of Property in Early America,* 66–79. Salmon argues that South Carolina legislators were opposed to divorce laws because it might open the door to claims by white women about their husband's adulterous actions in slave quarters. For examples of cases involving white women and African-American men, see Dayton, "Women Before the Bar," 97–100.

13. D'Emilio and Freedman, *Intimate Matters,* 7–9.

14. Jesuits, for example, were so upset at women's power to divorce and remarry among the Algonquin peoples that one missionary captured and imprisoned an Indian woman who had left her husband, holding her without

food, fire, or cover in January until she agreed to return to her husband. Devens, "Separate Confrontations," 28; White, *The Middle Ground*, 333.

15. D'Emilio and Freedman, *Intimate Matters*, 49; Mann, *Neighbors and Strangers*, 142–45; Wolf, *Urban Village*, 222, 258; Dayton, "Women Before the Bar," 156; Klepp, "Philadelphia in Transition," 87; Juster, *Disorderly Women*, 145–79.

16. Dayton, "Women Before the Bar," 199–215, 237, 256–62, 278; Walsh, "Community Networks in the Early Chesapeake," in Carr, et al., eds., *Colonial Chesapeake Society*, 239; Mary Beth Norton, "Gender and Defamation in Seventeenth-Century Maryland," *William and Mary Quarterly*, 3rd ser., XLIV (January 1987): 3–39.

17. For church officials concerned about cohabitation, see Wall, *Fierce Communion*, 136; for prosecution after long residence, see Fischer, " 'Disturbing the King's Peace,' " 5, 9. For another example of high status protecting such a relationship, and neighbors comments, see Mason, "Mama, Rachel and Molly," in Hoffman and Albert, *Women in the Age of the American Revolution*, 251–54, 257.

18. See Bolton, *Southern Anglicanism*, 122, for a description of brides pregnant at their weddings. D'Emilio and Freedman, *Intimate Matters*, 5–10, 13, 22, 41–49, 72; Hindus, *Prison and Plantation*, 48; Dayton, "Women Before the Bar," 152–56; Klepp, "Philadelphia in Transition," 87–93; Fischer, " 'Disturbing the King's Peace,' " 5, 9; Mann, *Neighbors and Strangers*, 142–45; Wolf, *Urban Village*, 222–58.

19. D'Emilio and Freedman, *Intimate Matters*, 5–13, 22, 32–33, 41–47, 72. Hindus, *Prison and Plantation*, 48–50, 67–68; Dayton, "Women Before the Bar," 89–92, 152, 163–68; Klepp, "Philadelphia in Transition," 87–93; Burnston, "Babies in the Well," 183–84; Rowe, "The Role of Courthouses in the Lives of Eighteenth-Century Pennsylvania Women," 10; Rowe, "Women's Crime and Criminal Administration in Pennsylvania, 1763–1790," 346–48, 353, 363–65; Fischer, " 'Disturbing the King's Peace,' " 5, 9.

20. D'Emilio and Freedman, *Intimate Matters*, 32, 72; Hindus, *Prison and Plantation*, 48–50, 67–68; Dayton, "Women Before the Bar," 89–92, 152, 168–69; Burnston, "Babies in the Well," 183–84; Rowe, "The Role of Courthouses in the Lives of Eighteenth-Century Pennsylvania Women," 10; Rowe, "Women's Crime and Criminal Administration in Pennsylvania, 1763–1790," 346–48.

21. Dayton, "Women Before the Bar," 89–92, 152, 168–69.

22. Dayton, "Women Before the Bar," 90–92; Klepp, "Philadelphia in Transition," 109–12.

23. Dayton, "Women Before the Bar," 95–106. See Diary of Jeffry Watson, 10 June 1741, in Cook, ed., "Jeffry Watson's Diary, 1740–1784," 90, for a mention of a woman transported as a servant as punishment for adultery. For the "Scarlet Letter" origins, see Hull, *Female Felons*, 114.

24. Dayton, "Women Before the Bar," 105–6. For examples of unprose-cuted adultery, see Klepp, "Philadelphia in Transition," 109–13; Walter J. Fraser Jr., "The City Elite, 'Disorder,' and the Poor Children of Pre-Revolu-tionary Charleston," *South Carolina Historical Magazine*, LXXXIV (July 1983): 172; Spruill, *Women's Life and Work in the Southern Colonies*, 183.

25. Kerber, *Women of the Republic*, 178–79; Cohen, "The Broken Bond," 68; Salmon, *Women and the Law of Property in Early America*, 61–67; Cott, "Divorce and Changing Status," 587–91; Dewey, "Thomas Jefferson's Notes on Divorce," 217–18.

26. Cott argued that the trend in divorce cases based on adultery showed a lessening of the double standard. Cott, "Divorce and Changing Status," 597–606, 611; Dayton, "Women Before the Bar," 285, 304–6; Cohen, "The Broken Bond," 70–72, 75; Kerber, *Women of the Republic*, 162–66.

27. Cott, "Eighteenth-Century Family and Social Life Revealed in Massa-chusetts Divorce Records," in Nancy F. Cott and Elizabeth H. Pleck, *A Her-itage of Her Own* (New York: Simon and Schuster, 1979), 121; Taves, ed., *Reli-gion and Domestic Violence in Early New England*, 58–68.

28. For an example of remarriage, see the account of Sarah Osborn Ben-jamin in Dann, *The Revolution Remembered*, 248–50. Rankin, *Criminal Trial Pro-ceedings*, 147; Dayton, "Women Before the Bar," 107; Cott, "Divorce and Changing Status," 597–99. For Revolutionary War cases, see Cohen, "The Broken Bond," 76.

29. Hawke, *Franklin*, 23–27; Van Doren, *Benjamin Franklin*, 70–71, 92–93.

30. Taves, ed., *Religion and Domestic Violence in Early New England*, 58, 66, 76–89.

31. Hull, *Female Felons*, 114; Dayton, "Women Before the Bar," 144–50; Taves, ed., *Religion and Domestic Violence in Early New England*, 58, 66, 76–89.

32. Axtell, ed., *The Indian Peoples of Eastern America*, 80; Kelsay, *Joseph Brant*, 52. The problem of slave marriages was discussed by Anglican missionar-ies, for example, who were unwilling to marry individuals who would not be able to live up to the vows through no fault of their own. As for potential incest, consider the infamous case of Thomas Jefferson and Sally Hemmings. It is not clear that Jefferson and Hemmings had a relationship; however, if they did, there is also evidence that Hemmings was related to Jefferson's wife. In the accusations in the press about Jefferson's morals, no one approached it as possi-ble incest.

33. For the extent of prostitution and concern about sexual license, see D'Emilio and Freedman, *Intimate Matters*, 44–45, 50–51, and Fischer, " 'Dis-turbing the King's Peace,' " 11–14; White, *The Middle Ground*, 333. The addi-tional connection to shifting standards of morality in general is my own.

34. D'Emilio and Freedman, *Intimate Matters*, 51; Rowe, "Women's Crime and Criminal Administration in Pennsylvania, 1763–1790," 346–47.

35. Norton, *Liberty's Daughters*, 138.

36. D'Emilio and Freedman, *Intimate Matters*, 31; Dayton, "Women Before the Bar," 112–17; Barbara S. Lindemann, " 'To Ravish and Carnally Know': Rape in Eighteenth-Century Massachusetts," *Signs: Journal of Women in Culture and Society*, X (Autumn 1984): 64–68; Rankin, *Criminal Trial Proceedings*, 86, 219–20.

37. Lindemann, " 'To Ravish and Carnally Know,' " 79–81; Dayton, "Women Before the Bar," 117–18, 141; Rankin, *Criminal Trial Proceedings*, 221–22.

38. For the rape incident in South Carolina, see John A. Hall, " 'Nefarious Wretches, Insidious Villains, and Evil-Minded Persons': Urban Crime Reported in Charleston's City *Gazette* in 1788," *South Carolina Historical Magazine*, LXXXVIII (July 1987), 166. Dayton, "Women Before the Bar," 117–27, 134–40 ; Lindemann, " 'To Ravish and Carnally Know,' " 71–81; Rankin, *Criminal Trial Proceedings*, 119–20.

39. Kerber, *Women of the Republic*, 140; Lindemann, " 'To Ravish and Carnally Know,' " 75–76; Dayton, "Women Before the Bar," 117–18, 127.

40. Gregory Evans Dowd, "Declarations of Dependence: War and Inequality in Revolutionary New Jersey, 1776–1815," *New Jersey History*, CIII (Spring/Summer, 1985), 54; Buel and Buel, *The Way of Duty*, 125; Chalou, "Women in the American Revolution," in Deutrich and Purdy, *Clio Was a Woman*, 83; Norton, *Liberty's Daughters*, 202; Kerber, *Women of the Republic*, 46.

41. Only one woman killed her husband in eighteenth-century Virginia, for example. Pleck, *Domestic Tyranny*, 18–23, 33; Brenda D. McDonald, "Domestic Violence in Colonial Massachusetts," *Historical Journal of Massachusetts*, XIV (January 1986): 53–61; Cohen, "The Broken Bond," 69, 74–75; Salmon, *Women and the Law of Property in Early America*, 54; Kerber, *Women of the Republic*, 172; Speth and Hirsch, *Women, Family, and Community in Colonial America*, 53–65; Dayton, "Women Before the Bar," 323; Spruill, *Women's Life and Work in the Southern Colonies*, 184; Rankin, *Criminal Trial Proceedings*, 224–25.

42. Salmon, *Women and the Law of Property in Early America*, 63–66, 76; Cohen, "The Broken Bond," 74–75; Cott, "Divorce and Changing Status," 597–99. For the case of the Virginia minister, John Brunskill Jr., see Gundersen, *The Anglican Ministry in Virginia, 1723–1766*, 134.

43. Rowe, "The Role of Courthouses in the Lives of Eighteenth-Century Pennsylvania Women," 11; Rowe, "Women's Crime and Criminal Administration in Pennsylvania, 1763–1790," 338–43, 358–59; Dion, "Women in the *Boston Gazette*," 91.

44. Juster, *Disorderly Women*, 148–57.

45. Pleck, *Domestic Tyranny*, 45–46.

46. Rowe, "Women's Crime and Criminal Administration in Pennsylvania, 1763–1790," 338–43, 358–59; Hull, *Female Felons*, 80; Rowe, "The Role of Courthouses in the Lives of Eighteenth-Century Pennsylvania Women," 11.

47. Hull, *Female Felons*, 80; Rankin, *Criminal Trial Proceedings*, 135–38; Rowe, "Women's Crime and Criminal Administration in Pennsylvania, 1763–1790," 339–42, 358–59; Pleck, *Domestic Tyranny*, 31–32; Dion, "Women in the *Boston Gazette*," 91.

48. Morgan, "Slave Life in Piedmont, Virginia, 1720–1800," in Carr, et al., eds., *Colonial Chesapeake Society*, 441, 455–60; Hull, *Female Felons*, 46.

49. Kealey, "Patterns of Punishment," 179–80; Hull, *Female Felons*, 65–67, 110–11; Rowe, "Women's Crime and Criminal Administration in Pennsylvania, 1763–1790," 338, 344; Rankin, *Criminal Trial Proceedings*, 156–57.

50. Susan Dion found the ads for runaway wives similar to those for slaves and servants. The evidence from divorce cases, however, shows a difference in treatment. Dion, "Women in the *Boston Gazette*," 91; Perdue, *Slavery and the Evolution of Cherokee Society*, 37–40, 78–82; Wright, *African Americans*, 94; Peter Wood, *Black Majority*, 239–63; Gerald Mullins, *From Flight to Rebellion*, passim.

51. Kruger, "Born to Run," 239; Kay and Cary, "Slave Runaways in Colonial North Carolina," 1–39; Mullins, *From Flight to Rebellion*, 103–5; Peter Wood, *Black Majority*, 241.

52. Ulrich, *Good Wives*, 224; Buel and Buel, *The Way of Duty*, 13.

53. Eliza Lucas to Miss [Bartlett], [June 1742], Pinckney, ed., *The Letterbook of Eliza Lucas Pinckney, 1739–1762*, 42; Hughes, *Populating the Back Country*, 140.

54. Juster, *Disorderly Women*, 147–79.

55. Dowd, "Paths of Resistance," 40–42; Devens, "Separate Confrontations," 78–79.

56. Mary Ann Jimenez, "Madness in Early American History: Insanity in Massachusetts from 1700 to 1830," *Journal of Social History*, XX (Fall 1986): 25–35.

57. Keyssar, "Widowhood in Eighteenth-Century Massachusetts," 98, 112–13; Fraser, "The City Elite, 'Disorder,' and the Poor Children of Pre-Revolutionary Charleston," 175.

58. Fraser, "The City Elite, 'Disorder,' and the Poor Children of Pre-Revolutionary Charleston," 169–70, 175; Nash, *The Urban Crucible*, 155–61, 232; Crane, "Dependence in the Era of Independence," in Greene, ed., *The American Revolution*, 259–60.

59. Wall, *Fierce Communion*, 102; Ulrich, *Good Wives*, 43; Nash, *The Urban Crucible*, 79, 116–17; Fraser, "The City Elite, 'Disorder,' and the Poor Children of Pre-Revolutionary Charleston," 175–78.

60. Fraser, "The City Elite, 'Disorder,' and the Poor Children of Pre-Revolutionary Charleston," 174.

61. Esther L. Friend, "Notifications and Warnings Out: Strangers Taken into Wrentham, Massachusetts, between 1732 and 1812," *New England Histori-*

cal and Genealogical Register, CXLI (July 1987): 185–202; Nash, *The Urban Crucible*, 115–16; Kerber, *Women of the Republic*, 142–43.

62. Nash, *The Urban Crucible*, 210.

63. Crane, "Dependence in the Era of Independence," in Greene, ed., *The American Revolution*, 259–66. For the general importance of the independence/dependence dichotomy in Revolutionary-era thought see Gundersen, "Independence, Citizenship, and the American Revolution," 59–77.

Chapter 8

1. Mary Beth Norton concluded that seventeenth-century defamation suits were gendered with public and private roles for both men and women. Norton, "Gender and Defamation in Seventeenth-Century Maryland," 39. See also Laurel Ulrich who noted "in the premodern world position is always more important than task." Ulrich, *Good Wives*, 238.

2. Dayton, "Women Before the Bar," 13, 55–56, 82; Gundersen, "Kith and Kin," 19; Gundersen and Gampel, "Married Women's Legal Status in Eighteenth-Century New York and Virginia," 122, fn24; Crane, "Dependence in the Era of Independence," in Greene, ed., *The American Revolution*, 258; Speth and Hirsch, *Women, Family, and Community in Colonial America*, 23; Shammas, Salmon, and Dahlin, *Inheritance in America*, 60, 120–21; Narrett, *Inheritance and Family Life in Colonial New York City* (Ithaca and London: Cornell University Press, 1992), 95–98.

3. Mann, *Neighbors and Strangers*, 9–10, 99, 122–23; Dayton, "Women Before the Bar," 36–38, 57, 66–70, 83–85.

4. Salmon, *Women and the Law of Property in Early America*, 7–27; Salmon, "Equality or Submersion? Feme Covert Status in Early Pennsylvania," in Berkin and Norton, *Women of America*, 102–4. For wives signing reluctantly, see Jeffry Watson diary, 13 July 1742, in Cook, ed., "Jeffry Watson's Diary, 1740–1784," 93–94, and the Mary Cooper diary, 16 May 1771, in Horne, ed., *The Diary of Mary Cooper*, 33.

5. Speth and Hirsch, *Women, Family, and Community in Colonial America*, 9–10; Gundersen, "Kith and Kin," 17.

6. Akers, *Abigail Adams*, 80–81.

7. Shammas, "Black Women's Work and the Evolution of Plantation Society in Virginia," 10–11; Kulikoff, *Tobacco and Slaves*, 177–78, 217; Norton, "Eighteenth-Century American Women in Peace and War," 395; Gundersen, "The Double Bonds of Race and Sex," 366–69.

8. Shammas, "Black Women's Work and the Evolution of Plantation Society in Virginia," 19–21; Jones, "Race, Sex, and Self-Evident Truths," in Hoffman and Albert, *Women in the Age of the American Revolution*, 294–97; Gundersen, "The Double Bonds of Race and Sex," 366–70. Shammas could only find two work designations other than field hand for women—cook and wash-

erwoman. Slave advertisements and correspondence from the period reveal a number of others, including dairymaid, spinner, and seamstress.

9. Kulikoff, *Tobacco and Slaves*, 183.

10. The Franklin home site is maintained as a museum with an archaeological interpretation. The house was 34 feet square. Van Doren, *Benjamin Franklin*, 316. E[liza] Farmer to Jack [?], 18 May 1774, Eliza Farmer Letterbook, 1774–1777, 1783–1789, Manuscripts, Historical Society of Pennsylvania.

11. Salinger, " 'Send No More Women,' " 36–37; Shammas, "The Female Social Structure," 78; Sobel, *The World They Made Together*, 104–5, 112–17. The Porters had six beds, 16 chairs, and three tables. This was not unusual for furnishing a two-room, double-loft house with a central passageway and separate kitchen. Thomas Porter inventory, 27 July 1767, CCR, W, VSL.

12. Elizabeth Trist diary, 3 January 1784, in Annette Kolodny, ed., "The Travel Diary of Elizabeth House Trist: Philadelphia to Natchez, 1782–1784," in Andrews, ed., *Journeys in New Worlds*, 206–10.

13. Smaby, *The Transformation of Moravian Bethlehem*, 100, 146; Thorp, *The Moravian Community in Colonial North Carolina: Pluralism on the Southern Frontier*, 204–6.

14. On traditional gender divisions and women's connection to agriculture in Indian communities, see Nash, *Red, White, and Black*, 237; Perdue, *Slavery and the Evolution of Cherokee Society*, 15; Theda Perdue, "Cherokee Women and the Trail of Tears," *Journal of Women's History*, I (Spring 1989): 16; Graymont, *The Iroquois in the American Revolution*, 291; Braund, "The Creek Indians, Blacks and Slavery," 622–23. On resistance, see Devens, "Separate Confrontations," 3, 10, 107–11. Franklin reported in 1763 that Indians "have received no presents. And the plan of preventing war among them, and bringing them to live by agriculture, they resent as an attempt to make women of them as they phrase it; it being the business of women only to cultivate the ground . . . ." For eighteenth-century missionary activities, see Margaret Connell Szasz, *Indian Education in the American Colonies, 1607–1783* (Albuquerque: University of New Mexico Press, 1988), 191–228.

15. Axtell, ed., *The Indian Peoples of Eastern America*, 92; Smaby, *The Transformation of Moravian Bethlehem*, 99–100. Neither Axtell or Smaby are responsible for the interpretation I have put on information gathered from their work.

16. Mandell, " 'To Live More Like My Christian English Neighbors,' " 568–77.

17. Guldenzopf, "Mohawk," 74, 77, 115; Graymont, *The Iroquois in the American Revolution*, 147; Kelsay, *Joseph Brant*, 49; Seaver, *A Narrative of the Life of Mrs. Mary Jemison . . . .*, 43.

18. Merrell, *The Indian's New World*, 204, 236; Mary E. Young, "Women, Civilization, and the Indian Question," in Deutrich and Purdy, *Clio Was a Woman*, 98–100; Perdue, "Cherokee Women and the Trail of Tears," 18.

19. Daniel Scott Smith, "Child-Naming Practices, Kinship Ties, and Change in Family Attitudes in Hingham, Massachusetts, 1641 to 1680," *Journal of Social History*, XVIII (Summer 1985): 543–53; John J. Waters, "Naming and Kinship in New England: Guilford Patterns and Usage, 1693–1759," *New England Historical and Genealogical Register*, CXXXIX (July 1984): 161–74; Cody, "There Was No 'Absalom' on the Ball Plantations," 567; Gunderson, "The Double Bonds of Race and Sex," 358–59. For choosing English forms of names see Wolf, *Urban Village*, 141.

20. Smith, "Child-Naming Practices," 544–46, 557; Waters, "Naming and Kinship in New England: Guilford Patterns and Usage," 161–74; Cody, "There Was No 'Absalom' on the Ball Plantations," 567–70; Gundersen, "The Double Bonds of Race and Sex," 358–59; Klepp, "Philadelphia in Transition," 154–55; Paul E. Johnson, "The Modernization of Mayo Greenleaf Patch: Land, Family, and Marginality in New England, 1766–1818," *New England Quarterly*, LV (December 1982): 509–11. Johnson argues that the Patch family chose all paternal names, but the children's names are also nicknames for the mother's family names. For a letter where a daughter apologizes to her parents for naming her child for a paternal grandmother, see Elizabeth DeLancey to Cadwallader Colden, [24 March 1743?] in Cadwallader Colden, *The Letters and Papers of Cadwallader Colden*, Vol. VIII, 292–93.

21. Morgan, "Slave Life in Piedmont, Virginia," in Carr, et al., eds., *Colonial Chesapeake Society*, 452; Cody, "There Was No 'Absalom' on the Ball Plantations," 580, 591; Gundersen, "The Double Bonds of Race and Sex," 358–59; Thomas Porter inventory, 27 July 1767, CCR, W, VSL.

22. Dion, "Women in the *Boston Gazette*," 93; Bailyn, *Voyagers to the West*, 83; Kruger, "Born to Run," 441–44; Soderlund, "Black Women," 67; Kelsay, *Joseph Brant*, 39–52. For missionary interpretations of traditional Indian naming customs see Axtell, ed., *The Indian Peoples of Eastern America*, 15, 24.

23. Gundersen, "Kith and Kin," 1–4; Kulikoff, *Tobacco and Slaves*, 207, 230–31, 287. For male friends, see Buel and Buel, *The Way of Duty*, xiv–xv; Lacey, "The Bonds of Friendship," 129; and C. Alexander to [ ] 2 April 1763, William Alexander Misc., Manuscripts, Box 1, New York Historical Society. Kulikoff argued that the poor and transient were excluded.

24. Gundersen, "Kith and Kin," 10–11; Kulikoff, *Tobacco and Slaves*, 205–9, 380.

25. Walsh, "Community Networks in the Early Chesapeake," in Carr, et al., eds., *Colonial Chesapeake Society*, 225–31; Gundersen, "Kith and Kin," 8–13. Walsh emphasizes the difficulties, Gundersen the possibilities. For mother with a nursing infant attending a ball, see Fairfax, "Diary of a Little Colonial Girl," 212–14. For a weaning trip, see Elizabeth DeLancey to Mrs. [Alice] Cadwallader Colden, 2 January 1746/7, in Colden, *The Letters and Papers of Cadwallader Colden*, Vol. VIII, 342–43.

26. Esther Burr Journal, 2 October 1755, in Karlsen and Crumpacker, *The Journal of Esther Edwards Burr*, 155.

27. For letters and visits, see Gundersen, "Kith and Kin," 12, 21–22, and Karlsen and Crumpacker, *The Journal of Esther Edwards Burr*, 22.

28. On roads, see Kulikoff, *Tobacco and Slaves*, 209–12, and Spruill, *Women's Life and Work in the Southern Colonies*, 89; Elizabeth DeLancey to Mrs. [Alice] Cadwallader Colden, 2 January 1746/7, Colden, *The Letters and Papers of Cadwallader Colden*, Vol. VIII, 342–43; Margaret Hill Morris Diary, 14 June 1777, in Evans, *Weathering the Storm*, 103–5. Mary Cooper's Diary records her daughter Esther traveling for social events about twice a month, except for April, June, and September. Horne, ed., *The Diary of Mary Cooper*.

29. For cousins referred to as friends, see Mary Jones to Frances Bland Randolph, April 10, 1769, and May 10, 1769, Tucker-Coleman Papers, Earl Gregg Swem Library, College of William and Mary. The phrase "Sister of my heart" appears both in the letters of Esther Burr and of Kitty Eustace Blair. Kitty Eustace Blair to Anne Blair Bannister, July 18, 1772, Tucker-Coleman Papers, Earl Gregg Swem Library, College of William and Mary; Karlsen and Crumpacker, eds., *The Journal of Esther Edwards Burr*, 53–54. For other examples of kin as friends, see Mason, "Mama, Rachel and Molly," in Hoffman and Albert, *Women in the Age of the American Revolution*, 259; Speth and Hirsch, *Women, Family, and Community in Colonial America*, 69. For the influence of religion and literacy, see Adams, *A Memoir of Miss Hanah Adams, Written By Herself With Additional Notices by a Friend*, 7–8; Grimsted, "Anglo-American Racism," in Hoffman and Albert, *Women in the Age of the American Revolution*, 344; Karlsen and Crumpacker, eds., *The Journal of Esther Edwards Burr*, 36, and Lacey, "The World of Hannah Heaton," 299. Kulikoff, *Tobacco and Slaves*, 229, suggests powerlessness as a reason. The testamentary patterns are in Gundersen, "Kith and Kin," 15.

30. Spruill, *Women's Life and Work in the Southern Colonies*, 94, 102; A[nne] Blair to [Mrs. Mary Blair Braxton], 1768, and 21 August 1769, Blair, Banister, Braxton, Horner, Whiting Papers, Rare Books and Manuscripts, Earl Gregg Swem Library, College of William and Mary; Buel and Buel, *The Way of Duty*, 21; Derounian, " 'A Dear Dear Friend,' " 498–510.

31. Horne, ed., *The Diary of Mary Cooper*, 1981.

32. Jeffry Watson diary, 18 April 1741, 10 August 1743, 18 May 1744, Cook, ed., "Jeffry Watson's Diary, 1740–1784," 89, 96–97; Gundersen, "Kith and Kin," analyzes the diaries of men for their content on women's visiting.

33. Eliza Graeme to Mrs. Campbell, 23 January 1763, Elizabeth Graeme Fergusson (1739–1801), Letters, Society Collection, Historical Society of Pennsylvania; Sarah Fisher to Deborah Norris, March 1780, in Sweeney, ed., "The Norris-Fisher Correspondence," 200. Annis Boudinot wrote a poem addressed to Esther Burr on their friendship. Susanna Wright's poem on women was in honor of Deborah Norris. Karlsen and Crumpacker, eds., *The*

Journal of Esther Edwards Burr, 256–57; Cowell, ed., " 'Womankind Call Reason to Their Aid,' " 795–800.

34. Esther Burr Journal, 4 October 1754, 17 June 1755, and Sarah Prince Meditation, 21 April 1758, in Karlsen and Crumpacker, eds., *The Journal of Esther Edwards Burr*, 49, 125, 307.

35. Dayton, "Women Before the Bar," 2, 198; Hull, *Female Felons*, 56; Ulrich, *Good Wives*, 89–125, 238–39, 283; Norton, *Liberty's Daughters*, 3–5, uses the "my" and "our" illustration. For women in court, see Gundersen and Gampel, "Married Women's Legal Status in Eighteenth-Century New York and Virginia," 130.

36. Axtell, ed., *The Indian Peoples of Eastern America*, 154; Nash, *Red, White, and Black*, 240; Kelsay, *Joseph Brant*, 450.

37. Dion, "Women in the *Boston Gazette*," 87–97.

38. This series is probably what led Esther Burr and her friends to ask Annis Boudinot to write a verse reply defending women. Paula Dorman Christenson, "The Colonial Family in New York: A Study of Middle and Upper Class Interpersonal and Institutional Relationships" (Ph. D. diss., Albany, 1984).

39. Dion, "Women in the *Boston Gazette*," 92.

40. Home, *Six Sketches*, 194–98, 242.

41. Grimsted, "Anglo-American Racism," in Hoffman and Albert, *Women in the Age of the American Revolution*, 379–80; Ulrich, " 'Daughters of Liberty,' " in Hoffman and Albert, *Women in the Age of the American Revolution*, 221, 234–35.

42. Karen Calvert, "Children in American Family Portraiture, 1670–1810," *William and Mary Quarterly*, 3rd ser., XXXIX (January 1982): 87–113; Ulrich, *Good Wives*, 115. Consider the novels *Pamela* and *Clarrissa*, both of which were popular in the colonies. Older women aid in Clarissa's rape, and Pamela is urged to conform by older women. Premo, *Winter Friends*, 112–13.

43. Dianne Dugaw, *Warrior Women and Popular Balladry, 1650–1800* (New York: Cambridge University Press, 1989), 1, 5, 132–77; Bailyn, *Voyagers to the West*, 409; Ulrich, *Good Wives*, 239.

44. For the Gannett story, see Evans, *Weathering the Storm*, 302–16; [H. Mann], *The Female Review*; Julia Ward Stickley, "The Records of Deborah Sampson Gannett, Woman Soldier of the Revolution," *Prologue: Journal of the National Archives*, IV (Winter 1972): 233–41. For specific concerns about Gannett's femininity, see Mann, *Female Review*, 113–17, 133, 256; Stickley, 240, and Chalou, "Women in the American Revolution: Vignettes or Profiles," in Deutrich and Purdy, *Clio Was a Woman*, 73.

45. For the emphasis on motherhood, see Wall, *Fierce Communion*, 128–37; Dye and Smith, "Mother Love and Infant Death, 1750–1920," 332–34; Calvert, "Children in American Family Portraiture," 87–113; Philip Greven, *The Protes-*

tant Temperment, passim; Philip Greven, *Childrearing Concepts,* passim. For expression of interest in children, see Elizabeth DeLancey to Cadwallader Colden [24 March 1743?], and Elizabeth DeLancey to Mrs. Cadwallader [Alice] Colden, 2 January 1746/7, in Colden, *The Letters and Papers of Cadwallader Colden,* Vol. VIII, 292–93, 342–43; Buel and Buel, *The Way of Duty,* 141, 196; Esther Burr Journal, 28 February 1755, in Karlsen and Crumpacker, eds., *The Journal of Esther Edwards Burr,* 95; and Eliza Pinckney to [Mr. Keate], February 1762, Pinckney, ed., *The Letterbook of Eliza Lucas Pinckney, 1739–1762,* 180–82. Lee, "Social Order," 122, notes the difference in will terminologies. For a eulogy stressing motherhood see Fountaine, *A Sermon,*. For catechizing, see Bolton, *Southern Anglicanism,* 123; Gundersen, "The Non-Institutional Church," 351–52; Seaver, *A Narrative of the Life of Mrs. Mary Jemison . . . .,* 20; Devereaux Jarratt, *The Autobiography of Devereux Jarratt,* 12–17. Smith, *Inside the Great House,* 103–5, 295–99, emphasizes fathers and sons, and gives little attention to the growing identification of women with their role as mothers.

46. Rosemary Zagarri, "Morals, Manners, and the Republican Mother" (paper read at the Annual Meeting of the American Historical Association, New York, 1990), 3–8, 21; Gundersen, "Independence, Citizenship, and the American Revolution," 65–67.

47. Deborah Norris to Sarah Wister, [18 April 1778], in Derounian, " 'A Dear Dear Friend,' " 501–2. Willing is quoted in Norton, *Liberty's Daughters,* 7.

48. Ruth Bloch, "The Gendered Meanings of Virtue in Revolutionary America," *Signs: Journal of Women in Culture and Society,* XIII (Autumn 1987): 44–47; Gundersen, "Independence, Citizenship, and the American Revolution," 61–62; Linda K. Kerber, "History Can Do It No Justice: Women and the Reinterpretation of the American Revolution," in Hoffman and Albert, *Women in the Age of the American Revolution,* 34.

49. Bloch, "The Gendered Meanings of Virtue in Revolutionary America," 44–56; Kerber, " 'I Have Don . . . much to Carrey on the Warr,' " 234–35; Kerber, *Women of the Republic,* 269; Lewis, "The Republican Wife," 698–715; Lester H. Cohen, "Mercy Otis Warren: The Politics of Language," *American Quarterly,* XXXV (1983): 490–92.

50. Dowd, "Declarations of Dependence," 60–61.

51. Linda Kerber argued that men saw the Revolution as a struggle against other men, with women providing some form of constant, rather than a changing factor. For women to claim a role in the Revolution thus required destabilizing relations with men. She makes the factors of destabilization flow from the ideology. I would argue that the destabilization existed, and women shaped it after the fact. Linda Kerber, " 'I Have Don . . . much to Carrey on the Warr' ".

Chapter 9

1. For women who seemed to approach the war as spice for their social lives see Sweeney, ed., "The Norris-Fisher Correspondence," 187–232; Derounian, " 'A Dear Dear Friend,' " 487–516.

2. For different views on virtue, denial of luxury, and secular or religious nature of virtue, see Ulrich, " 'Daughters of Liberty,' " in Hoffman and Albert, *Women in the Age of the American Revolution*, 215–25; Buel and Buel, *The Way of Duty*, 129; Lacey, "The World of Hannah Heaton," 301. For a more political interpretation of women's mobilization and spinning, see Filiaci, "Raising the Republic," 116; Kerber, *Women of the Republic*, 38–39; Cohen, "Explaining the Revolution," 209–10; Norton, *Liberty's Daughters*, 244–45; T[imothy] H. Breen, "Narrative of Commercial Life: Consumption, Ideology, and Community on the Eve of the American Revolution," *William and Mary Quarterly*, 3rd ser., L (July 1993): 495.

3. Breen, "Narrative of Commercial Life," 501; Norton, *Liberty's Daughters*, 157.

4. There is a satirical British engraving of the Edenton signing. The women appear as both masculine and promiscuous. Kerber, *Women of the Republic*, 77–83; Norton, *Liberty's Daughters*, 188–89; Breen, "Narrative of Commercial Life," 492–93; Nash, *The Urban Crucible*, 228.

5. Thomas Porter's inventory in 1767 included tea- and coffeepots, cups and saucers, and a tea kettle. Elizabeth appears to have served little tea after 1767, for her own inventory has no teapots or kettles. Her son William's inventory from 1775 has silver teaspoons and tongs, but only a coffeepot. Thomas Porter inventory, 27 July 1767, CCR, W, VSL; Elizabeth Porter inventory, 26 April 1773, ibid.; William Porter inventory, 18 October 1775, ibid.; Kerber, *Women of the Republic*, 39–54; Mary Cooper Diary, 25 May 1769, Horne, ed., *The Diary of Mary Cooper*, 13; Buel and Buel, *The Way of Duty*, 69; Breen, "Narrative of Commercial Life," 490.

6. Eugenia W. Herbert, "A Note on Richard Bache (1737–1811)," *The Pensylvania Magazine of History and Biography*, C (January 1976), 99–103; Bell, "Sarah Franklin Bache," in James, et al., eds., *Notable American Women*, 75–76; Sheila L. Skemp, *Benjamin and William Franklin: Father and Son, Patriot and Loyalist* (Boston: Bedford Books of St. Martin's Press, 1994), 50, 187–90.

7. Deborah Norris to Sarah Wister, [26 December 1778], in Derounian, " 'A Dear Dear Friend,' " 507; Akers, *Abigail Adams*, 33–36, 64; Buel and Buel, *The Way of Duty*, 69; [E. Farmer] to Jack [?], 19 September 1774, Eliza Farmer Letterbook, 1774–1777, 1783–1789, Manuscripts, Historical Society of Pennsylvania; Crane, "The World of Elizabeth Drinker," 7; Rachal Wells, petition as cited in Kerber, " 'I Have Don . . . much to Carrey on the Warr,' " 231; Spruill, *Women's Life and Work in the Southern Colonies*, 244–45; Norton, *Liberty's Daughters*, 157, 190; Evans, *Weathering the Storm*, 266–68.

8. Lacey, "The World of Hannah Heaton," 301; [Eliza Farmer] to Jack [?], 3 January 1774, Eliza Farmer Letterbook, 1774–1777, 1783–1789, Manuscripts, Historical Society of Pennsylvania; Rosemarie Zagarri, *A Woman's Dilemma: Mercy Otis Warren and the American Revolution* (Wheeling, IL: Harlan Davidson, 1995), 28–44, 83–85.

9. E. Feilde to [Mrs. Maria Carter Armistead], 3 June 1776, Armistead-Cocke Papers, Rare Books and Manuscripts, Earl Gregg Swem Library, College of William and Mary; Cohen, "The Politics of Language," 488–89; Zagarri, *A Woman's Dilemma*, 73; Norton, *Liberty's Daughters*, 170–71. Norton argued that women may have used pamphlets because they had less access to newspapers. The proportion of women among printers at the time of the Revolution, however, is quite high.

10. Zagarri, *A Woman's Dilemma*, 55–77. Kerber advances the argument of less access. Kerber, " 'I Have Don . . . much to Carrey on the Warr,' " 237.

11. Gundersen, "Independence, Citizenship, and the American Revolution," 75; Akers, *Abigail Adams*, 71.

12. Norton, *Liberty's Daughters*, 226; Coleman, "Two Lees, Revolutionary Suffragists," 18–21.

13. Dowd, "Declarations of Dependence," 53–57; Irwin N. Gertzog, "Female Suffrage in New Jersey, 1790–1807," in *Women, Politics and the Constitution*, ed. Naomi B. Lynn (New York: Harrington Park Press, 1990), 47–58; Taylor, "Women and the Vote in Eighteenth-Century America," 16–17; Norton, *Liberty's Daughters*, 191–93.

14. Caroline Gilman, ed., *Letter of Eliza Wilkinson During the Invasion and Possession of Charlestown , S.C. By the British in the Revolutionary War* (New York: Samuel Coleman, 1839), 27–35; Kerber, *Women of the Republic*, 46–47; Wylma Anne Wates, "James L. Petigru and the Revolutionary War Widow: The Petition of Christiana Teulon," *South Carolina Historical Magazine*, LXXXV (October 1984): 70–71; Gilman, ed., *Letter of Eliza Wilkinson During the Invasion and Possession of Charlestown*, 88; Buel and Buel, *The Way of Duty*, 145–58; Pinckney, ed., *The Letterbook of Eliza Lucas Pinckney, 1739–1762*, xxiii–xxiv; Chalou, "Women in the American Revolution," in Deutrich and Purdy, *Clio Was a Woman*, 77; Frey, *Water From the Rock*, 93, 102–3.

15. Eliza Farmer to [Jackey], 4 December 1783, and Eliza Farmer to Madam Kensington, 25 October 1783, Eliza Farmer Letterbook, 1774–1777, 1783–1789, Manuscripts, Historical Society of Pennsylvania; Mary Gould Almy journal, 7–8 August 1778, in Evans, *Weathering the Storm*, 255–57; Cynthia Dublin Edelberg, *Jonathan Odell: Loyalist Poet of the American Revolution* (Durham: Duke University Press, 1987), 56–59.

16. Chalou, "Women in the American Revolution," in Deutrich and Purdy, *Clio Was a Woman*, 79; Public Testimony, John Franklin, H. Mulligan, Ezekiel Robins, New York, 4 February 1784, New York Historical Society, Misc. Manuscripts, Box 14.

17. Evans, *Weathering the Storm*, 84, 294–96; Norton, *Liberty's Daughters*, 175; Kerber, *Women of the Republic*, 49–51, 121–22; Rowe, "Women's Crime and Criminal Administration in Pennsylvania," 345; Norton, "Eighteenth-Century American Women in Peace and War," 398–99.

18. Graymont, *The Iroquois in the American Revolution*, 147; Kelsay, *Joseph Brant*, 208; Kirkland, ed., "Three Mecom- Franklin Letters," 267 fn.

19. Chalou, "Women in the American Revolution," in Deutrich and Purdy, *Clio Was a Woman*, 83; Norton, *Liberty's Daughters*, 202; Kerber, *Women of the Republic*, 46.

20. Graymont, *The Iroquois in the American Revolution*, 196. Susan Brownmiller developed the interpretation of rape as an act of power and extension of war in her classic study, *Against Our Will: Men, Women, and Rape* (New York: Simon and Schuster, 1975).

21. Norton, *Liberty's Daughters*, 9, 198–99; [Eliza Farmer] to Dear Nephew [Jackey], 4 December 1783, Eliza Farmer Letterbook, 1774–1777, 1783–1789, Manuscripts, Historical Society of Pennsylvania; E. Feilde to Maria Carter Armistead, 13 June 1776, Armistead-Cocke Papers, Rare Books and Manuscripts, Earl Gregg Swem Library, College of William and Mary; Sweeney, ed., "The Norris-Fisher Correspondence," 187–232; Derounian, " 'A Dear Dear Friend,' " 487–516; Kerber, *Women of the Republic*, 52; Filiaci, "Raising the Republic," 148.

22. Graymont, *The Iroquois in the American Revolution*, 253; White, *The Middle Ground*, 384–88; James H. Merrell, "Declarations of Independence," in Greene, ed., *The American Revolution*, 199.

23. Graymont, *The Iroquois in the American Revolution*, 188–89; White, *The Middle Ground*, 384–89; Colin Calloway, "The Shawnees' Revolution," 5, 9–11; Braund, "The Creek Indians, Blacks and Slavery," 621.

24. Anna Oosterhout Myers deposition, Dann, *The Revolution Remembered*, 268–73; Kerber, *Women of the Republic*, 48; Braund, "The Creek Indians, Blacks and Slavery," 618–19.

25. Graymont, *The Iroquois in the American Revolution*, 196, 213–18, 222; Seaver, *A Narrative of the Life of Mrs. Mary Jemison*, 69; Calloway, "The Shawnees' Revolution," 4–7; Merrell, *The Indian's New World*, 216.

26. Akers, *Abigail Adams*, 53–54; Buel and Buel, *The Way of Duty*, 143–44; Kerber, *Women of the Republic*, 43–44; Smith, "Food Rioters and the American Revolution," 3–38. For the poem, see Rosemary Skinner Keller, "Women, Civil Religion, and the American Revolution," in Ruether and Keller, eds., *Women and Religion in America*, 390.

27. Evans, *Weathering the Storm*, 161, 249–50, 266.

28. For epidemic information see Akers, *Abigail Adams*, 38–39; Buel and Buel, *The Way of Duty*, 96–100, 118; Linda Grant DePauw, "Women in Combat: The Revolutionary War Experience," *Armed Forces and Society*, VII (Winter 1981): 214. On black experience see Norton, *Liberty's Daughters*, 210–11;

Smaby, *The Transformation of Moravian Bethlehem*, 39–40; Frey, *Water From the Rock*, 118–22; 169–71.

29. Norton, *Liberty's Daughters*, 204–5; Kerber, *Women of the Republic*, 63–65; Chalou, "Women in the American Revolution," in Deutrich and Purdy, *Clio Was a Woman*, 76; Evans, *Weathering the Storm*, 163–66.

30. For examples of pension petitions, see Dann, *The Revolution Remembered, passim*. Wates, "James L. Petigru and the Revolutionary War Widow," 68–71. For analyses of the petitioners to Congress, see Kerber, *Women of the Republic*, 87–93; Chalou, "Women in the American Revolution," in Deutrich and Purdy, *Clio Was a Woman*, 75–82; Norton, "Eighteenth-Century American Women in Peace and War," 404–7.

31. Hamilton, "Mary Brant," in James, et al., eds., *Notable American Women*, 230; Graymont, *The Iroquois in the American Revolution*, 147; Norton, "Eighteenth-Century American Women in Peace and War," 394–401.

32. Frey, *Water From the Rock*, 179–93.

33. Evans, *Weathering the Storm*, 234; Kerber, *Women of the Republic*, 75–76; Norton, *Liberty's Daughters*, 173.

34. Evans, *Weathering the Storm*, 202, 206, 248–49; Rowe, "Women's Crime and Criminal Administration in Pennsylvania," 345; Kerber, *Women of the Republic*, 123.

35. Evans, *Weathering the Storm*, 202–34; Edelberg, *Jonathan Odell*, 148–52; Kerber, *Women of the Republic*, 123.

36. Ardelia [Deborah Norris] to Sarah Wister [April 1778], in Derounian, " 'A Dear Dear Friend,' " 500; Evans, *Weathering the Storm*, 167–70, 184–88; Norton, *Liberty's Daughters*, 128; Kerber, *Women of the Republic*, 94–95.

37. Abigail Adams is one of the women who went from saying "yours" to "mine." Akers, *Abigail Adams*, 58–69; Buel and Buel, *The Way of Duty*, 105–12, 141, 177, 201; Wates, "James L. Petigru and the Revolutionary War Widow," 70; Norton, *Liberty's Daughters*, 216–21.

38. Kerber, *Women of the Republic*, 43. For other examples, see Elizabeth Drinker and Margaret Morris diaries, October, in Evans, *Weathering the Storm*, 94, 160.

39. Norton, *Liberty's Daughters*, 178–80; Kerber, *Women of the Republic*, 99–102.

40. Evans, *Weathering the Storm*, 288–89; Norton, *Liberty's Daughters*, 178–80. Other Philadelphia women involved in the effort included Julia Stockton Rush, Alice Lee Shippen, Sally McKean, and Mrs. Robert Morris.

41. No women from Germantown, Pennsylvania, for example, joined the efforts. Wolf, *Urban Village*, 179; Norton, *Liberty's Daughters*, 182–84; Kerber, *Women of the Republic*, 102–3; Filiaci, "Raising the Republic," 149–54.

42. DePauw, "Women in Combat," 209; Kerber, "History Can Do It No Justice," in Hoffman and Albert, *Women in the Age of the American Revolution*

(1989), 13–14; Chalou, "Women in the American Revolution," in Deutrich and Purdy, *Clio Was a Woman*, 85.

43. Kerber, "History Can Do It No Justice," in Hoffman and Albert, *Women in the Age of the American Revolution*, 40; DePauw, "Women in Combat," 209, 219, 221–22.

44. Curtis Carroll Davis, "Helping to Hold the Fort, Elizabeth Zane at Wheeling, 1782: A Case Study in Reknown," *West Virginia History*, XLIV (Spring, 1983): 212–25; DePauw, "Women in Combat," 222–24; Graymont, *The Iroquois in the American Revolution*, 134, 188–89, 236.

45. DePauw, "Women in Combat," 217–19.

46. Dugaw, *Warrior Women*, 5–54; Stickley, "The Records of Deborah Sampson Gannett," 235–40; Evans, *Weathering the Storm* (1975), 303–16; [H. Mann], *The Female Review*.

47. DePauw, "Women in Combat," 211–14, 217; Kerber, "History Can Do It No Justice," in Hoffman and Albert, *Women in the Age of the American Revolution*, 13–14; Norton, *Liberty's Daughters*, 213; Jones, "Race, Sex, and Self-Evident Truths," in Hoffman and Albert, *Women in the Age of the American Revolution*, 327. Jones does not identify as army women the blacks serving as workers, but the duties match.

48. Kerber says a General Order did establish the 1:15 ratio at the end of the war; DePauw claims that the measure was only discussed. DePauw, "Women in Combat," 211–16; Kerber, "History Can Do It No Justice," in Hoffman and Albert, *Women in the Age of the American Revolution*, 12, 15; Chalou, "Women in the American Revolution," in Deutrich and Purdy, *Clio Was a Woman*, 85.

49. At least one other woman besides Hayes served on a gun crew at Monmouth. DePauw, "Women in Combat," 213–16; Kerber, "History Can Do It No Justice," in Hoffman and Albert, *Women in the Age of the American Revolution*, 13–14; Sarah Osborn Benjamin pension depositions in Dann, *The Revolution Remembered*, 240–48.

50. The struggle women would have to go through to be allowed to be nurses during the Civil War is a measure of how completely this earlier service had slipped from view. Spruill, *Women's Life and Work in the Southern Colonies*, 271; Kerber, *Women of the Republic*, 59–60; Chalou, "Women in the American Revolution," in Deutrich and Purdy, *Clio Was a Woman* 84; DePauw, "Women in Combat," 213–14.

51. Chalou, "Women in the American Revolution," in Deutrich and Purdy, *Clio Was a Woman*, 84; Elizabeth Sandwich Drinker diary, 6–11 October 1777, and Margaret Hill Morris diary, 28–30 December 1776, 4 January 1777, 14 June 1777, in Evans, *Weathering the Storm*, 92–94, 101–2, 160.

52. DePauw, "Women in Combat," 210–11; Kerber, *Women of the Republic*, 57; Graymont, *The Iroquois in the American Revolution*, 208; Chalou, "Women in the American Revolution," in Deutrich and Purdy, *Clio Was a Woman*, 85.

53. Frey, *Water From the Rock*, 82–93, 118–22, 163–71.

54. Kerber, " 'I Have Don . . . much to Carrey on the Warr,' " 232–33; Crane, "Dependence in the Era of Independence," in Greene, ed., *The American Revolution*," 257; Norton, *Liberty's Daughters*, 176–77; Akers, *Abigail Adams*, 37–38.

Chapter 10

1. Abigail Adams to Mercy Warren, 9 March 1807, "Warren-Adams Letters," *Massachusetts Historical Society Collections*, LXXIII (1925). Mary Beth Norton, "Reflections on Women in the Age of the American Revolution," in Hoffman and Albert, *Women in the Age of the American Revolution*, 488–92, suggests a trade-off interpretation, as does Gundersen, "Independence, Citizenship, and the American Revolution," 59–77. For negative assessments of the Revolution's impact on women, see Crane, "Dependence in the Era of Independence," in Greene, ed., *The American Revolution*, 253–75; Joan Hoff Wilson, "The Illusion of Change: Women and the Revolution," in Alfred F. Young, ed., *The American Revolution: Explorations in the History of Radicalism* (DeKalb: Northern Illinois University, 1976), 393–400; and Kerber, *Women of the Republic*. For more positive views, see Norton's earlier work, *Liberty's Daughters*. For a review of the debate see Kerber, "History Can Do It No Justice," in Hoffman and Albert, *Women in the Age of the American Revolution*.

2. Gundersen, "Independence, Citizenship, and the American Revolution," 59–77; Dowd, "Declarations of Dependence," 47–67.

3. Gundersen, "Independence, Citizenship, and the American Revolution," 74; Cowell, ed., " 'Womankind Call Reason to Their Aid,' " 800.

4. For a discussion of the idea of equality in women's thought, see Cohen, "Mercy Otis Warren: The Politics of Language," 492; Cowell, ed., " 'Womankind Call Reason to Their Aid,' " 799–800; Norton, *Liberty's Daughters*, 252; Kerber, *Women of the Republic*, 30; Zagarri, *A Woman's Dilemma*, 111. For independence as religious or psychological, see Ulrich, " 'Daughters of Liberty,' " in Hoffman and Albert, *Women in the Age of the American Revolution*, 234–35; Grimsted, "Anglo-American Racism," in ibid., 379–80; Kerber, " 'I Have Don . . . much to Carrey on the Warr,' " 239.

5. Marylynn Salmon, "Republican Sentiment, Economic Change, and the Property Rights of Women in American Law," in Hoffman and Albert, *Women in the Age of the American Revolution*, 449–50; Salmon, *Women and the Law of Property in Early America*, 94–95, 112–15, 123–34; Crane, "Dependence in the Era of Independence," in Greene, ed., *The American Revolution*, 263. Salmon tends to emphasize the positive aspects of legal change for women, but her evidence can be read differently.

6. Bell, "Sarah Franklin Bache," in James, et al., eds., *Notable American Women*, 75–76; Salmon, "Equality or Submersion? Feme Covert Status in Early

Pennsylvania," in Berkin and Norton, *Women of America*, 95–96; Salmon, *Women and the Law of Property in Early America*, 94–95.

7. Kerber, *Women of the Republic*, 119; Kerber, "History Can Do It No Justice," in Hoffman and Albert, *Women in the Age of the American Revolution*, 34; Gundersen, "Independence, Citizenship, and the American Revolution," 68–74.

8. For more on women's economic dependence, see Crane, "Dependence in the Era of Independence," in Greene, ed., *The American Revolution*, 258–60. Evidence of Anne Porter's sewing is in the estate records of Benjamin Harris II, Chesterfield County, 1786, Will Book, Virginia State Library Archives; on her inheritances see Thomas Porter will, 27 April 1767, Cumberland County Wills, and Charles Sampson will, 19 February 1776, Virginia State Library Archives. Lee, "Social Order," 104–11, has a discussion of gender stratification in landholding.

9. Ulrich, " 'Daughters of Liberty,' " in Hoffman and Albert, *Women in the Age of the American Revolution*, 211–28; Cohen, "Mercy Otis Warren: The Politics of Language," 481; Dowd, "Declarations of Dependence," 48–49, 54–56; Kerber, " 'I Have Don . . . much to Carrey on the Warr,' " 234–35; Gelles, "The Threefold Cord," 1–2; Zagarri, *A Woman's Dilemma*, 48–77; Bloch, "The Gendered Meanings of Virtue in Revolutionary America," 39–57; Kerber, "History Can Do It No Justice," in Hoffman and Albert, *Women in the Age of the American Revolution*, 26–29.

10. Kerber, *Women of the Republic*, 280–83; Norton, *Liberty's Daughters*, 251; Zagarri, *A Woman's Dilemma*, 121–23, 148–49.

11. Zagarri, *A Woman's Dilemma*, 27, 93; Zagarri, "Morals, Manners, and the Republican Mother," 3–8, 21; Cohen, "Mercy Otis Warren: The Politics of Language," 492; Bloch, "The Gendered Meanings of Virtue in Revolutionary America," 44–47; Akers, *Abigail Adams*, 74.

12. Mathews, "The Religious Experience of Southern Women," in Ruether and Keller, eds., *Women and Religion in America*, 198–201; Kerber, *Women of the Republic*, 110–11; Nancy Cott, *The Bonds of Womanhood: "Woman's Sphere" in New England, 1780–1835* (New Haven: Yale University Press, 1977), 64–68, 128–30.

13. Akers, *Abigail Adams*, 74; Lewis, "The Republican Wife," 698–700, 715; Cohen, "Mercy Otis Warren: The Politics of Language," 498.

14. Lewis, "The Republican Wife," 698–715; for Thomas Paine's formulation of women surrounded by tyrants and seducers, see Crane, "Dependence in the Era of Independence," in Greene, ed., *The American Revolution*, 254–56; for the emphasis on freedom of choice at marriage, see Norton, *Liberty's Daughters*, 252; for an illustration of divorce theory, see Dewey, "Thomas Jefferson's Notes on Divorce," 214; for Mercy Warren's views on virtue, family, and republicanism, see Cohen, "Mercy Otis Warren: The Politics of Language," 490–98.

15. Kerber, *Women of the Republic*, 203–10, 227–29; Norton, *Liberty's Daughters*, 264–73; Melvin Yazawa, "Creating a Republican Citizenry," in

Greene, ed., *The American Revolution*, 282–83; Gordon, "The Young Ladies Academy of Philadelphia," in Berkin and Norton, eds., *Women of America*, 69–79.

16. Kerber, *Women of the Republic*, 200, 201, 220–21; Davidson, *Revolution and the Word*, 63; Norton, *Liberty's Daughters*, 266–73; Gordon, "The Young Ladies Academy of Philadelphia," in Berkin and Norton, eds., *Women of America*, 69–91.

17. Mary Brant is buried in the Anglican churchyard of what is now St. Paul's Church (then St. George's), Kingston. Hamilton, "Mary Brant," in James, et al., eds., *Notable American Women*, 230; Kelsay, *Joseph Brant*, 366.

18. Grimsted, "Anglo-American Racism,' " in Hoffman and Albert, *Women in the Age of the American Revolution*, 396; Soderlund, "Black Women," 49–61; Kruger, "Born to Run," 608–12; Benjamin Quarles, " 'Freedom Fettered': Blacks in the Constitutional Era in Maryland, 1776–1810—An Introduction," *Maryland Historical Magazine*, LXXXIV (Winter 1989): 299; Nash, *Forging Freedom*, 89; Ira Berlin, *Slaves Without Masters: The Free Negro in the Antebellum South* (New York: Vintage Books, 1976), 25; Frey, *Water From the Rock*, 240–47, 270–71.

19. The quote is from the will of Thomas Flournoy, 18 September 1794, Powhatan County Will Book, Virginia State Archives; Dowd, "Declarations of Dependence," 49–50; Grimsted, "Anglo-American Racism" in Hoffman and Albert, *Women in the Age of the American Revolution*, 338–41.

20. Gregory, "Black Women in Pre-Federal America," in Deutrich and Purdy, *Clio Was a Woman*, 62; Kaplan, *The Black Presence in the Era of the American Revolution*, 245.

21. Esther Harrison freed her slave Judah in 1776 in Maryland, for example, but required her to live with Harrison's grandchildren and do their washing, mending, and cooking until the children came of age. Quarles, " 'Freedom Fettered' " 300–301; Lee, "Social Order," 98; Berlin, *Slaves Without Masters*, 29.

22. Berlin, *Slaves Without Masters*, 33; for an example of an owner trying to ignore the servant status of mulattoes on his plantation, see Douglas Deal, "A Constricted World: Free Blacks on Virginia's Eastern Shore, 1680–1750," in Carr, et al. eds., *Colonial Chesapeake Society*, 301–3.

23. Gregory, "Black Women in Pre-Federal America," in Deutrich and Purdy, *Clio Was a Woman*, 61; Nash, *Forging Freedom*, 143; Berlin, *Slaves Without Masters*, 48; Daniel Branch will, 17 October 1782, Powhatan County, Will Book, Virginia State Archives. For emancipations by will in Powhatan County, see the will of Thomas Flournoy, 18 September 1794, Esther Langsdon will, 19 December 1793, John Maxey will, 21 December 1803, Benjamin Harris will, 20 October 1802, and Thomas Turpin will, 16 September 1790, PCR, W, VSA.

24. Grimsted, "Anglo-American Racism" in Hoffman and Albert, *Women in the Age of the American Revolution*, 408–9; Dowd, "Declarations of Dependence," 49–50; Wright, *African Americans*, 117.

25. Merrell, "Declarations of Independence," in Greene, ed., *The American Revolution*, 200–201.

26. Nash, *Forging Freedom*, 76–77, 89, 92–93; Buel and Buel, *The Way of Duty*, 208–10; Newman, "Black Women," 281–82, 285; Kruger, "Born to Run," 725–50; Kaplan, *The Black Presence in the Era of the American Revolution*, 243–44, 261–63; Gregory, "Black Women in Pre-Federal America," in Deutrich and Purdy, *Clio Was a Woman*, 67; Susan Lebsock, "Free Black Women and the Question of Matriarchy: Petersburg, Virginia, 1784–1870," *Feminist Studies*, VIII (Summer 1982): 271–77.

27. Kerber, *Women of the Republic*, 111; Norton, *Liberty's Daughters*, 614–15; Filiaci, "Raising the Republic," 161–82.

28. Bloch, "The Gendered Meanings of Virtue in Revolutionary America," 48–56. Terri Premo notes a growing gender differentiation in the understandings of aging. Premo, *Winter Friends*, 123; Norton, *Liberty's Daughters*, 7.

29. Guldenzopf, "Mohawk," 72, 101; Kelsay, *Joseph Brant*, 349; Dowd, "Paths of Resistance," 550–52.

30. Mary E. Young, "Women, Civilization, and the Indian Question," in Deutrich and Purdy, *Clio Was a Woman*, 99–106; Perdue, "Cherokee Women and the Trail of Tears," 17–21; Perdue, *Slavery and the Evolution of Cherokee Society, 1540–1866*, 50–52; Nash, *Red, White, and Black*, 241–42; Merrell, "Declarations of Independence," in Greene, ed., *The American Revolution*, 199–204; Calloway, "The Shawnees' Revolution," 11.

31. Devens, "Separate Confrontations," 74–77; White, *The Middle Ground*, 508.

BIBLIOGRAPHICAL ESSAY

The literature on women's participation in the American Revolution has grown greatly since the bicentennial of the Revolution, but general studies of eighteenth-century women's lives remain few. Much of the information remains scattered as incidental evidence or comparative data in gender-sensitive works. Scholarly editions of some women's diaries and letters have appeared recently, and new biographies of prominent women have appeared, but most research is on a single colony. Some of the interesting women's documents are now in print, but many are not. Of general background studies of eighteenth-century America, Gary Nash's book *Red, White, and Black* provided one of the few models for a synthesis of the colonial period integrating Indian experience with those of Europeans and Africans.

The story of Elizabeth Porter and her family is found in the manuscript records of Goochland, Cumberland, Chesterfield, and Powhatan Counties held by the Virginia State Library, in published primary sources on the Huguenot immigration, and in King William Parish records. The material on Peg and Amy came from these same sources and from studies of Chesapeake slavery cited later. Donald M. Sweig, "The Importation of African Slaves to the Potomac River, 1732–1772," *William and Mary Quarterly*, XLII (October 1985), and Walter Minchinton, Celia King, and Peter Waite, *Virginia Slave-Trade Statistics 1698–1775* (Richmond: Virginia State Library, 1984) helped put Peg and Amy's lives in the context of the slave trade.

Scholarly studies of the women of the Brant and Franklin families are limited to the short sketches in Edward T. James, Janet Wilson James, Paul S. Boyer, eds., *Notable American Women: A Biographical Dictionary* (Cambridge, MA: Harvard Press, 1971) and what appears incidentally in the biographies of the famous men in their families. David Freeman Hawke, *Franklin* (New York: Harper & Row, 1976), and Carl Van Doren, *Benjamin Franklin* (New York: Viking Press, 1938), both contain considerable material on Deborah. Some of Deborah's letters are accessible through the ongoing series of Benjamin Franklin papers. Information on Deborah Franklin's niece and daughter is found in *Pennsylvania Magazine of History and Biography* articles by Mary D. Turnbull, "William Dunlap, Colonial Printer, Journalist, and Minister," CIII (April 1979), and Eugenia W. Herbert, "A Note on Richard Bache (1737–1811)," C (January 1976). The Franklins' lives are put in context in the fine social histories of Philadelphia provided by numerous scholars including Gary B. Nash, *The Urban Crucible: The Northern Seaports and the Origins of the American Revolution* (Cambridge: Harvard University Press, 1986), abr. ed., and Susan Edith Klepp, "Philadelphia in Transition: A Demographic History of the City and Its Occupational Groups, 1720–1830" (Ph.D. dissertation, University of Pennsylvania, 1980).

Despite recent interest in the Iroquois, Mary Brant still lacks a full, scholarly treatment. Isabel Thompson Kelsay, *Joseph Brant, 1743–1807: Man of Two Worlds*, (Syracuse: Syracuse University Press, 1984), weaves information on Margaret and Mary into her account; Barbara Graymont's *The Iroquois in the American Revolution* (Syracuse: Syracuse University Press, 1972) was useful in providing a general context for Mary Brant's work during the Revolution. David Guldenzopf's dissertation, "The Colonial Transformation of Mohawk Iroquois Society" (Ph.D. dissertation, SUNY Albany, 1986), provided fascinating archaeological information on the Brants.

A study of women in the American Revolution begins with Linda K. Kerber, *Women of the Republic: Intellect and Ideology in Revolutionary America* (Chapel Hill: University of North Carolina Press, 1980), and Mary Beth Norton, *Liberty's Daughters: The Revolutionary Experience of American Women, 1750–1800* (Boston: Little, Brown and Company, 1980). Norton claimed that the Revolution improved women's lives, while Kerber characterized the Revolution as more conservative concerning women's status. In her essay, "The Illusion of Change: Women and the Revolution," in Alfred F. Young, ed., *The American Revolution: Explorations in the History of Radicalism* (DeKalb: Northern Illinois Press, 1976), Joan Hoff Wilson argued that the Revolution brought no substantive improvement. Other pioneer studies include George C. Chalou, "Women in the American Revolution: Vignettes or Profiles," in Mabel E. Deutrich and Virginia C. Purdy, *Clio Was a Woman: Studies in the History of American Women* (Washington, DC: Howard University Press, 1980), and a good collection of diaries edited by Elizabeth Evans, *Weathering the Storm: Women of the American Revolution* (New York: Charles Scribner's Sons, 1975).

In 1989 a number of scholars (including Kerber, Norton, and Laurel Ulrich) contributed essays to the collection edited by Ronald Hoffman and Peter Albert, *Women in the Age of the American Revolution* (Charlottesville: University Press of Virginia). These suggest a more complex set of changes and roles for women in the Revolution. Several essays in Jack Greene, ed., *The American Revolution: Its Character and Limits* (New York: New York University Press, 1987) include information on women. Linda Grant DePauw's "Women in Combat: The Revolutionary War Experience," *Armed Forces and Society*, VII (Winter 1981), has rewritten our understanding of women's roles in the military. For another form of activism see Barbara Clark Smith, "Food Rioters and the American Revolution," *William and Mary Quarterly*, LI (January 1994). The best work on loyalist women is Mary Beth Norton's article, "Eighteenth-Century American Women in Peace and War: The Case of the Loyalists," *William and Mary Quarterly*, XXXIII (January 1976). The pension requests for Revolutionary War veterans document the experiences of ordinary women during the war. See John C. Dann, *The Revolution Remembered: Eyewitness Accounts of the War for Independence* (Chicago: University of Chicago Press, 1980); Constance B. Schulz, "Daughter of Liberty: The History of Women in the Revolutionary War Pension Records," *Prologue: The Journal of the National Archives*, XVI (Fall 1984); and Julia Ward Stickley, "The Records of Deborah Sampson Gannett, Woman Soldier of the Revolution," *Prologue: Journal of the National Archives*, IV (Winter 1972) for examples of the accounts and their use.

Historians have explored how the ideas of independence and dependence, virtue, and civic actions relate to the political theory of the Revolutionary era. See especially the essays of Joan R. Gundersen, "Independence, Citizenship, and the American Revolution," and Ruth Bloch, "The Gendered Meanings of Virtue in Revolutionary America," in *Signs: Journal of Women in Culture and Society*, XIII (1987); Gregory Evans Dowd, "Declarations of Dependence: War and Inequality in Revolutionary New Jersey, 1776–1815," *New Jersey History*, CIII (Spring/Summer 1985); and Jan Lewis, "The Republican Wife: Virtue and Seduction in the Early Republic," *William and Mary Quarterly* 3rd ser., XLIV (October 1987). Caroline Taylor, "Women and the Vote in Eighteenth-Century America," *Humanities*, VIII (July/August 1987), and Irwin N. Gertzog, "Female Suffrage in New Jersey, 1790–1807," in

Women, Politics and the Constitution, ed. Naomi B. Lynn (New York: Harrington Park Press, 1990) document early requests for women's suffrage. Republican motherhood, first discussed by Kerber and Norton, is the theme of Anne Marie Filiaci's dissertation, "Raising the Republic: American Women in the Public Sphere, 1750–1800" (Ph.D. dissertation, SUNY Buffalo, 1982).

The starting place for general studies of women's lives in the eighteenth century is Julia Cherry Spruill, *Women's Life and Work in the Southern Colonies* (New York: W.W. Norton & Co., 1972 [paperback ed.]), and Laurel Ulrich, *Good Wives: Image and Reality in the Lives of Women in Northern New England, 1650–1750* (New York: Alfred A. Knopf, 1982). Linda Speth and Alison Duncan Hirsch in *Women, Family, and Community in Colonial America: Two Perspectives*, IV Women and History (Institute for Research in History and the Haworth Press, Inc., 1982), illuminate aspects of life for women in Connecticut and Virginia at mid-century. Carole Shammas has fascinating material in "The Female Social Structure of Philadelphia in 1776," *The Pennsylvania Magazine of History and Biography*, CVII (January 1983), and Lisa Wilson Waciega's "A 'Man of Business': The Widow of Means in Southeastern Pennsylvania, 1750–1830," *William and Mary Quarterly*, 3rd ser., XLIV (January 1987), provides a short taste of her recent book, *Life After Death: Widows in Pennsylvania, 1750–1850* (Philadelphia: Temple University Press, 1992).

Biographical literature of women during the era now includes the work of Joy Day Buel and Richard Buel Jr. on Mary Fish Noyes Silliman, *The Way of Duty: A Woman and Her Family in Revolutionary America* (New York: W.W. Norton & Co., 1984), and Rosemarie Zagarri's *A Woman's Dilemma: Mercy Otis Warren and the American Revolution* (Wheeling, IL: Harlan Davidson, 1995). Laurel Ulrich's *A Midwife's Tale: the Life of Martha Ballard, Based on Her Diary, 1785–1812* (New York: Knopf, 1990) re-creates the life and community of Martha Ballard in Maine. There are numerous works on Abigail Adams, but Charles W. Akers' *Abigail Adams: An American Woman* (Boston: Little, Brown and Company, 1980) is a good overview, as is the recent work by Edith Gelles, *Portia: the World of Abigail Adams* (Bloomington: Indiana University Press, 1992). Elaine Foreman Crane, chief editor of the Drinker diaries, *The Diary of Elizabeth Drinker* (Boston: Northeastern University Press, 1991), provides a short introduction to this prominent Quaker in "The World of Elizabeth Drinker," *The Pennsylvania Magazine of History and Biography*, CVII (January 1983). Barbara Lacey's articles, "The Bonds of Friendship: Sarah Osborn of Newport and the Reverend Joseph Fish of North Stonington, 1743–1779," *Rhode Island History*, LV (November 1986), and "The World of Hannah Heaton: The Autobiography of an Eighteenth-Century Connecticut Farm Woman," *William and Mary Quarterly*, 3rd ser., XLV (April 1988), add to our understanding of religious women's lives before the Revolution. For a prominent loyalist, see Mary Beth Norton's "A Cherished Spirit of Independence: The Life of an Eighteenth-Century Boston Business-woman," in Carol Berkin and Mary Beth Norton, *Women of America: A History* (Boston: Houghton Mifflin Company, 1979).

Women writers have gotten more attention. For Mercy Warren's plays and histories, see Lester H. Cohen, "Explaining the Revolution: Ideology and Ethics in Mercy Otis Warren's Historical Theory," *William and Mary Quarterly*, 3rd ser., XXXVII (April 1980), and "Mercy Otis Warren: The Politics of Language," *American Quarterly*, XXXV (1983). David Grimsted's essay in *Women in the Age of the American Revolution*; Charles W. Akers, " 'Our Modern Egyptians': Phillis Wheatley and the Whig Campaign Against Slavery in Revolutionary Boston," *Journal of Negro History*, LX (July 1975); and R. Lynn Matson, "Phillis Wheatley—Soul Sister?" *Phylon*, XXXIII (Fall 1972) are discussions of Phillis Wheatley. Pattie Cowell, ed., " 'Womankind Call Reason to Their Aid': Susanna Wright's Verse Epistle on the Status of Women in Eighteenth-Century America," *Signs: Journal of Women in Culture and Society*, VI (Summer 1981) gives background on another woman poet.

For diaries and journals exploring generally women's lives after 1750, see Carol Karlsen and Laurie Crumpacker, *The Journal of Esther Edwards Burr, 1754–1757* (New Haven: Yale University Press, 1984); William L. Andrews, ed., *Journeys in New Worlds: Early American Women's Narratives* (Madison: University of Wisconsin Press, 1990); Elise Pinckney, ed., asst. by Marvin R. Zahniser and introduction by Walter Muir Whitehill, *The Letterbook of Eliza Lucas Pinckney, 1739–1762* (Chapel Hill: University of North Carolina Press, 1972); and Field Horn, ed., *The Diary of Mary Cooper: Life on a Long Island Farm, 1768–1773* (Oyster Bay: Oyster Bay Historical Society, 1981).

Exploration of women's formal education in the eighteenth century begins with the debate over their literacy. Follow the debate through Kenneth Lockridge, *Literacy in Colonial New England* (New York: W.W. Norton & Co., 1974); Linda Auwers, "Reading the Marks of the Past: Exploring Female literacy in Colonial Windsor, Connecticut,"

XIII (Fall 1980), *Historical Methods* and the article by Joseph Perlman and Dennis Shirley, "When Did New England Women Acquire Literacy?" *William and Mary Quarterly*, 3rd ser., XLVIII (January 1991), with an exchange between Mary Beth Norton and Jack Perlman in the following issue. See also Cathy N. Davidson, *Revolution and the Word: The Rise of the Novel in America* (New York: Oxford University Press, 1986). For women's formal education, see the books by Kerber, Norton, Spruill, and Szaz, and Ann D. Gordon, "The Young Ladies Academy of Philadelphia," in Carol Berkin and Mary Beth Norton, eds., *Women of America: A History* (Boston: Houghton Mifflin Company, 1979).

General histories of eighteenth-century community life have become a veritable industry since 1970. Robert Gross, *The Minutemen and Their World* (New York: Hill and Wang, 1976); Rhys Isaac, *The Transformation of Virginia, 1740–1790* (Chapel Hill: University of North Carolina Press, 1982); and Daniel Blake Smith, *Inside the Great House: Planter Family Life in Eighteenth-Century Chesapeake Society* (Ithaca and London: Cornell University Press, 1980) focus more on male culture in planter society, but have some information on women. Allan Kulikoff, *Tobacco and Slaves: The Development of Southern Cultures in the Chesapeake, 1680–1800* (Chapel Hill: University of North Carolina Press, 1986); Darrett B. Rutman and Anita H. Rutman, *A Place in Time: Middlesex County, Virginia, 1650–1750* (New York: W.W. Norton & Co., 1984); and Jean Butenhoff Lee, "The Social Order of a Revolutionary People: Charles County Maryland, 1733–86" (Ph.D. dissertation, University of Virginia, 1984) provide contrasting, but sophisticated, gender-sensitive studies of the Chesapeake, as do several essays in Lois Green Carr, Philip D. Morgan, and Jean B. Russo, ed., *Colonial Chesapeake Society* (Chapel Hill: University of North Carolina Press, 1988). Frontier women are less noticed, although Susan C. Boyle, "Did She Generally Decide? Women in Ste. Genevieve, 1750–1806," *William and Mary Quarterly*, 3rd ser., XLIV (October 1987), and the 1985 dissertation by Kaylene Hughes, "Populating the Back Country: the Demographic and Social Characteristics of the Colonial South Carolina Frontier, 1730–1760" (Ph.D. dissertation, Florida State University), are exceptions.

The general studies of eighteenth-century religion have little to say about women. See, for example, Patricia U. Bonomi, *Under the Cope of Heaven: Religion, Society, and Politics in Colonial America* (New York: Oxford University Press, 1986), and Jon Butler, *Awash in a Sea of Faith: Christianizing the American People* (Cambridge: Harvard University

Press, 1990). The essays in Rosemary Radford Ruether and Rosemary Skinner Keller, *Women and Religion in America* (San Francisco: Harper & Row, 1983), compensate partially for this oversight. Anglicanism, however, is neglected. For that, consult Joan R. Gundersen, "The Non-Institutional Church: The Religious Roles of Women in Eighteenth-Century Virginia," *Historical Magazine* of the Protestant Episcopal Church, 1982, and Joanna B. Gillespie, " 'A noble part in the maintenance of religion': Eighteenth Century Episcopal Women in (what became the) diocese of Rhode Island," in Susan Hagood Lee, ed., *Remembering Our Sisters: The Rhode Island Herstory Project* (Rhode Island: Private Printing, 1987). For the Methodists, the dissertation by Doris Elisabett Andrews, "Popular Religion and the Revolution in the Middle Atlantic Ports: The Role of the Methodists, 1770–1800" (Ph.D. dissertation, University of Pennsylvania, 1986), has the best information on women. Susan Juster's sophisticated interpretation of gender relations in New England Baptist churches, *Disorderly Women: Sexual Politics and Evangelicalism in Revolutionary New England* (Ithaca and London: Cornell University Press, 1994), also provides a guide to the many articles on New England. See also the dissertation by Barbara Ellson Lacey, "Women and the Great Awakening in Connecticut" (Ph.D. dissertation, Clark University, 1982). William Lumpkin, "The Role of Women in Eighteenth Century Virginia Baptist Life," *Baptist History and Heritage*, VIII (1973), gives a basic overview of Southern Baptists. Joyce Goodfriend, "The Social Dimensions of Congregational Life in Colonial New York City," *William and Mary Quarterly*, 3rd ser., XLVI (April 1989), has written one of the few comparative studies sensitive to gender. Both Beverly Prior Smaby, *The Transformation of Moravian Bethlehem: From Communal Mission to Family Economy* (Philadelphia: University of Pennsylvania Press, 1988), and Daniel B. Thorp, *The Moravian Community in Colonial North Carolina: Pluralism on the Southern Frontier* (Knoxville: University of Tennessee Press, 1989), give good attention to women in the Moravian traditions. The best places to start for Quaker women in this era are Mary Maples Dunn, "Women of Light," in Carol Berkin and Mary Beth Norton, eds., *Women of America: A History* (Boston: Houghton Mifflin Company, 1979), and Jean R. Soderlund, "Women's Authority in Pennsylvania and New Jersey Quaker Meetings, 1680–1760," *William and Mary Quarterly*, 3rd ser., XLIV (October 1987). On black and Indian religion, see Carol A. Devens, *Countering Colonization: Native American Women and Great Lakes Missions, 1630–1900* (Berkeley: University of California Press,

1992); Gregory Evans Dowd, *A Spirited Resistance: the American Indian Struggle for Unity, 1745–1815* (Baltimore: Johns Hopkins University Press, 1992); Michael A. Gomez, "Muslims in Early America," *Journal of Southern History*, LX (November, 1994), 671–710; and Sylvia R. Frey, *Water From the Rock: Black Resistance in a Revolutionary Age* (Princeton, NJ: Princeton University Press, 1991). The research by Gomez challenges interpretations in Mechal Sobel's *The World They Made Together: Black and White Values in Eighteenth-Century Virginia* (Princeton: Princeton University Press, 1987) and Butler's *Awash in a Sea of Faith*, who see less persistence of African religion.

Recent studies of early American Indians use gender analysis. In addition to Dowd and Devens, the most helpful are James H. Merrell, *The Indian's New World: Catawbas and Their Neighbors from European Contact through the Era of Removal* (Chapel Hill: University of North Carolina Press, 1989); Theda Perdue, *Slavery and the Evolution of Cherokee Society, 1540–1866* (Knoxville: University of Tennessee Press, 1979); and Richard White, *The Middle Ground: Indians, Empires, and Republics in the Great Lakes Region, 1650–1815* (New York: Cambridge University Press, 1991). A handy compilation of primary materials is found in James Axtell, ed., *The Indian Peoples of Eastern America: A Documentary History of the Sexes* (New York: Oxford University Press, 1981). For assimilation pressures on women, see Margaret Connell Szasz, *Indian Education in the American Colonies, 1607–1783* (Albuquerque: University of New Mexico Press, 1988); Sylvia Van Kirk, *Many Tender Ties: Women in Fur Trade Society, 1670–1870* (Norman and London: University of Oklahoma Press, 1983); Marshall J. Becker, "Hannah Freeman: An Eighteenth-Century Lenape Living and Working Among Colonial Farmers," *Pennsylvania Magazine of History and Biography*, CXIV (April 1990); and Daniel Mandell, " 'To Live More Like My Christian English Neighbors': Natick Indians in the Eighteenth Century," *William and Mary Quarterly*, 3rd ser., XLVIII (October 1991). James H. Merrell, "Declarations of Independence: Indian-White Relations in the New Nation," in Greene, *The American Revolution*; Mary E. Young, "Women, Civilization, and the Indian Question," in Mabel E. Deutrich and Virginia C. Purdy, *Clio Was a Woman: Studies in the History of American Women* (Washington, DC: Howard University Press, 1980); and Theda Perdue, "Cherokee Women and the Trail of Tears," *Journal of Women's History*, I (Spring 1989), cover the decline in women's leadership.

Among the few pieces to focus on eighteenth-century black women are Joan R. Gundersen, "The Double Bonds of Race and Sex: Black and White Women in a Colonial Virginia Parish," *Journal of Southern History*, LII (August 1986); Jacqueline Jones, "Race, Sex, and Self-Evident Truths: The Status of Slave Women during the Era of the American Revolution," in Hoffman and Albert, *Women in the Era of the American Revolution*; Jean R. Soderlund, "Black Women in Colonial Pennsylvania," *Pennsylvania Magazine of History and Biography*, CVII (January 1983); Debra L. Newman, "Black Women in the Era of the American Revolution in Pennsylvania," *Journal of Negro History*, LXI (July 1976); and Chester W. Gregory, "Black Women in Pre-Federal America," in Mabel E. Deutrich and Virginia C. Purdy, *Clio Was a Woman: Studies in the History of American Women* (Washington, DC: Howard University Press, 1980). Some antebellum studies begin with the eighteenth century. Deborah Gray White, *Ar'n't I a Woman?: Female Slaves in the Plantation South* (New York and London: W.W. Norton & Co., 1985), and Carole Shammas, "Black Women's Work and the Evolution of Plantation Society in Virginia," *Labor History*, XXVI (Winter 1985), are among these inclusive works.

Luckily, many recent studies of African Americans provide information on women. For women's role in the Williamsburg school, see Thad W. Tate, *The Negro in Eighteenth-Century Williamsburg* (Charlottesville: University Press of Virginia for the Colonial Williamsburg Foundation, 1965). Besides the studies by Sobel and Frey, gender-sensitive works include Gerald Mullin, *From Flight to Rebellion: Slave Resistance in Eighteenth-Century Virginia* (London: Oxford University Press, 1972); Peter Wood, *Black Majority: Negroes in Colonial South Carolina from 1670 through the Stono Rebellion* (New York: W.W. Norton & Co., 1974); Sidney Kaplan, *The Black Presence in the Era of the American Revolution* (Boston: University of Massachusetts Press, rev. ed., 1989); Daniel C. Littlefield, *Rice and Slaves: Ethnicity and the Slave Trade in Colonial South Carolina* (Urbana and Chicago: University of Illinois Press, 1991); Gary B. Nash, *Forging Freedom: The Formation of Philadelphia's Black Community, 1720–1840* (Cambridge: Harvard University Press, 1988); and Donald Wright, *African Americans in the Colonial Era: From African Origins Through the American Revolution* (Arlington Heights, IL: Harlan Davidson, 1990).

Recent articles have likewise been inclusive. The essays by Douglas Deal, "A Constricted World: Free Blacks on Virginia's Eastern Shore, 1680–1750," and Philip D. Morgan, "Slave Life in Piedmont, Virginia, 1720–1800," in Lois Green Carr, Philip D. Morgan, and Jean B.

Russo, eds., *Colonial Chesapeake Society* (Chapel Hill: University of North Carolina Press, 1988), as well as studies by Jean Lee, "The Problem of Slave Community in the Eighteenth-Century Chesapeake," XLIII (July 1986), and Philip D. Morgan and Michael L. Nichols, "Slaves in Piedmont Virginia, 1720–1790," XLVI (April 1989) in the *William and Mary Quarterly*, are very good on women. Also useful were Marvin L. Michael Kay and Lorin Lee Cary, "Slave Runaways in Colonial North Carolina, 1748–1775," *North Carolina Historical Review*, LXIII (January 1986), and Cheryll Ann Cody, "There Was No 'Absalom' on the Ball Plantations: Slave-Naming Practices in the South Carolina Low Country, 1720–1865," *American Historical Review*, XCII (June 1987). There is a wealth of data on New York African-American women in Vivienne L. Kruger's unpublished 1985 dissertation, "Born to Run: The Slave Family in Early New York, 1626–1827" (Ph.D. dissertation, Columbia University). In addition, the studies of general plantation life and the Chesapeake contain much information on slavery.

Studies of eighteenth-century family life begin with demography, including Daniel Scott Smith, "Child-Naming Practices, Kinship Ties, and Change in Family Attitudes in Hingham, Massachusetts, 1641 to 1680," *Journal of Social History* XVIII (Summer 1985); James Matthew Gallman, "Relative Ages of Colonial Marriages," *Journal of Interdisciplinary History*, XIV (Winter 1984); and Robert V. Wells, "Marriage Seasonals in Early America: Comparisons and Comments," *Journal of Interdisciplinary History*, XVIII (Autumn 1987). Nancy Cott picked up the thread of women's friendships at the end of the era in *The Bonds of Womanhood: "Woman's Sphere" in New England, 1780–1835* (New Haven: Yale University Press, 1977). Among the many good studies on childbirth are Judith Walzer Levitt, *Brought to Bed: Childbearing in America, 1750–1950* (New York and London: Oxford University Press, 1986), and Laurel Thatcher Ulrich, " 'The Living Mother of a Living Child': Midwifery and Mortality in Post-Revolutionary New England," *William and Mary Quarterly*, 3rd ser., XLV (January 1989). Helena M. Wall, *Fierce Communion: Family and Community in Early America* (Cambridge: Harvard University Press, 1990), provides an overview of the family. Philip Greven, *The Protestant Temperment* (New York: Alfred A. Knopf, 1977); Barry Levy, *Quakers and the American Family: British Settlement in the Delaware Valley* (New York: Oxford University Press, 1988); and Karin Calvert, "Children in American Family Portraiture, 1670–1810," *William and Mary Quarterly*, 3rd ser., XXXIX (January

1982), 87–113, explore attitudes toward childhood and gender. For a fascinating look at courtship and sexuality see J. A. Leo Lemay's *Robert Bolling Woos Anne Miller: Love and Courtship in Colonial Virginia, 1760* (Charlottesville: University Press of Virginia, 1990) and John D'Emilio and Estelle B. Freedman, *Intimate Matters: A History of Sexuality in America* (New York: Harper & Row Publishers, 1988). Both Terri L. Premo, *Winter Friends: Women Growing Old in the New Republic, 1758–1835* (Urbana and Chicago: University of Illinois Press, 1990), and Lee Virginia Chambers-Scholler, *Liberty, a Better Husband, Single Women in America: The Generations of 1780–1840* (New Haven: Yale University Press, 1984), pay some attention to single women in the Revolutionary era.

Legal historians have long debated the "golden age" thesis. Marylynn Salmon questions the thesis in "Women and Property in South Carolina: The Evidence from Marriage Settlements, 1730–1830," *William and Mary Quarterly*, 3rd ser., XXXIX (October 1982), and *Women and the Law of Property in Early America* (Chapel Hill: University of North Carolina Press, 1986). For a contrasting view, see Joan R. Gundersen and Gwen Victor Gampel, "Married Women's Legal Status in Eighteenth-Century New York and Virginia," *William and Mary Quarterly*, 3rd ser., XXXIX (January 1982). The most sophisticated interpretation, however, is Cornelia Hughes Dayton, *Women Before the Bar: Gender, Law, and Society in Connecticut, 1639–1789* (Chapel Hill: University of North Carolina Press, 1995). *Inheritance in America From Colonial Times to the Present* (New Brunswick and London: Rutgers University Press, 1987), by Carole Shammas, Marylynn Salmon, and Michel Dahlin, summarizes an extensive literature on inheritance. See also David E. Narrett, *Inheritance and Family Life in Colonial New York City* (Ithaca and London: Cornell University Press, 1992), and Toby Lee Ditz, *Property and Kinship: Inheritance in Early Connecticut, 1750–1820* (Princeton, NJ: Princeton University Press, 1986).

On criminal and sexual offenses and criminal law, see N. E. Hull, *Female Felons: Women and Serious Crime in Colonial Massachusetts* (Urbana and Chicago: University of Illinois Press, 1987); Elizabeth Pleck, *Domestic Tyranny: The Making of American Social Policy against Family Violence from Colonial Times to the Present* (New York: Oxford University Press, 1987); Brenda D. McDonald, "Domestic Violence in Colonial Massachusetts," *Historical Journal of Massachusetts*, XIV (January 1986); and G. S. Rowe's two essays, "The Role of Courthouses in the Lives of Eighteenth-Century Pennsylvania Women," *The Western*

Pennsylvania Historical Magazine, LXVIII (January 1985), and "Women's Crime and Criminal Administration in Pennsylvania, 1763–1790," *Pennsylvania Magazine of History and Biography*, CIX (July 1985). Barbara S. Lindemann, " 'To Ravish and Carnally Know': Rape in Eighteenth-Century Massachusetts," *Signs: Journal of Women in Culture and Society*, X (Autumn 1984); Cornelia Hughes Dayton's, "Taking the Trade: Abortion and Gender Relations in an Eighteenth-Century New England Village," *William and Mary Quarterly*, 3rd ser., XLVIII (January 1991); and Ann Taves, ed., *Religion and Domestic Violence in Early New England: The Memoirs of Abigail Abbot Bailey* (Bloomington: Indiana University Press, 1989), cover issues directly affecting women's lives.

Studies of migration are poorly linked to women's history or the Revolution. There is scattered information in Bernard Bailyn's works on British migrants, *The Peopling of British North America: An Introduction* (1988) and *Voyagers to the West: A Passage in the Peopling of America on the Eve of the Revolution* (1986), both by Vintage Books. In addition to the work on Moravians, see A. G. Roeber, *Palatines, Liberty, and Property: German Lutherans in Colonial British America* (London and Baltimore: Johns Hopkins University Press, 1993), for a gender-sensitive study of German migrants. On servants, see David Galenson, *White Servitude in Colonial America* (Cambridge University Press, 1981); Sharon Salinger, " 'Send No More Women': Female Servants in Eighteenth-Century Philadelphia," *The Pennsylvania Magazine of History and Biography*, CVII (January 1983); Farley Grubb, "Immigrant Servant Labor: Their Occupational and Geographic Distribution in the Late Eighteenth-Century Mid-Atlantic Economy," *Social Science History*, IX (Summer 1985); and Margaret M. R. Kellow, "Indentured Servitude in Eighteenth-Century Maryland," *Histoire Sociale-Social History*, XVII (November 1984). On internal migrations, see Richard Morris, "Urban Population Migration in Revolutionary America: The Case of Salem, Massachusetts, 1759–1799," *The Journal of Urban History*, IX (November 1982); Eric G. Nellis, "Misreading the Signs: Industrial Imitation, Poverty, and the Social Order in Colonial Boston," *New England Quarterly*, XLIX (December 1986); and Paul E. Johnson, "The Modernization of Mayo Greenleaf Patch: Land, Family, and Marginality in New England, 1766–1818," *New England Quarterly*, LV (December 1982).

Several essays in John J. McCusker and Russell B. Menard, *The Economy of British America* (Chapel Hill: University of North Carolina Press, 1985), are helpful on women's economic roles, as are those in *Women in the Age of the American Revolution and in Colonial Chesapeake Society*. Extensive economic information is in Spruill's book, the various studies on slavery, servants, and in Gloria Main, "Gender, Work and Wages in Colonial New England," *William and Mary Quarterly*, 3rd ser., LI (January, 1994). Women's letters and diaries reveal even more. On the changing standard of living, see the Rutmans' book, Sarah F. McMahon, "A Comfortable Subsistence: The Changing Composition of Diet in Rural New England, 1620–1840," *William and Mary Quarterly*, 3rd ser., XLII (January 1985), and Stacy Gibbons Moore, " 'Established and Well Cultivated': Afro-American Foodways in Early Virginia," *Virginia Cavalcade*, XXXIX (Fall 1989).

INDEX

Page numbers in italics refer to illustrations

abortion, 55
abuse, 50
academies, 83, 89, 174
Adams, Abigail Smith, 168, 169; education, 82; property rights, 153
Adams, Hannah, 82, 91, 173; work, 65; writings, 93
Adams, John, 152; women's vote, 153
Adulator, The, (Warren), 152
adultery, 49, 50, 114, 116; divorce suits, 120, 121; grounds for divorce, 120; punishment, 120
African religions, 94
African-American women, tithe, 63
African-Americans, 121; British policy toward, 160; campfollowers, 167; economic status, 178; exiles, 160; free, 25; indentured servants, 178; kidnapped, 178; poets, 91, 92; population, 177; refugees, 159; republican ideology, 175; in Revolution, 36; sexual abuse by whites, 121
Africans, 3, 19
Albany, 11, 12, 14
Albany County, 28
alcohol, women and, 125
Algonkian Indians, 30, 85
almshouses, 129
Alphabetical Compendium of Various Sects, (Adams), 93
Amelia County, Va., executors in, 133

amusements, 145
Amy, 6, 15, 23, 24, 41, 155; death, 177; life, 181; sleeping quarters, 136; travel, 18; work, 63
Anglican Church, 5, 11, 12, 13, 15, 101, 102, 105, 113, 114, 175; established by law, 94; outreach to slaves, 99
Anglicans, 83
apprenticing, 79
army women, 165, 166; duties, 166
asceticism, 106
assault, by women, 125
Associates of Dr. Bray, 83
Associations, women sign, 150

Bache, Benjamin Franklin, 155
Bache, Richard, 39; courtship, 42; financial problems, 151; in Revolution, 151
Bache, Sarah Franklin, 10, 170; birth, 7; childbearing, 54; courtship, 42; education, 77, 82, 83; family, 155; finances, 171; flees mob, 151; fundraising, 162, 163; literacy, 81; marriage, 39; philanthropy, 179; refugee, 36, 155; religion, 100; after Revolution, 181; in Revolution, 151; sewing, 66; travel, 16, 18
Bailey, Abigail Abbott, 50
Ballard, Martha, 74
baptism, 109, 110, 118; limits on illegitmates, 119

Baptist Church, 98, 101; antislavery, 176; women's roles, 97

Baptists, 101

Barclay, Henry, 13

basket making, 64

Battle of Monmouth, 166

Battle of Oriskany, 34, 164

Battle of Trenton, 156

Battle of Yorktown, 165, 167

Beloved Woman of Chota, 180

benefit of clergy, 115, 116

Benezet, Anthony, 83, 84

Benin, Anthony, 3; inheritance, 26

Berks County, Pa., 125

Bethesda Orphan House, 81

Bethlehem, Pa., 33, 46, 159

Bibles, 105

bigamy, 120, 121

Bilbaud, Jean Pierre, 3

birth control, 55

Bishop, Elizabeth, 125

blacks. *See* African-Americans

Blair, Anne, 53, 82

Blair, Dr. James, 53

Blair, Kitty Eustace, 53, 54

Blair v. Blair, 53

boarding, 71

bonds, purchasers of, 152

Book of Common Prayer, 94, 95, 109

books, 5; religious, 95

Borden Town, N.J., 154

Boston, 7, 10, 15, 34; fire in 1760, 34

Boston School Act of 1789, 88, 174

Boudinot, Annis, 91

Boudinot, Susan, 151

Bowen, Penuel, 88

boycotts, 150; women's role, 149

Brafferton, 84

Brainerd, John, 84

Branch, Daniel, 27, 39; will, 177

Branch, Elizabeth Porter, 3, 4, 126; death, 181; inheritance, 26, 27; marriage, 39

Brant, Catherine Adonwentishon, 63, 86

Brant, Jacob, 113; birth, 14

Brant, Joseph, 12, 31; birth, 14; at Cherry Valley, 157; education, 29, 85; farming, 63; loyalist activities, 155; religion, 13; slaveowner, 29

Brant, Margaret, 1, 11–14, 29, 33, 86; adultery, 14, 113; birth, 12; children, 14; death, 158; home, 29; household management, 137; literacy, 81; parentage, 12; religion, 13, 84, 100, 104; in Revolution, 34; travel, 18

Brant, Mary (Molly), 13, 143; adultery, 114; assimilation, 181; childbearing, 54; death, 180; family, 139; farming, 63; household, 137; loyalist activities, 155; loyalist compensation, 160; marriage, 30, 33, 40, 46; names, 14; after Revolution, 35; in Revolution, 34; slaveowner, 29; travel, 18; wealth, 29

Braxton, Betsy, education of, 82

Braxton, Mary Blair, 82

brewing, 64

British: emancipation offer, 176; empire, 1; foraging by, 158; Indian policy, 33

bundling, 43, 44

Burgin, Elizabeth, 154

Burlington, N.J., 154

Burnet, Elizabeth, 90

Burr, Esther Edwards, 90

Butler, Mary, 177

Butler, William, 177

butter making, 61

Byrd, Mary Willing, 153, 160

campfollowers, 167

Canagaraduncka, Brant, 29, 72, 113

Canajoharie, 12, 14, 137

captives: Indian, 31; Iroquois customs, 12; white, 31–32, 157

Caribbean, 160

Caribbean immigrants, 19

Carroll, Molly, 55

Catawba Indians, 11, 14, 30, 137; losses during war, 158; war with Iroquois, 32

catechisms, 105

Cayuga Indians, 34

Chamberlain, Theophilus, 84

charity schools, 84

Charleston, S.C., 31, 74, 129, 150; poverty in, 128–129

cheese making, 61
Cherokee Indians, 62; assimilation, 180; Seven Year's War, 34; weaving, 138
Cherokee women: as leaders, 180; loss of status, 180
Cherokee–Creek War, 32
Cherokee–Shawnee War, 32
Cherry Valley, N.Y., 157
Chesterfield County, 155
Chickasaw Indians, 30
child abuse, 125
child support, 119
childbearing, 4, 6, 51, 55. *See also* mortality, 56
children: amusements, 79; chores, 79; clothing, 79; discipline, 79; Moravian, 80
Choctaw Indians, 30
Christ Church, 8, 10, 102
Christopher, Rebekah, 156
church governance, limits on women, 115
churches: finance, 179; national structures, 174; visiting, 102
citizenship, 147; women's, 171
clan matrons, 32, 40; roles, 62
Clarissa, (Richardson), 90
Clark, George Rogers, 158
clergy, 95; and women, 107, 109
Clifford, Ann Rawle, 162
Clinton, Henry, 36
cloth production, political meaning, 66
coffee, as replacement for tea, 151
Colden, Alice, 102
College of William and Mary, 84
Commissary General of Military Stores, 67
Committee to Inquire into the Condition of Freed Slaves, 178
Committee of Safety, 158
Common Sense Philosophy, 146
Conestoga Indians, 33
confiscation, 161; of women's property, 160
Congregationalist Church, 98
Connecticut, 105, 155; divorce, 8, 49; schools, 81
consumer culture, 78

consumer revolution, 68
Continental Army, 157
convict servants, 22
cooking, 21, 68
cooks, African, 69
Cooper, Mary, 50, 107
copyright law, 89
Corbin, Hannah Lee, 153
Corbin, Margaret, 165
courtship, 43
coverture, 46, 171; change during Revolution, 47
Coxe, Tench, 68
Cranch, Richard, 82
credit, 72, 75, 171
credit revolution, 64, 133
Creek Indians, 30, 157
crime, punishments for, 115
Croghan, George, 86
Croker, Deborah, 10. *See also* Dunlap, Deborah Croker
cross-dressing, 145
cruelty, as grounds for divorce, 125
Cumming, Janet, 74
Cummings, Anne, 150
Cummings, Betsy, 150
custody, 130

dairy farming, 4, 21, 61, 64
dancing, 43, 77, 82, 104, 135, 141
day labor, 10, 68
day laborers, 70; rural, 69
Declaration of Independence, 73, 155
Deerfield, Mass., 91
Defeat, The, (Warren), 152
Delaware, 11; private manumission, 177
Delaware Indians. *See* Lenape
dependency, 159, 168, 169, 170, 172, 178
depositions, home, 115
desertion, 48. *See also* divorce
Detroit, 32
Dick, 6
diet, 68
disease, 34, 159
divorce, 48, 50, 120, 173; among Indians, 48; attitudes toward, 51; in England, 48

domesticity, 106, 148, 149, 171, 173, 179, 182
double standard, 114, 119, 121, 130
dower, 47, 50, 62, 134, 160, 161, 170, 171
Doxtater, Honyery, 164
Dunlap, Deborah Croker: childbearing, 54; death, 181; marriage, 39
Dunlap, Frances, 39
Dunlap, William, 39, 111; ordination, 39
Durham, N.H., 98
Dutch immigrants, 28
Dutch Reformed Church, 98, 102
Dutoy, Barbara de Bonnett, 3, 18; inheritance, 26; literacy, 5; widow, 3
Dutoy, Elizabeth. See Porter, Elizabeth Dutoy
Dutoy, Isaac, 3; inheritance, 26; vestry service, 5
Dutoy, Marianne, 3. See also Loucadou, Marianne
Dutoy, Pierre, 3, 5; slaveowner, 5, 23, 43; vestry service, 5; will, 3, 26

economy, role of women in, 58–76
Edenton, N.C., 150
Edict of Nantes, revocation, 18
education, 174; advanced, 82; African-American, 83, 84, 88; classics, 82, 83; costs, 83; course of study, 82, 83, 84, 85, 88, 174; growth, 174; household skills, 79; languages, 77, 82; of poor, 77, 81; reform, 88–89; religious, 104; republican, 88; single sex, 81; value of, 87
emancipation, 176
English, 19
English Academy. See Bowen, Pennuel
entail, 47
Ephrata, 101, 106, 109
Episcopal Church, 119
equity trusts, 47, 170
Erskine, Margaret, 32
Estaugh, Elizabeth, 93
evangelical motherhood, 173

factories, employment of women in, 67
Fallen Timbers, 35
family, ideas about, 147

Farmer, Eliza, 154; as refugee, 156
farming, 63; Indian, 13, 62
featherbeds, 63
Female Review, The, (Gannett), 145, 146
feme sole status, 46
feme sole traders, 59
Fergusson, Elizabeth Graeme, 160
fertility, 25
fieldwork, 60, 63; African-Americans, 134
Fontaine, James Maury, 106
food riots, 158
food shortages, 158
forceps, 56
Ford, Judith, 32
fornication, 9, 114, 116, 118; laws prohibiting, 44; penalties for, 119
Fort Henry, 164
Fort Hunter, 12, 13, 137
Fort Loudoun, 62
Fort Niagara, 34
Fort Stanwix, 178
Fort Washington, 165
Fowler, David, 85
Fraier, Mary, 162
Francis, Ann Willing, 162
Franklin, Benjamin, 7, 71, 94; colonial agent, 151; courtship, 8; employer, 70; house, 135; marriage, 7; religion, 102; retires from business, 10; on Sarah's marriage, 40, 42; will, 171; on wives, 51
Franklin, Deborah Read, 1, 7, 11–14, 39, 71; business skill, 70; courtship, 8; death, 162; defends house from mob, 151; first marriage, 8; house, 135; investments, 76; literacy, 81; manages post office, 70; marriage, 7, 9; philanthropy, 179; religion, 94, 100, 102; shopkeeper, 70; slaveowner, 24; stroke, 151, 161; supports boycotts, 150; visiting, 17; visits schools for slaves, 83; weaving, 65
Franklin, Elizabeth, 97
Franklin, Francis, death of, 7, 10
Franklin, William, 7, 151; governor of New Jersey, 151; loyalist, 151; parentage, 8, 9; on sister's marriage, 40; warns Deborah, 151

free school, 129
Free Will Baptists, role of women, 108
Freeman, Elizabeth, 176
French immigrants, 19. *See also*
    Huguenots
French and Indian War, 26
French Protestants, 2. *See also* Huguenots
French settlements, 26
friendships, among women, 140, 141, 142
frolics, 142
frontier: cultural exchange, 28–32; women
    in combat, 164
fugitive slaves, 127, 140
funerals, 110

Galloway, Grace Growden, 160, 161
Gambia, 73
Gannett, Deborah Sampson, 79, 93, 146,
    165
gardening, 4, 21, 59, 60, 61
Garrett, Hannah, 85
Gatter, Christiana, 155
gender, ideas about, 143
Georgia, 21, 31, 73
Germans, 19; immigration, 12, 20, 28; in
    New York, 11; as servants, 21
Gleaner, The, (Murray), 93
Gloria Dei Lutheran Church, 42
Gnadenhutten, 33, 35, 157
Goddard, Mary Katherine, 73
Goochland County, Va., female literacy
    in, 81
Gray, Martha, 154
Great Awakening, 95, 98, 100, 106, 128
Greek immigrants, 19
Green, Anne Catherine, 73
Group, The, (Warren), 152
guardianship, 80
Guerrant, Daniel, 28, 39
Guerrant, Marie Porter, 4, 170; death,
    181; inheritance, 27; marriage, 28, 39

Half-Way Covenant, 99
Halifax County, Va., 135
Hamilton, Alexander, 68
Handsome Lake, 180
Harris, Eleanor, 88

Hatcher, Sarah Porter, 4, 28, 181; inheri-
    tance, 26; marriage, 39; travel, 18
Hatcher, Thomas, 28, 39
Hayes, Mary, 166
Heaton, Hannah, 105
Heck, Barbara, 104, 107
Hessian troops, 154
Home, Henry, 87, 144
Hooper, Anne, 156
Hopewell, 180
Hopkins, Samuel, 107
hospitals, 179
household(s), 132; accounts, 59; use of
    space in, 135; work, 4
housewifery, changes in, 134
housework, 68
Huguenots, 18, 102; immigration, 3;
    migration to Virginia, 18
hunger, among Indians, 33
hunting, 62
Huntington, Countess of, 92, 101
Huron, 12
Hutchinson, Margaret, 73
Hutchinson, Thomas, 152

Iliad, (Homer), 90
illegitimacy. *See* premarital pregnancy
Illinois, French, 68
immigrants, 19–20; adjustments, 20; mor-
    tality, 20; women, 19
immigration patterns, 21
incest, 50, 116, 121, 122
indentured servants, 23–24, 69; fieldwork,
    60; importation, 20; married, 21; sup-
    ply, 21
independence: definition of, 170; religious
    influence, 170
Indian cloth trade, 64
Indian women: education, 84, 85; in com-
    bat, 164; murder of, 157; religion, 180
Indians: allies in Revolution, 157; Christ-
    ian, 84, 100; converts, 103; cultural
    change, 30, 62; as dependent, 178; and
    domesticity, 138; disease, 30; educa-
    tion, 136; mobility, 30; new towns, 30;
    pressures for domesticity, 136; religion,
    98, 103; resist assimilation, 136, 137;

revivals, 104; servants, 2; trader's wives, 30; white misinterpretation of roles, 136–37, 148; women as leaders, 143; women sign deeds and treaties, 136
indigo, 60
infant care, 78
infant mortality, 57
infanticide, 114, 125–26
inheritance, 19, 26–27
intermarriage, 6, 31
investment, 75
Irish, 19; immigrants, 20; servants, 21
ironing, 83, 135
Iroquois: during Revolution, 34; war with Catawbas, 32
Iroquois Confederacy, 11; allies, 11; kinship, 13
Islam, 94
Italian immigrants, 19

Jefferson, Martha Wales, 163
Jemison, Mary, 32, 93, 137
Johnson Hall, 33, 40
Johnson, Mary, 165
Johnson, William, 12, 30, 114; Indian agent, 28, 143; marriage, 40, 46; ties to Brants, 33
joint deeds, 134
Joseph, 3, 5, 6; marriage, 5
Joseph Andrews, (Fielding), 90
juries of matrons, 115

Kaims, Lord, 87
Kentucky, 18, 28, 32, 35, 180; private manumission, 177; in Revolution, 35; war in, 157
kin, 139, 140
King George's War, 7, 14, 32; widows, 34
King William Parish, 2, 4, 5, 7, 18, 26, 41, 102, 199; slaves, 6
knitting, 31, 65, 66, 81, 84, 85, 98

La Brasseur, Anne, 128
lace making, 65
Lancaster County, Pa., 119
Lancaster, Pa., 33
laudnaum addiction, 55

Laurens, Martha, 105
lay preachers, women, 108
le Roy, Marie, 33
Lebanon, Conn., 85
Lee, Ann, 108; theology, 109
Lee, Richard Henry, 153
leisure, 135
Lenape, 33, 84, 85, 157
letters between women, 142
libraries, 89
liquor, 31, 104
Litchfield Academy, 174
literacy, 77, 80–81, 140, 144, 174; among Mohawks, 86; in New England, 80
literature, 89
livestock, effect on Indian farms, 62
Locke, John, 173
London, 18
looting, 154
Loucadou, John, 3
Loucadou, Marianne Dutoy, inheritance, 26
Loucadou, Marianne Porter, 5
loyalists, 36, 59, 134, 154, 155, 160; exiles, 160; resettlement, 160; women, 160
Lucas, Eliza. *See* Pinckney, Eliza Lucas

Madison, Eleanor, 163
Madison, James, 71
Maine, 27
malaria, 20
Manakin, 101; description, 2
Manakin ferry, 4
Manheim, Pa., 36
mantuamakers, 71
maple sugaring, 63
markets, 61
marriage: African-Americans, 41, 43; age at, 39, 40; attitudes toward, 46; in church, 110, 111; common law, 8, 45; for companionship, 51; customs, 45; frontier, 45; ideas, 54–55; laws, 44; Quaker reformation, 111; republican ideology, 173; role of kin, 41–42, 41–42, 45; slaves, 6; women's choices, 39, 42
Marriage Act of 1753, 45
marriage settlements, 40, 47

Martin's Station, 32

Maryland: divorce in, 50; private manumission, 177; slavery in, 23; tithe, 21

Massachusetts, 7; divorce in, 49, 120; education in, 88; emancipation, 176; infanticide cases, 126

Massachusetts Spy, 152

maternal deaths, 74

meat processing, 60

medicine, women practicing, 74

medicine lodges, 128

mental illness, 128

merchants, 73

Methodist Church, 98, 101, 105, 107; opposition to slavery, 176; outreach to slaves, 99

Methodists, 98

Midewiwin Societies, 103

midwives, 56, 74; and physicians, 75; in court, 115; skill, 75; training, 74

militia, Kentucky, 158

milliners, 73

Milton, John, 90

missionaries, and assimilation, 137

Mobile, 30

mobility, 16, 25; and kin, 140; patterns, 36–37

Mohawk, 11, 12, 13, 62, 85, 114; agriculture, 137; assimilation, 137; cultural accomodation, 29; diplomacy, 32; disease, 14; family, 13; land cessions, 28; literacy, 86; losses during war, 157; loyalist compensation, 180; marriage, 45; move to Ontario, 180; naming, 14; work, 13

Mohegan, 84

Molly Pitcher story, 166

Montauk, 85

Moor's Indian Charity School, 85

Moravian Church, 98, 159; choir system, 80, 96; discipline, 115; and domesticity, 112; education, 88; marriages, 42; theology, 109; women as leaders, 97; women's roles in, 96

Moravian Indians, 33, 35, 104, 157

Moravians: education, 81; families, 80; housing, 136; marriage, 111; sex ratios, 19; work, 136

Morris, Margaret Hill, 74, 167

mortality: child, 78, 80; infant, 74, 78

Mum Bett. *See* Freeman, Elizabeth

murder, 127

Murray, Judith Sargent, 88, 174; writings, 93

Musgrove, Mary, 31

music, 77, 104, 135, 142

musician, 97

Myers, Anna Oosterhout, 157

naming, 6, 14, 138

naming patterns, 138

Narragansett Indians, 85

Natchez, 30

Natick Indians, assimilation of, 137

neighbors, 140

Nelson, William Jr., 111

New Brunswick, 160

New Hampshire, 27; divorce in, 49

New Haven, Conn., sanctions for fornication in, 119

New Jersey, 155; disenfranchises women, 178; divorce in, 49; women's vote, 153

New London, Conn., 100

New Orleans, 30

New York, 120; divorce in, 49

New York Charity School, 81

New York Weekly Journal, 144

Newport, R.I., 74, 83, 101, 159

nicknames, 138

Norris, Deborah, 111, 147

Nova Scotia, 36, 160

novels, 90, 145

nurses, 159, 166, 182; pay, 167

Ohio Valley, 12

Ojibwa Indians, 180

Oneida, 85

Oneida Indians, 34, 85

orphanages, 179

orphans, 129

Osborn, Sarah (Conn.), 107; religion, 107; runs school, 74; school, 83

Osborn, Sarah (N.Y.), military service, 166

Ottowa Indians, 33

Page, Frances, 106
Palmer, Abigail, 156
Pamela, (Richardson), 90
Paradise, Lucy Ludwell, 47
paraphernalia, 47, 170
paternity suits, 119
Pearce, Mrs., 101
Peg, 3, 5, 11–14, 15, 18, 23–24, 23, 43; children, 6; fieldwork, 60; living arrangements, 5; marriage, 5; sleeping quarters, 136; work, 5, 6, 63
Pendleton, Edmund, 54
Pennsylvania, 2, 7, 82; divorce in, 8, 49; equity trusts, 48; infanticide cases, 126
Pennsylvania Gazette, 162
pensions, 160, 165
Pequot Indians, 85
Peters, John, 92
Philadelphia, 7, 10, 15, 67, 74; British occupation of, 159; immigration, 20; servants, 21; slavery, 24–25
Phillis, 126
piedmont, 2, 5, 6; slavery, 23
Pierce, Sarah, 174
pietists, 19
piety, 105, 175
Pinckney, Eliza Lucas, 60, 62; education, 83
poetry, 90–92
poisoning, by slaves, 126
Pontiac's Rebellion, 30, 33
poor, 128, 129–31
poor relief, after Revolution, 95
Pope, Alexander, 90
population, 118
Porter Family, 139; during Revolution, 155, 162; names of children, 138
Porter, Ann. *See* Sampson, Ann Porter
Porter, Dutoy, 3, 4
Porter, Elizabeth Dutoy, 2, 3, 4, 11–14, 126; childbearing, 51; family, 3; fieldwork, 60; home, 136; house, 5; inheritance, 26, 27; literacy, 5, 81; religion, 101; serving tea, 151; slaveowner, 5; spinning, 64; visiting, 18; work, 63
Porter, Elizabeth II, 4
Porter, Isaac, 4, 26, 101, 162

Porter, John, 3, 4, 26; death, 181; religion, 101
Porter, Magdalene Chastain, 39; serving tea, 151; weaving, 64
Porter, Marie. *See* Guerrant, Marie Porter
Porter, Sarah. *See* Hatcher, Sarah Porter
Porter, Sarah Watkins, 101
Porter, Thomas, 3; family, 3; marriage, 3; on vestry, 102; religion, 101; slave-owner, 6, 41; vestry service, 4, 5
Porter, William, 4, 26; death, 181
post office, 10, 11
poultry care, 61
Powel, Elizabeth Willing, 147
prayer meetings, 106
premarital pregnancy, 43, 114, 116, 118, 119, 173; among Indians, 40; rates, 44
Presbyterian Church, 84, 98, 119; out-reach to slaves, 99
Prince, Lucy Terry, 91
Princeton, 87
printers, 73
privacy, 132, 136, 174
processing skins, 64
Proclamation of 1763, 27
production, household, 162, 63, 150, 162, 171; cloth, 64–66; during war, 162; war supplies, 67
property rights, 170
prostitutes, 71
prostitution, 117, 122
public, definition of, 132, 146, 147, 174

Quakers, 102, 119; discipline, 115; free slaves, 176; marriages, 42; philan-thropy, 83; preachers, 96, 108; pun-ished as neutrals, 159, 161; reforma-tion, 97, 99; servant use, 21; women as leaders, 96; women's meetings, 96, 105
quartering, 159
Quok Walker case, 177

rape, 31, 116, 156; among Indians, 117; prosecutions, 123, 124; by soldiers, 124, 155
Ratcliffe, Ann, 90
Read, James, 8

Read, Mrs., 7
reading, 5
redemptioners, 21
Reed, Esther DeBerdt, 162, 163
Reed, Mary, 98
refugees, 34–35, 154, 156; African-American, 36; loyalist, 36; religious, 19
religion, 174; behavioral codes, 104; diversity, 94; family, 105; husbands as surrogates, 102
religious deviance, 127
republican ideology, 53, 114, 169; slavery, 176
republican motherhood, 88, 132, 147, 172; African-Americans, 175; influence on education, 174; slaves, 175
republican wives, 173
revival, in Newport, 107
Rhode Island, 120; divorce in, 49
rice, 60
Richmond, 2
riding, 141
rights, 169
Rind, Clementina, 73
Roman Catholic education, 89
Rose, Mary, 74
Rowson, Susanna, 88
runaways, 127
Rush, Benjamin, 88

St. Paul's Church, 102
Salem, N.C., 46
Sampson, Ann Porter, 4, 171; chooses guardian, 80; death, 181; inheritance, 26; marriage, 39; sewing, 69
Sampson, Charles, 39
Savannah, Ga., 88
Schenectady, 11
schools: adventure, 83; Indian, 84
Scots, 19, 20; immigrants, 20; as servants, 21
seamstresses, 66
Second Church, 107
Seneca, 32, 34; in Revolution, 35
Separate Baptists. See Baptist Church
servants, 68; abuse, 22; price, 23
Seven Year's War, 26, 32

sewing, 10, 31, 65, 66, 77, 81, 82, 83, 84, 85, 137; trade goods, 67; wages, 67
sex ratios, 26, 41
sexton, 97
sexual offenses, See also specific offenses
Shakers, 109; discipline, 115
Shakespeare, William, 90
Shankland, Katy, 157
Shawnee, 11, 28, 32; allied with British, 35; kill prisoners, 157; land pressure, 180; losses during war, 158
sheep, 4
shoemaking, 64
shopkeepers, 70
Shurtlef, Robert. See Gannett, Deborah Sampson
Sierra Leone, 160
Six Sketches on the History of Man, (Homer), 87
skating, 141
slander, 118
slave code, 127
slave trade, 5, 18, 19, 20, 23–25
slaves: childbearing, 6; as dependent, 178; education, 84; emancipation, 176; escaped, 36; fieldwork, 60; hiring out, 5, 60; housework, 69; marriage, 6, 41; names, 138, 139; naming, 6; population, 24; price, 23; as property, 47; purchase freedom, 178; religion, 99, 104; republican ideology, 175; schools, 83; suits for freedom, 177; travel, 6; work, 7
smallpox, 10
Smedley, Phebe, 106
Smith, Adam, 146
Smith, Elizabeth Murray, 73
Smith, Mary, 126
Smith, Obediah, 126
smugglers, 150
Society for the Propagation of the Gospel, 13
Society of Friends. See Quakers
soldiers: supplied by women, 162; women, 164
South Carolina, 60, 105; equity trusts, 47; frontier, 26; Seven Year's War, 34

spinning, 60, 64, 81; as political, 149; poor women, 65
spinning bees: political, 182; political meaning, 66
spouse abuse, 124
Stamp Act, 151; boycotts and women's work, 64
standard of living, 70
Stith, Elizabeth Smith, 97
Stith, Mary Smith, endowed school, 81
Stratton Major Parish, Va., 111
Sullivan Expedition, 156, 157; campfollowers, 167
surnames, women, 139
Swiss, 19

tavernkeepers, 71
taverns, 73, 72, 73
tea, 142, 151
teachers, 73, 84; women, 73–74
theater, 104, 135, 142
theft, 114, 126; penalties, 127
Third Communion, 128
Thomas, Mary, 137
Thorm, Mary, 107
tithe, 21, 60, 63
tobacco, 60
Townsend Duties, 150
Trabue, Daniel, 28
trade, 70; Indian, 12
traders, Indian, 30, 31; sexual abuse by, 31
travel, 141; during pregnancy, 140
treason, 160, 171; penalties for women, 155
Treaty of Greenville, 180
Treaty of Versailles, 35
Trinity Parish, 102
Trist, Elizabeth, 136
trustees, husbands as, 171
Tryon County Committee of Safety, 155
typhus, 159

Union Academy, 81
United Company, 66
Universal Friend. See Wilkinson, Jemina

Vermont, 27

Vindication of the Rights of Women, (Wollstonecraft), 172
Virginia, 2, 3, 6, 199; divorce in, 49; infanticide cases in, 126; private manumission, 177; slavery, 5, 23
Virginia Gazette, 72, 74
virtue, 52, 144, 146, 147, 172, 173
visions, 98
visiting, 5, 8, 139, 140, 142; elites, 141; among slaves, 140; as work, 140
visitors, 132
Vobe, Jane, 72
von Riedesel, Baroness Fredericka, 167

Wager, Ann, 84
wages: day labor, 69; midwife, 74; teachers, 74; women's agricultural, 63
Wahbino, 180
War for Independence: frontier, 156; impact on churches, 95
Ward, Nancy, 34, 180
warning out, 34
Warren, Mercy Otis, 169, 170; poetry, 172; political writings, 152; writings, 93
washing, 21, 68, 69, 83
Washington, Elizabeth Foote, 105
Washington, George, 67, 161; on army women, 165, 166; on women's fundraising, 163
Washington, Martha, 163; receives petitioning women, 161
Wayne, Anthony, 165
weaning, 78
weaving, 4, 31, 60; wages, 64
Weber, Jacob, 128
weddings, 38
Weissenberg, Catherine, 40
Wells, Ebenezer, 91
Wells, Rachal, 154
westward movement, 19, 27, 180
wheat, 60
Wheatley, John, 24
Wheatley, Phillis, 24, 91; poetry, 92
Wheatley, Susanna, 24, 101
Wheelock, Eleazar, 85, 104
White Plains, 165

Whitefield, George, 10, 65
widowhood, 7
widows, 59, 128, 159; as executors, 133; remarriage, 46; slaveowners, 60
wife, ideals, 52
Wilkinson, Jemina, 108; theology, 109
Williamsburg, Va., 72, 74, 82; schools, 84
Wilmer, Mary, 107
Wilmington, N.C., 156
Winchester, Va., 161
Windsor, Conn., female literacy in, 80
Winter, Mary, 127
witch, 128
women: acting separately from husband, 161; artisans, 70, 71; at Battle of Lexington, 164; consumers, 172; in court, 115, 133; declining wealth, 133; dependency, 7, 147, 178; family rituals, 109; farming, 59; fundraising, 162–63, 179; group action, 158; help prisoners, 154, 155; ideal, 53; ideas about, 143, 144, 148, 168, 173; land transfers, 133, 134; loyalists, 155; majority in churches, 98, 99, 100; manage farms, 62, 162; and men, 132, 148; military service, 164–67, 164; in newspapers, 143; nurses, 159; personal narratives, 93; petitioners, 159, 160, 161; piety, 105; poets, 91; political awareness, 168; politically active, 149, 151, 172; poor, 175; preaching, 108; reading, 90; religion, 94, 102; religious leadership, 107, 108; religious roles, 103, 107; in revivals, 97–98, 107; roles of, 52, 87, 106; running business for husband, 70; shopkeepers, 70; single, 46, 175; surnames, 139; tavern keepers, 71; travel, 16; virtue, 147; voters, 171; and war mobilization, 154; withdraw to private sphere, 133; as witnesses, 59, 141; work, 11, 171
Women Invited to War, (Adams), 173
Woodson, Constance, 74
Wollstonecraft, Mary, 172
work, 21, 134, 171; redefinition of, 146
worship, 104
Wright, Susanna, 82, 91, 170
writing, 81

Yale College, 158
yellow fever, 74
Young Ladies Academy, 88, 89, 174
youth, 144

THE AUTHOR

Joan R. Gundersen is Founding Faculty Professor of History at California State University, San Marcos, where she teaches courses in legal history, early America, women's history, and women's studies. She has published numerous articles on early America and women's history, two U.S. history textbooks and two monographs on the Episcopal Church, and serves on the editorial board of three journals. With degrees from Monmouth College (Ill.), the College of William and Mary, and the University of Notre Dame, she has also taught at Indiana University South Bend, Vanderbilt University, St. Olaf College, and as a Fulbright lecturer at the University of Oulu, Finland.